Praise for *A Sideways Look at Time*

"An exercise in Dharma, Poetry, and Philosophy."
—GARY SNYDER, Pulitzer Prize–winning poet

"This is smart, edgy work, from an original and exciting mind. Jay Griffiths's voice is a light beam in the fog of twenty-first-century debate."
—BARRY LOPEZ, author of *Arctic Dreams*

"A fascinating, highly original meditation on time. Jay Griffiths exposes the political nature of the linear, mechanical, and global time of industrial culture and contrasts it with the myriad 'times' embodied in nature's processes, known to indigenous cultures. Her writing style is rich and rhythmic, reflecting her main thesis. This is a book that needs to be read *slowly*."
—FRITJOF CAPRA, author of *The Tao of Physics* and *The Hidden Connections*

"Jay Griffiths is a dazzlingly original writer, a wordsmith of the first order. She writes like an angel: a funny, brave, passionate, and sometimes naughty angel. Her book is highly serious and yet playful; it is wise, wide-ranging, and radical. If it were a political party, I'd join it."
—ANITA RODDICK, founder of the Body Shop and author of
Take It Personally and *Business as Unusual*

"Jay Griffiths has the gift of insatiable curiosity. She is intensely aware of the world around her, its wonders, its horrors, and its absurdities. She questions and protests and celebrates—all in a language that is constantly alive, often sparkling and deep, like a good river. She is a revealer and a healer—to travel through time in the company of such a magical writer is a delight."
—ADRIAN MITCHELL, Britain's shadow poet laureate

"Like the seminal socialist, feminist, and ecological works, *A Sideways Look at Time* articulates what thousands have felt but no one has been able to put into words. . . . Cheeky, intelligent, always gripping, this book reintroduces us to a dimension we've utterly neglected. It will be the opening salvo in a new battle over the human spirit."
—GEORGE MONBIOT, author of *The Age of Consent*

"A truly brilliant and wonderful book, beautifully written—one of the best I've read in years."
—VANDANA SHIVA, author of *Monocultures of the Mind*

"A mine of ideas, of anecdotes, connections, angles."
—IVAN ILLICH, author of *Deschooling Society* and *Tools of Conviviality*

"Thoughtful, original and intuitive . . . amusing and erudite, fascinating and spirited. Bravo!"
—*The Times Literary Supplement* (London)

"Splendid, extraordinarily wide-ranging, emphasizing the political import of the subject. Impressive, absorbing, and radical, provocative, impassioned, often outrageously witty."
—*New Internationalist*

"A wonderful, delightfully humorous polemic against everything wrong with the way [in which] we deal with time today."
—*The Independent* (London; Books of the Year)

"An irresistibly provocative and political analysis of time . . . [Griffiths's] wittily enthusiastic thesis is that time has too long been used as a tool to power: as a manifesto, [this book] could cause a revolution."
—*The Times* (London; Books of the Year)

"A whirl of a book. Any page will get you hooked."
—*New Scientist*

"A compulsively readable book cleverly combining influences as diverse as Otis Redding, Beltane and Australian aboriginals. Griffiths does for time what Robert M. Pirsig did for truth-obsessed philosophy in *Zen and the Art of Motorcycle Maintenance*. It's also a sexual, playful, intensely female book. Griffiths argues that through their monthly menstruation cycles, often affected by the moon, women are much more in tune with cyclical concepts of non-linear time. With this book, Griffiths may just have beaten the clock. Passionately written and cogently argued, it's a book you should make time to read."
—*TimeOut* (London)

"A wildly exuberant and exhilarating polemic. Enormously intelligent, fresh, and innovative, this is a book unlike any other I have read."
—*The Age* (Melbourne)

"There are lots of books on time, but none like this lyrical account that proceeds via argument instead of examination. . . . Flowing with ideas, an audacious and exhilarating book."
—*The Sydney Morning Herald*

"Both revolutionary and a real pleasure to read. Certainly this must become one of the principal texts of anyone campaigning for social or environmental justice."
—*The Ecologist*

"A brave and novel rage against the machine of time. It oozes ideas as rich as a literary death-by-chocolate. Savour a spoonful at a time."
—*The Big Issue*

"Done with an energetic panache that will leave you mentally richer . . . A delight."
—*Earthmatters*

Wild

Wild

AN ELEMENTAL JOURNEY

Jay Griffiths

JEREMY P. TARCHER • PENGUIN
a member of Penguin Group (USA) Inc.
New York

JEREMY P. TARCHER/PENGUIN
Published by the Penguin Group
Penguin Group (USA) Inc., 375 Hudson Street, New York, New York 10014, USA · Penguin Group
(Canada), 90 Eglinton Avenue East, Suite 700, Toronto, Ontario M4P 2Y3, Canada (a division of Pearson
Penguin Canada Inc.) · Penguin Books Ltd, 80 Strand, London WC2R 0RL, England · Penguin Ireland,
25 St Stephen's Green, Dublin 2, Ireland (a division of Penguin Books Ltd) · Penguin Group (Australia),
250 Camberwell Road, Camberwell, Victoria 3124, Australia (a division of Pearson Australia Group Pty
Ltd) · Penguin Books India Pvt Ltd, 11 Community Centre, Panchsheel Park, New Delhi–110 017, India ·
Penguin Group (NZ), Cnr Airborne and Rosedale Roads, Albany, Auckland 1310, New Zealand (a division
of Pearson New Zealand Ltd) · Penguin Books (South Africa) (Pty) Ltd, 24 Sturdee Avenue,
Rosebank, Johannesburg 2196, South Africa

Penguin Books Ltd, Registered Offices: 80 Strand, London WC2R 0RL, England

Most Tarcher/Penguin books are available at special quantity discounts for bulk purchase for sales
promotions, premiums, fund-raising, and educational needs. Special books or book excerpts also
can be created to fit specific needs. For details, write Penguin Group (USA) Inc. Special Markets,
375 Hudson Street, New York, NY 10014.

Library of Congress Cataloging-in-Publication Data
Griffiths, Jay, date.
Wild: an elemental journey / Jay Griffiths.
p.   cm.
Includes bibliographical references and index.
ISBN-13: 978-1-58542-403-0
ISBN-10: 1-58542-403-X
1. Indigenous peoples—Ecology.   2. Human ecology—Psychological aspects.   3. Nature—
Psychological aspects.   I. Title.
GF50.G75   2006   2006026984
304.2—dc22

Printed in the United States of America
1   3   5   7   9   10   8   6   4   2

BOOK DESIGN BY MICHELLE MCMILLIAN

While the author has made every effort to provide accurate telephone numbers and Internet addresses at the
time of publication, neither the publisher nor the author assumes any responsibility for errors, or for changes
that occur after publication. Further, the publisher does not have any control over and does not assume any responsibility for author or third-party websites or their content.

Contents

WILD **WATER**

WILD **FIRE**

WILD **AIR**

WILD **MIND**

flight, silhouetted in the primal

—PENNY RIMBAUD

Wild Earth

ABSOLUTE TRUANCY

felt its urgent demand in the blood. I could hear its call. Its whistling disturbed me by day and its howl woke me in the night. I heard the drum of the sun. Every path was a calling cadence, the flight of every bird a beckoning, the color of ice an invitation: come. The forest was a fiddler, wickedly good, eyes intense and shining with a fast dance. Every leaf in every breeze was a toe tapping out the same rhythm and every mountaintop lifting out of cloud intrigued my mind, for the wind at the peaks was the flautist, licking his lips, dangerously mesmerizing me with inaudible melodies that I strained to hear, my ears yearning for the horizon of sound. This was the calling, the vehement, irresistible demand of the feral angel—*take flight*. All that is wild is winged—life, mind and language—and knows the feel of air in the soaring "flight, silhouetted in the primal."

This book was the result of many years' yearning. A longing for something whose character I perceived only indistinctly at first but that gradually became clearer during my journeys. In looking for wilderness, I was not looking for miles of landscape to be nicely photographed and neatly framed, but for the quality of wildness, which—like art, sex, love and all the other intoxicants—has a rising swing ringing through it. A drinker of wildness, I was tipsy with it before I began and roaring drunk by the end.

I was looking for the *will* of the wild. I was looking for how that will expressed itself in elemental vitality, in savage grace. Wildness is resolute for life: it cannot be otherwise, for it will die in captivity. It is elemental: pure freedom, pure passion, pure hunger. It is its own manifesto.

So I began this book with no knowing where it would lead, no idea how hard some of it would be, the days of havoc and the nights of loneliness, because the only thing I had to hold on to was the knife-sharp necessity to trust to the elements my elemental self.

I wanted to live at the edge of the imperative, in the tender fury of the reckless moment, for in this brief and pointillist life, bright-dark and electric, I could do nothing else. By laying the line of my way along another, older path, I would lay my passions where they belonged, flush with wildness, letting their lines of long and lovely silk reel out in miles of fire and ice.

I felt that my blood could only truly flow if it coursed into red, red earth. That I would only know my deepest glee if I could dive in an oceanful of trilling fish. I wanted to climb mountains till I cracked with the same ancient telluric vigor that flung the Himalayas up to applaud the sky. I was, in fact, homesick for wildness, and when I found it I knew how intimately—how resonantly—I belonged there. We are charged with this. All of us. For the human spirit has a primal allegiance to wildness, to really live, to snatch the fruit and suck it, to spill the juice. We may think we are domesticated but we are not. Feral in pheromone and intuition, feral in our sweat and fear, feral in tongue and language, feral in cunt and cock. This is the first command: to live in fealty to the feral angel.

I wanted to put my cheeks against a glacier, to drink direct from hot springs, to see vistas untamed. It's ferocious, this feeling: vigorous and raw. Wanting to touch life with the quick of the spirit, to feel the wind in my hair, the crusts of mud under my fingernails, the sun on my naked body, ice cracking my lips, tides flooding my body inside and out. Immersion is all.

I sketched out my journeys according to four elements of ancient Greece, earth, air, fire and water, but adding ice as if it were an element in its own right, which in a landscape it is. The only chapter I never planned to write was the last. It forced its way into the book, like a court jester with a dirty laugh and a deadly serious look in his eyes, leaping onto the stage just as Act

Five was closing, and offering an answer to the deepest question: the quintessential coupling of wildness with life.

I took seven years over this work, spent all I had, my time, money and energy. Part of the journey was a green riot and part a deathly bleakness. I got ill, I got well. I went to the freedom fighters of West Papua and sang my head off in their Highlands. I got to the point of collapse. I got the giggles. I met cannibals infinitely kinder and more trustworthy than the murderous missionaries who evangelize them. I went to places that are about the worst in the world to get your period. I wrote notes by the light of a firefly, anchored a boat to an iceberg where polar bears slept, ate witchetty grubs and visited sea gypsies. I found a paradox of wildness in the glinting softness of its charisma, for what is savage is in the deepest sense gentle and what is wild is kind. In the end—a strangely sweet result—I came back to a wild home.

I wanted nothing to do with the heroics of the "solo expedition." There was no mountain I wanted to "conquer," no desert I wanted to be the "first woman to cross." I simply wanted to know something of the landscapes I visited and wanted to do that by listening to what the knowers of those lands could tell me if I asked. I was exasperated (to put it mildly) by the way that so many writers in the Euro-American tradition would write reams on wilderness without asking the opinion of those who lived there, the native or indigenous people who have a different word for wilderness: *home*. I was angered by the nineteenth-century Europeans who called a landscape a "hideous blank" and who, knowing nothing of the land, ascribed their ignorance to it. And I was enraged by the modern species of "adventurer" who risks killing indigenous people by "contacting" them.

From shamans in the Amazon I learned something of how the wastelands of the mind, its dark depressions, could be navigated and from them I learned to see the world through feral eyes, through the eyes of a jaguar. From Inuit people in the Arctic I learned something of the intricate ice and how all landscape is knowledgescape. From whales and dolphins I learned how much we do not know, the octaves of possibilities, the maybes of the mind. From Aboriginal people in Australia I learned the belowness of things, how land is heavy with significance and how it sings. From West Papuan people I learned how freedom is the absolute demand of the human spirit. From a Buddhist monk I learned that you can cycle on ice and fall off laughing. From indigenous people all over the world I learned that going out into the wilds is a necessary initiation and that for young people, lost in the wastelands of the psyche, the only medicine is the land. Everywhere, too, I learned of songlines, how people who know and love a land can hold it in mind as music.

As I went, I found myself increasingly needing to distinguish wildness from wasteland. Wastelands, such as forests razed to the ground, are the inscriptions of tragedy while wildness erupts with the raw carnival of comedy, laughing its socks off, grace notes galore, honoring the erotic. For wildness is flagrantly sexual—the longest passion of all species, the longing of the daffodil for the spring sun, the thirsting of all roots for water, the sensual relationship between humanity and nature, humming with it, earthy to the core.

To me, humanity is not a stain on wilderness as some seem to think. Rather the human spirit is one of the most striking realizations of wildness. It is as eccentrically beautiful as an ice crystal, as liquidly life-generous as water, as inspired as air. Kerneled up within us all, an intimate wildness, sweet as a nut. To the rebel soul in everyone, then, the right to wear feathers, drink stars and ask for the moon. For us all, the growl of the primal salute. For us all, for Scaramouche and Feste, for the scamp, tramp and artist, for the furious adolescent, the traveling player and the pissed-off Gypsy, for the bleeding woman, and for the man in a suit, his eyes kind and tired, gazing with sad envy at the hippie chick with the rucksack. For us all, every dawn, the lucky skies and the pipes. Anyone can hear them if they listen: our ears are sharp enough to it. Our strings are tuned to the same pitch as the Earth, our rhythms are as graceful and ineluctable as the four quartets of the moon. We are—every one of us—a force of nature, though sometimes it is necessary to relearn consciously what we have never forgotten; the truant art, the nomad heart. Choose your instrument, asking only: can you play it while walking?

"Something there is that doesn't love a wall," wrote Robert Frost in "Mending Wall." Something there is in me, in so many of us, that detests a wall. Or a fence, reservation or golf course. That detests the tepid world of net curtains and the dulled televisual torpor of mediated living, screened experience in two senses, both life lived via screens and life itself screened out.

I know this chloroform world where human nature is well schooled, tamed from childhood on, where the radiators are permanently on mild and the windows are permanently closed. School seemed to me little more than a trooping process to educate the young to the cautious life of temperate contentment. Everything was made into corridors: corridors of convention, corridors from term time to term time, corridors from school to university, corridors from sensibly studying math to marrying an appropriate accountant. Intellectually, the corridors were supermarket aisles, tinned thought. Politically, the corridors offered one-brand, off-the-shelf, right-wing views. Outdoors the corridors were pavements of nonevents, pavements for those who take no risks. Pavements that trod past semi-detached houses, semi-the-same, semi-skimmed milk semi-tasted and always lukewarm. Emotions came only disinfected. The furies of grief or joy were somehow considered unhygienic, passion a nasty germ.

I was educated—as we all are—to stay inside, within the bounds of my tribe (physical bounds and intellectual bounds) and to stay within the protected zone, to let the traffic of routine smother desire for the real outside. I was taught—as we all are—to be scared of the prowling unknown, of the wild deserts of Beyond.

And we were taught to play golf. Golf epitomizes the tame world. On a golf course nature is neutered. The grass is clean, a lawn laundry that wipes away the mud, the insect, the bramble, nettle and thistle, an Eezy-wipe lawn where nothing of life, dirty and glorious, remains. Golf turns outdoors into indoors, a prefab mat of stultified grass, processed, pesticided, herbicided, the pseudo-green of formica sterility. Here, the grass is not singing. The wind cannot blow through it. Dumb of expression, greenery made stupid, it hums a bland monotone in the key of the mono-minded. No word is emptier than a golf *tee*. No roots, it has no known etymology, it is verbal nail polish. Worldwide, golf is an arch act of enclosure, a commons fenced and subdued for the wealthy, trampling serf and seedling. The enemy of wildness, it is a demonstration of the absolute dominion of man over wild nature.

So I wouldn't play golf, preferring to play Mozart as if he were the first of the great Romantics—it would have made a proper musician pale. I played Beethoven's furies and passions (badly) till I thought the piano would burst and detested the cool arithmetic Bach. I felt an unavoidable and total rejection of the nice, easy, convenient, narrow terms of life as offered, because those terms were stifling, life-reluctant, torpid.

I felt hungry. I've always been hungry. Whatever it is, I want more. When I was a child, it was a ferocious discontent: a feeling that this small and narrow place was not all, not nearly all and not nearly enough. There was a wide and wild world without, visible only through books, and though I could only see little fizzes of light from it like matches struck a mile away, I felt charged with desire for it.

There was a library in the house where I grew up. One wall was entirely covered with books, floor to ceiling. The children's books were on reachable shelves. I read them and stared upward for there, always out of reach, were the farther shores. I remember more than any other book the yellow spine that said *Seven Years in Tibet*. I climbed onto the filing cabinet, then up the shelves, fingertips on one shelf, toes on another, until about ten years old and ten feet in the air, I reached Tibet. But. If I let go with one hand to grab the book I would fall. I gazed at that spine for years. Tibet talked to me. Timbuktu too. Lapland lapped at the shores of my desire. Lhasa, Sahara and the Himalayas. Siberia and the road to Mandalay. When a math teacher said to me in class that I'd understood her about as well as if she were from Outer Mongolia, I was thrilled to bits. I'd never heard of any such place and yet it existed now—*plink*—suddenly in my mind. I was swept away. Outer Mongolia must be at the edge of the world. She had given me an Ultima Thule and I wanted to go there. Percentages could wait.

I ran away (for a few hours) when I was nine to sleep in the wildest garden in the street—a three-acre jungle where a tramp lived in secret. I ran when I was seventeen, hitching around the country, pitching a tent at night. (I'm a runner; I've run for hours until my feet were bleeding.) When I was eighteen I tried to go to Tibet but only reached India. When I was twenty-four I went to Thailand, living for six months with the Karen hill tribe in the northern forests on the Burmese border.

That time was profoundly important to me. It was the first time I had properly lived without construction, without shops, money, towns, artifice. You live on the Earth, in the seasons, right within nature because there is nothing that is not nature. You eat what is hunted—a wild cat once, bamboo rats, wild boar, including testicles. Rice with everything and sometimes only rice. For once, I felt what it was like to live essentially. Water was from a river, not a tap, fruit was from a tree, not a shop, and I felt life stripped, pared to the core. And while there were footpaths, there were no enclosures.

I wanted to live for the fire though it burns you in the process. And it has. After I walked the Annapurna circuit in Nepal with dysentery, I ended up in hospital when I almost stopped being able to breathe. I lost all my toenails climbing down from the peak of Kilimanjaro. I had frostbite once and when I've had altitude sickness up mountains I've continued climbing to the point of utter recklessness. I've known what it is like to whimper with sheer loneliness on a Christmas Day in a jungle on the other side of the world. I've felt the fear of being ill alone when in Ladakh I contracted a sudden and shocking fever and, just before I became delirious, I scribbled a note containing my passport number, everything I could remember about getting ill and my medical insurance details, then pinned the letter to my shirt, left the door open and passed out for two days. The kindly hotel owner found me and came up every two hours with a huge pot of ginger tea.

My feeling for wilderness or wildness was both a revolt from something and an impulse toward. Toward unfetteredness, toward the sheer and vivid world. Toward the essential freedoms, freedom of water, of fire, of ice, of earth, of air. This is political, for both the site and the idea of freedom depend on free nature and for us to be truly free, nature must be unenclosed, untamed by road building, logging and mining. And in conversations with indigenous people around the world I have felt a savage fury as they are thrown off their lands. My feelings now, personal and political, run to a savage love, and a savage rage.

It is a rage against the cruelties committed for the sake of this bland consumer culture. A rage against the effects of factory farming, so a bird, flying exhausted, without seeds or hedge margins, drops out of the sky, falling dead to a desiccated Earth. A rage against out-of-town shopping centers, placed on the last little chinks of commons, the wild places on the edge of towns where children play, teenagers fuck, the homeless sleep and the artist idles into life. The commons up for sale—another enclosure. And the common flowers of the commons, sweet heathens, are rare now, and the sparrow, little brown jug of a bird, is scarce. A rage against the hollow men, the stuffed shirts who are the agents of the wasteland, making the Amazon arid and the Arctic an over-heated suburbia.

When I was a small girl, awake on a long car journey one full-moon night while my brothers were fast asleep, I stared at the moon for hours, fascinated, compelled. I thought I was the moon's daughter. That common moon, that wild moon, belonged to me that night—and just as much it belonged to you. But the moon is being made a wasteland, a dustbin for detritus, the bibles and bunting of nationalist superiority. Outer space, the ultimate commons, the absolute wilderness, is being weaponized till there are rifles trained on every human being on earth and the stars look like searchlights.

There are two sides: the agents of waste and the lovers of the wild. Either for life or against it. And each of us has to choose.

DRINKING HEMLOCK AND STARS

The first part of this journey began by being lost. I had lost my way in a wasteland of the mind, in a long and dark depression, pathless, bleak and bewildered, not knowing which way to turn. Weeks leaked into months, lank and unlovely as greasy hair. I couldn't walk, couldn't write, and it felt as if I couldn't survive the violence of my unhappiness. I had a repeated image in my mind of a little night-light guttering in the wind and I had to wrap my hand around it to protect the tiny pale flame on the brink of being extinguished. I was protecting something very ancient and unmetropolitan: something shy, naked and elemental—the soul.

The sick body knows it lacks certain vitamins and minerals and seeks food containing them. As the body, so the soul. A handful of times in my life I have felt an absolute demand to go to a specific place or to know a specific person, recognizing immediately something my spirit needed. My journey to the forests began like this, in an imperative odyssey.

One May morning during this long depression I was sitting in my little rented flat in Hackney, in tears. The phone rang. It was an anthropologist I had never met but whose work with Amazonian shamans intrigued me and who had also admired my writing. He asked how I was, in the kind of voice that encourages an open response. I'm drowning, I choked.

He invited me to meet him in Peru the following September, to visit shamans he knew there, and to drink ayahuasca. Ayahuasca is a shamanic drug, the Amazon's most powerful medicine, which is used to treat—among many other things—depression.

Yes, I said.

Why don't you take a few days to think about it? he asked. It would be an expensive flight, a big trip.

No, I said. I knew a lifeline when I was thrown one.

So I learned Spanish, withdrew all the money I had in the world, bought an open return, dubbined my boots and left.

The journey from Lima to the shamans' center was long—a small plane, a car and a boat, a *peque peque*, one of the little motorized dugouts that zip up and down the rivers of the Amazon. The boatman dropped us off at a particular point of the riverbank where one of the shamans met us, and then we walked to their retreat, an area of natural hot springs. This retreat was called Mayantuyacu, meaning, in the Ashaninca language, "the water and the air"—a name that was so appropriate for my journey in the elements.

The walk to their center was my first meeting with the Amazon; Amazon stinging, itching and stroking you with velvet; Amazon biting, scratching and softly feathering you; the whole forest winks at you, rubs your warm thighs and grins. A tree bark smelled of nutmeg; certain plants smelled of rotting flesh; there were flowers sweet as honey and a fungus smelling of old and thoughtful mold. I could smell a fine mist of rain and a sour smell from a plant here, a fetid smell from a pool there, the consoling smell of moss, the zinging smell of sap. I could almost smell the sunlight, heavy and lovely as hops.

Palm fronds rattled like a snare drum in the hot moistness. The tower of an oil exploration mast jagged the horizon. A dove fluted in the trees. Logs that had fallen over the path were worn down by the passage of feet. Dalila, sister of one of the shamans, screamed as she saw a poisonous snake. The shaman knelt by the path to pick up a dead toucan, which he had shot on his way down to the river.

When we arrived, the anthropologist, Jeremy Narby, who had visited here before and worked on land rights for Amazonian people, was warmly welcomed back and Juan, the chief shaman, gave him an amulet whose base was the fossil of a prehistoric animal. It was adorned with agate, quartz and turquoise with guacamayo feathers, crocodile teeth and seeds at the cardinal points.

Juan was lying injured on a pallet in his house. A few weeks previously he had stepped off a path and straight into a trap set by a hunter. His leg had been splintered, he had lost a lot of blood and had nearly died. He interpreted his accident metaphorically: he had strayed a little way off his path in life.

Shamans say that ayahuasca shows you your path. Not "the" path, but your own. It is a songline of sorts, not as a map of the land but a map of your life. The songline can untie the choking riddles of your life and show you the winding way, deep in the green heart's forest, simple as sunlight and resonant with the motivation of a soul's journey.

Ayahuasca (pronounced "eye-er-*wass*-ka") is a powerful hallucinogenic drug widely used by shamans throughout South America. It is made from the vine *Banisteriopsis caapi*, boiled for twelve or more hours with certain other ingredients added and the bitter, foul-tasting liquid is drunk. It has many names, many properties; vine of visions, vine of souls. *Aya* means, in the Quechua language, spirit or ancestor or dead person, while *huasca* means vine or rope. It is thus sometimes known as the vine of the dead, because shamans say it puts you in touch with the ancestors, and through it they can communicate with the spirit world. (The name is perhaps influenced by the fact that drinking it can make you feel as if you're dying.) It is also known as *la purga*, the purge, for it dramatically courses through the body, often making the drinker vomit furiously. Perhaps the most common term for it, though, is *la medicina*, for it is used as a medical diagnostic tool, and as a curative for physical and psychological problems. Noe Rodriguez Jujuborre, a healer of the Muinane people of Colombia, told me once that under its influence, he sees the diagnosis of an illness, and the image of the plant that will cure it is "imprinted on my mind."

So that night I would drink ayahuasca. It was dusk and the insects of twilight were hissing and thrumming and all the forest's night players were coming to life, the fizzy, zestful *chicharras*, cicadas, were fermenting their song and frogs honked, bellowing for a mate. I took my notebook with me as ever, though writing anything in the near-coma that ayahuasca induces was hard.

In Juan's hut there were rugs, blankets and mattresses around the walls, with buckets if anyone needed to vomit. As well as Juan, there was another shaman, Victor, and an apprentice who poured out measures of ayahuasca into a carved wooden cup, like an egg cup. Just before I drank, I felt a vertiginous fear; this is a "pure alkaloid poison," I remembered reading, and the hallucinations may be terrifying. But then, I thought, my journey of depression was already frightening and I already felt poisoned. I drank. It was like drinking hemlock and stars; as foul as the one, as brilliant as the other.

Juan began to sing an *icaro*—a gentle song, thin as the wind in the reeds, ethereal, sweet and far away. As he sang, he repeated the word *ayahuasca* like an invocation; its sound onomatopoeic, soft and shimmering, a word of whispers and mystery.

Suddenly I wanted to be outside and I left the hut and went to watch the mists rise from the hot springs. After a while, Victor followed me out, asking if I was *mareada* (seasick). At first I didn't understand what he meant, but a few seconds later I felt a wave of strangeness and dizziness; then the visions began. I knew a little about the typical ayahuasca visions, of snakes, plants, eyes and rivers, but I was entirely unprepared for the visions I had. Garish and cartoonish, they were a kaleidoscope of tourist-shop junk, silly plastic toys, giddily repeating, row on row of fake London street-name plaques, tawdry key rings, cartoon traffic wardens with seaside-postcard bottoms. I felt mocked by the ugliness and stupidity of the city I had left. I've never taken acid, but I know of acid visions, and this seemed to belong in that category; a Xeroxed crazy paving, a zigzagging shopping arcade, jangling with febrile urban banality, the jag of enervation, the blaring buzzing of nothing, in a chivvying, gridlocked triviality.

I was grateful that Victor had followed me out and during the next hours I felt that he had not only found me physically but also psychologically. He put his hands on either side of my head and pressed his lips to my head and sucked. Then, still holding my head, he turned his face to the sky and spat out his breath far away. Each time he did that, my head felt cool at that spot. It felt as if he was sucking out of my head poisoned needles, some five inches long, hard and thin, dangerously sharp splinters.

We talk of being "stabbed in the back" by someone, being "needled" or "knifed" by someone's words. We refer to "barbed" remarks. Language is wise to the mind's experience and I had felt, as many people have, that such sharp, thin spikes had been shot straight into my head, where they lodged, creating the infection of depression and nothing I could do would dislodge them. My mind had been knifed. "An ugly word can be like the scratch of a needle on the lung," wrote Ibsen in *An Enemy of the People*. It felt now as if Victor were sucking out Ibsen's needles, saying, as he did so, "They're gone. Just gone. Away."

As I later learned, Amazonian shamans "use" such splinters or darts, either throwing them to injure someone or, as in Victor's case, extracting them from someone who has been wounded. I had "seen" these in the mind's eye, and experienced them as a powerful metaphor, before I'd had any idea that this was a common perception to them.

Then I nearly fainted, and Victor yanked me up from the earth and pulled me back into Juan's hut, where I collapsed on a mattress.

Depression is a wasteland all of its own. No animation, no vivacity. The psyche, hurt badly enough, will withdraw and won't come back easily—or, for some, at all. Like a plant without sap, the body is without dynamism, flair or potency and the psyche wanders far away, lost and lonely. Before I went to the Amazon, I wouldn't have used the term *soul loss*, because I'd never heard of the concept. Nor did I know anything about the "soul retrieval" practiced by shamans, who understand that if a person's soul is lost, it takes a sure-footed and skillful traveler in the landscape of the mind to find it. In the Amazon, shamans undertake these journeys into the deep forests of the psyche; they say they see their way to search for a soul as you would see a path in a dream, finding their way in the wildernesses of the human mind.

Previously, if I had believed in a soul, it would have seemed implacably bound to one's body till death. Now, though, *soul loss* is a term I would consider because that night I felt that my soul was found. I felt as if I were in a deep river, drowning, and that in these seasick visions Victor had sent his soul out of himself to come and find mine. I was too weak, too far gone in ayahuasca even to hear the *icaros* that Juan was singing. "Try to concentrate on the songs, use them like a rope to climb out of a bad place," said Victor, but I couldn't. He poured a little water on my head and it was like a benediction. "*Más tranquillo*," he said, gently. Be calmer. The words were half command, half comfort. They were like water when he spoke them, the quiet drops of water in the syllables of his words like the water on my head.

He held my face in his hands and I could feel his strength passing into me. For a shining moment, I felt as if I saw his soul in the river where I was drowning and he rose to his waist out of the water—so he came to me and in doing so he healed the devastation of my isolation. In finding me, he brought me back, unlonely. Then—*vamoosh*—on the instant the job was done, he was gone.

Day came up in a surge of song. When the creatures of the morning come to life, they soar for the dawn as if there's never been a sunrise before and to-day is the only day there'll ever be; they clamber out of the cocoon of night to shout up the day, swelling with warmth and light, and the hummingbird, for whom sunlight is the first and most necessary nectar of the day, bathes in the sun which warms it enough to give it first flight. (The hummingbird stores no fat so if it cannot find flowers it will die. It "hibernates" every night, wait-ing for the first sunlight to warm its wing muscles enough to fly to a flower.)

I heard the bird that sounds like a xylophone underwater and all the jun-gle birds were singing, in rattles and squeaks and octave-sliding hoots and whistles like a joke shop full of ten-year-olds.

The depression that had so darkened me for months had gone, and though during my months in Peru I had a persistent worry that it would re-turn, it did not and I was free of it for years. I said my good-byes to Jeremy and stayed on in the Amazon, my spirit as green, happy and elastic as a grasshopper in summer, tromboning in the grass.

TELLURIC THOUGHT

The world is wild-minded. Thought dialects thrive unknown to us: ants with their dictionary of pheromones; the dogged bee, trundling from flower to flower, for whose mind all that is not scent and color and waggle dance is mere refuse. "Wildness is the state of complete awareness. That's why we need it," writes Gary Snyder. Indigenous people have long extended their intellectual horizons by learning from the minds of other creatures. Claude Lévi-Strauss commented that many plants and animals were totemic because they were "good to think with." The Amazon forest itself, according to a Desana elder, "is a wide expanse, similar to a perceptive human head."

But the Western way of knowing has denied validity to every mind save its own. Socrates, pithily summing up an entire way of thinking, said, "I'm a lover of learning, and trees and open country won't teach me anything, whereas men in town do." Descartes said grimly that the aim of knowledge was to be "masters and possessors of nature." For the rationalists of the late seventeenth and the eighteenth century, there was a hatred of "enthusiasm," for its emotional, wild surges of knowing were too natural, too bodily, too animal. Rationalism demanded superiority to, and separation from, nature and nature's ways of knowing. The primacy given to literacy and the superior quality ascribed to written text over spoken words has deafened us to other voices and persuaded us that our meanings are the only ones that matter. So rooted is the idea that nature is stupid that one word for an idiot is a *natural*. Words for wisdom in the thesaurus include virtually no natural referents, whereas *fool* is full of them: "ass, donkey, goat, goose, owl, cuckoo . . . greenhorn, calf, colt, buzzard, clod-poll, clod, clod-hopper, bull-calf, bull-head, moon-calf."

In the Amazon it is not so. Here there is telluric thought, sunk deep in the earth, a wild way of knowing so utterly different from that of the West that while we use the term *vegetable* for a comatose mind and *vegging out* as a slang term for mindless laziness, in the Amazon the wisest men and women are called *vegetalistas*—plant experts steeped in plant knowledge. But there's more: people don't just learn *about* plants, they learn *from* certain plants called "plant teachers" or *doctores*, which teach people medicine. This is a contradiction in terms to the Western mind—it balks at there being intelligence in anything other than humankind. But to shamans who use it (*ayahuasqueros*) the vine is a wild intelligence of a vegetable kind. (Once in another part of the Amazon, drinking ayahuasca with a shaman, I "saw" a crown of speaking leaves on my head, vibrant in eloquence. The shaman interpreted it as an image of knowledge: the plants would speak and I should learn.)

Chief Luther Standing Bear, of the Native American Lakota people, wrote that for "the old Indian . . . to sit or lie upon the ground is to be able to think more deeply" and the earth was "a library, and its books were the stones, leaves, grass, brooks, and the birds and animals." In Russian, the term *Zapovednick* is a fourteenth-century concept denoting a protected land, and the root of the word means "knowing," as environmental historian Malcolm Draper points out.

Trees have long been associated with knowledge; the Buddha meditated under a tree and sought wisdom from it. In India, Saddhus have always retreated to the forests for wisdom; the pipal tree signifies universal wisdom and in traditional Indian thought, trees, in their previous lives, were great philosophers. The English language recognizes an association between wisdom and trees: an idea "takes root"; a book has "leaves"; a small book is a "leaflet"; an avid reader is a "bookworm"; you "branch out" into a new area of study—and even corporate language doffs its cap in the form of Amazon.com.

University thinking is "drily" academic and the term is important. Western ways of knowing use dryness not only for practical reasons (the dry books in dry libraries) but also because dryness itself is a characteristic of the unwild environment, no rain, no rivers, no lips. In the Amazon, by contrast, knowledge is wild and wet. Amazonian shamans feel they are drinking knowledge when they take ayahuasca and they say they are inebriated or "drunk" in trance. Their knowledge is passed on orally, wet and fluent from lip to lip, and in practical terms, knowledge travels along the liquid, flowing rivers, the communication system of the forests.

To the missionaries, this wild and wet knowledge was devilish: knowledge should come from dry Bible paper, made from dead trees, or be given soberly on dry stone tablets, not drunk, drunkenly, from the moist world of living plants. Christianity, like every other ancient system of thought, equated trees with knowledge, but—peculiarly—it chose to associate the Tree of Knowledge with *sin*.

A "wise man" of the Aguaruna people pointedly sums up his people's history of thought: they gained knowledge from plants, particularly ayahuasca and tobacco, but the end was abrupt: "This took place until 1953, when the school system of education began and the ILV prohibited the drinking of those plants." ILV is the Instituto Lingüístico de Verano, the Summer Institute of Linguistics, a right-wing American missionary outfit, responsible for cultural genocide. They consider indigenous knowledge evil in itself, because it deals with the relationship between the visible world and the spiritual world. For the Ashaninca, the story was the same: you cannot find *ayahuasqueros* or *tabaqueros* "unless you go looking in the deepest forests, where there are no schools." But if you do find such people, they will tell you of different ways of knowing. The Western way, they say, is merely theoretical; their own way is better, for it is both spiritual and practical, involving a constant moral dimension that includes respect for nature. Knowledge of successful hunting is knowledge of ethical hunting—because a hunter must learn never to be greedy, for instance. But with the arrival of missionaries and government agents and Western school systems, "we were taught to feel shame for our old beliefs."

There is a certain bitter irony in the fact that now prospectors come from pharmaceutical companies in order to exploit wild and public indigenous knowledge of plant medicine. "They rob us and make large amounts of money from our knowledge," I was told. Not for nothing is wild knowledge called "common knowledge." Common knowledge is free, open, unenclosed— and "free" financially: it must not be bought or sold for profit. But now in the Amazon an act of enclosure is taking place—people's common knowledge is exploited for commercial gain, often privatized with the patent laws, which are the PRIVATE: KEEP OUT signs in the open fields of knowledge.

Literacy is an epistemology of the built world, physically, in libraries in towns, but metaphorically too, the constructed artifice of our written culture, book-bound, which encourages our philosophies and values to move ever farther away from nature—to say nothing of the constructs of deconstructionism and postdeconstructionism.

I was tired of the tamed thinking and desiccated worlds of dry books, and I was following that wild call, familiar to us all: the young, the old, the sad, the curious, the footloose and all who yearn just to bugger off for a while. It is an ancient need, made heroic in the past: the anthropologist Hans Peter Duerr, in *Dreamtime*, writes, "Yvain, Lancelot, Tristan left culture behind to become mad in the wilderness. Only after having become wild could they rise to the rank of knight. Following this same path, the Tungus shaman runs out into the wilderness . . . until he finds . . . the 'animal mother' . . . and has experienced his 'wild,' his 'animal aspect.'"

Go to the wilds. The Amazon drew me and, once there, held me fascinated.

ON THE RÍO MARAÑÓN

After some time, I went north, with an Aguaruna woman, to the river where she was born on a tributary of the Río Marañón. She was taking twelve chickens and several baskets of chicks to communities in her area and the journey took days; by plane and then by bus, crowded with people, parrots and puppies and a man selling antiparasite pills. After the bus, a long car journey took us to the banks of the Marañón and she introduced me to the river as if to a close friend. We took a *peque peque* upriver.

Small, shiny children were playing like otters on the riverbanks and a dugout canoe softly paddled along the shoreline with a man at the back and an alert little dog at the front. There were biscuit wrappers in the water and trees dripping with moss and vines. A log, fallen in the river, looked like an alligator. If you come here without permission, you may well see your last arrow here; the Aguaruna shoot people who come uninvited. A little boy in a red T-shirt was fishing with a line from a canoe and a mother, surrounded by children, washed clothes. Smoke rose into low clouds from isolated shacks and "Bar. Rest" was marked incongruously on one hut. One of the chickens tried to eat my boots and a buzzard hovered over the bank. Bright green plastic Portakabin toilets, government-provided, stood in a comical row. They were locked. It didn't matter; no one in their right mind would want to use one of them, because if used they smelled awful and attracted mosquitoes. Outdoors, all excrement is gone in hours.

We began having trouble negotiating a shallow part of the river, until a couple of men appeared on the banks and shouted directions to us. After many hours, we reached the first of the communities Chinita wanted to visit, and we pulled up at the bank. A fishing net hung from a tree to dry, and close to it, a man was fishing. The river, canoe, man, paddle and line together created the elegance of sheer simplicity. There was a concrete schoolhouse, with iron bars on the windows. It was nearly evening and fires were lit, Aguaruna style, three logs pushed, tips together, so that one end of each log smoldered in the fire. Someone fanned the fire with a fan made from bird feathers sewn together. There was an accidental frog in the soup and a rat in the bedroom and on the steps crouched two huge rainbow-colored insects with fluorescent eyes.

Apart from the rivers, people can communicate here through jungle drums, made from dugout trees. The Aguaruna traditionally have three messages. The first is a lively dancing rhythm, an invitation to a fiesta. The second is for emergencies, a rapid series of sharp knocks. The third is a steady, calling song, which means that ayahuasca is ready. One man showed me how to play a tortoiseshell like a violin. With beeswax on the tortoise's arse, and using the edge of your palm like a violin bow, you draw your hand over it, scraping it till it sounds like a haunting violin string.

People talked fearfully of a religious sect that lives close to Aguaruna land and they were worried these people would start to build roads through the forests, which the Aguaruna are emphatically against. I mentioned Britain's antiroad protesters, and they were tickled pink at the idea of people living in treehouses to stop a road. But when I told them that some people had made tunnels and lived underground to prevent building work, they lay back and hooted with laughter.

At night, the palm trees were like fish bones, lively verdant skeletons, and Chinita and I swam in the river under a bright moon, while the stars vied with the fireflies on the riverbanks. There are parrots that sing at night, and their song is pure laughter.

We journeyed on, going to the confluence of two rivers for a rendezvous with a friend of Chinita's. At the rivers-meet, there was a sinister office building on the riverbank. It had been built by the Sendero Luminoso (the Shining Path guerrilla movement) and used for bulk coca transactions for cocaine. Most people happily chew coca; unprocessed and in small quantities, it's mild as tea, and is part of Amazonian culture. When coca is processed in large quantities for cocaine, though, the trade is dangerous and frightening for local people. Inside the building was a desk, a chair, a fridge and a pink plastic piggy bank. Chinita's friend was late and we spent hours and hours plagued by mosquitoes, listening to the wails of a funeral coming from a village in the distance; an old man had died of cancer the previous day and the forest was full of weeping. People here don't fear death, said Chinita: it's a "crossing to the other side" like crossing a river.

Chinita's friend arrived and we left together to go to another village to stay a night, but going upriver our *peque peque* ran out of gasoline so we stopped by a tiny path on the muddy bank and went to the nearest hut to buy gas. We were invited in to eat and drink; someone passed me water in a large hollow gourd and I played face-pulling games with a five-year-old girl. A big moth fluttered by and she caught it and pulled it apart matter-of-factly. There was a woman there, in her mid-thirties, with feet worn like leather from a shoeless life. Her heel was cracked as leather cracks; an unhealable split, deep into her sole. She scraped tiny mites out of my legs, which had bitten me and left dozens of swollen, itchy spots.

Outside, the moon was bright over the misty river. *Zapetas* (crickets) chuckled, and the lechusa bird called *wow* from deep in the forest. A storm crashed through the night.

People talked about the illegal gold miners in Aguaruna land and told me in angry indignation how functionaries from a mining company would fly helicopters over Aguaruna land, prospecting. One helicopter had landed, and the Aguaruna kidnapped everyone on board, except the pilot, whom they ordered to go back wherever he came from and fetch 13,000 *soles*, or $4,300, and return with this ransom; only then would the hostages be released. They were understandably proud of this, one of the few times when forest people have been able to robustly defend themselves.

In some areas, Aguaruna women are committing suicide because their culture is becoming "rotten" or "broken"—devastated by European contact, particularly when their lands are threatened. Here, deep in the heart of Aguaruna territory, it seems impossible to believe, but the edges of their lands are where people feel most vulnerable.

The days stretched into weeks, in the elastic time of wild lands, and we traveled farther and farther north until we got close to the Ecuadorean border. Here, there was a problem. The border guards were used to Aguaruna people paddling up and down the river but no Europeans ever come here, they told me. They were very suspicious. They called their chief. He studied my passport and didn't like the look of it at all. We talked. Nothing doing. So I took the only option and gently, firmly and unstoppably flirted with him. We went on our way, with his blessing.

Lianas the height of a three-story house dropped from tree branches into the waters and much farther upriver a man rafted past us, his craft made of bamboo with a small four-poster "wigwam" on the back. Our boat nuzzled its way into the mud of the riverbank and we went to visit a village, where people kept pigs, on reins, in the houses. I forgot to take off my sunglasses and a small child cried at the sight of me. "You look like a huge insect," I was told. We stopped for the night and stayed with a herbalist, whose knowledge of local plants was famous up and down the river.

Another night we stayed with relatives of Chinita's, whose house was full of chickens, children, cats, dogs and pigs. In the evening we ate hot banana soup, and oil lanterns lit the night as the fishing nets were hung out to dry. A small girl, with a laugh like a stream, sang catches of songs while her elder brother played a bamboo flute and I went to sleep in my hammock to the sound of laughter; laughter in the house, and in the forests the frogs seemed to be laughing with the birds. The women woke at about three in the morning for a long natter in bed and Chinita got the giggles. A coconut fell with a crash in the forest.

The next morning we went as far upriver as we could in the *peque peque*, before the rapids of the river became too dangerous. Chinita showed me a secret cave where Aguaruna people used to put the bones of their dead in baskets. There were boas in the deepest pits of the cave and birds nesting at the back. The boatman and a small boy with us went yodeling into the cave, to shoo out the birds before we went in. Every spring, Chinita told me, the river rises, washing away almost everything in the cave, but the ledge, where people put the bones and skulls, was above the high-water mark. She showed me the skulls, including one of a different shape which was, she thought, very old. A bright butterfly fluttered in on turquoise wings and alighted on the bones. The small boy stuck his finger into the eye sockets of a skull and dug out batshit. It was a strange place, gray, silent and ancient and I felt humbled to be shown it, the cave of the ancestors.

Downriver again, back in the green noisy world of now, sunlight was flashing on wet paddles and a child, showing off, did a backflip into the river off the end of a canoe. A group of boys played with their blowpipes on the banks— the blowpipes are about two feet long, made of green reeds, and good for hunting small birds. I spent a long time canoeing with the children in the dugouts. These tippy canoes sit high in the water and are very sensitive. Every wobble your body makes seems doubled by the canoe whose trembling in turn makes you wobble the more. The children were in charge, for sure; here, children can canoe almost before they can walk. I found it hard to paddle because just when I was ready to correct my direction they would pitch in with a deft flick of a paddle, not trusting me to know what to do. In the morning they were grindingly determined to push upstream and, easy in the afternoon, would glide back down to be home by dusk. Childhood, river and canoe all seemed spun of the same silk. Tranquillity is here; a canoe in a cool inlet, silent at twilight, reflected in the water under a cool and silent moon.

WILD LANGUAGE

Language expresses itself in the rivers. News travels along the rivers in the Amazon; communication and travel is primarily by boat, but beyond the practical reasons there is a deep affinity between rivers and language. Rivers flow like language—we say that someone is "fluent" in a language, their speech flows like a river. Languages, like rivers, run roughly the same course, but always change their details: you never step into the same language twice, because a meaning has newly shifted here, a connotation has just been formed there. Rivers and language are both gloriously wild. Careless of their courses, rivers won't run straight. Both languages and rivers are extravagant—who cares how a river wastes its meanderings? Who asks why language wastes its windings in splendid, luxurious, uneconomic curls of meanings? And then there are rivers that double back, meet themselves returning from an aside in the conversation they were having with the land. Picture a river that gradually makes a loop, like a U in a line. Then imagine how, in a season of fast-flowing water, the river would push for a more direct route, going straight from one tine to the other without flowing down and up the U. Then, after a while, the old loop would be cut off from the main line that the river is now following. Similarly language, finding a more rapid route to communicate, will leave unused obsolete words behind, still in the dictionary and perhaps in memory but no longer in the *currency* of language where language is flowing fastest.

Land seems to cross-fertilize language and language the land in an intricate chiasmus of mind and wildness, each a simile for the other. Land likens to language as the viridian green lichens onto trunks; creamy olive mold molds the fungus on the bark; the young green shoot shoots first and later asks questions of the sun, and the radical green root roots itself, complicated, into the simple earth. And the roots of words reach deep down into the earthy past. New leaves, cocky as new words, shine and gleam with sheer delight at being green, and chlorophyll spins sunlight to greenness in lively wordplay, a pun spun of the sun to make "life" from "light."

Metaphor is where language is most wild, spirited and free, leaping boundaries, and it may be no surprise that Amazonian languages can be as matted and dense with metaphor as the forest is tangly with vegetation. The Amazon seems a place of boundless allusion, this unfenced wild, where meaning is twined within meaning; words couple and double, knotted together. The wind twists a leaf's meaning and rain reflects the sheer fertility of language romping from sky to forest and back again. As metaphoric meaning is tucked behind revealed meaning, so the vivid green and wild language of allusion sings on the far side of the obvious, as mind is behind face.

The anthropologist Gerardo Reichel-Dolmatoff wrote breathtaking studies of the layered and allusive languages and thoughtways of the Amazonian people of Colombia, describing how they merge meanings into richly suggestive textures of thought, as association, that wild bindweed of language, makes one thing cling to another. "To be shining" or "to be resplendent" in the Tukano language is, for example, a metaphor for sexual arousal and erection. It takes five pages for him even to begin to describe the elegant and profound associations, through allusion and symbolism, of just one tree, to show how the "bow wood tree," or jacaranda, represents maleness, dominance, aggression and procreative energy. It also suggests a "package" and "thunder," "pollination" and the "semen spurt." So many concepts are held in one tree, says Reichel-Dolmatoff, that it suggests "dimensions of mind hardly suspected." Language reveals depth on depth of enfolded intimacy—softly erotic—between people and nature. He writes of the *uacú* seed, which can refer to sex, because that seed is reminiscent of a deer hoof; the deer hoof leaves a scent trail, the deer smells like the *uacú* seed and like a woman's cunt, while the V-shaped imprint of the deer hoof is like the shape of a woman's legs or the imprint of her buttocks in sand.

Reichel-Dolmatoff meticulously details one word root, *ahp*, which is the basis of words associated with hallucinogenic drugs, sex and creativity in the Desana language. *Ahpi* is coca, and *gahpi* is *Banisteriopsis caapi*, the narcotic vine used for ayahuasca. *Ahp* is the root of several words referring to sexual anatomy, including *ahpiri*, breast, womb; *ahpiru*, nipple; *ahpirito*, testicles; *yahpi*, vulva and *gahki*, penis. *Ahpiri*, meanwhile, means to create, and *ahpari* means to be essential. To me all these suggest wildness; the wild-mindedness of hallucinogens, the wildness of sex, the unboundedness necessary to creativity, and the essentialness of them all.

In the Congolese forests there are similarly dense textures and clusters of meanings in the Kikongo language and in Malaysia, traditionally, people going to get camphor from the forests had to propitiate the spirits of the forest by using a special allusive language called *bassa kapor*, camphor language; obsolete dialects mixed with Malayan words twisted from their original meaning. Language in forests flourishes in complexity and diversity and allusive meaning.

Green is around you, green above you, green below you in the Amazon; and in at least one Amazonian language, green is not a color term—as if green, being everywhere, is the one color not described; rather it is the norm from which others diverge. Reichel-Dolmatoff writes of the Desana language that "*Yahsári* . . . applied to a pale green . . . is not a color term; the stem is *gah, goh*, 'to germinate, to sprout,' related to *gohséri*, 'to shine.' The term is used in shamanic language when referring to the color of young coca leaves."

Intriguingly, if you look up *green* in the *Oxford English Dictionary*, you find something wonderfully similar. *Green* is from an Old Teutonic root *grô*, the same root for *grow* and *grass*. The rainforest is profligate with its greenness: the color of wildness, which grins and gurns, green the fire in the eyes, green the vivid shoot, green the light pouring through leaves, green the verb here; to grow is to green.

In the English language, colors are separate from one another; the words *white, yellow, red, green, blue* and *brown* are distinct terms which do not merge into one another. In the Desana language, Reichel-Dolmatoff shows, color terms melt into one another in a spectrum where one word gently hints at both the previous term and the subsequent term, just as colors themselves softly shift from one to another, yellow turning into orange into red. In this, the Desana language faithfully and subtly follows the truth of nature.

Thus: *bo'ré gohseró* means yellow-bright, for example sun rays;
bo'ré yahsáro means yellow-greenish;
yahsári-da means greenish-blue—for example, an aspect of moonlight; and
bo'ré yahsá diabiríro means yellow-greenish-strengthened-with-red.

For indigenous peoples of the Vaupés River, nature is bursting with signif-icance: shamans, concerned with the symbolic value of the forest's creatures, could be irritated if others only saw the physical or economic aspects of ani-mals rather than their value as carriers of image and meaning. Ralph Waldo Emerson writes, "The world is emblematic. Parts of speech are metaphor, be-cause the whole of nature is a metaphor of the human mind." The wild vision sees that nature, by relation and by association, is a metaphor for our truths, the slanted, hidden, enfolded truths of the spirit, and—as I was to discover dramatically—an emblem for our transformings.

One thing has struck me in virtually every indigenous community I've ever visited: when people are having a conversation in their own language and intermittently dip into the dominant language (Spanish in the Amazon, En-glish in Australia or the Canadian Arctic, Thai among the indigenous hill tribes of Thailand) for terms that they lack in their own, the words they need are words of measurement: measurement of money, of land and time. Words for meters and miles and hectares, virtually any number above about three, words for year or hour or days of the week. Their own languages express the wildness of nature, unfenced in extent; they lack terms for fencing wild time and for measuring wild lands. (A glorious exception to this rule is the relish with which the Papuan Kapauku people set up their own decimal system and can be obsessive counters.)

There are many terms (particularly for things in the natural world) that cannot be translated out of their local indigenous language—for example, be-cause they refer to a rare plant, or because they refer to a specific use of a root, or particular local knowledge. And when an indigenous language dies, so does a whole way of knowing.

Languages that are at ease in the wild world can express a speaker's mean-ing with precision by reference to nature. If I have a headache, for example, I would struggle to describe what kind of headache I have. Not so for the Ainu people on the Japanese island of Hokkaido, who could choose between having a bear headache, a musk deer headache, a dog, woodpecker, octopus, crab or lamprey headache.

In one sense all languages lean toward the wild world, through onomatopoeia. An owl sounds like an owl, 'owling in the dark. A river "splashes" waterily on the tongue as much as on the riverbank. All languages have long aspired to echo the wild world that gave them growth and many indigenous peoples say that their words for creatures are imitations of their calls. According to phenomenologist Maurice Merleau-Ponty, language "is the very voice of the trees, the waves, and the forests."

Places of the highest biodiversity (such as New Guinea and South America) are also the places with the greatest linguistic diversity. But there's more: just as biodiversity is threatened by a few agricultural species—wheat, barley, cattle and rice—so it is with languages; linguistic diversity is threatened by the dominant spreading varieties of Spanish or English. In the deep forests of the Amazon the land speaks in proliferating diversity of languages, each apt to, and expressive of, its locale, but where the forest has been felled for cattle the land no longer speaks its own languages but rather a kind of dumb Spanish, a wilderness roaring with eloquence turned into a wasteland.

In the Amazon, people refer to the forest as a speaking world, relating, talking and communicating. People can be interintelligent with their lands, the languages being formed from the land and then people in turn singing up their land. The roots of *intelligent* are *inter* and *legere*, which means both "read" and "gather"—people could gather plants and *words* from their lands. To gather, of course, itself means both "to collect" (for example, fruits) and "to understand." So we gather.

The Peruvian Amazon was called a Tower of Babel by early Spanish missionaries. Intended as an insult, it was actually a compliment, testimony to the luminous and tumultuous diversity of jungle languages, not just one tree of knowledge but millions, a forest of knowing. But the Church, the state and the education system together have deforested the human mind, forcing people to speak Spanish and aiding logging companies and others in a corporate land theft. If you take people out of their land, you take them out of their meaning, out of their language's roots. When wild lands are lost, so is metaphor, allusion and the poetry that arises in the interplay of mind and nature. To lose your land is to lose your language, and to lose your language is to lose your mind, as John Clare, England's peasant poet (born in 1793), knew. He was one of the very few poets in the canon who insisted on using dialect words, the language most specific to the land he described. This last English indigenous poet was torn up from his roots and shut up in a madhouse miles from his homeland.

Today the Amazon is full of mute inglorious Clares whose silenced words would sing the songlines of a stolen world if they could. For them, their lands had been lit with meaning, glowing with signs and messages, imbued with symbolic thought and without land, they say, they *are* not. Over three hundred people from the Guarani-Kaiowá people in Brazil committed suicide between 1986 and 1999. "Without land, the Indian becomes sad and begins to lose his language. He starts to speak with the borrowed language of the white man. He loses the memory of his people. Without lands . . . he starts to die," said Severino, president of Aty-Guasú, the traditional assembly of the Guarani.

The world's forests have not only been stolen, they have been badly misrepresented, portrayed as thickets dense with unmeaning, a glum dumbness mute as doom. Joseph Conrad did all jungles a terrible disfavor by his insistence on their inarticulacy, because he lacked the skills and experience to hear them and wanted them for a hollow echo to his story. He describes forests— "the wilderness without a sound"—with the shadow words, the negative prefixes *in-, im-, un-, op-*: "oppressive," "the extremity of an impotent despair," "the silent wilderness . . . invincible," "an empty stream, a great silence, an impenetrable forest."

The desire to tame what was wild—so strong in the days of empire— included a desire to tame the wildness of all languages, *even* the languages of empire. Philologist Otto Jespersen, in 1905, used land images to contrast French and English. French, he said, was like the formal, regulated gardens of Louis XIV, in contrast to the wild and open commons of the English *langscape*, "laid out seemingly without any definite plan, and in which you are allowed to walk everywhere according to your own fancy without having to fear a stern keeper inforcing rigorous regulations."

One reason for the massive project of the *Oxford English Dictionary* was a hatred of the wilderness of the English language. Wailed a pamphleteer, "We have neither Grammar nor Dictionary, neither Chart nor Compass, to guide us through the wide sea of Words." It was an attempt to fix the language, to fence it, to delineate it and establish its limits. The result was the opposite. The decades of work, the proliferation of page upon page, book upon book, edition upon edition, was glorious proof that language was unfixable and nomadic, wildly profuse and forever free.

Meanwhile, back in the Amazon, my perception could not have been more different from Conrad's: to me the forests seemed a riot of language in irrepressible gusto, life growling, flowering, leafing, hooting, wriggling and budding, flickering in a forest fiesta of verdant and noisy verbs. Far from Conrad's silence, it is a musical place, the tickety chopping sound of leaves in a breeze, the messianic birdsong in the canopies. Even in dead leaves or the carcass of a bird killed by a jaguar, life speaks out its stories, liana tangled, turquoise and elastic, the parrots that mimic a waterfall or a raindrop in a pool and would mimic the sunrise itself if they could; the tumescent and stretchy growths on trees; nests of tiny glistening worms, or thick snakes on a cold slink. Suddenly, bolt upright with curiosity, a monkey glances down at you, its eyes wide and its paws tapping a tattoo on the branches; the forest is chattering with language, a whole universe laughing with life.

GREEN SONGLINES

One evening at the end of our river journey, Chinita and I went to meet the local healer, or *curandero*, to drink ayahuasca. At dusk we were led down a steep path of thin, gnarly tree roots away from the village to a place apart—a small shelter by the river, with a sloping palm-leaf roof and a log to lean your toes against. The whole front was completely open onto the river and while we waited for the *curandero* we watched bats flutter and moths fly, carelessly thrilled by the full moon. The *curandero* was a small walleyed man in wonky boxer shorts, with a plastic Pepsi bottle of ayahuasca. The moment he arrived, he rubbed my arm and I loved his touch. It was warm, honest and healing. He spoke no Spanish so he talked to me via Chinita about depression, nodding and understanding. You are woundable, he said, succinctly.

He was too scared to call himself an *ayahuasquero* and wouldn't sing the *icaros*, for fear. He had good reason. When missionaries first came to his lands, they brought new sicknesses to the people which the shamans did not know how to cure. This severely undermined the status of the shamans. The racism of the Europeans added to the effect—the Collins Spanish dictionary shamefully translates *curandero* as "quack." But most devastatingly of all, ten to fifteen years previously, missionaries in this area had persuaded the Aguaruna to think their shamans were harming them so the Aguaruna killed their own wisest men. The missionaries, brutal and proud of their ignorance, murdered this gentle, deep knowledge and, bawling out their fatuous hymns, strangled the shamans' ethereal songs to silence.

I met many shamans in the Amazon, very different in their lives and temperaments, but there is a certain expression they share, something I saw in all their eyes, something long-sighted and intense: they were magnets to dreams. If you were a dream, it would be their sleep you'd swim toward, their minds you'd yearn to be dreamt in. Some Amazonian people call their shamans *soñadores*—dreamers—because they use their dreams to tell the future, to foresee hunting, to prophesy rain, and they aid people by the interpretation of dream language. Shamans have an immediate rapport with wildness, with wild mind in all its forms. They look as if they see the skeleton through the skin, the motive behind the gift, the pattern through the chaos, the death behind life, the life behind death, the invisible world behind the visible one. "Desana shamans say that, in order to be able to live well in the visible world, one must look at it through insights gained in the invisible world," writes Reichel-Dolmatoff.

They live on the edge, between the village and the forest, in the twilight borders between worlds, between the living and the dead, between the song-lines and the plastic Pepsi bottle, between sickness and health, between appearance and reality, between dreams and waking, between metaphor and matter. They are messengers, relating, telling, revealing and interpreting; they are travelers, moving between worlds. They are beyonders.

And they are the singers of the songlines of the Amazon. In the jungles, the drum. Shamans' songs, the *icaros*, are an extraordinary, wild music. Ethereal, quiet almost to inaudibility, they are sometimes whistled, sometimes voiced, and sometimes they sound like panpipes from miles away, music half-heard from a source unknown, where melody is more like scent, a sweet resin in the air from an unseen tree. The songs are wakeningly strange and dreamingly familiar. It is an Ariel enchantment, these "airs" of music, soft as smoke, curling and rising through the air and dissolving into it. A shaman in trance often draws on a reefer of pure tobacco and whistles out the smoke so you can almost see the shape of the melody in the smoke he breathes. The word *icaro* seems to be a loan word from the Quichua (a Quechua dialect) verb *ikaray*, "to blow smoke in order to heal."

They say that the songs themselves can heal, consoling the mind and creating harmony. Music and health both depend on harmony, as humanity has long known: in the tenth century, the monks of Cluny in France developed a healing practice based on plants and song. In the Amazon, they say the spirits are drawn by the compelling beauty of the *icaros* and then the shaman can use the spirits to heal a person.

For the Shipibo people of the Peruvian Amazon, the songs can be painted: their visual designs are a musical notation, so you can "sing" a design. They "see" patterns aurally and "hear" songs visually. The synesthetic element of songs is increased with the use of plants. By contrast one self-acknowledged sorcerer was heard singing his *"canciones apestosas"*—stinking songs, as German anthropologist Angelika Gebhart-Sayer writes, "concerning faeces, flatulence, kerosene and cheap soap."

There is a similar synesthesia in the Aboriginal Australian songlines, which are not the only songlines in the world though they are the most famous. Land is crisscrossed with invisible paths or lines which people can travel along: the paths are the ways the Ancestors took in the Dreamtime. These paths are memorized in the form of songs that describe the land, providing a map in music with which you can find your way for hundreds of miles. The synesthesia arises because the songlines are the aural version of the land and the land is the visual version of the song, so the song can be seen in the land and the land can be heard in the song.

In Australia, the songlines are a guide to the land and go horizontal. You learn them in order to travel the land. In the Amazon, *ayahuasqueros* say the earth has its songs, the songlines of each plant. The songlines are a guide to the mind and use the vertical plane.

There are drowsy intervals between *icaros*, when you hear again the cicadas outside or a whirring night bird; all the forest breathing and hunting, mating and purring, rustling and cocooning and watching. The shaman clears his throat and spits and there is a hollow knock of phlegm in a bucket. The song lies like a blind seed in hot silence for a while unsung, then from the shadows you hear a tiny leaf sprout of song. All the songs seem sung in the key of green. The song seems alive like a plant, and in a whistle you hear a wisp of slender stem, while some notes have a shaded pizzicato as if the song noted the nodes on a stem where leaves of a fresh melody may form. The music grows, elastic and gently energetic as a sapling sprung with green meaning; the songline twines like a vine in tendrils of trills, melody winding into leaf. This music is green and vivid and is so strongly suggestive of plants that I feel myself plantlike, rooted in brown leaf mold and thirsty for the sun. Vertical, the music jumps up to the light, clambers like a vine, streaks for the heat of noon and wetness. Then, at its height, the music descends a few tones and decrescendos as a leaf would drop, swinging down from the canopy to the forest floor. The music suggests to me how what is most precious is also most abundant: wild green life in myriad leaves, and shamans know an enormous repertory of songs by heart, singing aloud the immanent music of the forest.

Each plant, say shamans, has its own song and to learn about and use that plant you must learn its song. The songs of the plants come to you in dreams, an Achuar shaman tells me. They are a guide, a map; not a map of landscape but a map of a knowledgescape.

Under Western eyes, the Amazon is an un-understandable wilderness, an undifferentiated green of undefinable plants, a bewildering forest of obscurity where not only your body but also your comprehension can become fatally lost. It confuses and perplexes and is perceived as almost pathologically pathless for the mind. But indigenous people know how to "think" the forests, know that the paths through this wilderness are songs, the songs that each plant has. Song makes a thread of light, a path of the mind; each song tells of one plant's relationship to other plants and not only differentiates one plant from another but distinguishes between the uses of, for example, stem or leaf or root of the same plant. There is practical wisdom here but also psychological wisdom: you find your way and learn how to live unlost, not *through* the wild forest but *within* it. The songlines harmonize people with environment. There is no divide. Mankind is a full-singing part, not discordant but as necessary—and as beautiful—as a violin to an orchestra.

For the Yanesha people of eastern Peru, the songs are the result of an individual quest often involving hardship, fasting, sexual abstinence, vigil and drugs, done in order to obtain the revelation of a song. Anthropologist Hugh Brody writes of the Dunne-za people, of northeast British Columbia, "Powerful dreamers are the Dunne-za equivalent of shamans. . . . An elder once told me that those dreamers function rather like tape-recorders: they record a dream-song as they sleep, and find that they can play it back in the daytime." They are songlines, for through them the dreamers find a path to reach an animal they want to hunt. Brody writes, "The most powerful of Dunne-za dreamers . . . reported that they had found routes to heaven. This was a shamanic response to missionary ideas: if there was a trail to be discovered, the dreamer must find it."

Drinking ayahuasca can seem like being in a wilderness all of its own: while you are entranced you can feel bewildered and scared, as if you were lost in the forest and could see no path. But, shamans say, the *icaros* will guide you, the songs are the path, the songlines of the soul's journey. They can seem horizontal—a pathway through a mental state, a melodic map of mindedness so the psyche need not be lost. But they can also seem vertical—as if someone threw you a vine, a well-twisted rope, to climb upward, a lifeline, a vital liana for the mind to cling to, strong, green and true.

When I first went to Peru, I had lost my way, lost my path. Ayahuasca was the first lifeline thrown to me. Ayahuasca is made from a vine and is known by many metaphoric names, including the "vine of life," but metaphors themselves are known in at least one indigenous language as "twisted language," like a twisted vine, or a rope well twisted to be stronger—metaphor itself is a rope by which the mind can swing from one thought to another. The second lifeline thrown to me was the songs themselves. "Hold on to the *icaros*," Victor had said, and after a while I understood how you could focus on them, clutching them in your mind. Juan sang with compelling passion, as if he drew up all his kindness and strength and made it into good solid rope: if you are really lost, it is only love that can find you.

The *icaros* that Juan sang were of his locale, the particular stream, particular hills and particular plants he knew. In singing them, he made his land quite literally en-chanted. The Kuna people of Panama similarly have songs that describe real places in the jungle, and they also have "curing chants," which contain their most secret and most profound knowledge. But the younger generation are no longer learning the songs. They have little knowledge of the forests, so the chants are almost meaningless. And without the songs, the land in turn has little meaning.

Songlines offer meaning to wild places. Wastelands, by contrast, are places where there are no songlines, devastated places unpathed with song, unenchanted, the wastelands of missionary activity silencing earth wisdom, the devastated land whose meaning is destroyed by logging and mining. Mind, though, courses through wild places in those who, like the shamans, sing up the world and realize it in song.

"IF YOU GO TO THE RIVER MOUTH . . ."

"If you go to the river mouth you will become the owner
of machetes but if you go to the headwaters, you will
become the owner of feather crowns."

Rain fell softly in the night, precious and simple. In the morning, Chinita and I bathed in the stream, swam to a small waterfall, then walked back to the village where the boatman had packed up the boat and was ready to leave. So we journeyed on, following a different river's course, both of us shining with post-ayahuasca serenity. There was a sudden squawk and we all looked up, surprised. None of us knew we still had a chicken in the canoe. We passed rapids and whirlpools. At certain times of the year the water here was high and dangerous: seven people had drowned here six months before. The boatman read the river, working out a route that was deep enough for the motor, but not over rocks or rapids. The chicken, its feet tied together, looked as if it was almost dead from the heat and we periodically dangled it in the water to keep it alive. As we went, a strong gusting wind began whipping up squalls of rain.

After weeks of green in the forests, and seeing nothing larger than the tiny hamlets along the riverbanks, I was unprepared for our next port of call. It was a small town. When we arrived, we were told that the wind had just overturned a small *peque peque* and an old man, too drunk to swim, had drowned. Boats were revving, churning up the water, leaving to go to find his body.

Mestizos with donkeys sat drinking beer in the afternoon. A big YAMAHA sign gleamed red over a shack. The place was awash with coke, both brown and white. There was an atmosphere of underground hysteria and pickpocketing. Piles of rubbish slid down the bank toward the river: rotten, slimy bags, old clothes, toilet paper, Pepsi bottles and beer crates, the remnants of a hard party in the toilets. A young woman with thick makeup played cardsharp games at a little table on the pavement. A man set out a hoopla stall and scowled when someone won. The whole town seemed to lurch, smoky, drunk and stoned.

There were proposals amongst the Aguaruna people to go and kill the narco traffickers, but while the traffickers would have guns, the Aguaruna would have little more than bows and arrows. We stayed with Aguaruna people in the slum part of town. They welcomed us warmly but it was a miserable place even for a night, let alone for life. A dead, half-plucked chicken lay on the floor and a live one scrabbled for nothing under the bed. The squat toilet was slippery underfoot and feces were perched on the rim. The filthy tarpaulin that was wrapped around the toilet was so ripped that there was little privacy. A young woman followed me into the toilet out of curiosity, and I couldn't make her leave. Please go away, I said. She smiled. Go away. *Please.* She didn't. She was odd—maybe a little retarded. I suddenly wanted to scream in her face but I managed not to. My period was in full flood, I'd been in a canoe for hours and I had to change my tampon and my knickers, right now, without slipping on the foul floor. So I did. She watched. I hated her.

Filthy streams of water from one shack washed down onto the shack below. These people were, literally, living in a sewer. In the evening there was a competition to find the "prettiest" girl in town, and the hall was packed with sweaty, beery men. In this part of town, all domestic lighting was either ON or OFF. On, whether you like it or not, at sunset, and off at 11 P.M. I went to bed as early as I could, but I couldn't sleep; cheap pop music blasted into the night and a cockroach walked territorially across my bed and I imagined it in my mouth at midnight.

The headwaters of the rivers of the Amazon are often considered almost sacred and traveling upstream toward them is a kind of purification or initiation. The river mouths, though, are the "contact" areas, places of temptation and danger. I was reminded of the words of an old Tukano man: "If you go to the river mouth you will become the owner of machetes; if you go to the headwaters, you will become the owner of feather crowns."

To me, the forest had been wildly beautiful and the town was a hideous wasteland. But the history of the idea of towns and cities reverses those positions, and the ideal of "the city" has long been considered an opposite of wilderness.

UP, HEATHENS ALL

City walls were built as a physical boundary for the inhabitants, to protect them from the vile hordes outside, but they were also a kind of moral boundary, dividing the city dwellers from the devilish chaos of nature beyond, which was, quite literally, uncivilized. (*Civilized* comes from *civis*, a town dweller.)

Lúcio Costa, the architect of the city of Brasilia, wrote that the founding of a city "is a deliberate act of possession, a gesture in the colonial tradition of the pioneers, of taming the wilderness." The Manhattan grid, developed in 1811, segmenting and linearly dividing the land, was an amazing act of arrogance, notes historian Theodore Steinberg, in *Slide Mountain*: "Through the plotting of its streets and blocks, it announces that the subjugation, if not obliteration, of nature is its ambition."

The city, for the ancient Greeks, was the site of public life and its straight streets were the place of historic deeds in linear time: the stage of men, not women. Women were more associated with the cyclical time of wild nature, unfenced by linear history, in the unruly wilds.

To the Greeks, the city was a way of *thinking* and represented rationality. The city-state was associated with (male) reason and contrasted with the (female) irrationality of the wilderness. The city, with its plumb lines and right angles, represented the straight lines of logic, not the winding ways of intuitive, emotional thought. The cityscape was ruled, in the lines of its building, and it was also ruled in order while the wilderness without was unruly—in both senses. Unruly corkscrewing wiggling tangles of vines and creepers, inhabited by the villains of the piece.

The city represents law and order (the word *police* derives from Greek *polis*, "town"), while the "villains" dwell in the lawless wild nature outside. The word *villain* (a Middle English variant of *villein*, "peasant") once meant a rustic, and the root of the word is in villa—originally the word was merely a simple description of where someone dwelled. The word gradually shifted, coming to mean criminal.

The ideal of the city was partly founded on St. Augustine's *City of God*, and Christianity has long preferred the city to nature: cities were the home of bishops, the whole of Brasilia was laid out in the shape of the Christian cross, and Christianity used cities as a demonstration of its triumph over nature. Wild nature was associated with downright evil, and words originally denoting merely living in the country (heath dwelling, or living in a *pagus*, or small village) were turned into the derogatory terms *heathen* and *pagan*.

In the Amazon, these ancient battles are still played out. Missionaries try to keep people from living in the forests and force them to live in built settlements, in towns with a mission center, a church and a school, partly because the missionaries can exercise greater control in that situation, but also because of the deep affinities they perceive between the forest, the heathenry and nature-based spirituality.

There was, of course, an abyss between the ideal of the city and its actuality. For in the same way as there is a conservation of energy, by which total energy remains constant though it may shift from place to place, just so, there is what I'd call a conservation of wildness, so wildness, pent-up, blocked, bricked-over, fenced-in, built-on, suppressed too much, will erupt in the volcanic lawless havoc of urban wildernesses: knob rot, syringes and puke.

Shakespeare's London had its piss-seedy Southwark, which had London's City fathers in apoplectic rage, describing the "eavell practizes of incontinencye in great innes, haveinge chambers and secrete places adjoyninge to their open stages and gallyries, inveglynge and alleurygne of maides . . . the publishing of unchaste uncomelye and unshamefaste speeches and doynges . . . utteringe of popular bayse and sedycious matters, and manie other Corruptions of youthe and other enormyties." (Sounds fun. I'm allured already.)

The idea of "civilization," too, has long been opposed to wilderness. "The principal task of civilization is to defend us against nature," wrote Sigmund Freud. Today, it is nature that needs defending against civilization.

The word *civilization* was coined surprisingly late. Boswell quarreled with Johnson over it, for the latter didn't want to include it in his dictionary. From its inception it's been a conceited and dishonest term. The connotations of civilization include moral decency and it suggests that nature in general and wilderness in particular lack that quality. *Urbanidad* in Spanish means politeness, inextricably linking what is urban with good behavior or courtesy. The word *courtesy* itself, from the court, at the heart of the city, expresses a similar idea and to be courteous is to be at the very least civil, of course, and we're back to *civis*.

Civilization has also connoted culture and the fine arts, and its use suggests that people of the land are culturally inferior. The word is frequently used by dominant societies to pretend that only their kind of civilization is worthy of the name. In the 1987 edition of *American History: A Survey*, a standard textbook for high school students, the arrival of the Europeans in the Americas "is the story of the creation of a civilization where none existed"— one of the most false and bigoted sentences I've ever read. In 1975, a Kaingang woman of South America said, "Today, my people see their land invaded, their forests destroyed, their animals exterminated and their hearts lacerated by this brutal weapon that is civilization."

Lieutenant W. L. Herndon of the U.S. Navy, in a report to Congress on the Amazon in 1854, said, "Civilization must advance, though it tread on the neck of the savage, or even trample him out of existence." Andrew Johnson, in his message to Congress in 1867, said, "If the savage resists, civilization, with the ten commandments in one hand and the sword in the other, demands his immediate extermination." Quite which of the ten commandments encourages genocide is slightly hard to see.

The word *savage*—used so often to insult people of the land—comes from *silvaticus* (of woods or trees) from *silva*, a wood. In the Amazon, the forest is called *la selva*, while *salvaje*, the Spanish word literally meaning "person of the forests," is used to mean a savage and is a frequent term of abuse. (A word history remarkably similar to those of *pagan*, *heathen* and *villain*.)

In the Western tradition, not only *civilization* but *culture* too is frequently used as an opposite to nature—wild lands are uncultivated and the people of the land are supposedly uncultured. Denis Cosgrove, professor of human geography, writes, "Both classical and biblical traditions placed the city at the highest point in a hierarchy of imaginative environments built upon wilderness." Culture was decreed to be the opposite of nature and found in the city.

Interestingly, though, the roots of the word *culture* are inextricably tied to nature, through the idea of cultivation. Norwegian geographer Kenneth Robert Olwig, in *Landscape, Nature, and the Body Politic*, writes, "In its original, classical sense nature and culture were not polar opposites, quite the contrary. Culture was, if anything, the worship of nature." Culture comes from *cultus*, and *cultus* stems from *colere*. *Cultus* carries meanings including "cultivation," "tending," "care," "respectful treatment," and *colere*, "to cultivate," also means to dwell in a place, to honor and to worship. So the pagans, heathens, villains and savages were originally the most cultured of all.

Historian Polybius, a native of Arcadia, described how various meanings of culture merged: pastoral life in Arcadia involved cyclical "cultic" rites, involving nature and the arts. Culture was entwined in nature for the Arcadians. And that is exactly how Amazonian people live, where culture is woven with nature's vivacity and nature is intricate with culture's meanings.

The forests have been tended (cultivated) for millennia by Amazonian people. ("The wild is not the opposite of the cultivated," says philosopher and physicist Vandana Shiva. "It is the opposite of the captivated.") Nature and culture may be distinct; a house and the garden are domestic spaces, and have a different quality from the wild forests, but it is not an opposition. Further, one can be "at home" not only in a house but in the natural world outside. For nature and culture find trysting places in the forests, interweaving and reflexive in a lovely gyre of mutuality. Swedish ethnographer Kaj Århem writes, "Among Amerindians of the Amazon, the notion of 'nature' is contiguous with that of 'society'," and he notes that "the same can be said of many, if not most, indigenous peoples of the world." Sometimes, writes Århem, even animals "are attributed with 'culture'—habits, rituals, songs, and dances of their own."

For forest people, nature is defended by culture: many rules concerning hunting and the nonexploitative use of resources—blunt ecological truths—are encoded in the myths and magic, tales and enchantments that make up a society's culture. Shamans and thinkers of the forest know that the mind learns best this way. Myths, comments Århem, are "extremely efficient" for the purpose as they are "at once ecologically informed, emotionally charged and morally binding." If you scrape off the magic, then the raw facts and laws are harder to recall and harder to impose. So culture protects nature.

SELF-WILLED LAND

For me, the cities and towns of the Amazon were problematic. In one town, Maldonado, the atmosphere seemed fetid, unhealthy as a fly trap, people caught in a purple neon twist of poisoned sugar. It was a place where people ended up: thus far and no farther, a sink rather than a summit. The one road stopped there. There were flights to Cuzco, which most people couldn't afford. Or else there was Brazil. On foot.

It was as if wildness congealed here and turned to madness. There was too much alcohol, too much dope. People came and went mad, talking for days of William Blake, as one demented young man did to me. The most obviously insane person in town stood in the middle of the streets, amiably lunatic, directing the traffic. No one ever paid any attention, as he stood like a crazy conductor of a blind orchestra. In the stagnancy of the place, he chose—with that symbolic appropriateness of the sanely mad—to direct motion.

I left for Cuzco because I was joining some Harakmbut men there to trek through their forests. But when I arrived in Cuzco, I was suddenly ill. I'd barely been there two hours, and had many jobs to do, when I found myself faint and dizzy. I got a taxi to my hotel and crawled into bed and blanked out with the nauseous headache of altitude sickness. I felt too ill to move just four feet across the room to dig out my painkillers from my rucksack. After about six hours, I did manage that and about two hours later I got out of my room, staggered in to the hotel owner and asked her to bring me water and bananas. She brought them with steaming cups of *mate de coca*, the coca tea that is used to treat altitude sickness. I was in a strange delirium for hours. Sick in Cuzco, the hours crawling around the rim of the day like dying flies, I heard those hours drone.

The next day I had to go to the airport to meet the Harakmbut men. If I failed to show up, I had no way of contacting them and I would miss out on what promised to be an astonishing trek. I managed to pack and get to the airport, but once there, I nearly collapsed in a policeman's arms. He was kind, found me water, shade and a place to sit. I was shaking and my head felt cracked with pain. Someone gave me coca, someone else gave me unidentified local medicine, someone else found me water, and I took everything. In spite of the heat, my body was freezing cold though my head was on fire. I met the Harakmbut guys and we drove all day up to a high pass over the altiplano. The light and the motion were almost unbearable and I remember almost nothing about that day except that a woman in a café along the way rubbed my face with flower water and fed me banana and papaya like a child and I had to ask for help to go to the toilet.

The moment we reached the forests I felt better. Mainly it was simply being at a lower altitude, but also being out of the cities and back in the forests made me feel happy and well. The guides were wanting to set up an eco-tourism project here, called "Wanamei," and this trek was a practice trek. We would be trekking for days, walking by day and camping in small clearings at night and there was nowhere on earth I would rather have been.

The forest is never still. Wild vitality streams through it and all of life is on the shimmer, curling in the air, twisting up the liana, swimming in the rivers. Firefly and dragonfly take the plunge, leaping into the morning of life and gone by evening. A leakless, waterproof hyacinth leaf juggles a raindrop around its rim. Tiny insects sting, bite and itch. It is a world of contrasts; thunder and gossamer; the giant and the dwarf. A thousand-year tree, heavily buttressed like a well-anchored grudge, a moth with a wingspan of a foot, a butterfly seven inches across and a dwarf frog barely a centimeter long.

A light moth pretends to be a rotting leaf on moss, a moss-moth, a pun in sunlight. A rotten palm branch cradles fresh growth—death cradling new life in the palm of its hand. And on the branch an insect pretends to be a twig. There is a fecund, compulsive all-at-once-ness here, life thriving, twisting its way up to the sun, the green shoot poking through the decaying leaf. Everywhere is the signature of restless life; roots ripple into earth, vines stream from trees, leaves glimmer with green. The Amazon has many seasons, but it doesn't have a marked "spring" and "fall." Here, those two seasons are not separate times of the year but are verbs that take place concurrently, to spring and to fall. A sapling springs up and a mossy log falls, nudging another inch nearer earth. A glittering jewel of fluorescent green fungus is so new, sprung up brilliant overnight, while the forest itself is so old. Often what strikes me is the forest's sheer intensity of *now*. At twilight, the momentness is critical—cicadas zing up the volume, there is an increase of energy, of electricity, almost, at the zestful changeover between the day players and the night players. Now is all. Now the rain and new growth, now the hatching mosquitoes, now the ant and jaguar, now too the rotting snakeskin and dank woody stem, smelling of mushroom.

It takes vigilance to avoid being bitten or stung. I walked with my long-legged trousers tucked into socks, my long-sleeved shirt buttoned high. Given any opportunity, ants would start marching a column up my leg, crawling in awful army regularity: march, bite, march, bite. When we stopped to eat, flies would give us no reprieve. They swarmed together or needled us individually; they hovered in front of our eyes, their horrible persistence dementing. In the evenings, the flies would disappear and, to the minute, the mosquitoes would start up. (Mark Twain once noted the torture of mosquitoes inside his tent at night. Finally, he said, he could bear it no more and opened the tent flap, got them all in, and went and slept outside.) Writing notes was hard. We walked from first light until dark, going at a cracking pace, and when we stopped it wasn't for long. I would scribble the odd word in my notebook as I walked, trying not to trip. In the evening, the guides tied candles to the trees with shreds of plant tendrils and as they ate and slept, I would write my notes in almost complete darkness, for the light of a torch would attract a thousand moths and other insects. A guide saw my difficulty and caught a firefly for me, gently looping a thin thread around its body and tying it to the tip of my pen so it glowed its gentle green light on my notebook.

It had been a little hard for the leaders to persuade other local people to come on this trip because it was a journey through dense forest; paths once used were overgrown now (*cerrado*, closed, is the term they use) and it was almost impossible to see them. Much of the way, Hector, one of the guides, walked at the front with a machete, carving the way through, striking down saplings, slashing back thick vegetation, down a route he could not see but which he knew was right. Local people didn't want to stay a moment longer than necessary in the parts of the forest they considered wild. They were afraid of this area because it was unfamiliar, because they feared bad spirits and because it was an area where the wildest animals lived. Jaguars were there. How many? *Bastante.* Enough, plenty.

"*Terra viridis incognita*"—the green unknown land—was the way Europeans first saw this forest wilderness. American wilderness author Roderick Frazier Nash writes of the etymology of the word *wilderness* from the prefix *wild* and the Old English *dēor* (animal)—thus *wild-dēor-ness* meant the place of wild beasts. There is an echo in the Amazon as people speak of *monte real*—primary forest where people go to hunt or, indeed, where people are scared to go because they fear the wild beasts.

But what of the *wild* part of the word *wilderness?* This is to me the most interesting. Nash writes, "In the early Teutonic and Norse languages, from which the English word in large part developed, the root seems to have been 'will' with a descriptive meaning of self-willed, willful, or uncontrollable. From 'willed' came the adjective 'wild' used to convey the idea of being lost, unruly, disordered, or confused." And so, you could say, a wilderness is a self-willed land—easily my favorite definition. What is wild is not tilled. Self-willed land does what it likes, untilled, untold, while tilled land is told what to do.

The forest drinks rain, drinks sunlight, drinks sound. One ubiquitous sound is the bird that sounds like an untuned radio, a kind of high-frequency wolf whistle. The guides' hearing was far better than mine and often they would say, "Hush, listen; do you hear that?" A river, perhaps, whose sound in the distance they were using as a direction finder. I listened and heard whirrings, scrabblings and gnawings but no river sound at all, and they laughed and teased me for my deafness. When all the guides could clearly hear a *peque peque* in the distance, all I could hear was them saying, "Be quiet, sshh, listen." Some sounds were unmissable—the frogs' tromboning honk, one particularly loud at midnight as if it wanted something really badly. (I think it was sex.) Sometimes as we walked, we heard the mischievous monkeys giggling far above us. The guides saw a small monkey in the trees at one point, solitary and yeeping. They whistled to it and it came down in response but the moment it saw us, it stopped. Another time, a guide made a particular call, somewhere between a hoot and a chirrup, and a spider monkey replied. Once, the guides took me to see a whole monkey circus in the trees, bouncing, bum waggling, using the branches like a trapeze, rattling the treetops.

Plants in the rainforest have an audacious cleverness. Some can deliberately create the smell of rotting flesh to attract flies. The *Marantaceae* grow on
the forest floor and have dark purple undersides to their leaves so they collect
light on the topside but do not pass it through to plants below, rather every
leaf reflects light back to itself. (Light is food, down here.) A palm tree has
spiky needles, probably to keep monkeys from climbing up and grabbing its
fruit. Pitcher plants have flowers designed with hairs and glue so flies go in
but can't get out.

There are cedars and mahogany, rubber trees and chonta palms. The trees
grow at different heights, creating the forest stories, rising up to the highest
canopy. But the ground has its own levels too and there is no solid terrain for
the earth is a mass of roots and suckers, mosses, fungus and decaying leaves.

Wiry plant life riots here, tangling in creepers, ropes, vines and knots, a
matted greenness; vegetation first and last, above you, below you, surrounding you. In reckless zest, every protuberance and root is a sucker for rain, a
snorter of warmth, a guzzler of mold. Liana, rampant, rockets skyward, winding taut and hanging loose. Everywhere you look, the air is crazy with leaves,
tumbling and high-spirited, burgling the light.

BEWITCHED, BOTHERED AND BEWILDERED

Being lost in an English woodland, the one-night bewitching of a *Midsummer Night's Dream*, suggests a frisson of fear, but the be-wildering of being lost in the Amazon is terrifying. If you are lost here, you could die. The
paths themselves are uncertain: we often crossed rivers on the infamous and
ubiquitous *puentos podridos*, the rotten bridges that would collapse at a step. In
some places, a "bridge" was actually a log several feet underwater, which you
had to find with your toes and balance across. Wading chest-high through
rivers I would always ask one of the guides to take my notebooks for me. At
several points the guides would make an impromptu bridge by hacking down
a small tree, felling it over the river.

It was wise to follow the guides exactly, even going the same way around a
tree in the path, for there were always things they noticed and you didn't, and

you could find yourself with a mouthful of poisonous spider. The guides told me of one foreigner walking near here—not with them—who had gone for a swim without asking his guides' advice. They found him later, an arm here, a leg there. The pool he'd chosen for his dip was a caiman's pool. One night, we were near another caiman's pool and saw it from a distance. None of its body was visible, only its eyes, gleaming red rectangles reflecting in the light of our flashlights.

"*Pise donde yo he pisado*"—step where I have stepped—said one of the guides, Matteo, at one point, and he meant it precisely, for one step and a couple of footfalls wrong and you can lose the path. Forest people routinely snap twigs off plants as they go, leaving a tiny signage along the path for the person behind, or for themselves. If, for example, a hunter leaves the path to chase an animal, he should snap leaves off as he runs, to find his way back.

The trail we were on was a traditional hunting trail, but one unused for years. It was very much Hector's path. He walked first, leaving the campsite at dawn. Proud of his knowledge of the trail, he had kept the path open in his mind alone until he macheted his way through now. He used the position of the sun for direction for several days and then heard a river that he wanted to reach. He walked with his machete in his right hand, his bows and arrows and cooking pot in his left, and on his back a small rice sack tied up with forest rope. All the guides used machetes, not only to cut through paths but also as an extra leg, sticking it into a log for balance, or like a walking stick to climb a muddy bank. Hector's sense of direction was so perfectly judged that on part of the journey—a three-day walk in dense jungle, with no compass other than the sun, with (to me) no way of mapping a route at all, no way of seeing farther than twenty feet ahead, no hill, no land contour, with streams that may change their courses from season to season—he brought us to a river where we would wait for a boatman whom they'd asked to come there. After all the days and miles, we hit the river about a hundred yards from the meeting point.

A path in the forest can seem so visible, so inevitable when you're walking along it, but once you've stepped off it, you know it for what it is: a fragile skein too thin to see unless you're looking right down on it. Once you are off the path, it does not seem inevitable. Rather it seems extraordinarily lucky and briefly precious. On the instant of stepping off the path, a curtain of green confusion falls. A bare little patch of earth catches your sight. Is that the path? It goes nowhere. The path may be three feet away but be as invisible as if it were three miles away. What is completely revealed and what is completely hidden are so close, depending on angles of sight just a few degrees different. (If you do get lost, stop. Mark your position, light a fire if you can. Move in circles around it, trying to find the path.)

Where the path was most thickly overgrown, we would wait for Hector to swipe several times with his machete for every step we could take. As we waited, we were knotted up in the forest, the runners tripped us, liana twined around us, roots crisscrossed our feet, branches curled around us: we were held in the huge Gordian embrace of the jungle. But the path is not only a space, a thin absence of forest: keeping a path open is an act of care, for the path is a line of belonging and walking it repeatedly is an act of intimate love.

THE GENIUS OF THE FORESTS

The air of the rainforests is as damp as the exhalation of breath, steamy with the forest's hot, wild genius. *Genius*, that well-rooted word, refers in the classical pagan tradition to the spirit of a person and, also important, of a place. Across the world, people have perceived forest wildernesses to be full of spirit, as if the real and visible world had an equally real but invisible world folded within it. This idea is appropriate to the way one's vision works in the forests for you can look at the scene around you and yet fail to see what is there because the creatures' camouflage, from moth to jaguar, is so good.

Amazonian people speak of spirits everywhere in the forests. The Kukama people say there are spirits in streams, lakes, trees, salt licks and the small garden plots. One Shawi man comments, "We Shawi think that every living thing has its own spirit." For a Shiwilu man, Fidel Lomas Chota, there is a connection between wildness and spirit: domesticated plants don't have a spirit, but by contrast *las frutas sylvestres*, wild fruits, have spirits, and everything in *el monte* (the wild forest) has a *dueño*, spirit.

In the Amazon, there are four spirits of great power: *sacha runa*, the owner or guardian of the forest; *sacha mama*, the mother or creator of the forest; *yacu runa*, the owner or guardian of the river, and *yacu mama*, the mother or creator of the river.

In India, when an area of forest was cut down, people would often leave several trees standing as a sacred grove, where the forest spirits could take refuge. In Kerala, a sacred grove is called a *kaavu* and people describe it as "sacred," "fearful" and full of *shakti*, the uncontrolled, uncontrollable life force. They are places of fertility and danger. As more and more sacred groves are cut down, the people say, the spirits lose their dwelling places and move to the fewer and fewer groves left standing. In these groves now the spirits gather in ever greater numbers so the groves become ever more powerful, places of high potency. People believe these sacred places are "wild" in the sense of being self-willed—not subject to human will.

In Borneo, as in India, when trees were cut down, a grove would be left sacred for the spirits. The Khant people of Siberia had groves that they considered sacred and they were places where they would not hunt or fish. In Papua New Guinea, similarly, there are sacred groves where men do not hunt and women are not allowed: human life is believed to have originated there. For the Kaulong people of Papua New Guinea, the forest is the home of spirits that may be capricious and dangerous.

Anthropologist Carol MacCormack describes how the people of the Sherbro coast in Sierra Leone keep sacred groves that function as burial grounds and places for communication with the ancestors, sites for rites of passage. Children being initiated into adulthood "pass through the portal dividing the village and its mundane domestic preoccupations from the dangerous, potent, sacred forest. Initiates are carried straight into the maw of the great forest *min*" (*min* means "spirits" and, used as a verb, "to eat"), and the initiates "die as distinct social persons, and will be born from the vagina of the *min* after three or four months of liminality. This forest spirit symbolizes the potency of gender unity, and has both scrotum and womb/vagina."

The Harakmbut men told me stories of the "World Tree," Wanamei, which saved humans, and in Scandinavia there was also a tradition of a World Tree, the Ash Yggdrasil. At the twilight of the gods, everything would pass

away, but the earth would be repeopled from two who had hidden in the
World Ash, and their names were *Lif* (Life) and *Lifthrasir* (Desire of Life).
The Hindu World Tree similarly symbolizes generation and life. In the early
years of Buddhism it was thought that certain spirits or genii of the trees
lived in tree trunks and spoke from there.

Sacred groves abounded in the European classical tradition. In Greece,
the best-known was Dodona, and in Roman myth the sacred grove where
Romulus and Remus were suckled by a wolf became the site of the Luper-
calia, the riotous, lascivious festival in honor of Pan.

European countries have long thought that forest wildernesses were peo-
pled with spirits: the German Wood Wives, Wild Folk, Forest Folk or Moss
Folk; in Sweden Odin the Wild Huntsman and in England Puck, the spirit
of the woods and, widespread in Europe, the Wild Man of the woods, who
reportedly knew various secrets of nature lost to a more "civilized" age.

The European Wild Man struck me as astonishingly similar to the Amazonian spirit of the woods, called the Master of Animals, who has special
knowledge of plants. In Finland, a special forest god, Tapio, owned the wild
animals, so anyone wanting to hunt had to ask his permission and offer gifts
to persuade him to give up his creatures—which is exactly how Amazonian
people describe their relationship with the Master of Animals.

In the Amazon, I was also amazed by the similarities between the Master
of Animals and the ancient pagan figure of Pan: half goat, half man, shaggy
piece of nature and the player of panpipes who tends his creatures. Reichel-
Dolmatoff writes of the "Master of Animals of the Amazonian rainforest Indians, that supernatural woodsman, with his staff, his flute, his knowledge of
herbs, and his hidden abodes." He looked after the animals and guarded them
from overhunting, and if anyone wanted to hunt his animals, they had to seek
permission from him. "The figure of the Master of Animals is a projection of
a man's conscience; if he sees him or feels his presence in any way, he knows
he has violated some fundamental norm." A sign of him creates a feeling of
trepidation, even fear. For ancient Greeks, too, Pan was a frightening figure
and the word *panic* comes from Pan, from the fear that people could experience, journeying through the wild woods, hearing the eerie cries of wildness,
imputing them to Pan and feeling frightened if they had hunted his animals
too zealously.

NOTHING UNTHRUST

The Wild Man of the woods is famously lustful, a hairy, half-naked creature, on the lurk for sexual encounters, with hot breath and a smoky look in his eyes. In the classical tradition, the maenads of the wild forest—the female companions of Dionysus or Bacchus—suck each other's jugs, and lap up the forest juices with the satyrs. Pan, with capering goatishness and prolific masturbation, pings semen around the bosky woods, boasting that he'd shagged all the drunk maenads. Dionysus, god of having a wild time, was god of forest orgies and following in the same tradition the priapic Puck fucks everything in his grasp, lightfoot with reckless fertility and a restless, truculent horniness.

Meanwhile in the Amazon, the Master of Animals is a creature of "marked phallic attributes," according to Reichel-Dolmatoff. Rainbows represent his ejaculation and he is associated with the fertility of game; for Amazonian people, the animals' breeding grounds are considered places of strong spiritual energy, a domain of the Master of Animals, whose "universe is that of womblike abodes, seminal plant juices."

The Amazon, like the forests of Europe, throbs with an unmistakable pulse: the grinning green man, with a hooded wink, his green wand in one hand and his other—bolt upright—in the other. The forests of the world hum up the erotic; moss, damp and steaming, lust run riot in the liana, and a jaguar's throaty purr. Potency thickens every leaf and brims in every flower, tightly immanent in the bud then bursting with the urgent relief of dehiscence.

Language links sex with the forest: Reichel-Dolmatoff reports the language associations that join words for places where women wash and words for desire, with words for licking, including male sexual fantasies and secret places in the forest for making love. The sense of a wild, spirited life force is almost tangible in the Amazon—a rampant, thirsty energy, life shoving its way into rain and sun, splitting apart stone to get there, barging branches out of the way, while roots, in a concentrated drilling, corkscrew their way to water and the whole wild forest is an expression of the driven will to sunlight.

Nature swells with sex, cooing, licking, flyting, courting, hinting, mating and intimating: carnal knowledge, knowing, kenning, cunning. Every dragonfly is glued end to end to another. To every monkey an erection; to every insect, sackfuls of eggs; flowers bloom in smirking shapes of visual innuendo; leaves are protuberant; mushrooms conjugally fungal; every parrot on the squawk for it; every peccary rutting for it; every tendril internally sprung for it. Nothing unthrust. Nothing unfecund. Ripeness lusts till it rots, and its very rottenness makes a dank, warm bed for the next tight tip to poke through. For, nudging deep down in the chthonic nub of things, in the sweet and musky smell of a warm, rotting log, *eorthe* begins the cycle again.

Matteo was full of stories, including one that began, "In the end of the world"—the "end," though, was actually the beginning, long ago. The Harakmbut people had forgotten everything, said the story, including how to make love, so people tried to have sex with their belly buttons. One day, people noticed the monkeys with all their offspring and asked the monkeys how to make children. "Like this," said a monkey, taking his mate and illustrating. "Aha," said the people, and couples disappeared into the forests. "So, thanks to the monkeys," Matteo grinned and gave a thumbs-up, "we know how to make love and masturbate."

Wilderness and wild nature are sexual—if you had to choose part of the human anatomy as an analogy for wilderness, you'd have to go for the loins—and we humans lose an acute and vital part of our sensuality when we ignore the wild world; the grinding of shoots thrusting up into the light, the hungry torsion as snake squeezes snake, birds flightily dipping as they twang an orgasm in between wing beats, the delicate incipience of young sexuality in bud and blossom, lizards eyeing each other up for a darting lick of quick sex or basking with satisfied lust.

The Christian Church quite rightly identified wild nature with sex but then, in a cruel blow against life, decided to associate them both with the devil—fornicators were beasts and toads, the Devil was the Arch Beast. Othello's language of sexual "disorder" is of "goats and monkeys": their offense is their promiscuous, uncontrolled sexuality. Heretics of the Christian Church have always been identified with sex and beasts. The spirit of Pan is the spirit of lust, lust for sex, lust for life—the force that through the pink fuse drives the blood, the force that drives the green to green and grow. Pan was the personification of vagrant, extravagant sex in the wilds. The Christian Church, quite horribly, identified Pan as Satan.

All humans know the soft seduction of nature, how the wild world has its wild way with one's sexual senses; how it arouses, how we yearn for the touch of the warm summer breeze across the naked body, the naughty wink between friends looking at a marrow swollen in sun and rain: this is the longest love affair we humans have ever known, the lifelong intoxication of the senses, which is why even in the modern Western world, for many people their most lasting sensual satisfaction comes from their gardens.

The word for *wild* in Chinese, *ye* (Japanese *ya*), basically means "open country," but in combination with other terms, it means something sexually illicit. So an illegitimate child is an "open-country child," a prostitute is an "open-country flower," and "wild" can mean "sexually unrestrained." For the Laymi people of the central Bolivian highlands, sex within an official relationship takes place inside a house, but illicit, free or uncommitted sex takes place outdoors, in the hills or by the river—in wild places. For the Kaulong people of Papua New Guinea, the forest is the place where wild animals and humans have sex.

Sure-yani Poroso, a leader of the Leco people in Bolivia, tells me how his people used to have sex outside, in the forests, up trees, by the river, in canoes, all over the place, vagrantly wandering, but the missionaries came and insisted that people should only have sex enclosed, indoors, in bed, and in one position: the woman underneath. It was, of course, quite literally, the missionary position. "But no animal does it like two sticks. That was a law no one ever obeyed," said Sure-yani.

Bringing sex indoors was, I would argue, not so much to do with controlling sex between humans but rather controlling the sexual relationship between humans and nature. Because if *that* relationship was intimate and sensual— sexual, even—then there would be no space for the Judeo-Christian god. Only by prizing human sexuality away from nature, only by claiming this sexuality was filthy, could you make space for Jehovah. The pagan, heathen and sensual love between people and wild nature had to be destroyed so that the antiwild and abstract god could take control. God could only stamp out that intense and beautiful relationship by declaring that nature's sexuality was devilish. And thus we have centuries of shudder at wild, writhy beasts, fucking like goats, hung like donkeys, breeding like rabbits. Puritanism and its first cousin Pornography alike de-naturing sex, de-flowering the sweet love between mankind and nature.

Arthur Miller's play *The Crucible*, based on the history of Salem, Massachusetts, in 1692, opens with a note from the author: "The edge of the wilderness was close by . . . the Salem folk believed that the virgin forest was the Devil's last preserve . . . to the best of their knowledge the American forest was the last place on earth that was not paying homage to God." The play is full of references to "wildness," and the play's "villain" is the young woman, Abigail, whose fundamental sin is her sexuality, and her sensuous dancing in the forests.

American author Nathaniel Hawthorne, in *The Scarlet Letter*, 1850, wrote of the forest around seventeenth-century Salem as a place of freedom but of temptation, a moral wilderness full of sexual evil. Pearl, the illegitimate girl, beautiful and mischievous, the one character fully at home in the forest, is an "imp of evil, emblem and product of sin."

In the sixteenth and seventeenth centuries, the male point of view decreed that both women and nature needed to be constrained. What really got their goat was when wildness combined with woman *and* nature *and* sex, in the supposed orgies of the witches' sabbath. The witch-hunters thought nature's wildness was evil: wild weather, lightning and thunder, wildcats, toads and storms all became associated with witchery. Out on the heathen heath, frotting against tree trunks, witches would have sex *outside*, not indoors with the godly, and their wild infernal dancing suggested the very groin of wilderness.

But Christianity has never wholly succeeded in its attempt to separate sex and nature, for our human sexuality is wonderfully, hotly, happily linked to the natural world, as you would know if you'd ever licked your finger and gently stroked the pinkish smooth inside of a conch shell, or if you have ever flushed with understanding looking at a Georgia O'Keeffe painting, where petal and paint whorl inward, a curled world of lip on lip leading you in, or if you have ever planted leeks in deep puddles of wet compost, your hand straining down in the mud, gloopy and sucking, your fingers yearning inward and down into this dark, wet and lovely world.

I have my own personal wilderness, filthy, earthy, jungly, shaggy, roaring with its waterfalls, its white cascades—a self-willed, claggy swamp. There are caves with smooth, sheer, wet walls, cliffs within, a peak, salmon-colored, salmon-smelling, groves of vines and creepers, black and shiny, writhing like snakes. Sometimes it flutters as if a flock of birds is passing through its forest canopy and it has its moods and seasons, its cool fresh season, its burning, thundery season, its sweet-sowing, earth-for-seed fertility, and its angry autumn sheddings when red ore flows in the gulch and ooze congeals on its twisting gnarly hairiness. No one maps my wilderness, though they may come here. There are no tracks here, no books on the subject. A landscape unknown to science, infused though it is with mind. It's a fecund place of high humidity, steamy as a rainforest.

"NOT ENOUGH CUNT. THAT'S THE PROBLEM WITH GENESIS."

The path wound on, past plants with seedpods like Shakespearean money pouches, matte black mushrooms, sweaty tree roots aboveground like wigwams, leafcutter ants carrying bits of leaves like heraldic shields, parrots swooping to salt licks in the early mornings and evenings, a trace of a giant river otter (*lobo del rio*: river wolf), a spiderweb with hundreds of miniature spiders running arpeggios up and down the threads, a hole in the tree roots that is an "armadillo's fridge," used by the armadillo for storing insects, and a tree that was a wild pig's favorite back-scratching post. The guides showed me toxic plants and medicinal ones; plants that sting or ones to treat colic and diarrhea, one a painkiller, another antibiotic. (Poison and medicine, curse and cure, grow so close.) They showed me a tree of very hard wood, good for machete handles, and a spiky seedpod that is used as a hairbrush. We had to run part of the way through a bees' nest on the path, and at another point the guides leapt off the path, bows and arrows ready, chasing a wild pig.

When Matteo told me stories, I understood him for the most part. Every once in a while, though, I would not understand a term, but I didn't tell him, not wanting to halt his flow. He, though, seemed to have an uncanny knack of knowing the precise thing I hadn't understood. "Did you understand *that* bit?" he would ask, and I'd own up. Well, no, not that *exact* bit. After this had happened a few times, I saw the pattern. Whenever the stories got sexy (which they often did), Matteo would use demotic sexual terms and my dictionary Spanish would fail me.

The stories lit the journey, like pale orange luminescent fungus lighting a

log. Sometimes the stories were information rather than narrative. The walking tree, for instance, is a type of palm with roots like fingers, which the tree
will produce on the side nearer to water while roots on the other side wither
away so gradually the tree can "walk" to water. And, with the walking tree, the
walking fish, the "shuyo," six inches long, which can get out of water and move
across land to find new water.

In the evenings, Matteo told me stories of the "end" of the world (at the
beginning). The main story involved a great fire, which people thought would
destroy them all. So they took a naked virgin to the head of the river and
asked her to spread her legs. Various parrots had to try to drop a seed into
her. "There was a lot of cheating, but finally there was a parrot which managed to drop the seed of a *piyaho* flower right into her cunt, and in a moment
it began to grow into the tree called Wanamei. The fire got worse, and people
were frightened. The tree understood the Harakmbut language, and people
asked it to bend down a bit, so they could climb up its branches, because the
earth was melting. In this way, many people and animals were saved."

This story intrigued me for its inversion of Judeo-Christian themes: the
living tree is the savior rather than a dying man pinned to a dead tree. The
woman brings life and salvation rather than death and damnation. Wanamei
is a true tree of life and it suggests the vital necessity of forests, a rainforest
above all, for when the earth is dangerously hot and dry, the rainforest offers
wet, wet life, wet and very female, while the dry parchment of patriarchal religion blames both tree and woman. (In India, trees are "an abode of female
deities," says Indian writer Anees Jung. "In them rests a divinity worthy of
worship.")

Matteo told me another story, of a newly married couple. The woman was
up in a tree, her husband below. The woman was laughing unstoppably and
the man, perplexed, asked her why. "The tree," she replied, "is *flirting* with me."
And she changed herself into a termite. The image was very appealing; the
teasing tree caressing her, tickling her with its leaves until she nestled into it,
on the cusp between laughter and arousal, wanting to nuzzle into its nooks,
yearning for the intimacy that only a termite has with a tree.

In the punitive austerity of Genesis, the tree represents the "evil" of sexual
knowledge and the woman is sinful. Tree, woman and sex are tied into the
damnation of "the Fall," while here in the forests the stories tell the exact op-

posite; the lively flirtatious tree and the laughing sexy woman are the heroes of the story and she is wedded to the tree in the universal human truth of our long and necessary rapport with trees. Without them we truly fall. "Not enough cunt. That's the problem with Genesis," said one Ashaninca man to me.

In Peru, the *sierra*, the dry land, is often considered a "masculine" landscape. The culture of the *sierra* is macho and the *serranos* dislike the forest because it is hot, wet and threatening. *La selva*, meanwhile, the jungle, is moist with femaleness and in its dark deep thickets the Amazon drips and oozes a female fertility. Andean duality uses two ideas of Hanan and Hurin, with Hanan suggesting what is "higher," including the Andes, the sun and the male principle, and Hurin suggesting what is "lower," including the jungle and the female creative principle.

La selva is feminine, one Amazonian man said to me, because it is mysterious. "*La selva es una mujer*," a mestizo sculptor told me, categorically. "The forest is a woman because it is destructive, changeable, fecund, erotic."

When Amazonian people spoke to me of the Change of Worlds, when missionaries came with schools and settled communities, they described themselves as "coming out of" the forests (*salir*), for one is within the forests, *inside* them. Reichel-Dolmatoff says that the Indians speak of "entering" the forest, and the specific verb for this in the Desana language is *su'ári*, "with the distinct meaning of 'to penetrate,' 'to thrust into.' When used in an anatomical-physiological context, this verb refers to copulation."

For indigenous people of Colombia, says anthropologist Martin von Hildebrand, "women are the expression of earth; men of the heavens." Reichel-Dolmatoff says that for the Tukano, "woman was not created: woman always existed . . . she is identified with the earth" and there are no creation stories for the earth: "it always existed." He comments that the forest offers stimulation, as women do, and at the same time "harbours perils, poisons, uncertainties. The forest smells of woman"—in its deep muskiness. But this is a tensely paradoxical association: I was also told of strong menstrual taboos in the forests, because people believe that the forest spirits hate menstrual blood.

Woman at her wildest is identified with *wild-dēor-ness*: Desana people use the term "blood-carries-odor" to refer to menstruous women and certain animals, mainly those of the deepest forests. Menstruation means a woman "has passed from her normal, human state to an abnormal one that links her to the beasts of the forest. . . . People will say to her . . . 'animal-wild-are-you-words[norms]-hearing-not.'" For during those days a woman is outside human society, a creature of the wilds. Even in the tamest suburbs of modernity this wildness is within us—and it will out. Even in the most tedious job, the very blood rebels to be free. So we women get out of our heads, get drunk, run away, run with the wolves in our sleep, express our wildness in art or argument. That is when we experience our most feral nature—often in a carnal rage against restrictions, a compulsion to be what we are at that time: a creature of the deepest forest within, the undomesticated, unhousebound, unhusbanded woman, hungry for something beyond human society, restless, prowling, in thrall to a savage earth lust.

The whole idea of calling the Amazon "the Amazon" reveals how it is associated with female wildness. The name arose when Francisco de Orellana, having gone with the expedition of Gonzalo Pizarro in 1541, split off and reported being attacked by fierce female warriors, so they named the forests after the Amazons of Greek myth. Interestingly, some Amazonian people have a myth of a one-breasted woman who accompanies a spirit-being.

Freud was to argue that the association between wild woods and womanhood was a constant of the human mind: "All of these dark woods, narrow defiles, high grounds and deep penetrations are unconscious sexual imagery, and we are exploring a woman's body." In classical terms, landscape could be Apollonian or Dionysian: Apollo, sky god of intellect, was associated with what is harmonious, ordered, rational and male. By contrast, Dionysus, earth god (associated not only with Bacchus but with passion, sexual license, and the nonrational, intuitive, earthly forces), represented what was wild and female. The wilderness is utterly and incontrovertibly Dionysian.

The classical goddess of the wild woods was Artemis, footloose and reckless woman that she was. Hans Peter Duerr in *Dreamtime* describes her in various manifestations; there was Artemis Caryatis and her tree nymphs, who "swarmed and raged through the wilderness, uttering wild cries," and Artemis Lyaia, known as "one who looses," for she set herself free. The dances of Artemis Corythalia were notorious for the artificial phalluses that the female performers used, and the performance was "probably not very modest," said the Victorian understater F. G. Welcker. Artemis was associated with

Diana, goddess of wild animals, of wolves and of outlaws. Over the years, though, masculine culture couldn't stomach the wild womanhood she represented and Diana was tamed, subdued and made chaste; she came to be identified with—of all things—the Virgin Mary.

Land has been seen as virgin (explicitly in North America, Virgin-ia and Mary-land), and in 1656, John Hammond was to write of Maryland, "Twice hath she been deflowred by her own Inhabitants, stript, shorne and made deformed." The association between woman and land has the sinister and frightening overtones of rape: Raleigh, conquest in his eyes, in 1595 described Guiana as "a countrey that hath yet her maydenhead, never sackt, turned, nor wrought." John Smith in 1616 wrote of New England: "her treasures hauing yet neuer beene opened, nor her originalls wasted, consumed, nor abused."

Meanwhile American author James Fenimore Cooper, in *The Prairie*, describes a grove of cottonwoods being destroyed, and the sexual implications could hardly be clearer. One man buries his ax in "the soft body" of a cottonwood tree, which he regards with "contempt," and the tree is described as "in submission." The grove is "stripped" and the ax men move for "a general attack." In Cooper's *The Pioneers*, Billy Kirby comments that the wild forests are "a sore sight at any time, unless I'm privileged to work my will on them."

In classical sources, forest groves were considered to have a female aspect and cutting them down was an act of sexual aggression. Ovid, in his eighth "Metamorphosis," writes of a grove assaulted by Erysichthon: "His axe once violated Ceres' grove," the tree he cuts down is "wounded," and "Blood issued, flowing from the severed bark."

We reached the river to meet the dugout and piled in noisily. The skies were suddenly full of angry parrots and macaws, annoyed at the disturbance. We hadn't gone far downriver when the way was blocked by two enormous logs. We got out, wading in the water to push the dugout over, and went on our way patrolled by kingfishers. A kingfisher is very territorial and will follow a boat until it leaves its territory and will then scoot back as the kingfisher of the next strip of riverbank takes over the patrol. Along a river, you can measure the distance in kingfishers.

The river, like the forest path, was thickly overgrown in places and Hector would take out his machete and carve a way for the boat to go through. At a wide confluence of two rivers, he threw out a net to catch fish. There were brown bats in the dark, muddy banks and thunder in the distance; at one slope of riverbank there were hundreds of butterflies, and a small caiman slipped off a log into the water.

On the last night of our journey together the skies darkened, lightning glimmered almost constantly, and rain fell till the sky itself seemed thumping down on the earth. "The spirits were with us in the forests," said Matteo feelingly, "so they held off the storm till we were safely out." The next day, from a clearing in the forest, we took a tiny plane to Cuzco. All perspectives changed, up from the tree roots and fungus, up from the slippery paths, up the *aletas* of trees, up the liana, up the branches, up to clouds and sunlight. The deep and intricate world of the forest and its knowers disappeared from my view for a time.

A GENTLE RAPPORT

For indigenous people everywhere, nature is an enlargement of your mind and body, not a curse on your soul, as the Christian West has too often seen it. Pygmies of the Ituri Forest in northwest Congo explained to Colin Turnbull, "When we are the children of the forest, what need have we to be afraid of it? We are only afraid of that which is outside the forest. . . . The forest is our home; when we leave the forest, or when the forest dies, we shall die. We are the people of the forest."

The Malo people of northern Bangladesh used to have a custom of marrying a girl to a tree and a boy to the river, before their marriage to each other. For the Karen in the forests of northern Thailand, the umbilical cord of a baby would be tied to a tree; the spirit of the child dwelt there, and to harm the tree would be to harm the child; the ritual thus intricately linked person to tree.

Amazonian people live in a landscape of meaningful social interaction between themselves and animals, characterized by reciprocity, restraint and respect. (In the Xhosa language, a term synonymous with wilderness means "Forest of Respect.") Believing that nonhuman creatures have spirit, writes anthropologist Philippe Descola, "it is therefore possible for men to establish

with them rapports of protection, seduction, hostility, alliance or an exchange
of services." People look after the forest and the forest looks after them: it is
a relationship of allies. (This applies to the great majority of Amazonian
people—though not all. For the Jivaro people, for instance, the relationship
between people and nature is not reciprocal; rather it is a "matter-of-fact type
of predation," comments Descola.)

For Amazonian people, there are spirits or essences within reality, and
this essence takes different forms—human, bird or animal—but since the
essence is the same, the spirit in one form can transform into another form in
a kind of Ovidian metamorphosis known throughout the forests. The same
life force is in everything, animating you and the eagle, the glossy leaf and the
kingfisher, the jaguar and me.

There is a tender familiarity in this, a gentle ontology. The difference between creatures is just a trick of the light, a superficial thing, for underneath
we are made of the same stuff. On the surface there is an obvious difference
between you and the daffodil, the catfish and the monkey puzzle tree, but
what animates each is the same vibrancy and immanent energy, the one life
force expressing itself in differing guises. This understanding is learned
through the language of metaphor or through the intense experiences of the
soul. For Amazonian people, knowledge comes from communicating with
the wild world, through its plant teachers or through shape-shifting—that
strange, beautiful and entirely wild way of knowing.

Creatures are *gente* I'm told, everywhere I go in the Amazon: they are "people like us" with customs and homes and they are accorded gentleness for being *gente*. You must address the world gently, I was told, even to the wind you
should speak *con cariño*—with tenderness. The Harakmbut told me that all
animals were people *más allá*—long ago—and there is therefore a profound
equality between us and them; they are like distant family, and one has duties
and expectations as one would with family members. People are "familiar"
with the habits and ways of animals, can "talk" to them, and this familiarity is
cherished. (By contrast, in the West, close familiarity with animals was considered devilish: the witch and her "familiar.")

Animals should be treated kindly, even in hunting, for they are kin to humans. "We owe . . . kindliness to other creatures: there is an intercourse and

mutual obligation between them and us," wrote Michel de Montaigne, sound-ing uncannily like an Amazonian Indian.

The history of Europeans' actions in the Amazon—their murders and ex-tinctions and logging and land theft—is a demonstration of radical unkindness: the unmaking of the wild so it disintegrates into a wasteland empty of life. Behind those actions is the Western philosophy of a terrible un-kindness—the idea that the human animal is a different kind of creature, entirely sepa-rate from others. Luther Standing Bear said that "the old Lakota was wise. He knew that man's heart, away from nature, becomes hard; he knew that lack of respect for growing, living things soon led to lack of respect for hu-mans too. So he kept his youth close to its softening influence."

During the months of my journey in the Amazon, I met Antonio, who worked on a project to protect harpy eagles. He talked to me at length about this eagle; its nest five feet wide and four feet deep, its six-foot wingspan, its talons like bear claws that could puncture a person's lung. It has a twenty-year life span and no predator except humans. It feeds on monkeys and sloths—at fifty miles per hour, a harpy will slam into a sloth asleep on a liana and carry it away.

Antonio took me to a shaman he knew and we drank ayahuasca together at dusk, as the cicadas snickered, and coconuts crashed from the treetops at intervals through the night like a mad bell ringing the hours of its own choos-ing. I had been thinking about shape-shifting, the ayahuasca transformations where people feel changed into an eagle or other creatures, and on this night, in my mind's eye, I watched an eagle playing the air here where the air is thin, sweeping the wind in sheer glide and majesty; in pride and eerie silence it soars, flying alone far above the world. Shamans have long sought to remind us of our special relationship with other top predators—not only eagles but bears and jaguars too. These creatures are ourselves in a different guise, shamans think. We—every one of us—are no less wild than they. It's just that most of the time we forget our wild spirit, allow it to be smothered. Nonshamanic cultures forget the most, and this forgetting is a terrible loss, for we are wild in claw and feather, in glide and pounce and fury.

Shamans told me many times that a particular feature of their work was to communicate with other creatures. To listen, for example, to the messages of the birds. The Leco people, in their oral history, recall that when the Spanish tried to invade their lands, the Leco people had advance warning: "We would hear of their arrival because the parrots would squawk in a way we never heard otherwise. The parrots were like messengers," says Sure-yani Poroso. He tells me of how his people would hurl wasps' nests at the Spanish, and how they escaped from rubber barons who came hunting the Leco people with rifles and hunting dogs. The Leco fled, their path going through a river full of piranhas. So they took an anaconda, stuffed it with a local poison that they used as an anesthetic and flung it in the river. The piranhas ate the anaconda and were briefly stunned by the anesthetic so the Leco people could cross the river. A short while later, the Europeans came up and waded into the river, but by that time the piranhas were awake and hungry again and attacked the Europeans.

Nature brims with communication—the more wild the land, the more tellers and tales there are, relating their presence and personality: the flower that courts the bee in colors invisible (and scent unscentable) to humans; a monkey howling its personality from the trees; and a human dancer copying the movement of an eagle, a calling relationship that finds its most perfect expression when mind is so intimate with mind that an animal is your mentor.

Indigenous people perceive the wild epistemology of jaguar, or parrot, their own ways of knowing. They understand that a tapir has its way of thinking and that some plants can teach humans. The West, though, has long operated an intellectual apartheid, arrogantly certain that its own expertise is the only knowledge worth the name: it cannot manage to respect other human societies' epistemologies, let alone accept that an animal can think. In the days of empire, that single way of knowing invaded the wild world, and as it did so it claimed that it was an age of "discovery" and an expansion of the "known" world, the false claims of European history that knowledge increased in that era. It did not. The truth was the opposite. For, as Europeans destroyed human cultures and animals' habitats, there was in fact a net *reduction* in the world's knowledge.

Accepting that there are different ways of knowing, different ways of speaking, is the beginning of democracy, and forests are a model of a wild, tatterdemalion democracy, of seedpod, riverbank, wind and caiman. As if pollen mattered and the beetle had a vote, an ultimate *parlement* (literally, "speaking") where all voices can be heard. For democracy is not only a matter of voting, but of talking and discussion. Indian poet Rabindranath Tagore identified democratic pluralism and an ecological culture as the distinctiveness of Indian civilization. "From the forests, we learned democracy," says Vandana Shiva, "that every species has its place."

Democracy is falsely attributed to the ancient Greeks. Native Americans and other indigenous people practiced it generations before the Greeks and, moreover, extended democratic ideas into ecocratic wisdom. Luther Standing Bear writes that "The Indian . . . gave to all creatures equal rights with himself." Shipibo people in Peru say, "We believe that animals are our equals." Black Elk of the Lakota people saw trees as having rights equal to people, referring to them as the "standing peoples, in whom the winged ones built their lodges." The Lakota referred to the creeping people and the flying people and the swimming people, all of whom must be heard in human councils. A group of Oneida Indians, it is said, decided to move to a new territory, one where wolves lived. They decided to ensure that the wolves had their needs recognized in the Oneida councils, so at the meetings, someone was always required to advocate for the rights of the wolves, and they would ask at the beginning of the council, "Who speaks for Wolf?"

THE AX-MAN COMETH

While I was in Peru, several indigenous campaigners complained bitterly about missionaries. "They are responsible for the propagation of sicknesses and the annihilation of uncontacted indigenous people," they said and told me about one church in particular whose practices were, well, *evil* is I think the right word.

One of their missionaries would take a high-speed boat up one particular river, trying to trap the "uncontacted" tribes with biscuits and gifts, in spite of local indigenous campaigners trying to stop such deadly jaunts. It occured to me with a revolted precision, what *kind* of biscuits does he leave? Jammy dodgers? Ginger nuts?

In the forests around Cuzco, four Christian groups were competing with one another to reach the "uncontacted": they came in helicopters like raptors, or in the fastest boats for a smash-and-grab raid on the cultures they sought to destroy, predators all, bringing hell's fire and the news of the end of time to cultures that knew only eternity. The missionaries know full well that their contact can and does kill people; history tells them so, as well as activists. They know, too, that their arrival heralds the destruction of the wild forest itself, for missionaries willingly grease the path for logging and oil companies. This is part of an ancient battle of implacable animosity between Christianity and the forest wildernesses.

On one of my visits to Cuzco, I arrived on a Saturday night. Tomorrow, I thought, I would pay a visit to the church of American headhunters.

The pastor and his wife came from Texas. In most ways, they were still there. They had five children who sat chewing gum through the service and whose expressions—unlike those of typical children—were flat with a kind of murderous incuriosity. There was no communion. The only "bread" was the popcorn the missionary children ate, fought over and spilled, unshared with the nonwhite kids. The only drinking of "wine" was the missionary children sucking on cans of Coke.

Children are often the giveaway to the true soul of the family, because they haven't learned to overlay their expression with social niceties. One of the children, a girl of about five in a pink frock, had a cruel look of superior, self-righteous hatred that I have only ever seen on the faces of American evangelical children. She had a dead-eyed violent look, as if Judgment Day were a week from Wednesday and she was anticipating with glee watching the damned writhe in torment. Her father, the bull-faced pastor, shouted at the congregation, "How many people have their Bibles today? Lift them so I can count them." Dry Bibles fluttered like dead butterflies. "Amen," said the pastor. "Genesis 29." Count, count.

On stage, a teenage mestizo girl sang sickly love songs to the lord god almighty (*te quiero, señor*), licking her lip gloss, leaning her head back and shutting her eyes, telly-pop style. The pastor punched out the hallelujahs with a clenched fist. His wife chewed gum in time to the chorus. After the service she came to meet me and shook my hand. She had red-painted fingernails; I had the dirt of the Earth under mine. She smelled of Johnson's baby powder; I smelled of the jungle. I had wood smoke in my hair, river water in my clothes and ayahuasca in my soul. We recoiled, mutually. I knew why; she didn't.

I talked to the pastor, who said he wanted to help uncontacted people co-operate with oil workers. "I think we should make a responsible contact," he said. "What's an irresponsible one?" I asked. "One that doesn't weigh the cost of contact—for example, medical needs," he replied suavely. But he was perfectly happy to bring diseases, I pointed out, that the healers couldn't cure. This brought him to ayahuasca: "A lot of people don't ever come back from that trip," he said sternly. "It's extremely dangerous. You can die. It takes people into the spirit world. It's pure witchcraft." (SIL, the Summer Institute of Linguistics, calls ayahuasca "Satan's business.") I countered his comment, saying that it was used for healing and for the diagnosis of illness. Diagnosis, he thundered, is divination, "and that's a definition of witchcraft" (which would put millions of doctors in a tight spot). To the Christian mind, in ayahuasca all evils meet: drunk in the dark, producing visions of the forests, associated with snakes, giving people access to a supposed tree of knowledge and involving shamanic communication with the spirit world. No wonder they get their knickers in a twist.

"We're too afraid of impinging on their culture," he said grandly—which frankly was not something I'd noticed. American culture needed to be respected just like any other, he said, and one part of its culture was to spread, to force itself on others. He pointed to a boy sitting next to me. "We cast twelve devils out of him three weeks ago," he said casually, as if he'd just unblocked the toilet.

The Amazon has long been associated in the European mind with darkness, and to the missionaries, darkness is of itself evil; the devil is the "Prince of Darkness," while Christ is the "light of the world." In the Middle Ages, monasteries were deliberately established in forest wildernesses, the abodes of the devil, partly to be away from the temptations of society and partly to represent the moral vanquishing of the dark, wild world. So the monks took up their axes and chopped down the darkness of the heathen heath, seeking to bring literal light into darkness. The connections persist: right-wing Christian fundamentalist groups are linked with the antienvironmental "Wise Use" movement in the States, both of which seek to attack wilderness conceptually and destroy it in actuality.

Christianity sees forests as *benighted* places. The Puritans of New England described their battle between the "cleare sunshine of the Gospell" and the "thick antichristian darkness." For Nathaniel Hawthorne, wild country was "black" and *dark* deeds are done in "the tangled and gloomy forest." A "shady character" or "shady deal" is tinged with wrongdoing. If you look up *vice* in Roget's Thesaurus, you find "black" and "of the deepest dye." Conrad's *Heart of Darkness* famously equated the darkness of the jungle with evil, writing of "the lurking death . . . the hidden evil . . . the profound darkness of its heart." Earth itself, being dark, came to be seen as morally bad. Soil could "soil" a person, and mud was a mundane stain on the blank white sheet of the soul.

The Pygmies of the Ituri Forest of northwest Congo thought the opposite, singing their great song of praise to the forests: "If Darkness *is*, Darkness is Good." Knowledge is mothered by darkness in the Amazon; knowledge from the "plant teachers" learned at night, while the *soñadores*, the dreamers, find their wisdoms in the dark. In the forests, you see the tenderness of darkness, how it folds things into itself, nature *nurturans*, for all good things are cradled in darkness first: seeds and babies, sleep's dreams and the heart's love, compost and starlight.

"And when you fail, and are defeated, and in pain, and in the dark, then I hope you will remember that darkness is your country, where you live. . . . Our roots are in the dark; the earth is our country. Why did we look up for blessing—instead of around, and down? What hope we have lies there . . . in the dark that nourishes, where human beings grow human souls," Ursula Le Guin writes in *Dancing at the Edge of the World*.

Edmund Burke, whose ideas of the "sublime" influenced Western thinking about wilderness, championed darkness, as Simon Schama writes: "While the eighteenth century is conventionally thought of as the epoch of light— the Enlightenment, led by what the French called their *lumières*—Edmund Burke set himself up as the priest of obscurity, of darkness. . . . So it would be in shadow and darkness . . . in the shroud of the cloud, in the fissures of the earth, that, he insisted in his *Inquiry*, the sublime would be discovered."

In the Amazon, the shamans' authority was undermined and their laws governing land use were weakened by missionaries, and one result has been a marked loss of wild creatures around mission compounds, for without traditional controls, animals are overhunted to the point of scarcity.

There are extinctions, too, of ways of knowing. "The evangelical church extinguishes our knowledge, that richness," says a Shawi man in Peru. Under

Christian eyes, shape-shifting was satanic. Moreover, the ecocratic beliefs that underlie shape-shifting, the essential democracy of the forests, was anathema to the Christian Church which insisted that man alone was king of creation. To this end, *mirrors*.

When missionaries have invaded some new territory, they have often brought mirrors. There's a shallow reason for this and a deep reason. The shallow one is a desire to frighten or impress people with technology they haven't come across. It certainly works. Sure-yani Poroso tells the story of the missionaries' arrival among the Leco people. They arrived in a plane, the first plane seen in Leco territory. (The Leco people thought it was "male" because it had prongs of wheels that stuck out. But it landed painfully on its balls, which was why it howled when it landed. Then, they conjectured, it had its arse on its side which produced the white people—but perhaps that meant it was female. When it took off, it did so by a flaming fart of such power that it flew.) The missionaries brought a big mirror for the chief, who, looking into it, fainted with shock. "God has the power to see your spirits," claimed the missionaries. The Leco thought it represented spiritual power and were persuaded by the mirror that the priests were god's representatives. "We were tricked by the mirror. Not defeated by arms but by a mirror."

The shallow reason, then, is to up-puff a priest. The deeper reason is to destroy the intimate and equal relationship between people and nature. For Amazonian people, the forest itself is a mirror; people are reflected in nature, and nature in people. Looking in a mirror, though, you see yourself as both central and enormous—nature a mere backcloth. The mirror divorces people from nature; it is both symbol and tool of anthropocentricity, reflecting only the observer, suggesting that self-consciousness can be outside nature and introducing a way of knowing that obliterates nature.

Early American settler Edward Johnson, in 1654, wrote with delight that "the admirable Acts of Christ" had changed Boston's "hideous Thickets" into "streets." Christianity spread most easily via towns and along roadways and has always loathed the tangly, matted jungles and shaggy forests where earth-religions survived the longest. To the Christians, there was a moral allegory in the "hideous Thickets"—to them, the jungles' very *tangliness* was equated with sin. (Hawthorne's dark deeds in the "tangled" forest.) Exodus 14:3 records that "Pharaoh will say of the children of Israel, They are entangled in the land; the wilderness has shut them in." In the Christian mind, forests were the lair of the Hairy, the Wild Man of the forest, the hairy satyrs. In the Semitic tradition, hairy demons were supposed to inhabit wilderness places, and in the *Epic of Gilgamesh*, the Wild Man, Enkidu, is described thus: "All his body was covered with fur. His hair stuck out from his head like hay."

Women's foresty wildness, shaggy and hairy as a wolf on the heath, with tangly groves and underarm thickets where the devil pheromone may muskily, lustily lurk, has been tamed over the years—the name of one product to get rid of unwanted hair is "Immac," for women must be immaculate as the Virgin Mary (not for her, hairy legs). The archetypal wild woman has long and tangled hair, wild as thickets, and when witches in Europe were "shorn" of their hair, it was a demonstration of society seeking to control them. The wild woods, too, have been shorn, cut down for symbolic as well as actual control.

The missionaries hated the feral shagginess of the Amazon, and early Christian monks considered that the groves and thickets harbored the devil, and did so in a peculiarly *female* way. To the missionaries, the godless jungle of the Amazon represented the lawless lust of the hairy cunt which could ensnare a man. Not so much *vagina dentata* as *vagina dendrida*. (It was a visceral loathing and a mutual one, though the cunt's point of view is rarely recorded.)

Conrad expressed the European hatred of the jungle, writing of the forest rivers as "streams of death in life, whose banks were rotting into mud, whose waters, thickened into slime, invaded the contorted mangroves that seemed to writhe at us"—in a passage that seems to suggest an obscene and female sexual corruption: slimy, slippery and infested with vines, hair and snakes, the opposite of the cool, sexless serenity of the Garden of Eden. Everywhere in the jungles something is always rotting, for sure, but to me this suggests life in death rather than death in life. And its wet and steamy dankness is not an obscene corruption but a shining necessity.

Christianity likes things straight. Jungles, though, wiggle. Christianity likes the straight path, the straight lines of the cross, the straight Roman roads by which it traveled to convert the wiggling pagans, and the straight linear time of history, as opposed to the cyclical time of nature. In the forests, though, time wiggles, rivers wiggle, paths wiggle, vines, plants and tendrils wiggle. All things that represent life at its most vital and wild wiggle. Words wiggle into metaphor; sperm wiggles; dancing and jokes and giggling wiggle; the shape and character of tumultuous life is a wiggling one.

The forest as a whole was a wiggling labyrinth to the linear missionaries, a place of zestfully unsubdued disorder, chaos in dendros; *scene di disordine o confusione*, as Italian translates "wilderness." The missionaries loathed the involuted woods, for in them a person's will or intent could be inextricably entangled by the forest's will—Conrad's "implacable force brooding over an inscrutable intention." This wild will was considered to be opposed to their god's will: in revenge, the god would come down on the Amazon like an almighty ax.

His will could hardly have been clearer. Exodus 34 commands, "Ye shall destroy their altars, break their images, and cut down their groves." Judges 3 reports that "the children of Israel did evil in the sight of the Lord, and forgat the Lord their God, and served Baalim and the groves." Judges 6 has a command to cut down the grove. In the second book of Kings, chapter 18 sees Hezekiah cutting down the groves, while in chapter 23 Josiah is at it. The commandment of Deuteronomy 12 is that ye shall "burn their groves with fire." In the second book of Chronicles, chapter 14, Asa cut down the groves, and by chapter 31, all of Israel cut down the groves. And just in case ye have not got ye message, Isaiah 17 stipulates that a man "shall have respect to the Holy One of Israel" but "he shall not . . . respect . . . the groves."

A love of trees seems rooted in the heart of humanity and if Jehovah could not uproot that love from the human heart, he would order his servants to uproot the trees from the earth.

The Finnish word *Hiisi* originally meant a sacred grove, but with the arrival of Christianity the groves were destroyed and the meaning of *Hiisi* was altered to mean a devil.

The Boora people of the Peruvian Amazon called the first white man the "maker of axes" and the white world "the World of the Ax." They call a mestizo or a European "the ax man," as they came to the Amazon acting out the will of their ax god. An old Wintu woman of California, reported by Dorothy Lee, said, "We don't chop down the trees. . . . But the White people plow up the ground, pull up the trees, kill everything. . . . The spirit of the land hates them. They blast out trees and stir it up to its depths. . . . How can the spirit of the earth like the White man?"

Matteo told me of the arrival of missionaries in his lands. They came in a plane, flying low over the forests. The Harakmbut tried to shoot the plane down, with bows and arrows, and the plane dropped machetes and underpants. (Since their first forays, missionaries in the Amazon have given people machetes and axes.) The Harakmbut, chuckled Matteo, kept the machetes but sniffed the underpants, thought they smelled odd and threw them down the river. We both got the giggles at the idea that somewhere deep in the riverbed or the sea there are hundreds of sensible (doubtless white) and virginally unused underpants.

The place where these missionaries made their first inroads was called Itahuania. There is a white space on the map around Itahuania now, as if someone had taken an eraser and rubbed out the forest; logging has been heaviest here. Blank white paper now stands for the dark forest's groves of earlier times. The road built by the missionaries has facilitated the work of a local logging company and a gold mine. In a similar pattern, in Ecuador, missionaries from SIL lured Huaorani people into a reservation, helping Texaco blaze a mining trail through their lands and opening the area to colonization.

I spoke to one Catholic priest in Harakmbut territory, to ask him about the arrival of the first missionaries. "We came like saviors and messiahs," he commented modestly. The people they "saved" told me a very different story. Within two years of missionaries' establishing a base, 50 percent of the local people were dead, killed by diseases the missionaries brought. When people first started dying of diseases brought by the whites, the deaths were blamed on female shamans and the Harakmbut killed the women. In South America as a whole, when a tribe's fate is known, between a third and a half of people have died within five years of first contact. The number of native people who died as a result of European invasion, from Alaska to Patagonia, is disputed, but it varies from about two million to over one hundred million. Jared Diamond remarks that the population decline among native people in the century or two following Columbus's arrival is thought to have been up to 95 percent. A holocaust.

ᘐ

Go and talk to Tarzan, I was told by several people. Ask him about the missionaries. Tarzan, a Harakmbut man in his nineties, remembered the time
when the missionaries first came to his lands. A local indigenous-rights activist radioed ahead for me to Tarzan's village, to introduce me, to vouch for
me. I took a car with two of his colleagues as far as Laberinto, where we had
to wait for the president of a community called Diamante. Then we would
get a boat together up the Madre de Dios River. Waiting in the Labyrinth for
the King of Diamonds to go up the Mother of God to find Tarzan. It could
only be the Amazon.

We bought food and gasoline, more than the tank would hold, so we
fetched out a big cooking pot from the canoe prow, and filled that as well, till
the canoe was slopping with gasoline and old stew. After several hours of
waiting for the president, I was very bored, so I started asking around to see
if I could hitch a lift in another boat. Two old people were juddering past
us upriver in a *peque peque*; someone recognized them as the parents of an indigenous campaigner I already knew—as luck would have it, they lived in
Tarzan's village. Everyone started shouting from the banks, but the couple
were old and a bit deaf, I was told. Their motor was loud. So we started up
our boat's motor and caught up to them. They were happy to take me, and I
swapped boats midstream. Their *peque peque* was full of bananas, buns and
broomsticks. The wife wore layers of clothes to keep the sun off her head and
cataracts hooded her eyes, but she smiled at me broadly when I awkwardly
said the few snatches of phrases I knew in Harakmbut. The boat was slow
and the motor like a jackhammer in my ears and the sun like a jackhammer
in my head, but I was pleased and relieved to be on my way.

When we arrived, someone took me to Tarzan's house and my heart
dropped to my boots. A tourist guide from Maldonado and two unsmiling
and rigid-eyed tourists were photographing Tarzan and Carlos, another elder,
who had donned traditional clothes and feathers specially for the tourists.
The guide, gimlet-eyed, was giggling shrilly, talking in a false-friendly voice to
the old men. When her tourists had taken their pictures, she gave some
money to the old men and she and the tourists left in a hurry. The moment
they were gone, the atmosphere became toxic. Carlos's face was lined with

fury: humiliated, he shoved his palm at me. "Thirty centimos," he said in disgust. Seven pence. And the coins were filthy. Thirty dirty centimos: the price of degrading old men. It's the fourth time in a year that tourists have come and abused people here. (I confronted the guide later. She first said the old men were lying. "I saw the coins," I said. Then she said it was none of my business, because I wasn't Peruvian. The mestizos could treat "their" tribal people however they liked.)

Tarzan and I spent hours talking, with various others coming and going, adding their own thoughts. Gradually, the story of the missionaries unfolded.

The missionaries came in a plane, which, said Tarzan, "we thought was a huge and frightening eagle, of a type we'd never seen before. We fled to the hills. Every day, the missionaries came searching for us. When the plane saw us, it flew very low, which was all the more frightening, and it dropped machetes and sweets and clothes and mirrors. It frightened us, and we didn't use them." (The sky religion that would conquer their earth religion did actually come from the sky, swooping deadly as an eagle on its prey.)

The other old men nodded enthusiastically as Tarzan went on: "We took our arrows and tried to shoot it—we did think we'd hit the plane's backside." They remembered it all perfectly, and the old men leaned back, as if reenacting it all, shooting arrows of the past, at a plane long flown, in a sky unchanged.

Tarzan was old, so steeped in years that even the old men called him *tío*—uncle. After a while, he went into his house and brought out a stone ax head. This is what we were using when the missionaries arrived, he said, and I realized I was holding in my hands a relic of the Stone Age that ended only twelve years before I was born.

Before the contact, "everything was good for us, the plants and animals and fish. We lived *fuerte*, strong; we wore no clothes, only feathers. We were painted and singing." Was life better then? "There were no illnesses, worries or problems. Of course life was better then, *antiguamente*. We were rich in what we were." In the old days, people would blow a large shell for a fiesta and wear face paint, body paint and feather crowns and dance all night. It was "clean," I was told: there was no alcohol. That evening, as I sat with Tarzan, most of the village had gathered in a house with a television, watching an awful Peruvian soap opera with some thirty cases of beer, and the yard around the telly was a junkyard of broken bottles.

The New Tribes Mission, working in parts of the Amazon including Paraguay and Bolivia, used hunting imagery to refer to uncontacted people: "We were hot on their trail." Unsurprisingly, indigenous people often say they felt like prey: "They trapped us; they captured us." The New Tribes Mission refers to "tame" Indians used to hunt the—presumably—wild ones, including capturing them by force. Missionaries often used the term *civilizados* instead of *tame* and they have taught people—for example, the Huaorani of Ecuador— that "to go into the forest was uncivilized."

The missionaries began approaching Tarzan's people via other tribespeople who were already *civilizados*—I hated hearing Tarzan use this word—and at one point Tarzan's people had encircled a *padre* with bows drawn. "But the civilized tribespeople said, 'Don't hurt him, he talks of god.' The people were split, half wanting to kill him, half not. The padre was on the far side of the river—" Tarzan broke off to stand and imitate the man pacing up and down, his hands like an open book in front of him: thus the *padre*, his Bible in his hands and his life in theirs. "In the end, we called the padre over across the river and when he arrived we put our arrows down on the ground and received his goods. He brought machetes and clothes and sweets. We tried to sow the sweets like seeds but of course they never grew."

The missionaries set up a mission station and a school. "We were scared and threatened by them," said Tarzan. "No one wanted to go to school, and anyway after the missionaries came, our children died. We learned things, though: we learned money and Spanish and work. We learned that we had to work for money for needs we didn't have before; matches, salt and sugar. Why were we civilized? For what were we civilized? To be taught that we needed sugar and oil and money and clothes and food from the markets, more and more."

Tarzan stopped, angry and upset. A small boy crawled over his body, splatting flies. A duckling pattered underfoot and a woman was picking nits out of an older woman's hair. I changed the subject, asking him about his name. The colonists called him Tarzan, because he was so tall and strong. He'd never seen the Tarzan films, but he was pleased with the name. And he quietly told me his true name. A passing grandmother, Ursula, thought I looked hot and tired, so she guided me to a dugout in a stream, waited while I washed and guided me back.

Dusk was falling and Tarzan sat on a low bench by his hut, singing catches of songs, whistling the four-note song of the *punkwana* bird. He played a sweet panpipe, a low flute that fitted snugly in his hand, and with it he called the birds. ("And when they're close, you shoot it with an arrow! *Rico*." He beamed. "Very good to eat.") A small boy came up to me with the "tourist smile"—half proposition, half contempt. "Gringa, gringa," he called. Tarzan frowned and sent him away. Then he leaned over to me and held my wrist. "You don't have a husband." I don't. "*No te vas*," he said. Don't go. I didn't want to.

Another of the elders, Manuel, hearing that we had been talking about the missionaries, came to join us. At first, he said, "we were scared of their white skin, and we were scared they would kill us. They did actually kill us. They brought illnesses *como un plago*, like a plague. These were illnesses we couldn't cure with plants. Six or seven thousand people got ill, and almost all of them died; influenza, fever, measles. The missionaries brought some medicine to cure the diseases they themselves had brought, but not enough." Here as elsewhere, when the local shamans couldn't cure these new diseases, their status was undermined. "We became embittered," said Tarzan.

I stayed talking till night and slept near Tarzan's house. In the morning, half the village came with me to the riverbank to flag down a boat and say good-bye. The river was wide, here, and a boat purled past, far on the other side. An old woman took off her white blouse to wave it—the Amazon equivalent of thumbing a lift—and the boatman saw her and steered over. I got in, and looked back. As the boat pulled away, you could make out the shack of a gold mine and the devastated land around it, logged and mined. This was the outward and visible sign of the missionaries inward and invisible crime: they ensured the gold miners could enrich themselves by impoverishing the forest's *riqueza*. The Indians see it clearly. "They are missionaries of money," say people of Paraguay and Bolivia, bluntly. The missionaries said they wanted people to know god, but Tarzan doesn't see it that way: "Now we know *money*." Further, thanks to the missionaries, he says, "now we know we *lack* money, which we hadn't known we lacked before."

Martin von Hildebrand speaks of the Tanimuka, Letuama and Makuna people of Colombia: "In their view, the guardian of white people is Christ.

What distinguishes whites from indigenous people is merchandise. So Christ is the guardian of merchandise."

The spread of missionary activity is, in fact, the spread of capitalism. In the forests, life is free in a financial sense, and missionaries have immediately grasped that they must deny people this freedom first, to make them dependent on the money economy. In Colombia, the New Tribes Mission (NTM) has given "gifts" to tribal people in order to force them into debt. In Paraguay and Bolivia, the NTM has sold empty tin cans to Indians so that "they might learn that not everything in life is free." The director of SIL in Bolivia (quoted in *Is God an American?*, an anthropological exposé of SIL's activities), described how missionaries would leave gifts for Amazonian people until a relationship developed. "Sometimes it comes as a surprise when we explain that from now on if they want to possess them they must work for money. . . . They settle down to it when they realise that there's no going back." Elsewhere, missionaries say, "We taught them to save." For the missionaries have sensed that out in wild nature, where life is free, people perceive themselves to have other fundamental freedoms. The missionaries have sought to prevent people living "for free" in the forests because once they are made dependent on money, their other, more conceptual, freedoms can be taken away: freedom of will, freedom of time and freedom of thought. (SIL also operates to further the political power of North America. In Bolivia, Che Guevara's guerrillas were in hiding and betrayed by missionized Indians, while SIL missionaries supplied the Bolivian army with maps of the guerrillas' area of operation.)

Around the world, in Nepal, Thailand, West Papua and South America, I've seen missionaries at work, busy converting people not so much to Christianity as to a specifically middle-class capitalism, taming the spirited modus vivendi of wild places into a tepid, orderly, punctual, fenced suburbia, every woman a housewife, every man a nine-to-five employee, every child in a clean white blouse off to school to learn how to be a good Euro-American consumer.

The missionaries exemplify a hatred of wilderness, which for hundreds of years has been associated with the lowest orders of the social hierarchy. In Europe, the vast majority of those wild women associated with the wild heath and murdered as witches were from the lowest social classes. (Caliban in *The*

Tempest and Bottom in *A Midsummer Night's Dream* are lowlife creatures of the wilderness.) The attitude has been transferred to indigenous people, and missionaries have tried to prize them out of their wild forests in order to place them in the civilized middle class, controlled and tamed. In practice, however, the effect of missionary activity is that a tiny minority of their converts achieve middle-classness. The majority, torn out of their forests, are dumped in the slums of towns, on the lowest rungs of the social ladder. Out of the wilds and into the wasteland.

CAGING THE LAND

The oldest Indo-European root of *wild* is *welt*, meaning "forest or wildwood," and Roderick Frazier Nash comments on the possibility that the word *wild* is in part related to *weald* or *woeld*—the Old English terms for forest. Gilbert White, the great eighteenth-century English naturalist, referred to "the wild or Weald" as if they were interchangeable. *Weald* is "a formerly wooded district," from Old English *wald, wold.* Language, gentle in the dark like felt, softly rolled and pressed the words close to one another; *wold, weald* and *wild.* What is wild is self-willed, and *wold,* formerly *wooded,* would be wooded if it could. The wild weald has a quality of self-willedness—there is energy in free and open land—which is why common land, land running wild, seems so vitalizing, for we were born wild to a wild Earth.

Indigenous people all over the world have owned land communally. John Locke wrote of "the wild Indian, who knows no enclosure, and is still a tenant in common," and reminded his readers, "Thus in the beginning all the world was America." Heinmot Tooyalaket (Chief Joseph) of the Native American Nez Percé said, "The country was made without lines of demarcation and it is no man's business to divide it."

But the resemblance between Native Americans and British peasants was unwelcome, and the social reformer and economist John Bellers (1654–1725) wrote, "Forests and great Commons make the Poor that are upon them too much like the Indians." Common land was "a hindrance to Industry" and the commons were "Nurseries of Idleness and Insolence."

The enclosures that began in Britain in the thirteenth century had a peak in the fifteenth and sixteenth centuries and a more extreme peak between 1725 and 1800, though continuing thereafter. John Clare identified the loss of common land as a loss of wildness. He describes common land as "wilderness"; the "wild" and "wild pasture" were a "common right." For Clare, the loss of wild lands was a loss of freedom: he speaks of England as the land of liberty but now, "Like emigrating bird thy freedom's flown," "Inclosure came, and all your glories fell." As a result of enclosures, wilderness was turned into wasteland, "all levelled like a desert." Enclosed, land is no longer self-willed, and becomes listless, subject to the will of its owner, subdued in spirit.

Enclosure also crushed the spirits of the common people. For centuries, communal carnivals were held on the commons, common people celebrating a common time on common land. These carnivals were wild in character; bawdy, exuberant, unfettered, they were a commonwild of the human spirit, which, demented by claustrophobia, hates to be cooped up, enclosed, indoors. But traditional carnivals were tamped down and stopped by one thing: enclosures. When people lost their common rights to land, they also lost their rites, their common—wild—time.

In the Amazon, land was enclosed by cattle ranchers, logging companies and mining companies, stealing huge tracts of common land and profiteering from it. The missionaries preferred to enclose and crush the human spirit, and they created reservations, where they forced people to live, fencing them out of their wild, free lands. As nature had been a mirror to Amazonian people, so they had previously seen their freedom reflected in the land's, but when their land was fettered, subdued and listless, so were they.

On part of my journey, I stayed with Shipibo people who had a couple of hundred illegal gold miners on their lands. The mines were polluting the rivers with mercury and the Shipibo planned to drive out the miners. They wanted me to go with them, for a white face is protection as far as the local police are concerned. So we went. The Shipibo got their canoes ready and dressed in *achote*, "war paint," feather headdresses, clothes of tree bark (bra straps underneath), and picked up their bows and arrows. In previous encounters, the miners had shot at the Shipibo and set dogs on them, so the

Shipibo regalia is partly done because it puts the wind up the miners (*the Indians are coming*) but in large measure they wear it to boost their own morale, because it symbolizes action, valor and force, they told me. They were reclaiming not only their land but also their tribal power, and when they were about to set off from their village, whistling and clapping, there was an ancient justice in their eyes. I asked one of the men if he was scared. "Yes," he said simply, and he didn't look like someone accustomed to saying that. (In Lima, I'd asked the advice of a human rights lawyer about joining them, and what the worst outcome might be. "*La muerte, claro,*" she said bluntly. Death, clearly.) As we set off upriver in the direction of the headwaters, one of the women came to me and gave me her feather headdress—beautiful, many-feathered, old. Thank you, she said, for taking our side. What other side is there to take? I said. As I held it, she took my hand. "I know where paradise is," she said.

The canoes were stuffed to the gunnels with rice, hunting guns, bananas and machetes. As we arrived at the first outpost of the mine, two of the miners saw us, jumped into a boat and skimmed off fast across the water. The other miners stayed. Their camp was littered with cigarette packets, Panasonic film and tuna tins, a TV, which it was hard to believe could possibly work, a chicken and piles of potatoes. The Shipibo lit a fire and started cooking. The miners' shacks were pieces of tatty tarpaulin; they had a Heath Robinson–style jungle radio and tiny scales for weighing gold. The miners' faces were mean, with a burnt-out look, which made me feel briefly sorry for them: it was as if in the smelting processes of gold they were themselves part of the discharge, just another waste material.

One Shipibo man awkwardly wrote a paragraph in a blue school notebook, detailing an "agreement" to leave the site, which he wanted the miners to sign. (It seemed like a reenactment of a historic theme, where indigenous people, politely, earnestly and truthfully try to make a paper agreement with men who will not honor it.)

The *dueño* of the mine showed up, listened for a few minutes and offered the Shipibo people dollars. All hell broke loose. "Tranquillity is worth more than dollars," said one of the women, scornfully. The shaman took out his machete and began sharpening his arrows.

A couple of the younger men took up positions on slightly higher ground around the camp, and pulled their bowstrings taut, pointing their arrows at the miners. Someone else torched the roof of a shack. "*Vamos*," said one of the leaders. "Let's go. We give you two hours." The miners did not budge.

We went farther upriver to find a larger mine site. The Shipibo looked at this land with shock and bitter sadness. There were fires burning in tree stumps, huge barrels leaked diesel, and rusty machinery turned lake water orangey brown. The miners had dug out everything, leaving a cruel landscape, oil oozing into a lake and slag heaps slicing the sky. The wasteland had come. One of the leaders, Ernesto, said softly, "If the earth is maltreated, it's as if we ourselves are maltreated." Rain began to fall and people cut large banana leaves as umbrellas.

Then, quite suddenly, the Shipibo got moving, and they physically "undid" the mine, pulling it apart with their bare hands, bit by bit. Some people untied ropes, others pulled pipes apart, others brought down platforms. Some of the younger men looked angrier by the minute as they did this. "*Tranquillo, tranquillo*," said the elders.

Night fell and the Shipibo left to find a quiet spot on the riverbank to make a camp. They cut down a few saplings and erected a couple of wigwam structures and several instant houses, roofed with leaves and with special sleeping platforms. In the night, a huge storm blew up, the river rose and rain fell in ropes like lianas. The lightning flickered almost constantly like a child playing with a light switch. No one got much sleep, but all I heard at dawn was the laughter of soaked, tired people.

The previous day, the miners had called the police, who now arrived. The police, mestizos with precious little sympathy for *los Indios*, began haranguing the Shipibo, who listened calmly and then gave the police a lecture in international law with specific reference to indigenous rights in their own land. The police were flummoxed and one of them sidled up to me: Was it true? Was this mine illegal? Without a doubt. The Shipibo then returned to the fray: not only had they given the police a legal lesson, they had also confounded the officers by having committed no crime that the police could identify. That was the beauty of their action: they had not stolen any pipe or platform, they had broken nothing. They had simply dismantled an entire gold mine with their bare hands.

THE WASTELAND

Often, the word *wilderness* is used interchangeably with *wasteland*. To me they are not so much synonyms as opposites. The missionaries came to the Amazon's wild land and made of it a wasteland: a literal wasteland as they axed the trees; a social wasteland of perceived poverty; an emotional wasteland of fear and shame at their nakedness; a conceptual wasteland of the world of mirrors, where humans were no longer part of nature; a natural wasteland as animals were hunted to extinction; a bodily wasteland of disease and alcoholism; a spiritual wasteland as their relationship with their own land was crushed and an epistemological wasteland as shamanic ways of knowing were destroyed.

For Amazonian people the use of forest resources is an ethical affair. It is considered wrong to be greedy or to take more than you need. But the Younger Brothers (as many indigenous people around the world call the whites) are recklessly greedy, careless of such a gentle relationship with nature. The corporations and industries have followed the example of the missionaries, going to wild lands and turning them into wastelands.

During the Vietnam war, the United States is thought to have sprayed 77 million liters of the herbicide Agent Orange on the jungles of Vietnam—the worst chemical warfare in history. It continues to devastate the lives of hundreds of thousands of Vietnamese, causing horrible deformities and neurological disorders. In the current vicious campaign in Colombia, crops and water supplies are "fumigated" by the United States, opening the way for corporations such as Exxon Mobil and BP to exploit resources. This is, says Vandana Shiva, "a jihad against wilderness."

If you fly over the Amazon, you fly through smoke like a war zone—an infinity of trees made finite by fire. If you want to know what stupidity looks like, here it is—the devastated rainforest, stumps of trees and charred underbrush. If you want to know what stupidity sounds like, listen to it here—a chainsaw in a muted land, songlines devastated, birds and animals gone. Without trees, nothing can speak. It is an assault on nature and human nature.

"We do not use the word *environment*," said a Yanomami man from Brazil. "That is your word for what is left of what you have destroyed." By 2011, there could be virtually no more tropical rainforest to save, warns one researcher. In Ecuador, American oil companies have demanded that oil production should not be hindered by laws protecting nature reserves, national parks or indigenous rights.

So kill pity. Crack down on kindness. Pour mercury over metaphor. And destroy the creatures that bring their characteristics to the menagerie of the world's mind: the sloth's slothfulness ("lazy" in every language that names it); the bee's diligent drunkenness in its petal pub crawl; the ant's order in crowdedness; the butterfly's delicate legacy of light; the monkey's indignation, lust and mischief.

In the Amazon, the assault against nature *is* an assault against culture, hundreds of tribal cultures. So burn their books, hack down their languages and ax their philosophies. Tip Agent Orange into the eyes of a forest Picasso. Tie a Shakespeare's hands behind his back—with razor wire. Break Nureyev's ankles, stamp on Fonteyn's feet. Crack Joyce's head against a wall until the words whimper and fail him. Daub graffiti over an El Greco. Bulldoze the sculptures of Rodin. Burn the entire *Oxford English Dictionary*. Slash every copy of Dylan Thomas. Napalm the Berlin Philharmonic.

And when the guffaw of the macaw is silent and the artistry of weaverbird gone, and the last tribal people are living in slums, morosely selling postcards of how they used to live, then take the Amazon as a mirror, as they used to. For there is a radical hollowness now, an empty gauntness in the soul of the world, a savage nothingness that blankly taunts you with your own reflection; the razed Amazon a mirror of terrible truth for the soul of modernity. Only waste survives in a wasteland; Harakmbut villagers, wasted alcoholics, wasting days watching cheap soap operas, as the mercury wastes their rivers.

But beyond indignation, beyond anger, there is only a terrible and infinite sadness: sadness to the treeless and gaunt horizon for the end of a whole way of knowing, a wild epistemology, knowledge gained through dream and song and shape-shifting. The generous Harakmbut *soñadores*, courteous to dreams, their dreams wasted and all the Amazonian *ayahuasqueros*, who learned from plants and sang the songlines of the forest, silent.

Native American Black Elk was born in 1863 (in the Moon of the Popping Trees in the Winter When the Four Crows Were Killed). When he was nine he had a dream, a vision of being taken to the sky world, where he saw the wild animals of the Plains all dancing. At the heart of the dream was a vision of the end of the Plains way of life and a dream of the end of dreaming itself. After the massacre at Wounded Knee, Black Elk said, "I did not know then how much was ended . . . now . . . I can see that something else died there in the bloody mud, and was buried in the blizzard. A people's dream died there. It was a beautiful dream. . . . There is no center any longer, and the sacred tree is dead."

THE JAGUAR'S APPRENTICE

Before I left the Amazon, I wanted to return to the shamans Juan and Victor with whom I had drunk ayahuasca at the start of my trip. I was frightened of returning home, to the depression I feared would find me again. I made arrangements to travel back to their center, and Victor sent me a message to say he would come the day after I arrived *para cuidarte*—to look after you. The day drew to dusk. Victor arrived and hugged me. An eagle came today, he said, and landed in the center of the compound. "I've never seen that before. It's a good sign for you. It's never come before but it came today for you. Because you fly with eagles." I felt honored, undeserving and touched. Juan called us to drink.

When I had drunk, I wondered if I was going to die. My heartbeat felt so weak it was barely palpable, I couldn't feel my breath, and my muscles were completely unstrung. I got aural hallucinations, like radio frequencies, and lightning glimmered on the horizon, silhouetting a tall tree. So what if I did die? At that moment, death seemed just a quick trick; a slight (if splendid) sleight of hand, the pack shuffled, mortality cast off and a new round of life dealt out.

Then Juan's *icaros* began to include Christian references, terms such as *El Señor, hallelujah, gloria* and *Jesu Criste*. Amazonian shamans sometimes use a diversity of influences, and Juan may well have thought that as a European I would appreciate hearing familiar words. I did not. They made me feel physically sick, as if I saw afresh how Christianity is an enemy of nature in general and the Amazon in particular, this vicious cult pulping the forests.

Then the visions started like a waking dream. I could see the High Street in Oxford with people milling up and down. And then I saw a jaguar in the middle of the street, a female, adult jaguar, a wildcat pacing past the Queens Lane Coffee Shop. Everyone else was scared of it and ran away, but I was not frightened. Quite the opposite. I was drawn to it, feeling a kinship with it. I recognized it as if we were from the same tribe and I approached it, slowly, coming closer and closer. The jaguar light was shining in its eyes, and I stared, mesmerized. I was drawn to it as if it were my teacher and I urgently wanted to learn from it.

I am the jaguar's apprentice. That thought came to me clearly, in Spanish and English. I was drawn to what it would teach me, so compelled that I felt myself dissolving, melting into it, slowly. The boundaries of person and jaguar are permeable, I found, and I wasn't surprised. I was still "me" but now in a different form, or shape.

This was shape-shifting. I knew the term but never thought I'd ever experience the feeling. At one level, and only dimly, I was aware it was a hallucination, but underneath that, I felt it was true; a slanted, metaphoric truth. I felt a wild empathy, and so much did I feel a rapport with this animal that what was "I" and what was "she" were indistinct. I was the jaguar. I felt like her, inside me, and then that feeling grew more intense, more vigorous, more violent, and what was inside began expressing itself outwardly. I felt as if I had whiskers, twitching, tense and alert. I felt as if I had a tail, and it was switching back and forth in slow anger. I could put my front "paw" to my mouth and tug out a thorn from between a claw and paw pad. As I prowled, I could feel the folds of pelt ruck under my armpits. My paws were soft and sensitive, so I could stalk silently without breaking a twig or shifting a stone.

I smelled everything; noticed, watched and heard everything. People had fled. The High Street was deserted. I was stalking something by scent: not the scent of a creature, rather it was the scent of anger, the trail of an injustice, and I was prowling with a fury far older than me, far larger than my individual concerns. I could smell myself. I plunged my nostrils deep toward the fur of my groin and I sniffed up the satisfying, heady musk of wild female jaguar, and I roared, a ferocious roar of wild and perfect contempt. I felt an untetherable rage at the Bodleian, which houses with such care all the dry knowledge of years, *while the Amazon burns.*

The wet and current knowledge of the forest mind is disrespected by the dry academies of science—even while indigenous knowledge is stolen for profit. The West's intellectual apartheid, which refuses to recognize indigenous wisdom even as it steals it, made me livid.

Oxford was my university but I was now apprenticed to a jaguar out of revenge for centuries of wrong. I stalked through the Bodleian, prowled its stacks and shelves, growling and snorting people away like dry dead leaves. I came across a couple making love in an unsupervised room, and I purred them on. I went to the Radcliffe Camera—the center of a center of Western learning—and I paused a moment at the threshold. This was the heart of the epistemology that had bred me (the horses of instruction) but I returned to it in the form of a jaguar from the Amazon (tiger of wrath) and I stalked in and roared in the very heart of the building, roaring in anger and disgust at how my culture can know so little for knowing so much.

And the vision faded. Are you okay? one of the shamans asked me. "*Estoy in otro mundo.*" I am in the other world.

The following night, too, I drank. Juan was singing. I had told him that the Christian references made me feel ill and this evening he avoided them altogether, singing forest songs only, with forest terms. He sang songs of protection and then, softly, he whistled as if whistling up the spirits and played a simple forest flute. Victor blew smoke over me and I was aware of the power of this gesture—his breath wreathed me like a benediction. He put my hands together, as if in prayer, and blew smoke over them, healing my hands. (In my depression, I had been able to write nothing. It was as if someone had stamped on my writing hand and crushed every bone in it.) His hands were healing and he held the sides of my head gently.

I vomited suddenly and violently and then the lights came on in my head, the drug taking effect with a brilliant, radiant *fuerza*, strength and energy. I felt ransacked with wonder and charged with life. And then I felt an extraordinary sensation, as if I were giving birth to myself—as a jaguar. This was nothing like vaginal birth but rather birth as transformation. I was concentrating, straining, pushing out of my body the image of my soul. With each breath out, I pushed myself "through" into jaguarness, like a runner forcing herself through the pain barrier into a transcendent state beyond. It felt like straining and pushing something into being, but the "something" is not other but oneself in a new form, a process like all difficult works of creation.

The previous night, I had been the jaguar's apprentice and the first thing I learned was how my body felt. This night, I learned how to mother my jaguar self into being, in the agony and ecstasy of birth. When, with one last effort, the process was complete, the first thing I did was sniff myself. I smelled of meat and musk and damp hot fur. Jaguar, in groin, pelt and whisker, panting and alert.

I was willful, I was hungry, I was solitary, I was proud. The jaguar walks its own sure way, treads its own path with certainty and a tender ferocity. Beyond love, hate or complexity, things fell into two categories, those on the side of death and the wasteland, and those who walk with the jaguar on the side of life and the wild. From a hunger for life, I roared myself into being, and now sheer life brimmed me to overflowing.

"We can send you to the stars," one of the shamans had said to me. (They were pleased because they felt I had an aptitude for ayahuasca, that I could use it and learn from it, and from what they could teach me.) And now, in my hallucinations, I saw the stars and leapt for them, pouncing from star to star until I wanted to lick the moon. So I did. The crescent moon, like a slice of white papaya, was small enough to be held in one paw. I caught it gently with my claws and licked its wet smoothness with my rough tongue. What flavor is the moon? Cool water.

Sexual desire was steaming through me. I was panting and my paws were kneading the earth. Sex glistened me, every cell of me. Every sinew in me, every pore, every vein was glinting with the hot, slow glow of it, that vibrant hunger, smoldering me. Sex prowled through me, purred in me, growled in me. The inheld *riqueza* of desire, the deep drumming of chthonic sex, as if my entire body were a part of the fecund sexuality of Earth, her hot mud steaming in me, through me, her deep slow breaths my own.

Victor stayed by me for much of the night, bringing water in a cup and scooping it onto my head with his hand. I couldn't speak, but I was purring, my mouth was open, and I wanted to suck the water off his fingers. (Keep sucking the marrow out of life, in Henry Thoreau's words.) Victor's touch was a curing and a caress. He leaned my head back against the wall and stroked my hair away from my face. At one point, when I felt my head was exploding with the sheer vividness of it all, he sucked at my temples, smoothing my hair away. I never wanted it to stop. It was intimate and healing. I leaned my head into his hands, my head heavier and heavier, my nose squashed, his hands strong. His shoulders looked three feet across and his black hair fell in waves. My hair was loose and tangly, with streaks of vomit in it. I couldn't have cared less.

The comedown was quick. "We've come back to earth," said Juan, with a quiet laugh, and in my still-influenced state I accepted, matter-of-factly, that it was obvious we'd all been to the moon.

What happened? he asked me. *Fui tigre*, I was a jaguar, I said, surprised. (*Tigre* is the Amazonian-Spanish word for jaguar.) For even in the darkness how could they not have seen that? I felt genuinely puzzled; neither of them had seen my paws kneading the earth, or heard me growling, or smelled the jaguar.

I have never forgotten this wild apprenticeship, by which I began to feel for myself how a jaguar might sense things, how its body might feel and react. It was a sensual knowledge, an emotional one—carnal knowledge—a feral way of knowing. Thoreau wrote, "The Spaniards have a good term to express this wild and dusky knowledge, *Grammatica parda*, tawny grammar, a kind of mother-wit derived from that same leopard to which I have referred."

When I got back home, I was keenly curious to read about this phenomenon of transformation and I realized how my experience had elements in common with other people's, including the anthropologist Françoise Barbira Freedman, who had a similar experience of feeling that the jaguar was her teacher, and a similar hatred of prayers.

Transformation is to do with experiencing one's full powers. Hugh Brody, in western British Columbia, visited a Nisga'a elder, Harold Wright. What is power? asked Brody. "Without a blink of hesitation, he answered: 'Transformation. Transformation is power.'" The Kandozi people of the Peruvian Amazon say that the man who walks in his full power has the spirit of the tiger. Across the Amazon, jaguar transformation is known as a shamanic initiation. Reichel-Dolmatoff comments that ayahuasca hallucinations often include visions in which "the person becomes his own begetter," and many sources suggest that the jaguar is associated with revenge and with the moon: in many myths the jaguar is the moon's descendant. Amazonian people say that a jaguar transformation is often sexual, and the jaguar is associated with fertilizing energy: the Desana people use the word *yee* to mean both "jaguar" and "shaman," while the related verb *yeeri* means "to copulate." The jaguar is associated with wild weather—it is a "thunder animal" in Desana cosmology— and thunder and the jaguar alike have strong fertility associations.

Associated not only with wild weather but with a quintessential wildness itself, the jaguar is an outsider and "for the Indian the jaguar embodies raw nature in her most uncontrolled and aggressive sense," wrote Reichel-Dolmatoff. Unlike most or all the other forest animals, the jaguar tolerates no fixed pattern, no order. It is truly wild, free, untrammeled. In many myths of the Amazon, the jaguar refuses to eat cooked food and detests fire, the method by which raw (wild) nature becomes cooked, processed into culture.

The jaguar epitomizes *wild-dēor-ness*, as the Harakmbut had told me on our trek, and it's a widespread understanding. For the Siona, a western Tukano people living along the Putumayo River, the deep forest is the place of wild animals and the dominant, the wildest of them all, is the jaguar. Free, the jaguar roams all terrains, at home in all wild worlds: land, water and forests. If anything embodies pure, raw wildness, it is her, essential and *ecstatic*, standing outside the ordinary.

FERAL SONG

The wild. I have drunk it, deep and raw, and heard its primal, unforgettable roar. We know it in ourselves, for we are wild to the core. We know it in our dreams, when the mind is off the leash, running wild. "Outwardly, the equivalent of the unconscious is the wilderness: both of these terms meet, one step even farther on, as *one*," wrote Gary Snyder. "It is in vain to dream of a wildness distant from ourselves. There is none such," wrote Thoreau. "It is the bog in our brain and bowels, the primitive vigor of Nature in us, that inspires that dream."

And as dreams are essential to the psyche, wildness is to life.

For the Native American O'odham people, the term *doajkam*, wildness, is etymologically tied to terms for health, wholeness and liveliness. "Life consists with wildness," wrote Thoreau. "The most alive is the wildest. All good things are wild and free" and "In wildness is the preservation of the world."

We are animal in our blood and in our skin. We were not born for pavements and escalators but for thunder and mud. More. We are animal not only in body, but in spirit. Our minds are the minds of wild animals. Artists, who remember their wildness better than most, are animal artists, lifting their heads to sniff a quick wild scent in the air, and they know it unmistakably, they know the tug of wildness to be followed though your life is buckled by that strange and absolute obedience. ("You must have chaos in your soul to give birth to a dancing star," wrote Nietzsche.) Children know it as magic and timeless play. Shamans of all sorts and inveterate misbehavers know it; those who cannot trammel themselves into a sensible job and a life in the sterile suburbs know it.

What is wild cannot be bought or sold, borrowed or copied. It *is*. Unmistakable, unforgettable, unshamable, elemental as earth and ice, water, fire and air, a quintessence, pure spirit, resolving into no constituents. Don't waste your wildness: it is precious and necessary. In wildness, truth. Wildness is the universal songline, sung in green gold, which we recognize the moment we hear it. What is wild is what drives the honeysuckle, what wills the dragonfly, shoves the wind and compels the poem. Wildness is insatiable for life; neither truly knows itself without the other. Wildness is the luminousness of a bluebell wood at twilight, massing clouds boiling up their rain, the weed that cracks the pavement and the river that floods its banks, the creeping jenny run riot. It is the first "fuck" on television, it simmers in the feral intoxication of jazz, it explodes exuberant in carnival, it honks with laughter in the magic-mushroom season, it smashes the clocks above the factory gates and sucks up the now, it blazes in your eyes and it glories in everyone who wilfully goes their own way.

Wildness loves language, roaring with pleasure at the Tower of Babel and leaping at the Internet; it loves myriad diversity, it whistles through scene changes and plays happily on new stages. Wildness is the spirit of shape-shifting, the metamorphoser-at-large. We come from its wild song—in music was the creation of the universe—and we are most fully alive when we resonate to its wildest pitch with intense and necessary love, in jaguar forests or deserts or mountains or in the lands of essential ice, or the water that first coaxed the story. Humanity's highest purpose is to be fluent in the streaming cadences of all our world's languages, making our earth more vivid and realizing it in song. For that is how the spirit deep within all life leaves the unforgeable signature of its wild authenticity, in the songlines of this wild world.

Wild Ice

ICE MUSIC

The Arctic is a soundscape. Under an iced sea, a wave surges, knocking on an iceberg underwater, sounding like the muted thud of wind on icy canvas. The movement of the wave rubs the sea ice against the berg, which squeaks and whistles. A little chip of ice falls and shatters a high and fragile timpani at a distance, while water sucks through a cave of ice in a sonorous glug and the berg grinds its molars on the gravel shore. As the sun melts the end of an icicle, small drops fall like the cool, dipping melody of a bamboo water fountain.

Giant plates of ice growl and roar as they cross antlers with each other, a splinter of ice scuttles off half a mile. Ice whines, plinks and grunts.

In the autumn days of freeze-up, the sea ice as it forms makes sounds that are lumpy and phlegmatic, a turgid and inarticulate sound of thickening ice. What is yet water hisses—one last hot sound—as a new wave tries to heave upward, but the heavy, greasy ice coldly squashes its protest.

Gulls sob like creaking ice, and three snow buntings flying past mew in the cold air. It is hard to get a perspective on sound, here. Is that a distant ruffle of paw on snow, or the breeze in your hood? In the Antarctic, even the names sound cold: the Weddell Sea, for instance, is ice forged like iron, a welded whiteness.

The composer Peter Maxwell Davies described the sounds of the Antarctic as he spent time there to research his *Antarctic Symphony*, and writes of the vessel ramming its way through frozen seas, the ice breaking beneath, "with electric zippings and cracklings sounding off into the far distance as fissures extended for miles from the ship." On land, he writes, "There is almost no wind, but occasionally an astonishing sound whistles gently from the peaks to the south, almost subliminal at first, but growing into an alto-flutish lament." I listened to him conducting the premiere of his symphony and I was swept up by its synesthetic magic: I saw what I heard. In the xylophone there were drops of meltwater, and sounds of iced air in the harp. In a sliding scale, penguins made an exuberant glissando descent, and the deadliness of cold itself was sounded by a distant drum. There was a yaw of shifting, creaking ice and in a curved S of strings, the contours of ice sculpture.

People have lived in the Arctic for hundreds or thousands of years: people including the Inuit (the word means "people") of Canada and Greenland, the Saami of Scandinavia and various people of northern Siberia, including the Chukchi. Europeans (Southerners, or Qallunaat, as the Inuit call them) have long maintained that the Arctic is a wasteland; they came to these northerly places and saw yawning emptiness, barren, lifeless lands. Often they also portrayed the land as hostile. The landscape, described by these explorers, is given a malevolence it does not—cannot—possess. It is cold according to the facts of its nature, not as an act of malice. And it is full of cold integrity. There is no lack in the land unless you decide it lacks a tulip. Only the eye accustomed to elms sees elmlessness here. Polar bears need their vast territories of ice, the land requires so much cold, and ice is no enemy.

For the peoples of the north, by contrast, this land is full of life and meaning. It can be hard, for sure, but it is not a wasteland. The biggest reason for the difference in perspective between them and the Europeans could be summed up in one word: *knowledge*. Only to those ignorant of the land could this be a wasteland. I asked one Inuit elder, Joseph Koonoo, if he felt that calling the Arctic a "wasteland" was just a Qallunaat concept. He agreed, politely. Why is it not that to you? "Because," he said slowly, "we really *know* the land, and this knowledge means we're in the safety of our zone."

I went on a journey to Nunavut, Canada's Inuit territory, flying from Iqaluit (formerly Frobisher Bay) in southern Baffin Island up to Pond Inlet in the north, and to Igloolik, an island off the Melville Peninsula, to Resolute on Cornwallis Island and to Grise Fiord on Ellesmere Island. These are tiny Inuit communities; Resolute and Grise Fiord have fewer than two hundred inhabitants each.

SIGHT AND ICE LIGHT

I spent a lot of time on Ellesmere Island walking and watching. Sight is strange in the Arctic. The air is so clear and the whiteness so ubiquitous that perspectives are deceptive: what is actually far away can seem sharp and close, while what's near can seem far. As you trudge through snow on uneven land, you may have no idea where your foot will fall as the landscape zooms in and out of proportion. What looks like a mile across a valley is in fact a distance that you can stride over in one step. Then you shrink to nothing as a ridge of snow, seemingly two feet high, takes you twenty minutes to crawl over. Or a day. Trudge on.

Arctic explorer Vilhjalmur Stefansson watched what he thought was a grizzly bear. It was in fact a marmot. A Swedish explorer carefully drew a map of what he thought was a rocky headland. It was in fact a walrus. Antarctic explorers reported seeing what they thought was their dogs' encampment. It was in fact an empty biscuit barrel. European sailors have had the eerie sense that their ship was adrift not at sea but in the air; a mist around them, above them and, frighteningly, below them. Or they saw reflections of the ship hanging in the air. Upside down. Mock suns heralded summer snowstorms, mock moons winter blizzards. Seeing what was apparently more than one sun or moon was a trick of the light, and similarly fata morgana bewildered the sight. Ships of the mind, phantom cities, false forests, nonexistent but visible islands, irreal mountains and archipelagos of the imagination alone bewitched them. The European psyche had a hard time with this, for to them sight was champion of the senses and the most trusted route to knowledge. (Aristotle said that the sense of sight was to be trusted "above all others." An "observation" is a statement of knowledge, and "I see" means "I know.")

The Inuit, cannier to the Arctic's sleight of sight, depended heavily on what they heard as well. Author of *Eskimo Realities* Edmund Carpenter writes that for the Inuit, the eye is "subservient to the ear. They define space more by sound than by sight. Where we might say, 'Let's see what we can hear,' they would say 'Let's hear what we can see.'" Nonetheless, Inuit have certainly had odd visions: Sarah Haulli, an Inuit elder of Igloolik, said she was certain she had seen *Tariassuit*, illusionary shadow beings. She described being out on the land with her husband when they saw two dog teams driven by people at a distance, which she guessed was a group coming to meet them. It was very slow going and she had plenty of time to prepare for them. The shapes gradually began to turn white, though, and as she and her husband got closer "we found they were nothing but two ice ridges." So sure had she been that they were people that along the way she had boiled up a kettle and made tea for them.

When the land itself is a shape-shifter and when the Arctic practices an optical legerdemain from inch to infinity and back, little wonder that Inuit stories are full of transformation and size-shifting and they caution you against judging by appearances, even as they pocket the moon.

Larry Audlaluk, an elder of Grise Fiord, told me a story of a shape-shifting creature who changed into a walrus, then a musk ox, then a wolf. The wolf, he said, was beautiful, sensitive, easily offended and always traveling ("even to the land of trees"), but he was thin and hungry and couldn't keep up with the pack, so an older wolf told the young wolf how to run: "You have to reach out for the horizon to keep up, as if you're seizing the horizon in your paws."

So the hungry wolf pounces forward as if he is hunting at the edge of the world, seizing pawfuls of skyline, as if the enormous horizon, halfway to the stars, is nothing more than a hare to be caught in the wolf's claws, and he plunges on, giving chase to the future, where land meets sky and never does, just at the point where mind meets time and never does.

"*That* is how to run."

The shape-shifter finally becomes a polar bear—young, ignorant and cocky—and meets a skinny two-legged creature. An old bear warns the young one, "That two-legged is more dangerous than it looks." And the last thing the young bear remembers is the skinny two-legged with its spear raised.

From the quality of light, the future could be seen: the elders say that shamans would read the future by the sparkliness of the air. Sparkles extending beyond the horizon would mean a period of plenty.

The Northern Lights is a special instance of the Arctic's irrealities: while the snow is softly drinking moon, the aurora borealis rains down huefuls of greenlight. The night sky is tie-dyed and spun, in centrifuge from the sun, in hesitance and light; the wind wrests color from the night and secret light is wrung from the dark.

In Inuit traditional belief, the Northern Lights are the ancestors playing ball with a walrus skull. The souls of the dead (specifically those who have died through blood loss, in childbirth or murder) wish to come back to Earth, so they softly whistle to the living and, if people on Earth gently whistle or whisper back, the ancestor lights can be enticed closer to Earth out of curiosity. The Northern Lights are also sometimes thought to be children who are not yet born, reeling out the light. Another belief was that they are gifts of light from the dead to those on Earth, to lift the gloom of winternight. By another belief, they are a strange polar dreamtime, visible in the present but containing happenings of the future and of the past. Inuit elder Simon Tookoome, in a book of his life, says people thought the lights could be dangerous. "If you whistled you might bring them too close . . . they are very beautiful but they are like dangerous water."

No light is simple here. A sky heavy, pregnant with snow, can be gray-yellow. Sun can be silver on a cold sea, and icebergs green. An inukshuk, a traditional stone carved figure on the land, glows yellow against cobalt skies. And in a sunrise after winter, the sky can be red and the snow purple. As I looked out the windows of a Kenn Borek plane, the sky had a streak of blue, a smudge of pink and an offhand sun. There were ten passengers: me, eight Inuit and a husky puppy. One pilot rummaged through his bags to find a plastic container of limp Caesar salad, croutons and baby carrots, pre-peeled, and he offered us all "grape nectar." Sailing over Baffin Island, drinking grapes and my heart was singing.

A massive iceberg was anchored in the waters by Pond Inlet. The pilots told me it had been there for a year and they could see it eighty kilometers away, in summer, against a dark sea, and they could steer by it. The flight was long. At Pond Inlet, all the other passengers disembarked but we refueled and headed on, north. Dusk and winter were falling and there were only the two pilots and me, so they invited me into the cockpit as we flew higher into the gray snow, while coral pink sun fell on the peaks. The sun seemed to tatter the clouds as if its last burning wish of the year was to rend them completely. We flew up, cloudfogged at first, then broke through it entirely, and there above the cloud the sun was setting to glory, the skies were blue and the cockpit was full of gold. "Sunset in the Arctic for you." The pilot smiled. "Last month the sun didn't set. Just went round and round the sky."

NIGHTWINTER, DAYSUMMER AND THE TWILIGHT OF FALL

The Arctic is "sudden with summer" in Canadian poet F. R. Scott's beautiful phrase, and the midnight sun is a two-word song.

It is autumn now, the twilight of thaw. Summer's vowels are swallowed by the first howl of autumn, before winter, consonantal, cracking, shocks the last whisper out of the land. "We're right on the edge of day and night, here. In the winter below the shadow. We're stuck in the shadow," says Paul Amagoalik from Resolute Bay. Below them is day, above them, night. Night and winter are one and the same: the Arctic doesn't swing to a daily rhythm but to an annual one: nightwinter and daysummer.

Dark is a stalking, hungry season, preying on summer, stealthy and watchful. It doesn't have to pounce or chase, for it is a predator half made of time. It need only wait, shadowing the days at the covert end of fall; it prowls on the back of blizzards and steals up on the last small bird, migrating a day too late. And snaps its wings. Because that is its nature.

Deeper into winter, time seems more frozen, for little moves through which time-alive can express itself. The small jubilation of a stream is a relief to hear. It is a faint, buried sound, for the water is running under a layer of ice, which itself lies below a layer of snow. There are marks on the snow where a bird has landed and skidded eighteen inches on ice. Comic, cartoonish, like arrows on a prisoner's uniform, this wee prisoner of winter grabs a last bag of swag: a beakful of fresh water. Then midwinter comes, so implacably black that even frost mist is dark.

But the year's twilight is an undersung moment, when the psyche looks both ways, when summer is still all but present even while the darker shades creep up on you.

The Inuit see shaded seasonality; in Igloolik they name eight seasons of the year and these can be emotionally nuanced. Larry Audlaluk says, "This time of year when winter is coming, the lives of my parents and my memories become very real. I see the land through my parents' eyes as well as mine. I get tears in my eyes at these times. In the summer, the feeling of being dominated by the wilderness is not as intense. But here in September it feels dangerous. Here in April, I feel safe, yet it's the same place. In the summer, it calls you, it says, 'I'm not dangerous. I'm safe. Get to know me.' Two faces of the same land. Fishermen say the same of water. It's scary and menacing but also beckoning, beautiful, irresistible."

It's the light they've told you about . . .
But it's the darkness they mean,

writes American poet David Rothenberg.

From the plane, and more so on the ground, you see how the landscape is drawn by the wind. If you could read the wind as Inuit hunters can, you would rarely be lost. The wind inscribes the snow, leaves its signature on the water, it delves and inclines, writes the narrative tension of a cornice, an overhang of snow, then dictates a long regular line of a ridge on a flat plain, where it almost always blows from the same direction.

The authoring wind writes its playful riffs when it whistles around a rock, it doodles with bergy bits and scribbles graffiti in brash ice, or etches a deep memory of moods in the miles of a glacier, it blows a Miltonic univocal deadset gale or, in changeable tempestuous gusts, this many-tongued wind writes what it will:

the wind
time's restless infinite unruly wind

wrote Saami poet Nils-Aslak Valkeapää.

THE POLES OF MEANING

This land doesn't chat. It won't squabble. Plea bargaining cuts no ice with it. It demands and states but can never apologize. There are absolutes here, death, winter, birth and ice. It has a quality of simileless essentiality, for the poles are at the poles of meaning, the Ultima Thule of comparison. Colors have reached their apex here, in the black of the ravens, the white of the snow, and the red of blood. Red, at its most northerly point, contends with no southerly shades—red wine or roses. Only blood. And you see blood on the snow a lot: the killed whales, a seal bleeding.

Here at the poles more than anywhere on earth you feel the spiral truth of the world, at midsummer the topmost point of the year's gyre and midwinter the dark below. Driest, highest, whitest, iciest, Antarctica is the pole of superlatives, the coldest place on earth, yet this "wilderness" is of all continents the most a friend to humankind, as its unmelted ice protects the world's climate. So implacably iced is it—the Antarctic ice cap can be three miles thick in places—that the land beneath it has been submerged well below sea level. (In Greenland, ice lies so heavy on land that the land is shoved 1,180 feet below sea level.) On average it is three times higher than any other continent, 5,000 meters high in places. It never rains and seldom snows, it is sheer, utter ice. It has a strange relationship to life, for very few creatures can survive here and yet, and *yet*, without it, how damaged would life be.

THE WHALE HUNT

The day after I arrived in Resolute was the day the belugas came in. At a distance, I saw one person suddenly start running from the community down to the sea. Two more people made for the boats, someone got on an ATV (all-terrain vehicle) and headed along the shoreline. Then, everywhere I looked, people were furiously yanking their boats loose from the moorings, slinging their rifles by the windshields and revving up. I didn't know what was happening, but I ran too, full pelt for the shore. A man passed me on an ATV and screeched to a stop. "Wanna ride?" "Certainly do." "They're having fun over there," he said.

A gaggle of boats had collected in one spot and we heard the dull thud of a rifle shot over the icy water. One whale looked as if it was heading west and we followed along the shore. Close by, perhaps sixteen feet away, another whale was swimming. It was shot once, then twice more. A minute before, spray was jetting from its blowhole. Three cracks of rifle fire, and now blood fountained into the air; plumes of blood in the water blooming, hot and flourishing. The beluga was hauled onto shore, its smooth white body bleeding; the violent perfection of blood on snow. And its smile curled shy like a child's while the whale head snuggled down onto the shore ice, its dark gray eyes wise to death.

Hans, a hunter in polar bear skin trousers, was reloading cartridges into his rifle, fast. The boats were cruising the bay in different directions, chasing other whales. Various ATVs were charging around the bay one way, then another. There was a cracklingly festive atmosphere, animated and alert, people whizzing around, eyes peeled, happy and high-spirited, the boats careering in a circle after a turning whale, giving chase. A crowd of people had gathered on the shore about half a mile away, presumably around another dead whale. Near to me on the shore, a whale mother had been struck, the harpoon was embedded in her flesh, and attached to the harpoon was a red plastic gasoline canister to mark her where she swam: she was towing her own target with her, a bobbing indignity. Her calf followed, just a gray smudge in the water, an anxious orphaned shadow. (Traditionally, Inuit used floats of inflated sealskins attached to their harpoons so the hunters could see where a struck whale swam.)

I passed a husky, its white furry body red with whale blood—it must have shoved almost its whole body into the guts of a whale.

It was all over in a few minutes. Ten whales killed and the rest had fled. It was an enormous catch, as sudden as it was large. This is how life is in the Arctic; hunters must seize the moment or starve. It is a place with few margins or second chances.

I walked around the shoreline to where people had been butchering a whale. A bunch of skinny kids in jeans were playing with it. Its lungs were still warm to my touch. There was a drop of blood in one of its eyes and a boy squeezed the eye with his finger so more blood oozed out. Another tried to pull out a tooth and another yanked its mouth open and felt its warm tongue. I did too, and touched the heart and felt sorry. Its heart was as warm as my own and later, alone, I felt sorrier still. For hours, my fingers smelled of the warm-blooded heart of this whale. A child pulled out sausages of intestines. A kid on crutches dropped them accidentally into the bloody body and the other kids laughed. There were claw marks on its body where a polar bear had tried to kill it. I walked back past another carcass; its guts lay in snow on the shore and the snow was pitted with ravens' claw prints. Paul Amagoalik told me how whenever a whale or seal is killed, people put something (intestines, for instance) back "for the sea," out of respect. The whale carcasses along the beach would draw polar bears from miles around, people said.

At Grise Fiord, I went out hunting on the boats with a hunter, Christian, and two of his friends. In his shed, next to two dead eider ducks, he found piles of warm clothes for me, layers on layers till I was wrapped up like an onion. For himself, he chucked into the boat a pair of gardening gloves, a thermos of tea, rifles and bullets. We cruised out over the sea, with bits of brash ice bumping and knocking at the underside of the boat, past a bright blue berg.

A harp seal popped its head up, sleek and sudden, whiskers dripping water, nose high, sniffing, alert, but it was gone in a flick of water before anyone could reach a rifle. Christian radioed to other boats, speaking in Inuktitut, the Inuit language, punctuated every once in a while with "Channel 3. Over." A bearded seal in the distance stuck its nose up and scooted down, and the three hunters were immediately lined up, rifles aimed, all still, tense, waiting to see if it would come up again. Intellectually, I am on their side. This is their land, their culture, their food: we Qallunaat should not presume to tell them how to live, and it is commercial whaling, not Inuit hunting, that has driven sea creatures to extinction. My emotions, unfortunately, were in conflict with my mind on this; my sympathies are always with the prey, and the line of rifles looked like a firing squad.

A small ringed seal emerged, someone shot, and it disappeared. The bergs were bloody with previous kills. Eider ducks flew past. The men shot at them, but missed. "Nah," said Christian. "Too thin, anyway." I saw two seals that no one else saw, and I said nothing. I felt guilty for this because I should have justified my place in the boat with at least some observation. But I couldn't do it. Snowflakes were falling on the sea without melting. One of the men quietly pissed over the back of the boat.

Another small ringed seal came up, inquisitive and doglike, its curiosity a warm thing in this cold sea. The rifles cracked fire but it got away. Immediately, though, another came up and was shot and injured. It sank for a moment but soon reemerged to breathe. Christian swung the boat fast at it and one of the other hunters harpooned it and pulled it to the boat, still alive. At that point, he clubbed it with his fist against the side of the boat, but it was not yet dead, so another of the hunters put a gun to its head and shot it straight through the forehead. At this point my handwriting in my notebook (which until then had been cramped with cold, disturbed by the boat's movement and thickened by mittens) goes tiny and trembly; four little words are all there is: "shaky weak at knees," it says. For an awful moment I thought I was going to faint, I felt very sick and sat down suddenly. My face betrayed me, and Christian saw. He said nothing then, and very little to me after that. I felt angry with myself too, to be honest.

A second seal was shot, virtually its whole face shot off, but it was still moving, so it was clubbed with a fist against the boat. (Once an animal has been injured, the hunters do all they can to kill it quickly.) The smell of rifle fire was acrid in the clear air. Another boat, with one man aboard, drew parallel, and the men swapped whale sightings and seal kills; then the other man accepted a cigarette and was off. The sea was glassy and an iceberg appeared with strange ice formations like snowy reindeer horns, lit by thin winter rays of pale yellow light.

We landed on an island and I wandered off for a piss. It took me ages to undo all my clothes and by the time I'd finished my hands were numb and stiff. The smell of urine was strong in this cold and almost smell-less place. Christian cut the seals open and their bodies steamed hot on the snowy shore.

The sight of blood hummed intensely in my mind and I wanted to eat it, partly from a strange sense of bodily intimacy with something that had died so near me, and partly because I felt Christian was now regretting letting me come, assuming that my near faint was a "moral" revulsion. When he offered me a slice of seal liver, I took it. It melted in my mouth like fudge. Christian had blood dripping from his lips. I didn't know if I did or not.

In the afternoon, the sky was like mercury and the sea was as gray and cold as metal. Another seal was sighted and shot. It was badly injured, the water was red with blood, but the seal sank and the hunters were truly sorry, not only because they wouldn't have the seal to take back home, but also because they had left it injured. "It doesn't want to give its life up to us today," said Christian. It was a simple remark but reveals a very widespread philosophy among hunting people. According to many hunters of the north, animals choose to offer themselves to be killed. They give themselves to hunters who treat them with respect.

Late in the afternoon, we turned for home. The harpoon in the bottom of the boat was iced over. It had been hours since I had any feeling in my toes. Christian lined his boat up with that of another hunter, Oolat, who very nearly went into an iceberg. "Are there trees where you're from?" he asked. I nodded: Loads. "I wouldn't know a real tree," he said. "I've only seen fake Christmas trees." I was too cold to judge whether he was teasing me, but Christian was staring at him. "You're *joking*," he said, and I was quite relieved. Even Christian was unsure. We landed the boat, its sides spattered with blood, and Christian showed me an eighteen-inch-long bone. "You won't know what that is," he said. I didn't. "It's a walrus penis bone." He smiled. Two kids playing with a rifle were shooting a Coke can off a wall. The next day I had a terrible headache and my eyes were swollen with cold.

These were strange days, the last boating days of the year before the seas froze, and I asked people to take me with them in the boats. One of the elders suggested I offer to pay for the gas, which I was only too happy to do, and more. But still . . . I was too heavy, too female, too thin, would get too cold, I was told. Too Qallunaat, really. I would wait around the boats, and felt like a kid hanging around a newsagent's pestering grown-ups to buy me some fags. I tried to hide my disappointment every time a boat left without me.

One evening, I was visiting a hunter, Jaypeetee Akeagok, when Christian dropped by. The two of them began talking in Inuktitut, about me, as I thought. Christian switched into English only to say "make-me-feel-un-com-for-ta-ble" and switched back into Inuktitut. I blushed. A moment later, Jaypeetee threw me a question, like a hunter scoring a direct hit. "When you were on the boat and saw the seals being killed, how did that make you feel? Suddenly nauseous?" He gestured almost angrily at his stomach. I felt embarrassed and cross with myself, again. Inuit are sick of Qallunaat telling them it's wrong to kill seals and whales. My mind and my politics agree with the Inuit. My body, apparently, does not.

I was lucky, everyone told me, for being at Resolute when the whales came in. It happens like that barely twice in a year. And then I was lucky again: the whales came in at Grise Fiord when I was there. I was indoors when I heard, and I grabbed as many warm clothes as I could and legged it down to the boats. Can I? No. Please can I? Not today. I could feel the pricking of hot near tears of frustration, as I watched the hunt-happy vivacity spreading along the shore, one boat after another being launched into the water. One more try, just as a boat was being dragged over the last icy yards of shore, "Please can . . . ?" "Yes. Jump in." I hopped into Eugene's boat. The metal was so cold that my glove stuck to it, and part of it was torn off when I pulled my hand away. My notes of this day were hard-won, as I would whip off a glove to write one single word; even that made my hand crooked with cold, and I had to nurse it back to feeling under my arm or tucked between my legs.

Eleven boats in all were out on the water, each barbed with harpoons. Snow was falling from a dark gray sky. The engine of our boat kept cutting out and it was frustrating to see the other boats wheeling around in the waters. People hurled jabs of information at one another from boat to boat, words thrown like harpoons, somewhere between orders and advice to one another; each boat was working both alone and in concert. "Go *that* way," "It's gone *under* your boat," "*Now*, you're closest," "I've *got* it."

It was tense and nervy in the boat. Someone dropped all the bullets on the floor and swore. We caught sight of one whale close and went after it—one of the hunters grabbed the harpoon, which was tied to a rope made of bearded sealskin. We were close enough—the whale rose to breathe—the harpooner lunged—but the rope attached to the harpoon was twisted and, worse, the harpooner was standing on the coil of rope. The harpoon was jerked to a stop in the middle of its flight and plopped, impotent, into the water. (Coitus interruptus.) I felt some deep fright at the smell of gunpowder. I ignored this. I was also very, very cold—in an aluminum boat in freezing water with snow in the bottom of the boat. I ignored this too.

At each fresh sighting, the excitement grew, giving the men a little more information on the whales' direction, how many there were. Everyone's gaze swept the seas, over and over; the boats scudded fast after a sighting, stopped dead and cut the engine right where the whale had been seen. Then the intense, silent watching. The harpooner was frozen in his posture with the harpoon in his raised arm. Only his eyes moved, stroking the water, double-focused: focused to look for the clear line of spoon-back as the whale breaks the surface, and focused also to look for the smudge of pale light nudging its way underwater. Eugene was at the engine and two hunters were poised with rifles readied; everyone was on edge, hyperalert. The whale's need for the breath of life is what kills it, and as it broke the surface to breathe, the harpooner hurled again. This time the whale was hit; the harpoon rope trailed a ludicrously pink buoy, and the whale gave a fast tail flick and tried to get away, frightened. The hopeless struggle to escape began. The harpoon went in like an arrow but then hinged into its T-shape, which wouldn't come out. Between the first harpooning and the final rifle shot, it does seem sexual, as hunters tell you.

Hunting and fucking share an intensity, a drivenness to a culmination, and a sense of the universe being tightly drawn into this drama here; all senses heightened; a concentration of both mind and body, tight muscles, thoughts urgent and tense. There is a strange ejaculation of spirit, and an involuntary shudder, like the vulva's repeated contractions.

With a final rifle shot, it was over. The boat was flooded with an atmosphere of laughing, postcoital relief, someone lit a cigarette, and after one whale had been shot, the keenness was taken off people's appetite. One of the hunters remembered that he hadn't had a cup of coffee all day.

The whale whistled as it died; a sad sound, only air, just a breath, no articulated sound, certainly no whale song, just the escaping air in a thin and final surrender—life reproaching death for striking too soon, but with the reproach a kind of Arctic absolution: we all must live, we all must die, we all must eat, and such is life, so long. "Life's greatest danger lies in the fact that man's food consists entirely of souls," an old Igloolik shaman, Awa, told Knud Rasmussen, the Greenlandic explorer and anthropologist. (To eat he must kill, and all the animals he kills have souls, which can be angered if they are not hunted with respect.)

The sigh, the whale's life breath, pours into the air just as the warm red lifeblood billows out into the frozen water. The whistle is to the air what the blood is to the water, the last signature of life in each element. The whistle is warm with life and language, and plumes out into the cold, unwhistled and unlanguaged air.

One day, I went out in a boat with Jarloo, one of the hunters from Ellesmere Island. He was happy to be out on one of the last days of the year before the seas froze. "Look like I belong to this place," he said softly. There was a slushy patch of ice forming in the sea in our path, one or two hundred yards across. It was stiff, you could hear its susurrus under the boat as Jarloo headed into it, and it slowed the boat down a little. Then slowed it down a lot. The boat was staggering forward, the engine struggling, the boat shoving its way more and more slowly. I was nervous, suddenly. If the boat got stuck, you could hope for a sudden wind or rise in temperature to break up the ice, or that enough ice would form to walk back to the shore. Neither was likely, neither was safe. And in any case, you could die of exposure in the boat. These things were going through my mind. Jarloo swung the boat around to make for the nearest line of open water; the boat strained, the engine sounded raw with effort. It inched forward, then shot free. Jarloo turned to me, his face pure relief. "Oooooops," he whistled softly. I hadn't been the only one worrying. (Later, another hunter told me that he had been out in his boat when wind blew the ice in, and his boat was jammed into ice several miles from home; he had had to spend two weeks out there before he could get home.)

After a little time, Jarloo began to steer the boat toward a large and flattish berg or floe, perhaps some thirty yards square, with scat on it. He drew the boat up, cut the engine and reached for the anchor, and we anchored on the ice, climbed off the boat and looked around. It was polar bear scat, with fur in it from perhaps an arctic hare or fox, and there was a yellow patch of frozen piss. There were paw prints too, big, soft round ones, going down to the edge, and there were three burrows, one large and, on either side, two smaller ones, scraped out of a high-sided ice ridge. A mother bear had curled up here last night with a cub on either side. It was magical—a polar bear's bedroom.

"Polar bears are wild when they're hungry," said Jarloo, and told me how he had been out on the land in the winter. It was very dark and he hadn't seen the bear coming. He hadn't heard it either; their paws on the snow are almost silent. Then it was suddenly upon him, "and one little slap from them can kill you." Right at the last minute he saw it and jumped to get his Ski-Doo started—"and the bear just about managed to get sat on the sled behind the Ski-Doo! Eeeee," he laughed.

Near the house where I was staying, a team of huskies was chained to rocks, restrained in such a way that they couldn't attack one another. They snarled at me, one leaping up at the flutter of my notebook, each a ball of bored, cold and angry hunger. A husky puppy was chewing the tail fluke of a beluga whale as a raven first barked like a dog then poured out a streaming melody like a songbird. One of the hunters told me of a husky that had a litter of eight pups; all were left out over winter and all froze to death. Their owners said if they didn't survive that, they wouldn't have survived later. Huskies are usually kept on sea ice in winter, not land ice, because the sea ice is warmer.

One evening a gaggle of children accosted me for sweets or cigarettes. Their eyes gleamed weirdly. Are you stoned? one of them asked me. No, I said. Are you? They shrieked with laughter. I wasn't smiling—they couldn't have been more than ten years old.

ON ICE

Herman Melville wrote pages of loathing for the Arctic's white, claiming it represented death and atheism, that it was utterly colorless. It is as if he never looked. If you take a snow crystal, perhaps two or three millimeters in diameter, there is a rainbow of colors within it, a mandala of tiny and perfect jewels; silver, red and turquoise, soft gold opalescence, mother-of-pearl. Like the music of Arvo Pärt, the clear bell sounds; music that first comprehends (absorbing all colors into itself) and then shines, transcendent.

Ice is strangely alive: glaciers "calve" an iceberg; there are "parent" ice fields, and ice is active—it crushes ships, explodes and swims. "Young ice" is formed in the sea at autumn, while "old ice" has been knocking around for years, creaking a cold and idiosyncratic biography—this particular ice formation, which has never been seen before and will never be seen again. The lightest, freshest, youngest ice just kisses the water; the thick old ice plates shift unevenly, lapping one another, clasping them—new ice in the old ice's arms.

There is a phenomenon called *ivu* in Inuktitut: a midwinter explosion when an enormous block of sea ice can rocket hundreds of feet inland, crushing people to death. Rivers of ice can thaw in summer, so a block of ice the size of a small house, torn from the river by sheer force of thaw, is flung half a mile away.

You can get rolling fissures and waves of fractured ice. The warmer it is, the crazier the ice goes, say the Inuit, and they speak of ice "rotting" and "decaying"—when ice melts unseasonably, or has been trodden too much. Ice acts on the land, chiseling up a new cliff or making of itself a wall to lock a whale in a fjord, or becoming a nutcracker to crack open a ship.

Ice is an artist generous with its sculptures. Beyond audience or applause, it creates in profusion for only one reason—that it has need to create. Ice has a wide vocabulary of touch: ice crystals in the wind can sting; an emerald icicle melts as smooth as cream; an iceberg can be etched by wind to a knife edge or blunt snow can nub a thumb of ice.

An iceberg the size of a church, with pillars and spires, a mile away, catches the last light of twilight. (The sun at twilight has little more strength than a full moon.) Through holes and caves of ice, the icebergs gurgle. The ice in icebergs can be twenty thousand years old. Four-fifths of a berg is underwater, and seven-eighths of its mass.

One berg has a strange row of icicles like the baleen of a whale. One is an exaggeration of a whale's tail fluke. Another has an inner grotto of ice. Sometimes they resemble Inuit carving: a shaman wrestling with a monster, or the bergs sculpt the abstracts of the psyche, expressing the intrinsic, doing away with the vocabulary of the actual in order to express the landscape of the mind, leaning in contented curves, concave and clownish, or in the shock of protrusion, a dog's hind leg of ice, an unwelcome and ugly soul event, or the soft lines of sheer serenity, the honeycombed dents, a pattern of frozen ripples, a snatch of time when one breeze touched one water, now both held in the lasting hour of ice.

Bergs have characters: some are shy, all hollows and retreats, while others, "tabletop" bergs, flatfootedly chart a turgidly pedestrian course through life, and there are those who sing their unrepentant arias of a glacial age while some are eloquent—but only in turquoise.

During the week I stayed on Ellesmere Island, the seas froze. When I arrived, the sea was still a summer sea and not one crystal had formed. I watched it daily, sometimes hourly, because although I knew the facts, it still seemed miraculous to me that a whole sea could freeze. By contrast, more than one Inuit person expressed their great surprise that where I lived the seas never froze.

I watched tide after tide coming in and going out as water. One day, though, one tide was different. It left tiny wave-signatures, shallow U-shaped links of frozen froth with fragile, crinkly stars of ice so delicate that when I breathed over them, they melted away.

The huskies howled nearby and a small girl, perhaps five, ran up to me affectionately. Her face was gashed with scars, ear to mouth, nose to chin. "Look," she beamed proudly, pointing at her face, "I'm scared of dogs." (When she's older will she hide her face from strangers?)

The following day, the wind blew intermittently, and whenever there was no wind, the sea was stilled as if a skein of thin gray silk were cast on black water. (When hexagonal crystals form in the water at the surface, it is called "frazil ice.") The following day, ice was forming where the water was windless and the ice was as shiny as scar tissue. The next day, the seas' ice crystals became "grease ice"—so aptly named, for the ice forms like congealed white fat in a black baking tin. The following day there were plates of ice in the water, several inches across; this is "pancake ice" or "bear-paw ice." The icebergs out at sea no longer seemed to float free, but were caught on the claw of winter, and the waves were like cold metal. You could no longer hear any waves on the shore because the water was iced some two hundred yards out to sea. It was too cold to stay out long, and I returned home, past sealskins pegged up on frames to dry. The following day, there were plates of ice underwater by the shore, and snow was settling on the frozen sea.

The ice had pinioned the very waves. The waters were flattened by cold. Heavier blocks of blue ice seemed to form by the hour, while the water at the shore was a crusted sheet. Big, soft snow was falling from gray skies, and the mountains had disappeared in fog. Perfect snowflakes fell on my black notebook, and my fingers hurt to write. It was as if the seas themselves had migrated, as if "sea-ness" must retreat southward come winter.

Several days later, I was flying in a small plane about two hundred meters above the sea, now composed of pack ice in huge plates, with gaps between them, lines of water called "leads" (which you pronounce *leeds*). The sun was dark yellow behind us, which made the leads ahead look black while those behind us were soft gold. Shards of ice were scattered in enormous flakes like broken slate. (Solid sea ice is broken into pieces called ice floes, which collectively are called pack ice.) Twice I saw bear paw prints on the ice. So did the pilots, scanning the horizon, banking the plane steeply till my stomach gave way, and I was dizzy and nauseous. The sun set and the hills and valleys of northern Baffin Island were like a black-and-white etching washed with ink.

One time, days later, the sky at sunset was deep gray but vivid as gray so seldom can be. The snow was creamy yellow and it seemed as if the sun was shining from below, as if the sun were rising under the snow and pouring up through it.

Back in the nearby community, blood spattered the snow. A man was shot dead here two weeks ago.

When one Inuit elder of Igloolik, Michel Kupaaq Piugaattuk, was asked for different words for snow, he reeled off fifteen, hardly pausing for breath. Some Europeans have scorned the idea of there being a famously large number of words for snow in Inuktitut, calling it a "vocabulary hoax" and claiming that there is just one word for snow used with a variety of prefixes and affixes. This is simply untrue, and rather overweening for Europeans to pretend they know Inuktitut better than the Inuit. Anthropologist and Inuktitut speaker Hugh Brody says bluntly, "There is no root term, no category that is equivalent to the English 'snow.'" When Igloolik residents were asked for compilation of words for ice and snow, they provided a hundred or so.

Michel Kupaaq Piugaattuk uses entirely different words for snow, expressing snow's uses and its formation. In Inuktitut, the word *mauja* means deep snow, which is soft and you easily sink into it. *Pukakjiujaq* is hard snow turning ever so slightly soft; the best for igloo-building because it will heat faster. *Qikuutitsajaq* means powdered snow applied to the cracks in the wall of an igloo. (Arctic Polyfilla.) *Uqalurait* means snowdrifts arched toward the northwest wind. (Their windward tips are tongue-shaped and *uqaq* means "tongue.") *Tissujaaq* is the term for a snowdrift covering a large area on the leeside of an ice floe. (Where the polar bear and her two cubs had scooped out their sleeping places on the ice.) *Irrarliniq* means that the top layer of snow is iced but underneath it is soft, and no matter how strongly the wind blows, this snow won't be blown away. I could go on. But I want to tell you about words for ice.

The English language has many evocative terms for ice formations. *Bergy bits* describes small icebergs, rising less than five meters out of the sea. A *growler* is a small floating piece of ice, a hazard for ships. *Nilas* is a thin crust of sea ice that moves according to the wave motion beneath but does not break. *Sastrugi* is almost onomatopoeic, meaning windblown furrows in snow. "Needle ice" can form in second-year ice and it is, as you might guess, sharp and painful for people, polar bears and huskies alike. There are "ice clouds" of Antarctica and types of sea ices, including ice rinds, ice flowers and vuggy ice. Coastal ices include anchor ice, rime ice and ice haycocks. Mountain ices include cirque glaciers and ice pipes. Polar plateau ices include ice domes and ice rumples. Atmospheric ices including ice crystals and ice dust.

For Inuit hunters, knowing the words for ice is a matter of life and death, because the words discriminate between how ice is formed, which in turn tells you how it will—or might—behave. And how the ice behaves is what your life depends on. The language takes you into a delicate, intricate kenning of ice and time. Will it support you or crack? Will it sail away for a week and a day . . . with you on board? Only knowledge can protect you from the cold; knowing which type of ice would be warmer than another, how not to slip into the killing water.

I stopped writing by the time I'd noted thirty-three words with full descriptions, and what follows is not an exhaustive list but an illustration of a land where ice is all the world; ice behind you, ice under you, ice the past and the future ice. In this world, the Edge is an electric idea: land-fast ice is the safest to travel on, so you need to know when you're reaching its edge. But a hunter may want to cross over, out onto sea ice, to get to an *aglu* (a seal's breathing hole) or he may see a bear right out on the floe ice at sea, and want to chase it; you have to get there by crossing moving ice, so you need to know where that moving ice meets the floe edge. The moving ice moves according to the state of the tide beneath it, coming crushed together or spreading wide apart. The hunter has to judge this very carefully. And if he misjudges it, that line would spread out into a wide and fatal margin.

Mark Ijjangiaq describes *nipititaaq* and this term shows language carved to precision to meet the demand of ice. To define it, you have to tell the life story of part of ice. Moving ice meets land-fast ice, and the two are interlocked for a period; then when the wind shifts to the north from the direction of the land-fast ice, the moving ice will dislodge from the land-fast ice, leaving some of it cemented to the land-fast ice. This new addition is *nipititaaq* and is usually rough with pressure ridges. You need to recognize that you are on that kind of ice, because soon this ice pan in turn will move out but separate from the main block. Now the terminology gets more precise still, for if this separate pan is high with pressure ridges, it is called *ijukaqut*. Mark Ijjangiaq comments, "When hunters were taken out with the moving ice, they used to take refuge on these as it is warmer to be on them, because they are much dryer than newformed ice, it feels like ice blanketed with snow. And if there were some snow on it, some kind of shelter could be made."

Uluangnait is when snow has fallen on newly formed ice and that ice has not yet become strong, so that the ice underneath is warmed by snow, and then pushed underwater by snow. The ice then is being warmed not only by snow above but by water below, leaving effectively only snow. This, of course, is highly dangerous.

But the words for ice are being lost. The younger generation, forced to go to Qallunaat school instead of learning from the land, know fewer and fewer terms. Land that had been intimately known is now shadowed with ignorance. And it is ignorance that makes a wasteland. As the words for ice and snow are melting away with each elder's death, so the knowledge they contain is melting. Pauli Kunnuk says, "Since we no longer use vocabulary that was common in the past, we tend to forget the words as soon as they are no longer used." The elders are word-artists of a melting world.

SURVIVAL

I asked Lamech Kadloo, of Pond Inlet, if there was anything in the world he would call wild. "Cold," he said, "and blizzards. Sometimes it seems nature wants to take away a life." Author Richard Nelson reports that Koyukon elders considered cold weather to be "a conscious thing, with a potent and irritable spirit. They warn the younger ones to speak carefully about cold, lest they incite its frigid wrath."

This cold can kill in seconds. People tell of their eyelids frozen into saucers of solid ice. The cold stupefies, paralyzes you. A man sinks to his knees, mouth open, lips torn with cold, snow filling his mouth. People lose fingers, toes and noses to frostbite. Once, an elder tells me, someone found his feet were frostbitten; the man had to cut off his own leg to save his life.

In the past, each winter brought the threat of starvation when severe frosts turned *aglus* and leads to ice. Chukchi people describe having to scrape the walls of their meat caches for any last scrap of flesh stuck on the ice; they would cook leather straps of sealskin, and eat anything, from the material of their tents to hare droppings.

In the harsh winter of 1957–58 the inhabitants of several Inuit communities starved to death. Joe Haulli, an Igloolik elder, recalled being a small child in a starvation time, and wanting to eat so badly that he couldn't stop crying. His older brother and sister had died of sickness already, and Joe's father took him by the hood, lifted him, told him not to cry because there *was* no food to cry for, and then tried to choke him to death. Another man came past, and his father let him go.

When Captain Oates famously walked off into the snow ("I may be some time"), to give the rest of Scott's South Pole expedition a chance of survival, it was called a "sublime sacrifice" by Herbert Ponting. Inuit did it all the time. Traditionally, in a period of starvation, the old would walk naked out into the snow. Both suicide and cannibalism were a horrific necessity but done with consent when people knew that one person might survive by another's death.

So harsh was life and so necessary the hunter to the life of all that it was common for baby girls to be killed at birth. Knud Rasmussen lists the numbers in one village where there were ninety-six births and of this number thirty-eight girls were killed. He records Manêlaq, mother of twelve children of whom eight were girls. Seven of the eight were killed at birth. Tatqêq was mother of two boys and two girls. Both the girls were killed. Saquvluk had eleven children and of these seven girls were killed. This is the moral context of whale hunting for, given that whales could be as intelligent, or more so, than humans, their killing is no more or less shocking than infanticide. Sheer survival demands it.

Igloolik elders Joe and Sarah Haulli speak of going out hunting with another man and being adrift on moving ice as the wind picked up and blew them farther away from land-fast ice. They were cold. Their winter clothing, which had been buried in the ground during the summer, had been unearthed and eaten by dogs. The three of them were adrift on an ice pan for about a week. They tried and failed to shoot a walrus, so they killed a dog, skinned it and ate it. Sarah Haulli found her mittens had got wet, so, for warmth, her husband strapped her arms and mittens inside her coat, straitjacket style, so that her hands would stay warm and her mittens dry out. It worked. Up to a point. She walked too close to a lead and fell through the ice. They did all finally make it back to land-fast ice. In such a situation, comments Pauli Kunnuk, "you consider the land-fast ice as home."

Kunnuk once found himself on an ice pan being blown out to sea, blown south all through a long night, using his rowing boat for a windbreak. Then the ice pan began breaking up. Seals that they had caught dropped through the cracks and they were running out of water. They were stuck like this for five or six days, during which time, hunters say, you strain your ears to listen to sounds from the edge of the ice pan because the sound you most want to hear is the crunching sound of pressure ridges being built up as the moving ice rubs heavily back onto shore ice and home.

They made it. Many didn't. One man, George Kappianaq, described how he and his brother were asked to go looking for his father's cousin, whom they saw, at a distance, on his knees on the ice. Kappianaq went to him, asking, "Are you awake? Are you cold?" There was no answer, so Kappianaq grabbed the man by the shoulder and his face became visible, lit, now, by moonlight. His mouth and nose were frozen, and the man was dead. The brothers loaded him onto their sledge, one taking off his jacket to make a pillow for the dead man's head, and they traveled all night home to his widow, who collapsed at the news. "It was so sad and remorseful and so much pity toward her."

Some hunters court difficulties. When I was in one community, people were worrying for a hunter who was out on the seas. "He likes to travel on rough seas, that guy," I was told. "Once, in rough seas, he was boating back and forth and we all thought he was crazy but that's what he enjoys." He was gone two weeks, but did return, safe.

So scarce could food be in the winter that it was vital for people to turn nomad, following the caribou or moving to a new area for seals. Nothing could stand in the way, neither old age nor even childbirth. There are descriptions of a woman about to give birth on a sledge journey. She stopped the dogs while a circle of men gathered around her to protect her from the bitter winds. She gave birth to the child and tucked it inside her furs and they climbed back onto the sledges once more and were away into the dark.

The cold affects how you breathe. If you overexert yourself, your lungs will freeze, so you need the fur hood of a parka, which enables you to breathe warmed air. Eating seal meat, an elder told me with a wink, "keeps your feet warm for months," while a young man explained to me how if someone's hands were becoming dangerously frozen you could cut open a dog to warm your hands in its stomach. I stayed with a family for a few days where there was half a skinned seal on the kitchen floor—in an igloo, the air was warm while the floor was ice and snow; that was therefore the best place to keep food fresh.

Although Inuit may balk at calling these lands a wilderness, they know them to be harsh, and they have worked out lifeways that are precisely adapted, sinew to niche. Although it may be dark and blowing a blizzard outside, igloos can be very snug. People do still make them: when you're out hunting, one person told me, "they're warmer than tents and you don't hear the wind so much." In the traditional igloos, a lamp was made with a wick of Arctic cotton, or willow catkins or moss soaked in whale blubber, seal oil or caribou fat and set in a stone dish. It would glow a soft yellow, offering both warmth and light. Some igloos were built adjoining others with corridors so people wouldn't have to go outside in order to visit a neighbor. Igloos usually had windows, sometimes made of a sheet of clear freshwater ice, or sometimes the intestines of the bearded seal. But, explains one elder, "my mother always preferred the oesophagus because it stays flat even when it's wet but the intestines crumple and tended to flap in the wind."

One Inuk woman (Inuk is the singular form of Inuit) told me that an igloo window could be made of a walrus penis. It's very long—she grinned—the right length for a window. The skin was cut around and around along the membrane (she gestures, a bit like turning a kebab and slicing off a slither), so as the penis turned, a thin piece of membrane was produced.

Tents for the summer could be made out of caribou skin and struts of whalebone. Some Inuit and Chukchi people made boats of walrus skin stretched over driftwood. What is more, these boats were translucent so people could see down into the green sea through the bottom of the boat. "People who had never been in one before were filled with fear," writes Chukchi man Yuri Rytkheu. Spears were made with narwhal tusks or a bear's thighbones. Sledges for the Inuit were traditionally made of whalebones with runners made of walrus tusks or the jawbones of whales. Cross-slats could be made of frozen meat or fish.

A hazard of traditional travel was that the dogs, hungry, would occasionally find it irresistible to eat the sledge. On the other hand, for a hunter to lose his dogs to starvation was a terrifying prospect, and a sledge could, after all, be rebuilt. (Sledges may yet be the best mode of transport, for no hungry husky has yet been able to eat a Ski-Doo.)

For Inuit hunters, well-made clothing could be a matter of life and death; clothes made so skillfully that they were waterproof could save your life, while an unmended mitten might cost you a hand. Women, usually, made clothes, and had to know the properties of all their materials. Sealskin was strong and more or less waterproof but not warm. Polar bear skin was warm and waterproof but very heavy. Hare, eider duck and fox were warm and light but delicate. Caribou skin was the best—strong, light and warm. A baby's clothing might include the fur of an arctic hare for a hat, underwear made from the feathers of birds and a hood made of a small caribou fawn. (When you realize quite how important good clothing is, you see the reason for what is supposedly the foulest oath of the Inuit: "Your mother does not know how to sew!")

In every community, I noticed something that at first looked odd to me: people pulling a sledge behind a Ski-Doo, and on the sledge blocks of icebergs. "It's the elders," I was told. "They won't drink anything else. They won't touch tap water—their taste buds are too sensitive for chlorine." The elders find store food "makes them weak" and are only satisfied eating "wild country foods."

Useful material from the world of whites is treasured by the Inuit. Inuit hunters have always needed to be able to make or repair equipment and clothes along the way, and Richard Nelson remembers "an old Eskimo hunter named Kavvik, advising me again and again, 'Never go *anyplace* without dental floss.'"

LOST, UNLOST AND TEMPORARILY MISPLACED

One Igloolik man, Theo Ikummaq, was asked if he knew of any hunters who had been really lost. "No, not really," he replied. "That's a mark of a seasoned hunter. You are only temporarily misplaced." He described being in Greenland, while his brother was some distance away, calling him on the shortwave radio to ask where exactly Theo had cached seven caribou. From the brother's description, Theo could "see" where his brother was, and then could describe exactly where the caribou were buried by describing all the rocks coupled with the wind directions as compass points to tell him where the caribou were. So precise was the information that the brother found six of the seven.

Joseph Koonoo, an elder of Pond Inlet, described to me how even when you could see no sun, or moon, or stars, you could find your way because you would know the direction of the prevailing wind and you can see how wind shapes the land, so you read the land by the wind-design. People also use "sky-maps": when it's overcast, the sky will be dark above open water or above snow-free lands, while when the land is covered with snow but the earth still shows brownly through, the sky will be lighter. Brightest of all is pure white sea ice, which is reflected white up onto the sky.

At sea, if it's foggy and windless, you can read the floating seaweed for directions; it streams out with currents and wind, though you have to bear in mind how the currents are running and the tidal times. If you are at sea in fog, you should always aim for either one side or the other of your destination, so when you hit land you'll know which way to walk. People would also listen for wave sounds along fogbound coasts and would sniff for scents of shore and surf. And you can always rely on the Arctic tern, for if it has anything in its beak, it is headed for land. You can also read the seals: if a wind is blowing up, watch marine animals, for they will all come up for air facing the same way. Dogs, too, says Abraham Ulaajuruluk, an elder from Igloolik, "were useful, for they knew things that we did not"—if a hunter lost his bearings, the dogs would often not be lost.

Qallunaat often died in snowstorms because they believed that you must keep moving to keep from freezing to death. The Inuit rule is the opposite.

As soon as you realize you're lost, stop, make a shelter and wait it out. Don't move until you know where you're going. If you walked until you were more lost and too exhausted to build a shelter, you might die. But this knowledge is less common now: one young man said to me with rueful honesty, "I tried building a snow igloo once but it fell down."

I was told about an Inuk man who had recently come to a community, gone off and got lost in a blizzard and died. Elders worry aloud and often that young people who do not know the land as they themselves do are easily and dangerously lost. When people lose the knowledge of how the land lies and where they stand within it, the land can become a frightening wasteland.

THE PEOPLE WHO CHANGE NATURE

All land has a story unto itself," said Susannah Singorie, a Pond Inlet elder, to me. "All the land that surrounds us has stories to tell." When the Anglican missionaries arrived, they banned storytelling, an Inuk man tells me. Talking to Joseph Koonoo, I mentioned Australian Aboriginal people's songlines. He listened, intently, then gently whistled a long breath. "*Piujuq,*" he said. "That's beautiful."

Knowledge was held in stories, in customs and in the rules by which people lived. One of the most important of these was not to take anything away from the land, no rock, no fossil, no stone, nothing. "In the past, before we were Christians, we had our own belief of not bothering the land—that was before Christianity was put upon us," says Susannah Singorie. The reason is partly to shape oneself to the land, to honor it. One young Inuk man told me it was "disrespectful" to change the land. "Someone who was respectful of the land would not even move a rock unless he needs to use it." It was also a practical rule, because every feature in the landscape was a map: someone might have memorized a particular route, taking directions from the relationship of the prevailing wind between two rocks. If another person moved one of the rocks, the first man, returning on the route he had learned, might fatally lose his way.

When Inuit first met whites, they called them Qallunaat (singular Qallunaaq), a white person, a Southerner, one having values different from Inuit.

The word is said to carry various meanings, including "the people who change nature." According to Inuk woman Minnie Aodla Freeman, the word suggests "people who are powerful, avaricious, of materialistic habit, people who tamper with nature." It was not a compliment. It was, in fact, more ominous and apt than they could ever have known.

If whites were those who changed nature, the peoples of the Arctic chose not to alter it, but to study it, to observe it closely. They were first noticers of nature and then revealers of it. Inuit carvers would watch an animal with a hunter's gaze, needing to know it and, with a piece of ivory in their hands, would seek to "reveal" the shape or figure within the material. (Michelangelo carved marble similarly, to let the statue emerge, as it were, of its own accord.) I watched an Inuk carver, with half-carved stone in his hand, who explained his wish to "let it tell itself, to let the stone speak."

Edmund Carpenter comments, "Language is the principal tool with which the Eskimo make the natural world a human world. . . . Words are like the knife of the carver: they free the idea, the thing, from the general formlessness of the outside." When language was fluted into song and poetry, it was considered not a luxury but a necessity for life. The hunter, shaman and poet Orpingalik, a Netsilik man, talked to Knud Rasmussen about one of his songs titled "My Breath." "This is what I call my song because it is as important for me to sing it as it is to draw breath."

An Inuk woman told me how for the Inuit, all the surroundings have spirits, and are "aware." Even ideas, such as "sleep" or "weather," are alive. The Inuit felt *ilira*—an awed, respectful and slightly nervous feeling—toward nature, and lived accordingly. Elders still stress that no animal should be killed unnecessarily, or made to suffer, or be mocked or made fun of. Everything, even vegetation, should be treated with care. Even bees or spiders have minds "and in their own kind they are adults," says an Igloolik elder. "That is why you do not mistreat them. Because . . . they can think too." Even glaciers can be considered "animate" and passing a glacier you should not speak or laugh, eat or smoke.

For the Saami people, the *yoik* was a kind of songline—a way of singing the land that to an initiate could evoke a landscape or people, animals or moods. The song was part evocation and part intercession, for Saami people, believing as they traditionally did that nature had "soul," would sing a *yoik*, asking mountain passes or lake ice to be kind to a traveler. But when the missionaries came, they said *yoik* was of the devil, and these good Christians killed people for it. Nils-Aslak Valkeapää writes, "Even an old man of more than eighty years of age was executed because he was irresponsible enough to *yoik*."

For the Inuit, says Simon Tookoome, "in the old days, the animals and the people were very much the same. . . . They thought the same way and felt the same way." It was a minded world. With the arrival of the people who changed nature, these two worldviews collided heavily, jolting in shock like the pressure ridges of ice when an ice floe at sea crashes into land-fast ice. A whole way of thinking was jarred. Inuit knowledge and language began to melt, and all the aware, animated spirits of the land were termed "satanic."

THE NOTHINGNESS, THE NOTHINGNESS

Wilderness is not an easy concept to translate into Inuktitut. There is a word *inuillaq*, which means people-less places. *Silainaq* is a place where no one lives but people just pass through. There is a word that can be translated as "wild"—*nujuaqtaq*—which usually applies to an individual character trait of, for example, a dog that is hard to approach, difficult to use as part of a team. But even this is qualified. Joseph Koonoo says, "We really don't know how to say 'wild' in Inuktitut. We say they are just animals; themselves." Several Inuit said that although animals were certainly not controlled by man, they controlled themselves, living according to the rules of their being.

Chief Luther Standing Bear said that for the Lakota people "there was no wilderness; since nature was not dangerous but hospitable." "Only to the white man was nature a 'wilderness' and . . . the land 'infested' with 'wild animals' and 'savage' people." (Anthropologist William Brown comments that the idea of "wilderness" in Alaska is "ethnocentric to the point of being insulting.")

John Amagoalik, several times president of the Inuit Tapiriit Kanatami of Canada, spoke with scorn of the journalists who would refer to the Arctic as a "wasteland where nobody lives." It angered him twice over, first because their land was beautiful and precious and second because they were not "nobodies."

Paul Amagoalik in Resolute, said, "To me, cities are wild: the concrete jungle." Elders going to Ottawa for medical appointments have found themselves totally lost. Alexina Kublu spoke of being "be-wildered" in London. She was speaking in English and her English was flawless. She chose the word carefully, for to her the word *bewildered* suggests the psychological experience of wilderness. "In China, too, I was bewildered. Because there was noise but no meaning; I couldn't understand anyone." She added, "To me, trees are wilderness, because you could get lost in a forest. Here, you wouldn't, because you would have the shoreline." She, as all Inuit do, spoke of going "out" onto the land; these are places of long horizontal vistas. Several Inuit, though, use the word *into* when they talk of entering the bewildering woods, the vertical forests.

One day in Igloolik, I was sharing *maktaaq* and soy sauce with an extended Inuit family. *Maktaaq* is the skin and fat of whale; a delicacy. (We ate off the floor. Store food is eaten off the table.) I asked one man whether he thought the land could ever be termed a wilderness. He frowned, slightly uncomfortable with the word, and turned it in his mind, fashioning it into a truth he could recognize. "The land controls itself," he said. "The government thinks it controls it, but it doesn't." "The land is self-willed? To you?" I asked. He nodded. Exactly.

A small child came in wearing a sealskin coat and trousers with a fur-lined hood. He got cuddles from everyone and the conversation changed to the film *Atanarjuat* (*The Fast Runner*), which was made here in this small community, in the Inuktitut language, by a local Inuk film director, with an Inuit cast. The film has won international plaudits, and Qallunaat love its storyline: a woman is in love with the hero, Atanarjuat, and he with her. But the woman has been promised in marriage to another man, cast as the villain of the piece. Atanarjuat wins her, in line with the Qallunaat romantic aesthetic. One of the men sharing the *maktaaq* was the actor who played the "villain," and Inuit men seemed overwhelmingly on his side, not that of the supposed "hero." It wasn't fair that he lost her; he was promised the bride, so he should have had her, they grumbled. "Instead that asshole Atanarjuat got her."

I met the film's director, Zacharias Kunuk, with John Arnatsiaq, a hunter, and we talked about the land. "If you know the land," said John, "it's not a wilderness. The only place I would call wilderness is a place I don't know."

"If I'm out on the land, it *is* wilderness," Zacharias countered. "I could *die*. If you can't radio to anyone and you get stuck and you run out of bullets, then you're in the wilderness."

"You'd be on the *land*," John said, correcting him.

Zacharias wouldn't be corrected. The land was wild, he said, because animals are always wild. "And they're wild because they're free."

"If I see animals," John replied, "I don't see them as wild; that's part of their life. To me 'wild' would be fierce and dangerous. To me, not even polar bears are wild."

Zacharias stuck to his guns. This is wild, he said, and by contrast, "If you go down South, you see what is *not* wild. All cities are not wild. All the hotels are the same." ("I've never seen a hotel," said John.) "You really see it down South, what's not wild. It's *dull*." Zacharias pulled a face and laughed.

At Resolute and Grise Fiord, though, people have experienced the land as wilderness. In the late 1950s, the Canadian government brought several Inuit families from Quebec up to these northern places, allegedly as a means for Canada to stake a territorial claim. The distance was at least as far as Oklahoma to Winnipeg or London to St. Petersburg.

The Inuit were promised good hunting grounds and were also told that if they did not like the new land, they could move back in two years. This proved to be a lie, as Larry Audlaluk told me: "I can still hear the silence of the RCMP when he's refusing my father to be allowed back." The government boats dropped six families at Resolute. It wasn't the intended destination, but, said Paul Amagoalik, "they were in a hurry because it was September, so we were just dumped on this bleak gravel island." An elder from Resolute recalled, "We had no idea where we were," and explained that you need to know the land, how to travel across it, for instance, in order to hunt for food. "Lots of children died in the first year because it was too cold and there wasn't enough food." She remembered her mother worried and weeping for months. The family's youngest child died. People are bitter about it still. Larry Audlaluk remarked, "The government attitude was this. 'They are Eskimos. This is the Arctic. They will survive.' It hurts because there's no feeling. Indifference." The respect that Inuit would accord to a spider was not accorded to them. They still recall the cold, and the shock of the bleak. "The nothingness. The *nothingness*," said Paul Amagoalik.

At Grise Fiord, Minnie Audlaluk, Larry's sister, remembered the journey, "the high mountains getting higher and higher, the weather colder and colder." She remembered her mother "mostly crying" for years. Her family was dropped at Grise Fiord with nothing, no way to make a shelter, no food and, worst of all, no knowledge. "I don't know how we survived," she said.

As we talked, five-year-old Olaf walked through the room. He looked Danish but he spoke only Inuktitut. He wore a Washington Huskies sweatshirt and switched on a loud computer game. He left tiny red footprints from his left sock; he'd walked through a seal's body while it was being cut up.

"There were no people here; we wanted to go home. We were homesick. And we were *used*. It was frightening," Minnie recalled. "And dark all the time." Talking to me, her eyes filled up with tears from the memory of it. "Let's stop talking about it," I suggested. "No, no, it's fine. I want to tell you." Every elder, men as well as women, who talked to me about that time, cried.

People were freezing cold and they were terrified of the winter when the sun disappeared. They had never experienced a season with no sun at all. In Grise Fiord in the winter, people didn't know how to hunt in the dark, and had to learn to hunt by the light of the full moon.

Resolute is known as Qausuittuq in Inuktitut. There are several translations for this but the most popular (and historically apt) is "place with no dawn." And reflecting the cold that caused the first people here such misery, Grise Fiord is Aujuittuq, "the place that never thaws out."

Larry Audlaluk described the feeling of "dramatic bewilderment" when they first arrived, and he added another dimension to the story. It wasn't only a matter that there were no people there, but also that there had been no people there in the past. His sense of "isolation, excommunication, hardship" was not just in the immediate vicinity, but a sense of isolation in time; they were following in nobody's footsteps. There was no map, no memory, no former knowledge. "For me, when we came here, we came to a wilderness."

ARKTIKÓS—THE COUNTRY OF THE GREAT BEAR

Late one afternoon on Ellesmere Island, when snow was falling and clouds mulled low over the land, I walked alone out of the village. I'd often walked alone along the shore or on a clear day walked out of the community, but never when it was snowy. Beware of the bears, I was told, as I left. They are more likely to attack people alone, and at freeze-up the bears are hungry.

They mainly come toward the sea east of the village, so I headed off on the west side. A raven's cry echoed from the cliffs, then silence, and the cold alone clanged metallic in my face. This cold has weight.

The Arctic lies beneath the constellation of the Great Bear and is named from the Greek Arktikós—the country of the great bear. The wildness in the eyes of a polar bear should shock us with recognition, not alienation, for we share its dreams of wide horizons, cublove and denning up for winter. We share a kinship. Like us, it is a hunter on land, in water, on ice. Like us a tool-user and traveler, builder and map-minder. Like us a top predator. Bear and human, both seal-hungry in autumn, prowl the shores, watching the seas freeze, watching out for the other too, for we are both each other's predator and prey, strangely balanced, mutually wary and aware.

The polar bear can change its mind, make decisions, have a plan, get bored, frustrated or curious. It can lie lazy on its back in the summer, belly to the sun, or toboggan down a snowy hillside just for fun. Its solitary nature is part of its charisma, and the polar bear was the most powerful of the "helping spirits" of an Inuit shaman. A bear will wait patiently at an *aglu* for a seal, waiting motionless for hours, then leaping *kerpow*, batting the seal with its paw, pulling it right out of the water. And if no seal emerges, it may finally get fed up, roar with frustration and shimmy off. Usually, though, says Mateussie, a hunter from Pond Inlet, polar bears are "very wise"; they know when to wait for a seal at an *aglu* and when not.

Polar bears can easily get too hot because their bodies are so well blubber-lined, over four inches thick in some parts of their bodies. They lose so little heat that they don't show up on infrared cameras and the only thing such a camera would see is the warm pawprints left behind on the snow. Polar bears can hide behind blocks of ice when they are hunting seals, say Inuit, and evidence has been found of a bear using a 45-pound block of ice to break into a seal's den. They are architects of ice, designing dens that will keep tiny cubs warm through the winter. The cubs are blind, deaf, unable to walk or smell, have no insulation and are small enough to be scooped up into their mother's left paw. (Inuit say polar bears are left-pawed.) The mother needs to be an expert in coziness to build and maintain a den sufficient to protect her cubs. So good is their design that it is thought that Inuit learned some of their techniques of igloo-building from the bears.

Polar bears are known to have swum sixty-two miles from a shore, and on land they can travel some two thousand miles in a year. In northwest Greenland, the bear is called *pisugtooq*, the great wanderer. "The bear is a great wanderer not solely because it travels far, but because it travels with curiosity, and tirelessly . . . successfully and intelligently," as Barry Lopez writes, in his extraordinary love song of ice, *Arctic Dreams*, which deeply influenced my own journey and informed so much of this chapter.

I wanted to walk beyond the human horizon, beyond the point where I could see anything made by people. I wanted to be alone in the snow. As I walked, ravens croaked above me, their blackness cross-hatched by driving snow. My compass was slowly spinning, drunk, lazily veering through 180 degrees and back. I was also stumbling like a drunk because all perspective was gone; there was almost nothing to guide the eye. Ahead of me, inland and northward, the sky was as white as the land, so the two merged into each other. Behind me the sky was darker over the water. That was my direction-finder, my only sign in a vast and abstract canvas. Sight confused, I realized I was walking uphill only when my foot bent up toward my shin, or knew I was walking downhill when I "missed a stair" and fell forward. So white was it that I could see all the tiny flickering things on my eyeball, like gazing at white paper. The whiteness of the snow changed, after a while, and my eyes began seeing blue and gold in it, like—of all things—a hazy, warm English June.

There were few sounds, the skitters of snow flung out from my footsteps and my body's internal noises. Polar bears come silently, and I was nervous of them. I wanted to see a polar bear, but not here, not alone. My curiosity, pushing me forward, met my fear pulling me back. I strained to listen into the silence, for any catch of sound, my nerves taut, open to a flicker of movement. No one so alert as the predator. Except the prey. In wild lands, people always seem to speak of the hunter, the backwoodsman, the survivalist, explorer and predator. Men talking. With few exceptions, men seem to want to be more predatory than a wilderness, to "conquer" it. Ask women, and perhaps they understand more quickly how they might be prey; how to hide, be silent, not to obtrude, to draw no attention to yourself, listening like a deer or a hare, fluttering with adrenaline and exhilarated by it too.

It occurred to me how you could die happy in the snow, how it could be a release from a strange struggle to stay alive, a letting go, drifting, like snow yourself, to sleep, with a lullaby in the key of ice. The pity of this land is what strikes me now, not its supposed pitilessness. It stills the unquiet and peculiar ambition to stay alive, it hushes the frantic, noisy pursuit of your own tomorrow.

When I was out of sight of the human horizon, completely alone in the whiteness, I wanted—as I only realized when I was there—to lie in the snow and feel this world fully as an animal, as the animal I am. I took my clothes off. I sank into only my body, a few bones clogged with blood, strings of muscle, scraggy flesh, a few rolls of belly fat and thin skin. No culture clings to a naked body, no nationality, no language. You can slip off your life here, shuck it away like clothes; this is all that I am. A small, thin, female animal, cubless, alone, naked and prey. The human animal, somewhere between a walrus and an arctic fox but far less well adapted than either, clever toolmaker perhaps, but simply not fat or furry enough to survive. No mate is here, no herd; I do not have antlers or fangs or claws. I cannot swim in this icy water. I will be lost within another mile in this land. I cannot smell to hunt, but my own smell will betray me to a bear.

This is not a "hostile" environment—there is no enmity here, no spite or unkindness. You might die here, yes, for the laws of nature are strict of necessity, but death is laconic, just a part of existence, not malicious. If a polar bear snagged my arm off and gashed my thigh, plunged a claw into my neck till I bled to death at its feet, it wouldn't have done that because it took pleasure in my pain, only because it needed my meat to survive and it had cubs to feed.

What is kind and what is wild do not contradict each other.

THE KIND WILD

Kindness is not a characteristic lauded by modernity. At best it is portrayed as a pastel quality, something meek and mild: tame. At worst, it is foolish. A naïve characteristic in this dog-eat-dog world. To me, it is the opposite. Kindness is both wild and wise.

In its etymology, what is kind is natural: the word stems from *ge-cynd* in Anglo-Saxon, a noun that means, among other things, "nature." The adjective *ge-cynde* translates as "natural, innate, genial," suggesting that we are born innately kind.

Our wild ancestors needed kindness as much as food, for a law of kindness toward their own kind was the only way they could all survive. Life was full of small children and young fires to be tended, big game that could be hunted only cooperatively, and in the entirely unsentimental tenderness of the tribe, people would know that to help someone else is to help yourself. (The prevailing idea of the nasty, brutal, wild "caveman" seems to me motivated by vanity in order to claim that "progress" has led to the Apex of Us.)

What is most natural is most wild and what is most natural—most *ge-cynde*—is most kind. Shakespeare's *Timon of Athens* illustrates the unkindness of the unnatural world of wealthy civilization as the disillusioned Timon comments, "Timon will to the woods, where he shall find / Th'unkindest beast more kinder than mankind." In so many hunting societies, animals are considered kin, and must be treated kindly.

Wild creatures hunt and kill, but they do not act unkindly to humiliate other creatures. What is wild needs to cage nothing, mock nothing. The kill is swift, the motive simple hunger. Cases of cruelty in the animal world are rare and may be nonexistent. The cruelest, most unkind creatures are those that are most unwild: the caged. If you want to make a wild animal learn cruelty, put it in a cage.

The wildest things and people are the most self-willed, self-governing, anarchic. Since will is wild, to damage someone else's will is both unkind and unwild. By contrast, to be truly an-archic is to follow a wild and radical kindness. Anarchy refuses to impose one's will on another. In this is kindness. By contrast, cruelty and the abuse of power always involve imposing one's will on another. My Will Be Done, the Christian god thunders at the self-willed world, which thrives—so kindly—without him.

For hundreds of years, Christian propaganda has pumped out the lie that what is wild is unkind. It's a lie of consequence, for imputing unkindness to the wild world justifies a murderous attitude toward it (dehumanizing your enemy to justify a genocide). European philosophy, which sought to place mankind "higher" than animals and "outside" nature, manufactured the ferocious hatred of wildness, the annihilation of whole species and the vicious destruction of wild lands.

To kindle means to "bring forth young"—the same Old English root as kind: *ge-cynde*. All the wild processes of life are generative, regenerative, genial, kind—the Arctic ice kindling polar bear cubs in a den, Earth like a wildcat kindling kittens in her hot womb. Kindness kindles life. To be kind is to be part of the boisterous, generous, creative life, while to be unkind is anti-natural. Kindness is nothing less than a force of nature—meek and mild it is not. It springs from the loins, it brings forth young, it is a lust within all wild things, a lust to kindle, the will to make kind, not only as strong as the will to make love but actually, in the word's root, identical with it. To be kind is to be on the side of life. Fucking, lovely, kind, wild life.

The Anglo-Saxon word *ge-cynd* has been suggested as a word root for "cunt" and, though this is debated, it seems a likely derivation, particularly since Anglo-Saxon also gives you the word *ge-cynd-lim*, "womb" or "vulva"—literally, a "birth-limb"—while *ge-cynd* also translates as "generation, nakedness" (and in Latin is translated as "genitals.") Wildness is generous and generative: both words that share the same Indo-European root with *kind*, *germinate* and *genital*.

My cunt is kind and cannot be otherwise. It is a well of self-willing, which responds to all that is kind and all that is wild. Both *kind* and *cunt* are said by some to be linked to *ken*, meaning "to know." Cunning in wild knowledge, canny in the country of kindness. Within us all, as the wild animals we are, is a hot kindled kindness, and in the wildness within, the wisdom.

WE ARE WILD

We need what is wild, we thrill to it. If a tiger stares right at you, wild lightning blasts your heart. If you hear wild horses across the plains, then you feel their exultant gallop explode within you. I was walking up a bracken hillside in Wales recently and a horse picked its way nervously toward me and then stopped. I turned away from it not to frighten it, and waited. I could not hear its approach on the soft and fertile earth but suddenly I felt its breath on my neck, where my sweat scent curled up from my collar and my hair smelled of wheat. It sniffed me for ages and did not leave. It filled me with rapture.

We crave these epiphanies because we are wild. "What then is the wild human? Is it savages? It is us! Mind in its untamed state as distinct from mind cultivated or domesticated for the purpose of yielding a return," writes Claude Lévi-Strauss. In Jack London's *The Call of the Wild* the hero, Buck the dog, hears wolves calling and "remembers" it from a distant past, the wild wolf from which the dog has been domesticated. The call is irresistible. "Life streamed through him in splendid flood, glad and rampant. . . . It was the call, the many-noted call, sounding more luringly and compellingly than ever before." And we read this with a shiver of recognition; we too hear the luring, compelling call and know it for the truth. We are wild, far wilder than Buck, because we have never been domesticated. Ecological philosopher Paul Shepard, in *Coming Home to the Pleistocene*, writes, "'Domestic' means a 'breed' or 'variety' created by the deliberate manipulation of a plant or animal populations' reproduction by humans with a conscious objective. We ourselves are genetically wild rather than domesticated. . . . We are also tame . . . conditioned to accept the human environment. . . . The tameness of captive wild animals is like our own tameness."

We are wild but tamed by television, controlled by Captain Clock, hemmed in by routine and obedience to petty convention. The more suffocatingly enclosed we are, the louder our wild genes scream in misery, aggression, anger and despair. In wildness is our self-willed, self-governing freedom, and such wild freedom blossoms within us, bubbles over with an anarchic *ivresse* of feeling. And we glint when the wild light shines.

We are drawn to derangement and drugs and—living in a way that denies our natural wildness—we choose self-induced wildnesses of mind when we can. And you still hear the call, the many-noted call, in the torrential emotions we are heir to, and you see it in the streak of sheer wild sanity in the eyes of the supposedly mad. "You've got to be careful of your bewilderness," a psychiatric patient confides—kindly—in a wild whisper.

THE POLAR PSYCHE

The polar regions perhaps draw people who understand the polar emotions, and for a few days during my journey—very bright days of late autumn—I spent time with Henry Morgentaler, survivor of Nazi concentration camps, doctor, and hero to a million Canadian women by going to prison in order to win for them abortion rights. Almost eighty when we met, he was in a kind of brilliant ecstasy—very bright days of late autumn in his own life. Together we imitated Topol, roaring out "To Life!" as we stomped across an ice field, and we jumped together in a river to smash plates of ice, bellowing in primal delight. He used joy as his rage against the dying of the light. "*La Liberté*," he bawled into the frosty sunshine. What's the Yiddish word for freedom? I called out. "*Freiheit*," he shouted back. Mateussie, the Inuk hunter who took us out in his boat across the bay, smiled in a combination of disbelief and fond indulgence as Henry stood up in the boat, belting out Italian opera, pausing only to shout out, "I'm in love with the universe!" It can take you that way, the Arctic. Barry Lopez glosses an Inuktitut word, *nuannaarpoq*, as "taking extravagant pleasure in being alive."

The polarities of the mind are analogous to the polarities of season. At the summer pole, all is hope and optimism, desire and possibility, and summer's radiant serenity is *quviannikumut*—"to feel deeply happy," comments Lopez. At the winter pole, all is despair, hopelessness and fury, the so-called Arctic hysteria known in Inuktitut as *pibloktok*. Yuri Rytkheu writes of the same experience for the Chukchi people: "In that state a man was liable not only to lay hands on himself, but to murder his whole family." The Inuktitut word *perlerorneq* means "to feel the weight of life," says anthropologist Jean Malaurie, quoted in Lopez. It means being "sick of life," and people maddened by it may run half-dressed into the ice, screaming and eating dogshit, stabbing at things and people. The shaman is the intermediary in these cases, because he has *qaumaneq*, which Lopez so beautifully describes as "the shaman light, the luminous fire, the inexplicable searchlight that enables him to see in the dark, literally and metaphorically."

This is a minded world, where the spiritual world is only just contained in the actual world, the symbolic world is splitting at the seams to get out, bursting the confines of the real.

In the winter, the seas freeze up like the subconscious storing its seared pain, putting it on ice. The first heaviness of winter is like mind, muddled and confused. Words seem like water stirred with icy silence, and the few faltering waves that still fall tell their small parts to the shore, but if ignored they peter out. Winter is deaf to its effect. The mind hardens into bearpaw ice, each plate a paragraph dewritten, a visible silence, the space where words should be, a blanking out. The face of the ocean moves less and expresses less, the mind freezes over. In the dark, lonely silence, all the lovely, lapping tongues of waves and all the uproarious shouts of the seas falling to the shores are gone, the summer of the psyche silenced. No wonder that when, on occasion, the sea ice cracks, it can do so with a scream, the pain echoing along a fault line of the mind, as memory repressed now explodes ferociously, buckles ships and crushes icebreakers and when it comes howling back its rage is frightening and shocking. The hurt mind, iced to protect itself and silent for years, can turn savage in its anger, shattering on its release.

Inuit traditionally insisted on the importance of people speaking out their hurts before they were iced in, before their wounds became frozen and dangerous. They knew how the repressed mind ices itself into psychic violence, and there was a strong confessional tradition. People would lose their minds if they didn't express themselves, said the elders. If they didn't, or couldn't, then it was a job for the shaman.

Only shamanic fire was bright enough to reach people lost in this kind of darkness, for the shamans knew how to negotiate the mind's wildernesses, through shamanic songlines. But the white invaders hated them. The shamans of Siberia were imprisoned by Communists, and under Stalin shamans were often shot or thrown out of helicopters, taunted with the remark that if they thought they could fly they should prove it now. The shamans of the Arctic were hounded out by the missionaries, who called their work satanic.

When the rinky-dink church arrived, neat and tidy, chalet-style, with its clean fingernails and a mindset to suit, the wild extremes of psyche that the shamans understood were driven out into the blizzards, where the missionaries thought they belonged. It was not a clash of right and wrong, as the priests pretended, but a clash of mental geography. The church's mindset was of the temperate zone, the narrow emotional register where there is no fury, only tepid annoyance, no semen blast and bloodlust, only a careful, best-bedlinen position where petty benignity is all you need from a plastic cradle to a well-tended grave. But with the shamans gone, the specialists in the psyche are gone, and now when people go mad, as they do with "Arctic hysteria," there is no one to bring them back, no burning brilliant flame of one mind to guide another.

"FEAR NOT,—THERE IS A BRITON AT THY DOOR!"

Inuit place names suggest a snug and intimate acquaintance, so intimate in fact that even some boulders have names. Their names include the hunt-helpful names—for example, Kiggavialaaq ("peregrine falcon chicks nesting") and the broad description for Ellesmere Island as Oomingmannuna (alternatively spelled Umingmak Nuna), which translates as "Muskox Land." Some names are lovely in their simplicity: Igloolik means "has igloos." (One Koyukon place name is equally beautiful in its specificity: there is the "hill shaped like the nape of a snowshoe hare's neck," as Richard Nelson reports.) Some Inuit names include a story: there is the "Place Where Qallunaat Are Buried," and Inukturvik, "The Place Where People Were Eaten," named out of respect for an Igloolik woman, Ataguttaaluk, who had to eat her husband and some of her children to survive. The school in Igloolik is named in her honor.

Some Inuit names are quietly droll: near Igloolik is a lake called Tasilugjuak, which translates as "Big Lake Having Little Purpose." Some are robust: one island, with very little vegetation or moss, is called Iquutiksaqtaittuq, meaning "there is nothing to wipe one's arse with." One camp was called Uttuusivik, "Vagina Place." There are several stories of how this place got its name, including one where the men of the community were carried out to sea on moving ice; another where the men were killed; another where the men had gone inland to hunt caribou. Whatever the cause, the result was that the community was long occupied only by women.

The British have named places at the poles with the imperialist voice: mountains in northern Ellesmere Island are called the British Empire Range, and there is a Buckingham Island and Admiralty Island. Others have been named with dusty-hymnal Anglican intonation (the Sons of the Clergy Islands) or with the academic tones (the Royal Geographical Society Islands) or with the note of dreary bureaucracy (Committee Bay). All demonstrate ownership, but none as clearly as the bay named by Captain Cook Possession Bay, at the island of South Georgia: "I landed in three different places, displayed our colors, and took possession of the country in his Majesty's name, under a discharge of small arms." In Inuit society, land could not be owned.

Sometimes the names given by European explorers speak in the language of emotional heraldry, stark statements of the mind's experience: Invincible Point in the Parry Islands and Resolute Bay, and the places where courage failed: Repulse, Terror Point and Deception Fjord. (There is a little poetry in the naming: Scott called one place in the Antarctic Inexpressible Island, a whispering paradox. And also in the Antarctic there is Pourquois Pas Island. And why not?)

The U.S. government told explorer Robert Peary in 1903, "The attainment of the Pole should be your main object. Nothing short will suffice. The discovery of the poles is all that remains to complete the map of the world. That map should be completed in our generation and by our countrymen." The *Times* wrote of Scott's final journey, "The real value of the expedition was spiritual, and therefore in the truest sense national . . . proof that we are capable of maintaining an Empire." Herbert Ponting writes of the news that the whole of Scott's party had died, "This shocking news struck deep into the heart of every civilised nation . . . the whole Empire mourned, whilst priding itself that these undaunted adventurers, who in death had found immortal fame, were British."

This sanctimonious, preening nationalism would probably have amused and irritated the Inuit at the time, as would the Qallunaat preoccupation with northness, that strange obsession of the whites, searching for years for the so-called Northwest Passage. (Which only has meaning if the speaker's mind locates itself south and east. Somewhere like Greenwich, in fact.)

With a few exceptions, the explorers ignored Inuit place names, because it would have given the lie to all their myths: the myth of the land's enmity, the myth of the blank and unknown land, the myth of their solo heroics, the myth of the land's emptiness, the myth of the ice as enemy.

"The land itself was a desolation, lifeless, without movement. . . . There was a hint in it of . . . a laughter cold as the frost and partaking of the grimness of infallibility. It was the masterful and incommunicable wisdom of eternity laughing at the futility of life and the effort of life. It was the Wild, the savage, frozen-hearted Northland Wild," writes Jack London in *White Fang*. It is a lie, of course, however superb the language. For ice is friend to humanity, as the Inuit know, not an enemy.

The European explorers frequently portrayed it as hostile, often with the unlit expression of a military mindset. Grace Scott described one motive of her brother's as "the hoped-for conquest of raging elements." Shackleton wrote in his journal in military terminology, "The strongest forces of Nature are arrayed against us." Shackleton called his journey to the so-called wilderness of Antarctica "the White Warfare of the South." You can't translate this idea into Saami. The Saami language has no word for wilderness and no word for war. Peary wrote of the Arctic as "the frozen wilderness. . . . Nothing but the hostile ice, and far more hostile icy water," and described "our conquest of the unknown spaces," and in crude militarism the Canadians named one polar island "Air Force Island."

The image persists. A puerile television program about polar bears was broadcast recently that cast the entire Arctic in military metaphor: the program was entitled "Wild Battlefields." It was a jangling piece of anthropomorphism, projecting onto the polar bear the ugly militarism of modernity. It used computer-generated images of hexagonals over the land to illustrate the polar bear's "command-and-control" center, the bear gazing over its battlefield domain. At one point, again supposedly through the point of view of the bear, the screen showed the crosshairs of a rifle's sights over a "target" seal. The voice-over spoke of "victory," "massacre," "organizing an assault," "enemy territory" and "window of attack."

For the most part when European explorers went to the poles, they took their toys with them, the trinkets of their culture to shore up their minds against the wild strangeness of the land. With their silver dinner plates, a copy of *The Vicar of Wakefield*, a cigar case and kid gloves, they did amateur theatricals—Parry's Arctic expedition performed Sheridan's *The Rivals* (appropriate for the national rivalry of the polar expeditions)—and many expeditions wrote "local" newspapers: Parry's *Winter Chronicle* and *North Georgia Gazette*, Nansen's *Framsjaa*, Scott's *South Polar Times* and *The Blizzard*. They took a mental drawing room with them, with bourgeois parlor games and a petty class system. Contemporary writing about Antarctica can leave a similar impression, of rule-bound, claustrophobic research stations where characters jostle one another at close quarters, chummily telling private jokes amid a round of parties, superconnected via e-mail, and sending one another recipes for chocolate cake.

The European explorers made much of the supposed blankness of the Arctic—Grace Scott writes of her brother that he felt keenly "the call of the vast empty spaces, silence; the beauty of untrodden snow." They wanted to pretend these lands were silent in order that their voices could be heard the louder, and they wanted to create these blank white spaces in the public mind in order that they could write in bigger, inkier letters "I was here, I and I alone." "There is nothing worth living for but to have one's name inscribed on the Arctic chart," wrote Tennyson. (One explorer, whom I will take a mischievous delight in not naming, said of the North Pole: it was "MINE . . . to be credited to me, and associated with my name, generations after I had ceased to be.")

The Inuit are having none of it and can speak with utter scorn of the European explorers. The hunter Jaypeetee Akeagok commented disdainfully, "They were not the first explorers. We were." Joseph Koonoo at Pond Inlet remarked of the Europeans in these lands, "The firstcomers were saved by the Inuit. They got stuck in the ice and the Inuit would go and start helping them. White people got so cold they couldn't move even to pee, so the Inuit helped them undo their trousers. White people made themselves proud and made it sound as if they went alone, but they had so much help. I wish it were written in books that white people only survived with the help of the Inuit." Some explorers did admit that the Inuit had saved their lives: explorers Ross and Parry were rescued by the Inuit who warmed them, fed them and treated them "with the same tenderness they would have bestowed on their own infants."

Twenty years after Parry's visit to Igloolik, he was still remembered kindly there because he had killed a bowhead whale and shared the food with the Inuit, but munificence could become a fatuous boast. Chandos Hoskyns Abrahall wrote of supplies given to an Inuit community from an expedition of Parry's,

> *Poor child of chance! Hath Winter shrunk thy store?*
> *Fear not,—there is a Briton at thy door!*

Parry's journal of his 1821–23 expedition has a wealth of detail about the Inuit, but on his return he was rapped over the knuckles for spending too much time with Inuit and too little searching for the Northwest Passage.

For the most part, the explorers tried to blank out the Inuit altogether. In 1909, Ooqueah was thought to have reached the North Pole, with Ootah and Egingwah and Seegloo and a manservant—"the Negro Henson" in the words of Robert Peary, who accompanied them. You wouldn't know this from the usual sources of public memory.

Inuit had trouble comprehending the Qallunaat desire to reach the North Pole, because as an endeavor they thought it was a bit of a silly exercise. All that bother, all that effort, all that pointless dying—they were too practical to understand how an abstraction could justify such pain. Some of them thought there must be a pragmatic reason, and the Inuit of Annotoak in the twentieth century translated the North Pole as the "Great Nail," and thought that anyone who accompanied the Qallunaat explorers and found the Great Nail would always have iron to make spearheads and axes.

Certainly the polar explorers suffered: cutting butter with a chisel and finding their tongues frozen to their beards, while ships like Shackleton's *Endurance*, trapped in ice, were crushed, shivering their timbers quite literally. European explorers found themselves eating their boots, sucking putrid bone marrow from carcasses of caribou and eating warble-fly grubs. They died in droves, largely because they were blinded by their own sense of superiority. Inuit knew how to dress to stay warm but many explorers turned up their noses at their "savage" ways and wore wool, which turned their sweat to ice. (There were exceptions, such as the Scottish John Rae, who adopted Inuit ways of travel and survival.)

Inuit used to be referred to as "Eskimo," a term that has a hazy etymology. It is thought to be a Cree word, and different meanings have been given to it, including "stranger" and "eaters of raw meat," a term assumed to be derogatory but may well not be. Inuit got necessary vitamins in their diet precisely because meat was eaten uncooked. (Almost no fruit, and no vegetables, will grow up here.) To Europeans, raw food was culturally inferior to cooked food and they often died of scurvy from lack of vitamin C.

In 1818, on John Ross's expedition, the Europeans met Inuit of North Greenland who asked the whites whether they were from the sun or the moon. Before the Europeans came, the Inuit of North Greenland had genuinely believed themselves to be the only inhabitants of the world. Many Europeans, by contrast, dishonestly erased the presence of the Inuit, writing of the unknown, unmapped, untrodden, empty, uninhabited wilderness lands, because it suited their narrative to pretend they were alone.

Many explorers treated Inuit shamefully. Peary not only stole the meteorites that had been used by the Inuit as an important source of iron for their tools, he "stole" some Inuit. Minik and other Inuit were brought to the U.S.A. as a curiosity by Peary. The other Inuit died not long after arriving. Minik survived, and asked to be allowed home. Peary refused to allow Minik to return. On other expeditions, the Europeans kidnapped and killed as they went. On the 1913 expedition of Donald MacMillan, a British man, Fitzhugh Green, was being guided by an Inuk man, Piugaattoq. Green had wet feet, which was a potentially fatal circumstance. Piugaattoq insisted they turn back, and set a fast pace so that Green would have to move quickly to keep up. As Piugaattoq knew, that was the only way for Green to stave off frostbite. The Briton, however, thought his guide was abandoning him, threatened Piugaattoq with his gun and told him to walk behind him, where he belonged. Piugaattoq at that point grew frightened of this rifle-wielding maniac and tried to walk away from him. Green shot him dead.

Yuri Rytkheu comments that in many Chukchi legends, the words for "white man" and "enemy" are synonymous. The newcomers were identified "as the physical embodiment of the evil spirits, as the personification of avarice and contempt for the rules of human conduct." Yi-Fu Tuan writes that "Greenland Eskimos thought that Europeans were being sent to Greenland to learn virtue and good manners from them."

The American Elisha Kent Kane, who led the 1853–55 expedition in search of John Franklin, wrote of his first impression of "the Esquimaux" that they were "wild and uncouth, but evidently human beings." His first act was to kidnap a man and hold him "hostage." He then refers to "the Esquimaux" as "very rude and difficult to manage." He imprisons more ("I had given orders to detain them"). The Inuit, as was their custom and indeed law, shared out some of the ship's tools. Kane correctly surmises that "they had some law of general appropriation" but decides that in revenge he will imprison another man, who escapes. He gives an order that in the case of attack, his men should shoot to kill. In further revenge for the "thefts" he seizes two Inuit women, orders them to be stripped and tied up, then forced to walk to the ship.

"The thirty miles was a hard walk for them." He writes of their terror with a sardonic, self-amused sadism:

> They were prisoners in the hold, with a dreadful white man for keeper, who never addressed to them a word that had not all the terrors of an unintelligible reproof, and whose scowl, I flatter myself, exhibited a well-arranged variety of menacing and demoniacal expressions. . . . For five long days the women had to sigh and sing and cry in solitary converse.

And he refers to *them* as "savages."

But the history of Arctic exploration is written by the victors. Written you note, not spoken. The Inuit have their oral history, but it is considered third-rate compared with the written history of the Qallunaat. Even in Nunavut. Even today. Elders from all over Nunavut held a conference in 1998, which called on the government to implement an immediate and systematic documentation of Inuit traditional knowledge, in every community in the territory, based on a project in Igloolik. The government failed to respond.

The Igloolik project is an extraordinary program dedicated to recording interviews with the few remaining elders; their knowledge is precious and disappearing with every elder's death. I am indebted to this, the Igloolik Research Centre, and to John MacDonald who is the spirit behind it. Most of my quotations from Igloolik elders are from their work—work that is painstaking, difficult and urgent. It has insufficient funds. Rather than spend money on this priceless culture, though, the Nunavut government, I was told, was considering spending many thousands of dollars on some old copy of some white explorer's book, which they could quite easily photocopy for a fiver.

SOLOISTS IN THE ICE

Herbert Ponting, famous for his photographs of the South Pole, refers to "this godforsaken wilderness of ice and lava . . . these ghastly, uninhabited solitudes" and "this desolate realm." An early explorer to the Arctic wrote, "*Praeter solitudinem nihil video*"—I see nothing except solitude.

European individualism has colored its attitude to wilderness, making wild lands the right place for the solitary hero, on a solo mission, the myths of all Lone Rangers. Polar explorers were very often men from the army or navy, swaggering with the boast of a solo mission.

The European idea of individualism was compounded by the idea of the void, and in the Arctic the Europeans looked at the land with the eye of the I alone, and frightened themselves with *horror vacui*—the fear of emptiness. Julius Payer, painter and mapmaker, who went on the Austro-Hungarian North Pole expedition of 1873, wrote, "The road to the Arctic interior is a hard one. . . . Only the ideal of his goal can support him; otherwise he will wander, a victim of mental ambiguity, through an internal and external void." For the European mind had the zero, the void and the vacuum as a concept and applied it to land in a way that would be politically expedient, declaring *terra nullius* in Australia, stealing the "wildernesses" of Africa and usurping land rights all across the Americas.

It is hard to find any indigenous people who have the idea of a zero, let alone would apply it to nature. Luther Standing Bear recalls, "There was no such thing as emptiness in the world. Even in the sky there were no vacant places. Everywhere there was life, visible and invisible." Richard Nelson, describing the worldview of the Koyukon, writes, "There is no emptiness in the forest, no unwatched solitude, no wilderness where a person moves outside moral judgment and law."

There have been others, though, the true soloists, who have sought to add their pennyworth of anarch to the wild world, whose individualism was not the fake pretense of having boldly strode alone over the icy wastes, but an authentic idiosyncrasy. Those who have gone to the wilds not to conquer, map or subdue but to find the only place worthy of their vivacity: wilderness, where the ebullient punk plays with lightning and the unimprisonable Puck and the shaman of the ecstatic mind casually shower the vivid world with diamond words, artists of vodka and teeth and tempest, self-willed, wild-minded, willingly lonely.

Henry Thoreau describes the way he had tried to live and think: "I did not wish to take a cabin passage, but rather to go before the mast and on the deck of the world, for there I could best see the moonlight amid the mountains. I do not wish to go below now." Gary Snyder writes, "One departs the home to embark on a quest into an archetypal wilderness . . . on the mythical plane this is the source of the worldwide hero narratives. . . . It can mean seeing . . . the people of your old place as for the first time. It can mean every word heard is heard to its deepest echo. It can mean mysterious tears of gratitude." Jean Genet in *The Thief's Journal* of 1949: "Solitude is not given to me; I earn it . . . I want to define myself in it, delimit my contours." He wrung his selfhood from a social wilderness. Others have drawn their characters from the land, like Fridtjof Nansen, that estimable nutter who crossed Greenland, sailing across parts of the ice using the groundsheet of his tent for a sail, and who wrote, "In the wilderness, in the loneliness of the forest . . . this is where personalities are formed."

It is this aspect of individuality in wild places that is understood by many indigenous people. In the Siberian and Inuit traditions, young potential shamans would often go to the wilderness, either by choice or because they felt commanded to do so by spirit voices. Rasmussen relates a shaman, Igjugarjuk, telling him, "True wisdom is only to be found far away from people, out in the great solitude, and it is not found in play but only through suffering. Solitude and suffering open the human mind, and therefore a shaman must seek his wisdom there." Snyder writes in *Earth House Hold* that "in many American Indian cultures it is obligatory for every member to get out of the society, out of the human nexus and 'out of his head' at least once in his life. He returns from his solitary vision quest with a secret name, a protective animal spirit, a secret song. It is his 'power.' The culture honors the man who has visited other realms."

VAGABOND FUNGI

The age of European exploration was also an age of classification by which wildness was conceptually tamed. Unruly, unrowly nature was put into rows and lines, and wildness was neatened into degrees, indexes and catalogues. It was an age of measurement, fencing what was wild with barometers, microscopes, astrolabes, callipers and pedometers. It was an age obsessed not only with classes and orders within nature but also with social hierarchy and class classification.

Carl Linnaeus, Swedish botanist, conflated these two ideas. Using the widely held Aristotelian belief in a "Scala Naturae," Linnaeus described "kingdoms" of plants and animals and divided the plant kingdom into different "tribes and nations." He called grasses "plebeian," for "the more they are taxed and trod upon the more they multiply." Lilies were "patrician" and were associated with "the splendor of courts." Fungi were "vagabonds." Ants were "monarchical" but storks were "republican," while sparrows were the "Irishmen of birds" because of their "noise, squabbles and ubiquity." We are perhaps so used to Linnaean classification that we hardly see the falsifications that his metaphors produce. For what they suggest is that it is appropriate to impose eighteenth-century European social structures onto the natural world and that it is then correct to argue—by means of those metaphors—that some creatures and plants have more value than others. That some wild animals are "pests" and some wild plants are "weeds," an allegory designed to portray wild nature as morally inferior.

Not everyone sees things that way. Inuktitut has no word for either "pest" or "vermin" or "weed." And, adds Hugh Brody, there are no words for these in Athapaskan, Algonquian or San. The Koyukon believe that no animal should be considered inferior or insignificant. Luther Standing Bear said, "Plants which the Indian found beneficial were also 'pests.' There is no word in the Lakota vocabulary with the English meaning of this word."

In the Western tradition, for thousands of years, nature was made to seem hierarchical and hierarchy was made to seem natural. And this naturalness of hierarchy was used to justify genocide, by arguing that civilized "cultivated" cultures were like the superior—cultivated—plants, while "wild" and "savage" people were like pests and weeds. Luther Standing Bear writes, "The white man considered natural animal life just as he did the natural man life upon this continent as 'pests.'" Indeed they did, openly so: Father Biard, a French missionary in Canada, described the First Nations people there as "like a great field of stunted and ill-begotten wild plants."

J. C. Loudon, writing in the early nineteenth century, states that one should "compare plants with men, consider aboriginal species as mere savages, and botanical species . . . as civilized beings." De Quincey writes of Southern Asia, "The part of the earth most swarming with human life. . . . Man is a weed in those regions." Richard Walther Darré, one of the Nazis' chief race theorists, spoke of Jews as "weeds."

VIRGIN

Captain James Cook "made three penetrations of the Antarctic" writes Peter Kemp, editor of the *Oxford Companion to Ships and the Sea*. Right opposite this note is Herbert Ponting's extraordinary photograph of an oval cavern in an iceberg so the viewer looks out through the hollow which is whorled within in folds of ice, dark inside, glistening with a trickle of meltwater at the base and fringed with hairy icicle fronds. And, through the oval hole, you see the explorers' ship, its dark and phallic lines ready to penetrate the virgin-white and female ice.

Admiral Byrd, who, avian by name, was appropriately the first person to fly over the South Pole, wrote, "At the bottom of this planet is an enchanted continent . . . pale like a sleeping princess. Sinister and beautiful, she lies in frozen slumber." The poles have not only been seen as ice princess but as the Snow Queen of the folktale. She is exquisitely beautiful but has a heart of ice and glass; she is alluring but frozen, numbing and dangerous. Though the polar ice was interpreted as female, real women were—and sometimes are—not welcome. Peter Maxwell Davies writes of the Antarctic research stations, "There are women here, but you feel they must somehow fit themselves in: if they become pregnant, they are sent home."

Philosopher of the sublime Edmund Burke argued that what is beautiful is tame, pleasing, neat and sweet. The sublime, by contrast, contains greatness and awe. It can be terrifying and noble, the category for wildness and wilderness. It was a gendered categorization for what was beautiful was female in character, and while women could appreciate and represent beauty, only men could recognize and be identified with the sublime.

It wasn't only that ice was sexed as female but also that the explorers penetrating her were made more "manly" by the endeavor. George S. Evans in 1904 wrote, "The wilderness will take hold of you. It will give you good red blood. It will make you a man." In 1899, Peary wrote that he was pursuing the

North Pole because "it has value as a test of intelligence, persistence, endurance, determined will, and, perhaps, courage, qualities characteristic of the highest type of manhood."

To be *really* manly, one must penetrate a virgin, I suppose, and being the first to the poles was a huge part of the allure. Scott's January 1912 diary describes how bitterly disappointed he was by not being the first: "Great God! This is an awful place and terrible enough for us to have laboured to it without the reward of priority." Ranulph Fiennes writes of expeditions to the North Pole in the 1980s, "It was not enough merely to reach the North Pole without support or air contact. We must be the first to do so."

To the white gaze, with its tendency to see land as moral allegory, there was something very alluring about this world of white, which suggested purity. Alaska, said John Muir in 1879, was "pure"—the white of virginal sheets and virgin bridal gowns. The explorers could project onto the white screen of these white lands their fantasies of woman, pure, virginal, vacant and waiting.

CAGING WILD TIME

ooty Pijamini, a sculptor, spoke furiously to me about the effects that the Qallunaat have had, italicizing his words with gestures. "This was not a *wilderness* but my *home*, which you guys ran over and invaded. White people are like a *disease.* You came and took as much as you could: whales and muskox, and then after you'd hunted everything out then you tell us *we're* not allowed to hunt more. White people came as a great holy man and *took my land.*"

The great holy man took something else away too: Inuit time. European missionaries, in the Arctic as all over the world, wanted to control the minds of the people whose cultures they conquered, and one of their ways of doing this was to order and command people's freedom of time, that most metaphysical of all the freedoms. They brought the clock, which tamed time, caged it, enclosing its natural wildness. The missionaries insisted on punctual church services and regular prayers, they banned hunters from hunting on the Sabbath, and they brought the calendar of the Christian year.

The traditional Inuit calendar had moon-months, named for events in the land's cycles. In his book *The Arctic Sky*, John MacDonald details the Igloolik calendar, which begins the year with "Sun is possible" (mid-January) and moves through the rest of the thirteen moon-months: "Sun gets higher"; "Premature birth of seal pups"; "Birth of seal pups"; "Birth of bearded seal pups"; "Caribou calves"; "Eggs"; "Caribou sheds hair"; "Caribou hair thickens"; "Velvet peels from caribou antlers"—more poetic than October, eh?—then "Makings of winter"; "The hearing month" and "The great darkness." (By "The hearing month," at about the end of November, the seas are frozen and all ice strong enough for people to travel by dog team to scattered camps, where people would visit and hear news of their neighbors.) Through this transparent calendar, one can "see" the landscape. The white calendar, though, hangs like thick blank white paper, preventing you from seeing the land.

Inuit have no word equivalent to *time*. John MacDonald recalls asking a young Inuk man for his definition of time. "Time?" he wondered. "Time is nine to five." Hunters are sensitive to—and deeply dislike—the commandingness of the Qallunaat hour. People out hunting "did not have a timepiece that dictated to them," said an elder. Theo Ikummaq refers to "these days, when time governs." Joseph Koonoo says that "in the community, time—watch time—is overriding," and he strikes his watch with his finger to emphasize his frustration. "In the settlement, watch time is the only time you've got, but out on the land, come spring and summer, there's always light and time and freedom." Out on the land, time is wild and one feels one's own freedom through it.

STIR-CRAZY

The whites brought the clock and the Bible, alcohol and drugs and another thing that has been perniciously dangerous. School.

Together with the missionaries, the teachers insisted that children stop living in the wild time of the land, the times of hunting, the times of free hibernatory sleep in winter, and enclosed them with white time, tamed by the clock. The teachers tried to make children punctual to school hours. (It still happens. I met a head teacher who told me he was ordering caseloads of alarm clocks up from the South to get the kids out of bed in the winter.)

Schooling caused a crisis of knowledge, because there was no knowledge of the land taught in schools. "We were taught Columbus, Cabot, maths and spelling," says Theo Ikummaq. "What is taught in school is just . . . 'The Three Pigs' translated into Inuktitut. Little Red Riding Hood. Traditional knowledge is only acquired out of school." (This is changing, but only just. Inuit knowledge is just beginning to be formally taught in schools.) *School* is not a synonym for *education*. You might, if you're lucky, get a bit of an education at school, but for Inuit children, the land was their education.

White lawmakers forced Inuit children to go to school, insisting that their parents settle in communities and, in some instances, shooting people's dog teams so they couldn't leave. In two generations people lost the knowledge of the land, for the young were not learning how to hunt, or how to survive on the land. They grew up unable to negotiate the land outside the communities. Maurice Arnatsiaq at the Igloolik Research Centre commented that "young people today struggle between white people's ways and Inuktitut ways. It's mixed up." And, he suggests, young people are lost in both grammars, both in Inuit learning and white learning. "They don't know enough of either." He describes a time in his youth, when he was about fifteen, traveling alone with a dog team for two weeks from Igloolik to Crown Prince Frederick Island, then Committee Bay and Melville Peninsula. "Maybe only three or four young people would be able to do that journey now. They don't know about the land."

One result is that people are dependent on store-bought food, and if they have no cash they go hungry. One woman described how her husband, in his thirties, had been unemployed and the family had needed food, so he had gone hunting with his son, though he was inexperienced and barely knew how to cope on the land. They never returned. They were found later on a beach, their boat having capsized. They were frozen to death and the son's face was eaten by ravens.

That is a stark physical example of the effects of not knowing the land. But the psychological effects are everywhere. Without knowledge, you cannot be out on the land. Without the language for precise aspects of ice, the winter sea can be fatal. Without knowledge of where you are, the land is a terrifying and dangerous wasteland. Without survival skills, you can barely set foot beyond the perimeter of the community. Young people are effectively imprisoned by this ignorance into the small and claustrophobic communities where they go stir-crazy. And there, all the symptoms of urban wilderness lurch out at you.

The communities seem bleak as industrial estates, as maddening as prisons. Every community has a store with clanging metal doors at the entrance, noisy metal stairs, graffiti (FUCK YOU AMANDA) and then barren lobbies with a cold metal pay phone, nothing to blow away in the wind, nothing to be stolen, like inner-city police stations or welfare offices. Inside one overheated supermarket entrance is a mean sign that says NO LOITERING OR WILL CALL RCMP. (Just in case a few bored, shivering teenagers might hang out there for a smoke.) The communities seem overheated, overcrowded, places of junkyard dreams, with rusting trucks dumped everywhere and a sense of unfreedom that makes people go ballistic.

I was told of a Southerner who went and shot at a ten-ton dynamite container two kilometers from town. He lost both his legs and the school shifted four inches on its foundations. There's a kind of *South Park* cartoonish quality to this and other acts of violence that I heard about: the crackpot, hotheaded idiocy in which people are so careless of themselves that they scrawl out an afternoon taking pops at dynamite as carelessly as they'd piss against a wall. In a hotel at the Northwest Passage there are kids hanging around playing pool, their eyes are red-balled, yellow-balled, glazed with dope smoked for misery's sake. "It's not a sane place," says one woman, whose brother committed suicide.

I stayed with a woman who was the mother of eleven children. Four had died violently. One son had died of hypothermia because he was drunk and collapsed outdoors. Another son was murdered in Iqaluit. A daughter had died in a plane crash. Another daughter had been beaten to death, by her own brother.

I saw six-year-olds, locked into themselves, thirteen-year-olds careless with their one-dollar lives, their eyes crazily bright, swimming with alcohol and dope and sniffing gas. For a second you glimpse in their minds the burning hieroglyphs of the world as they see it, their laughter has a strange and senseless calligraphy, raucous ink swipes of no meaning. The Innu people have similar problems. At Davis Inlet and Sheshatshiu, Innu communities in Labrador, the majority of the children are chronic gas sniffers. They do it all night, out in the woods, in subzero temperatures. Some pass out, some have become brain-damaged, several have accidentally set themselves on fire, and one eleven-year-old died recently, burnt to death. The RCMP comment that sniffing gas is not illegal, so they are not allowed to take the bags away from the children. All the police can do is put them out when they set themselves on fire, said an officer.

The land is becoming too hot.

Outside Iqaluit, I went for a walk one afternoon up a hill in bluff winds and I wandered for an hour or so, up to an inukshuk with a metal bell sounding in the wind. (On the bell was inscribed, "May this bell ring you safe passage.") Turning, I saw another single figure walking over the hillside and we let our paths cross, me and a twenty-nine-year-old Inuk man from northern Baffin Island who was, as it turned out, one of Nunavut's most notorious drug dealers. We sat together for a while and he told me his story. He'd tried to be a sculptor but he couldn't carve anything. He couldn't hunt—school had ensured that he didn't know the first thing about it. When he was eleven, he "felt low," he said, and his face suddenly belied the casualness of this term—his expression was wrenched just saying the words. So he turned to pot. He was thrown out of school for smoking it, so he turned to dealing and he had, he said boastfully, recently been stopped by the police and searched and found with forty thousand dollars' worth of drugs. He'd done everything. "Paris hash is good," he said, and coke and ecstasy and "herolin"—his English comes a little awkwardly. "It's a medicine when you're down and it's good for the body and 85 percent of Nunavut takes drugs." This is a huge overstatement, but the percentage is still about four times the national rate in Canada.

His words were angry and defiant. "Everyone knows me. Everyone saw me on TV, but I say fuck them. It's my life. I don't listen to anyone. Fuck them. Fuck everyone. It's my life. I'm looking ahead and I don't care if I go to hell." A wilderness wind seemed to howl in his mind in blizzards of defensive nihilism. He said he was "pleased about September eleventh," and that he watched the United States and Afghanistan at war with the same indifference with which he'd watch a football match. "And anyway Afghanistan hash is good." His words were all a kind of brutal boast, but his eyes were so lonely and so hurt that I felt intensely sad. Why was I being nice to him, he asked, did I want some dope? No, I said, I just feel really sorry for you, to be honest, and his face crumpled for a second like that of an eleven-year-old trying not to cry.

I met a musician, Jimmy Ekho, in a museum in Iqaluit. "Are you stuck here?" he asked. I laughed. No, I'm here by choice. He laughed in turn. "Oh, sorry, they're all stuck, most white people who come here." We talked a lot. "Too many bad things came when the whites came in: alcohol and drugs and social problems. It's a wilderness we're in now, a clash of two cultures." He showed me some of the museum's sculptures. One had a heavy impact on me; it was a man wrestling with a spirit and it looked to me like Jacob wrestling with the angel but without the intervention of dawn. This is a morningless Arctic winter of the mind, filled with anger, despair and loneliness, the solitary agony that precedes suicide. "It would be better if we went extinct," said Jimmy, in a moment of savage cultural despair.

Physically immobilized, the younger people are often emotionally disturbed with a restless, vertiginous violence. Many of them are maddened by the widespread abuse and rape that Inuit children have suffered at the hands of priests and missionaries teaching in the residential schools. The figures are overwhelming. A whole generation, I was told, has been left traumatized, psychologically damaged and in many cases suicidal.

Young people's inability to spend time out on the land, their lack of survival skills or hunting prowess, the ancient depression of winter, a boredom that could drive you to tears in days are compounded by unemployment, poverty, low cultural self-esteem and, more than anything, sexual abuse. There is nowhere for them to go except South or suicide. The former is too expensive to achieve. The latter is too cheap to ignore.

Nunavut has a suicide rate some five times the national average. Many people I spoke to told me of a son, a brother, sister or cousin. They happen, says Michel Kupaaq Piugaattuk, because people are in limbo between cultures. An eighteen-year-old commits suicide on Broughton Island. "My son suicided three years ago." My notebooks are littered with these asides, simple statements, rarely elaborated, betraying an abyss of grief. One woman tells me of another: "Two of her children—suicided." (The suicide rate of the Innu is thirteen times as high as the rest of Canada, making them the most suicide-ridden people in the world.)

People who are dangerously close to committing suicide give one clue—how they speak. Toneless, barren-voiced, hollow and flat-sounding, without intonation, an empty sound, a dead sound, the wasteland of the human voice.

That is the sound of the mind on the far side of tears, a shore of cessation and stasis, where no one can reach you, where no one can hear you over those waters.

In one family I stayed with, the young son was obsessed with a computer game called Spyro, the name of the character in the game. He would play all afternoon, and when forced to switch it off would be stupefied and bad-tempered for hours. Another character in this game, a gray-bearded old man, says to Spyro, "And now let me tell you a story." Spyro pulls a face. "Aw, no thanks," he says in a repugnance at such a passé pastime. "Stories. Aw, no thanks," mimics the small boy watching. It's a tiny but revealing thing, for the Inuit world used to be full of stories, stories that could guide your life. This boy's own grandfather is a fund of stories that the child is now being taught to despise. "My mother knew many songs," says Simon Tookoome. "She was a Keeper of Songs for the people. . . . But the missionaries told us to stop. They thought it was a shaman's teaching."

In many of the houses I visited, the TV was on constantly. The TV is itself a kind of a wall. In one place, the "community channel" of the local TV played programs from the community to itself. It was a virtual world where fewer than 150 people living less than ten meters apart communicated with one another by staring at the walls. The channel relayed messages and requests: it reported that a child's watch, a present from her grandmother, was lost on Saturday. The watch was yellow and black with a happy face. There was a lottery being held and a For Sale bulletin—including a helmet, a coffeemaker and an eighteen-speed bike. There was an ad for church services, where the church is shown in a green field with Noah arriving with a white dove, in an icebreaker.

One man shows me a "flight simulator" on his computer so, he says, you can simulate being right here. I feel claustrophobic in minutes, inside these walls of simulacrum. In one community, a jukebox is bawling out Pink Floyd's *The Wall*—an understandably popular choice. Walls frustrate your view, block you off, pen you in. Simon Tookoome says that in the past "everyone knew all the stories. It is no longer that way." Why? "It is the walls. In the igloo there were no walls. In these buildings we are separated. We do not see or hear each other. We have become different." Some of the walls are literal prisons: Nunavut has twenty thousand people—and four jails and they're all full. It seems to me another example of the conservation of wildness. Wildness, apparently walled out, is actually walled in, so it erupts violently in people's minds.

Some of the children are physically walled into their homes by cold—they are too skinny for subzero temperatures. This is also an effect of television, for the children eschew both traditional food and traditional clothes in order to wear the clothes and eat the food they've seen on TV. "These days our children get colder than us because the kids eat white man's food and don't like raw meat," says Joseph Koonoo. Seal meat is rich in fat and keeps the body warmer than white man's food, says an elder. In one house I visited, there was a whale fin on the floor, resting on a packet of instant mashed potatoes. (Two types of food for two generations.)

The kids want ice cream, flown up here from the South, and the French-Canadian store manager jokes, "I never thought I'd find myself selling ice cream to the Eskimos at the North Pole, but here I am," and he sells out of ice cream within twenty minutes of the plane's arrival.

There is a sense of stifling heat, too: one woman told me she and her baby had a heat rash, and in one home I visited, while the outside air temperature was well below zero, women in sundresses were watching Harry Potter with the heating on full blast, the windows wide open and heat pouring out like hair driers.

The hunters and elders, by contrast, have the cool of the land in them, still and serene. The movement of their lives on the land has brought about the stillness of posture that goes with a quiet mind. They are tranquil and calm and do not seem to suffer from the ferocious sense of cramped and maddening suffocation that the young people are prey to in the communities. The elders and the hunters seem by far the happiest people in the communities: they alone, having knowledge of the land, are not imprisoned. They can—and do—appreciate many things brought by white culture. They remember how hard life used to be on the land and are quick to point out the advantages. "White man's igloo," said Joseph Koonoo. "We used to have just sod houses, so thank you, guys, for bringing nice houses." (When I met him he was sitting cozily on his sofa playing solitaire on his laptop.)

When I asked younger people about the land in the present tense, people answered in the past. One woman, in her thirties, told me she had only been out of the community once in two years, to go berry picking. It is this sense of people being stuck in the communities, unable to go out onto the land, that gives the settlements, tiny though they are in the great expanse of the Arctic, their atmosphere of overcrowdedness. I asked another woman about the land. Her answer was poignant. "I remember it was beautiful," she said. She was living two hundred yards from thousands of miles of open land.

LAND AS MEDICINE

From the ghettos of Southern Africa, I heard it. In the deserts of central Australia, I heard it, and in the Arctic I heard it. That the young people were dangerous to themselves and others, that they were violently out of control, that they lived in a wasteland of the mind. And in Africa, Australia and the Arctic, I heard people telling me the one and only solution.

The land.

"Violence comes from being outside nature," says Jimmy Ekho. "Alone on the land," says Joseph Koonoo, "you can feel freedom. Anyone can. You can feel your *own* freedom."

Out on the land, there are no petty orders of community life. Officious Southern hours are scattered to the winds, and the grand and calm seniority of land sets the psyche in order. The coldness cools your mind and the clear air brings a clarity of thought.

"People think more clearly when they're out on the land," said James Angnetsiak. "The land clears my mind, there's more solitude there; and then I can see the hurtness in my heart and I can start seeing what I can do."

"The land helps people heal," says Terry Iyerak. "You're not seeing things that might make you feel mad. You feel freer to talk about your emotions when you're out there." The insane and dangerous wildness of the young seems comprehended out on the land, comprehended in two senses, both "understood"—this land understands wildness—and comprehended meaning "contained." The land holds your mind safely in its enormous embrace, and violence resolves into wildness without injury.

Farley Mowat, writing of the Ihalmiut people, is told that anger is "a source of great shame. It is the only really indecent thing in the land." Anger was very dangerous in these lands, for anger makes it more likely that mistakes would be made out hunting and, as a result, that people could get lost or starve. Within communities, anger was dangerous because people had to live very closely together. But land is stronger than anger and can sufficiently contain it. The Inuit have a custom whereby if someone is angry, they walk right out on the land, walking out their rage until it is gone, and they mark that psychological point by putting a stick in the ground, testament to the strength of their fury.

There is a sense of well-being, satisfaction and happiness that those of the older generation associate only with being on the land. "You go back to the land to be yourself," more than one person told me. The mind's health and wholeness come from the land, I'm repeatedly told. James Angnetsiak describes *silainaq* (the land where no one lives) and says, "If you're in a lonely mood, *silainaq* is dangerous, but if you're happy, *silainaq* means freedom. If someone is crying and wants to go out on the land, people would stop him, but if someone is quiet and wants to be alone, they let him go."

There are programs to take young offenders out onto the land for a couple of months, living in "survival camps." One man explains, "They get rid of their anger there where it's safe. It works. There are kids who behave badly in town, but if you take them out onto the land, they behave perfectly and really come alive." These programs have a very high success rate. Young people are physically removed from drugs and alcohol on the land and they are also given a sense of freedom that they lack in the settlements.

Hugh Brody writes of three teenagers in the Arctic who had injured three people. Some of the men of the community decided that the boys should be taken out trapping. There the boys would learn "the right ways to live.... Everyone seemed to think that the trapline was something of a local correctional institute."

When the maelstrom of adolescent wildness begins, the boiling pandemonium, cock-a-hoop with kicking hormones, many societies send their adolescents out into the wilderness. Teenagers, jousting at petty or parental authority, need real Authority: Ice, Fire, Thirst, Hunger, Predator. They need to take on the unbreakable laws of the wild, which, disobeyed, may kill you.

In months of initiation, teenagers are thrown into the only place truly able to cope with their rebel wildness by being far wilder, more complex and tougher than they are.

One Aboriginal Australian woman talked to me of her son who had alcohol problems and had spent time in prison as a punishment for his wild behavior. Prison was the opposite of what he needed, for, imprisoned, his wildness turned frenzied and nasty. His mother longed for the opposite. He should be "out on the land. Yeah, then he'll be all right."

In South Africa, there are projects to get young gangsters out onto the land, to experience, temporarily, the wilderness. I talked to Quentin Fredericks, who spent five years in gangs in the ghettos of Soweto, between ages twelve and seventeen. He told me about the blood rituals, including having to steal or stab a person. To be a full-fledged member you have to kill a member of a rival gang. "I refused to kill, so I couldn't go back—because if you refuse, your life is forfeit. This is a thing about blood: lifeblood must flow. These rituals bind you for life. There are rape rituals; you have to rape a woman. I didn't do that."

When Fredericks was seventeen, he was sent to prison. He now works taking young people out bush for "purposeful and constructive" rituals. He speaks of the role of wilderness in traditional initiation and of how it can be recast as a way of dealing with gang teenagers today. (The judicial system is beginning to recognize the success of these projects, one judge saying recently that he wouldn't send young people to prison if they agreed to go on such a wilderness course.)

"With the destruction of wilderness and the displacement of indigenous cultures, the young men's transition and the older men's empowerment has been destroyed, so there is a dislocation of wilderness," says Fredericks. "The wildness within young men needs a container. But without the actual wilderness, the wildness in young men is unencumbered. So gangs have invented rituals, which have a mystique, which is as powerful and compelling as traditional rituals, except that they are warped, so there's no *end* to initiation in the gangs, it continues till death. Rituals should mark a beginning, middle and end—you come back from the bush."

The rituals focus on the psyche's wildness, articulating its relationship with wild nature. In the wilderness, you can "fly like an eagle and look skywards where your destiny lies, not in the dust. It restores dignity and self-respect. In the wilderness, we are contained by elements beyond our control. Storms are raging and we use it as a metaphor for storms inside. We have all those elements in ourselves. We need to recognize danger when elemental forces rage within."

There are an enormous number of studies being done showing the overwhelmingly positive effects of "wilderness therapy" on "behaviorally disordered adolescents"—naughty teenagers. What is shocking, though, is why it has taken urban cultures so long to realize that exile from wild lands is harmful.

All human mind is free and wild and needs wild land, its objective correlative. Societies that cage the mind, removing it from wild land, imprisoning it with clocks and enclosure and routine, pettifogging it with paperwork in a dreary photocopied world, run the risk of creating dementia and misery. The human mind developed in wilderness and needs it still.

The Inuit have until very recently been living out on the land and never settled in any one place for long. Living a settled lifestyle will make the ice "rotten," they say. Hubert Amarualik, an elder interviewed in Igloolik in 1993, said that land could be occupied for a maximum of three years. "The land itself was prevented from 'rotting' by this requirement . . . otherwise people would face peril. . . . No one should live on that land for another winter so that the land be given a chance to cool down." Traditionally they believed that if people stayed too long, and the land got too "hot," then sickness, discomfort, crime and social breakdown would occur.

"We are run by coldness and our natural laws. When the white man's law comes to a cold place, it never works out," says an Inuk man.

But the Arctic is warming in a weirder way than the Inuit could have known; the ice is rotting unhealthily.

A MELTING WORLD

There'll always be an England. That's not saying much. There'll always be a North Pole if some dangerous clown doesn't go and melt it." (Michael Flanders and Donald Swann.)

The weather in the Arctic has been called *uggianaqtuq*. An Inuk explains the word: If you meet someone you know well, you can see immediately that something is amiss, that they are not themselves. So with the climate today.

Spring comes too early, so ice that has been thick and firm is thin and dangerous. While I was in the Arctic, I was told of a herd of three thousand Peary caribou that died because they fell through thin ice on a thousand-year-old migration route. The Inuk woman I stay with in Grise Fiord tells me that this was the first year when people could hunt polar bears from boats, because the seas were so late to freeze. Jimmy Qallik says that five years ago at this time of year people would be out Ski-Dooing on the shore, but now no ice has formed. "And the glaciers above us seem to be melting faster." Other hunters show me a glacier melting worryingly.

"The elders are less confident in their knowledge because of climate change; an elder went through the ice and drowned in Pond Inlet last spring, in a place where it never would have happened before," says Hugh Lloyd.

"Funny weather," says Minnie at Resolute, pulling a face. "We as kids would wish for rain because it was so rare, it was fun. But this year it rained all summer."

The sun is hotter than it used to be, I'm told, and people have sunburns and skin rashes, attributed to sun exposure and a damaged ozone layer.

An Inuk man told me how Inuit will chase a polar bear but are frightened of a fruit fly. He intended it to be a gentle joke about the difference of worldview, but actually a fruit fly *is* more frightening than a bear, because of what it represents: a heat that is horribly unnatural here. Jarloo tells me there are mosquitoes now, on Ellesmere Island, where there have never been any before. It's a jarring observation, for mosquitoes are so emblematic of steaming tropics. Local people from Sachs Harbour in Canada's Northwest Territories report seeing species never before seen so far north, including certain beetles and sand flies, salmon, barn swallows and robins.

Polar bears need the seas to freeze so they can travel across the ice to hunt seals to build up their fat reserves for the winter, and warmer weather means their dens can collapse, crushing the cubs or forcing them out on the land before they are big enough to survive. Polar bear and seal populations seem to have halved in the Arctic, and scientists predict that the polar bear could be extinct by 2020. According to current computer models, the Arctic will have no summer ice by 2070.

In the Antarctic, the New Zealand yachtsman Peter Blake sailed through a hundred miles of open water that had been frozen for hundreds of thousands of years and, appalled, he telephoned an urgent Mayday for the ice. "I am speaking from an area of water that has never been water before. It has always been frozen solid."

Inuit I spoke to felt directly threatened by this. Some Inuit of Canada and Alaska are taking the U.S. government to court, arguing that they face extinction because of climate change and saying that in failing to address climate change, the U.S. government is violating their human rights. We're north of everywhere, they say, and the first to feel these changes. "I'm the last man standing, so be careful with me," says one, in elliptical vulnerability.

Every culture depends on nature and nature's seasons, on the backdrop of *natura naturans*, the turning world doing what comes naturally, a rite of spring, a midsummer night's dream, an ode to autumn and a winter's tale. But we are indeed the people who change nature—the Inuit term for the whites was as astute as it was underestimating.

Anxiety may shrill you awake every morning. A hurricane may terrorize your neighborhood, the tongue of a typhoon from the seas comes ashore to lick off the roof of your house like ice cream, as the whole of Kent slides into the sea. It would be a world where almost nothing could matter except survival. A world where friendship would count for little and the only humanity you knew was a savage *sauve qui peut* in the eyes of strangers. A world of untrusting shadows, insecurity gnawing at you like cancer, a world where traveling outside your immediate vicinity would be all but impossible, a world without films or pubs or parties, where childhood would be a cruel learning experience, not charmed years of play. In such a world you would know the pitch and roll of fear, angrily, hourly and for all of your life. (How many dead? Most of us. Starving or drowning, take your pick.)

The language of the world's climate would become chaotic of meaning, its words buckled into an upjerk of spasmic, unpredictable incoherence, whose sense was maddened off to catastrophe. Its seasons would no longer be smooth sentences of regular—comprehensible—meaning but would bang with typhoon and dust storm and tidal wave. Its proper nouns scrambled, perhaps Siberia in Somerset perhaps Sahara in Surrey. Its verbs cracked and contorted. Its tone of voice an explosive scream of jangled unmeaning. An unknowable language. What is "land" submerges into what is "sea." What they called "north" melts ineluctably into what they called "south." A word-blur that smudges all geography.

The elders referred to ice "rotting"—overheated by people settled in one place too long. When they said they feared the land would grow too "hot," running an unhealthy and unnatural temperature, they could not have known how right they would be. And when they were saddened that their words for ice were melting away, lost between the cool minds of the elders and the over-heated minds of the younger generation, they knew that their culture was melting away with the language melt, but they could not have known that the land, the ice to which those words referred, would itself melt and vanish, this ice that was no enemy but a friend to humanity.

A white icicle hangs like frosted glass. Ice it has been in a world of ice for aeons. Fragile and original as a snowflake, each crystal of ice hangs in the balance. The frostedness disappears to plain white ice. The white thins out to transparency and then the crystals of ice dissolve, leak into shiny water, thin and helpless. And at this drop of water civilizations fall: two hundred million environmental refugees run like water, and chaos at its most brutal leaks out in the melting. Ice melts, language melts, a culture melts, a climate melts, and all the music, the songlines of ice-alive melt to the engineered unmusic, the silence of a melting world.

Wild Water

SEA GYPSIES

I must go down to the seas again, for the call of the running tide
Is a wild call and a clear call that may not be denied.
—John Masefield

To those of an island home like Britain, the call of the sea can be a compulsion from childhood, drawn by the poetry of the names, the Sea of Marmara, the Coast of Coromandel, the Seven Seas, the South Seas. If two words could ever catch your imagination, it must surely be these: *sea gypsies*. So romantic, so remote, over the South Seas roam the sea gypsies. I visited the Bajo people, sea gypsies living at the edge of one small island off Sulawesi, one of the islands of Indonesia. Their lives are traditionally spent on boats at sea, though recently they have made settlements on land as well. The little motorboat I had chartered bounced and smacked its way hard over a choppy sea, while the burning Pacific sun fell down from the sky, fell up from the water, fell sideways off the waves, and for hours we—a translator, the boatman and I—careered over the water, into blue mist and horizons.

The Bajo people can live at sea virtually all the time, cooking on stones or flat coral on the bottom of the boat. People sleep on the boats, and women sometimes give birth at sea, and if someone is sick, they use the traditional medicine of the seas. Some people take children to school on the land, these days, but apart from that the only two reasons why they would have to go ashore are to collect fresh water and to bury their dead.

Near to the Bajo people's island, I made out something strange in the water. It was a gray, lucent shimmer, as if the sea was shining with more than its own light. Close up, I saw it was plastic drink bottles, upside down, bobbing in the water by the thousand, encircling the island by half a mile. Each bottle was tied firmly over strands of sea grass. The Bajo "farm" the sea grass and have discovered that this litter of modernity makes a perfect miniature greenhouse. A problem, though, for us. The boat's rudder and propeller were being strangled by the thick sea grass. The motor was clogged up and we could see no passage. Eventually a Bajo man saw our difficulty, swam out to us and guided us down a waterway, invisible to us, which he knew.

There were rickety wooden houses, seeming no tougher than balsa wood, and the houses and walkways between them were built on stilts over the water. Sea grass was drying in the sun and there was litter everywhere in the waters under their houses: rags, Coke bottles, biscuit wrappers, tin cans, cigarette packets, plastic bags and broken shoes. There were small canoes everywhere and children flitted between houses on the shaky walkways, peering at us through slatted walls. As for the sea, imagine a set of allotments, but instead of fences there are buoys and markers to show one person's "sea-field," and from the buoys poke up sticks and flags and plastic toys, leaves or flowers, to show whose sea grass garden is whose.

We were invited in to talk with various old people, and we talked of the sea. They believed that there was very deep water with fish that are unfamiliar even to them, in spite of the fact that they know the waters here so intimately. They believed in a spirit of the sea, which would be angry if they acted in an immoral way, and would show disapproval by withholding fish. They prepare food sacrifices for the sea, because the sea likes to eat, they say, just as people do.

Quite by chance, the day I arrived the community was making such a sacrifice. A group of women and girls were weaving leaves into miniature boat shapes, then loading them with rice, eggs and fruit. When the boats were ready they would be floated out to sea with a traditional dance. Only one old woman knows when to do this ceremony and the timing is her secret—it isn't good for too many people to know this, she said. The boat sacrifice would placate storms and all the spirits of the sea would eat and, in return, would offer fish from the deeps to the fishermen. The old woman would talk with the spirits, going to the sea and asking for its protection.

The woman inherits this role from her parents and only one woman in this village has this gift. The magic comes to her in a dream. It is as if the voices of her parents speak through her, she said. I asked her if she thought the sea was wild, and she paused. "Yes," she said quietly, "but I don't want to say why." When she goes to talk with the sea, she said, she travels on the back of an invisible crocodile, which will bring her to the right place. (It's as if she's walking on water, other people told me.)

Aboriginal Australians of the coastal regions also have a profound sense of communicating with the seas. In the Great Australian Bight, the Yirkala Mirning people use gong stones, musical stones from the local cliffs and caves, and say that by striking the gong stones they can call southern right whales, and that the musical stones are used in song ceremonies and dance ceremonies in which both the people and the whales take part. The Bajo people would have understood this elusive co-enchantment, seeing the oceans as a spirited place, alive with character and emotion. Under Western eyes, though, the seas seem barely inhabited, let alone enspirited.

A MARINE RATTLEBAG

A funny thing happened on the way to the Americas. A funny thing happened on many voyages of "discovery" and it is this: the sea was barely seen. The ship was of interest. Any sighting of land was noted but the ocean was merely an absence, not discovered but ignored. *Aqua nullius.*

When I look for the deeps in the so-called literature of the seas, all I find is navigation. When I yearn to read of oceanry, all I get is shippery, quadrants and compasses.

It persists, this strange absence. *The Oxford Companion to Ships and the Sea,* reprinted throughout the 1990s, has almost nothing about the sea in it. There are some seventeen and a half pages under the entry "ship" but "sea" merits no entry at all. There is no "abyss," no "Mariana Trench." "Whale" gets just six words but there are full entries for whale catcher, whale factory ship and whaleboat, while "whaler" occupies half a page and "whaling" gets two and a half pages. There are no turtles at all, but there are entries for the "turtle-deck" of a vessel and a "turtle-boat." "Wave" is given a quarter of a page, but "yacht" and "yacht-ing" eleven pages. "Coral" gets seven and a half lines, while the Battle of the Coral Sea gets sixty-seven lines. The lovely creature the dolphin merits four and a half lines, while the HMS *Dolphin* gets eighteen and a half lines. Captain Cook gets four pages, Krupp Von Bohlen, the German steel-and-armaments firm, gets a fulsome eighteen lines, while Rachel Carson, preeminent marine biologist, is not listed at all. Sir William Parker, Victorian British vice admi-ral, gets a mention, the First Duke of Albemarle gets a whole page but there is no entry at all for William Beebe, who brought the underwater world right into the public consciousness with his invention of the bathysphere.

The sea is a strange blank to many writers. Coleridge wrote of "that round objectless desert of waters" and Francis Calderón de la Barca described Colum-bus, the "Discoverer of a World," gazing over "the unknown and mysterious waste of waters." Even when the oceans do become the subject of literature, the representation of the seas concentrates almost wholly on the surface of the seas. Conrad, the éminence grise of ocean literature, who writes of it so evocatively, only concentrates on the face of the waters, from the malice of storm to fetid stillness. All that is beneath the waves—where the sea's charac-ter, meaning and music exist—is somehow not his concern.

The age of discovery was an age of measurement and control, while the seas were an unfathomable and uncontrollable wildness. Samuel Purchas in the *Art of Navigation* wrote that shipping enables man to "manage this untamed Beast . . . with the Bridle of the Winds, and Saddle of his Shipping." Early European sailors did not love the sea so much as love their conquest of it.

Thank god for Thor.

With the writings of Thor Heyerdahl and William Beebe, Rachel Carson and Heathcote Williams, the oceans open to us. With the camera of Jacques Cousteau the underwater world washed into people's minds, wave on glorious wave, and recently the BBC's *Blue Planet* series brought the oceans crashing through television screens, flooding a million sitting rooms with penguins, sharks and fish of the deeps.

Heyerdahl actually noticed the element he moved across, and all its creatures: the flying fish, the creatures at night, glimmering with phosphorus. The reverse of the Christian explorers who thrust their god on the people they met, Heyerdahl called his raft the *Kon-Tiki*, in honor of the founding hero of the Polynesians. Heyerdahl also saw the early signs of oil pollution and became a powerful environmental campaigner for the oceans. And I can't resist telling you about the London cabbie. Thor Heyerdahl had just broadcast at the BBC TV center and was waiting in the lobby for a cab that had been called for him. After a while the cabbie arrived, took a look at our man Thor, then turned away and sat down. You have to say the following exchange aloud. The cabbie has a strong Cockney accent.

THOR: Excuse me, but I think I'm the one you're looking for.
CABBIE: Nah, not me, mate, I was told to come and pick up four Airedales.

William Beebe, in his pioneering underwater journeys from 1930, was courageous, for he couldn't know for sure that his bathysphere would withstand the pressure as he sank underwater, and in noting various points at intervals on their way down, he seems trying to keep his panic in check: "We have just splashed below the surface. . . . We are at our deepest helmet dive. . . . The *Lusitania* is resting at this level. . . . We are passing the deepest submarine record. . . . Only dead men have sunk below this. . . . We are still alive and one-quarter of a mile down." At such depths, the water pressure would be so great that you would not drown but rather "the first few drops would have shot through flesh and bone like steel bullets." He found aspects of it hard: "the complete and utter loneliness and isolation . . . a loneliness more akin to a first venture upon the moon or Venus than that from a plane in mid-ocean or a stance on Mount Everest."

He is an ecocrat in wilderness, right down to the plankton. In a tiny scoop of water, he collects, and lovingly counts by the thousands, the feathery copepods, short-eyed shrimps, siphonophores, helix-snails, nautilus-like flying snails, and comments "As regards beauty and variety I can compare copepods only with snow crystals," and a little later he thrills to "that exquisite violet sea-shell with the euphonious name of Ianthina."

Jacques Cousteau's voice intoxicated me when I was small: my brothers and I would watch him on TV and then gleefully imitate his accent and swim through sharks in the garden. He describes in his books another kind of intoxication, the effects of nitrogen narcosis, which he and his fellow divers did not understand at the time. They experienced its "drunken" effect, and one diver, under the influence, found himself worrying about the fish, thinking they couldn't breathe and offering them his breathing apparatus. "We called the seizure *l'ivresse des grandes profondeurs*"—the rapturous intoxication of the great depths. And the phrase seems to suggest the wildness of the world's waters and the play of the ocean creatures.

Spinner dolphins in a superpod of hundreds chuckle and corkscrew to glory as they leap, sheer exuberance—exuberance for exuberance's sake—curling their way. They play "pass the seaweed," passing a strand on from fin to fin. They chortle with bubbles, show off with them and even hunt with them, corralling a shoal of mackerel or sardine into a tight ball, then making a wall of bubbles that the fish hate to cross.

In the haunting eyes of a whale there is wistful wit, wisdom and memory: the largest can live for over a century, and the layer formation in the earplugs of whales demonstrates their longevity like rings in the trunks of trees.

Whales and dolphins spyhop—rising vertically out of the water—and they sound, diving deep down. They breach and lobtail, slapping their tails or flippers down on the water (and when it comes to humpbacks and sperm whales, you can distinguish individual whales by their tails). The enormous blue whale is the largest animal ever to have lived, on land or in water. Its tongue is said to be the weight of an elephant, it has a nine-foot penis and seven-gallon testicles, and no one knows where it goes for a seven-gallon shag. No one, that is, except the blue whale. Pounding up a fountain of spume, it rolls across oceans, an ancient Atlas shouldering the Pacific out of its way, making inches of the miles, its tail fluke falling, colossal cymbal clapping on the ringing water. Humpback whales sing, serenading their mates, and perform ultramarine acrobatics in the waves, sensing each other slowly in a foreplay of exquisite, gentle asking. The male whale offers his penis voluntarily, uninsistent but yearning, thrilling with desire, to lick its thoughtful laps around the

female's pink lips, and they hug each other with their flippers, pressing themselves together, "standing" face to face, sometimes needing a third to help them
hold each other close. As they climax, their tail flukes thrum the water in
their ecstasy and they pulse upward, up through the water surface, becoming
mountains for a moment, their peaks high in the air with waterfalls cascading
from them, two whales coming together in a burst of bright sky.

And then there's the dugong, enormous and tender, slow-rolling with its
paddling fins and bowl of a nose, the dugong, gentle vegan, more closely related to the elephant than to other marine mammals, round of snout and soft
of heart, among whom the males, to impress the females, splash. That's all. At
full moon the dugong nocturne serenades the moon and others; soft squeaks
and chirps, crooning for seagrass greenery, for splashing, for love and for being left alone. They can bark if they need to, to scare off intruders.

In the water wilderness, a turtle, like a fat happy thought, has nothing on
its mind but paddling and keeping one eye on the moon while, with slow and
creaking grace, it spoons its way away into the endless blue, as it has done for
150 million years. The furry sea otter, the teddy bear of the oceans, lies on its
back hammocked in seaweed for a snooze. (The otter wraps itself up in
fronds of kelp and is anchored by the kelp's standfast so it doesn't float away
as it naps.) Cradling itself and rubbing its cheeks with its paws, it dreams perhaps (who knows) of small fry in the shallows.

Dolphins chase mackerel, swimming below the shoals, while in the sky,
shearwaters wheel. The eloquently named shearwater can dive down perhaps
as much as fifteen meters, and the desperate mackerel, to escape the dolphins,
jump up into the air—flying fish and swimming birds.

Diving in the coral reefs off Sulawesi, I once found my vision completely
filled with fish. I was swimming in five shoals: blue and gold fusiliers, pyramid
butterfly fish, big gray snappers, lunar fusiliers and striped fusiliers. They
swam together, then separated out into their own shoals, then swam together
again. The vivid powder-blue lunar fusiliers remained longer than the others,
then the whole shoal was suddenly skittish and rang out for a different angle,
swimming a blue streak. Soaring and falling, they shot vertically downward
like a thousand shooting stars plummeting together down a mercurial plumb
line. Shoals of fish, alerted by a movement or flicker of a shadow, turn around
on a fin-instant as a flock of birds can turn on a wingtip's timing. They move

as if the flash of a current swung them, but the impetus is their own, fluent in the languages of struations of light and the confluence of waters.

A shoal of herring is a carousel of synchronized pizzicato, and any tiny movement is a miniature flash of sound, as they accelerate and turn, fin to fin, sound made sudden silver. When fish move, the movement vibrates through the water, the quick motion making a sharp sound, inaudible to humans. Flashes of light, too, are mirrored from their bright scales, so fish in shoals re-act to touch, sound and sight in virtual synchrony. But then an orca whale ap-proaches with a low rumble of sound and thuds the water around the herring with its tail, effectively clubbing the shoal till its quicksilver is stunned to bruised gray slowness, and the bright and singing sphere of the wheeling her-ring orchestra is now broken, stuttering, smashed.

The seas glow with phosphorescence (from the Greek word for "light" and "to carry or bear"). Evanescent flickers of electric current evoke the wonder-light of the mind, quick as a joke. An octopus, surprised, will blush brick red, then turn to mottled red and gray. The blue-ringed octopus is small and gold but, if stressed, can flash bright blue rings. And then there's an octopus's gar-den beneath the sea. Each "house" has a stone doorway propped by two lintels and the floor is "excavated" some five inches. And the garden contains crab and oyster shells, stones, sea anemones and urchins.

A coral reef is a marine medley, of shuttlecocks and foxgloves, parachutes, mushrooms and the mosaic perfection of Islamic art; crystals, ferns and frozen reindeer horns, frosted trees and snowflakes, Borobudur and the pyr-amids, elephants' ears, modernist pottery and pawns of an underwater chess set. There is a dark coral like the charred remains of a spent volcano, extin-guished by ocean. Soft coral looks like feathery fireworks, blazing with sparks but wafting with current. There are fans of gold, elkhorn coral and octocoral, a white lattice feather-skeleton and a lace shroud (of his bones are coral made). There is whip coral like an ancient anchor, sea squirts blue and soft as gos-samer, and a polka-dotted deep purple sponge. A rope of coral hangs like a strand of necklace that has been underwater for years, moss crushed with di-amonds, sapphire and shells. One pinky maroon sponge is six feet long with open undulating wave-folds of labia. The first time I saw a coral reef, the won-der of it brought tears to my eyes.

Coral reefs are by far the largest structures created by living creatures.

Rich with fish, if you dipped a spoon in the water you'd pull out a fish. But they are brittlely, bitterly fragile. There are fragments of coral like smashed Ming Dynasty vases. A harlequin shrimp—yellow, blue and orange-dotted, with blue and white striped legs, daft as bagpipes—gleefully tows away a starfish to eat it alive.

Small fish, anthias, rill a brilliant yellow scherzo in their hundreds over the reefs with the bursting orange anemone fish, who come with bowler hats on, sure they do, their bodies striped with ribbons of boisterous, boastful camouflage. (If this is camouflage, they're just doing it for show.) The surgeonfish of turquoise and gold—the exquisite complementary colors of perfect pitch—laugh like grace notes over the reef. Each parrotfish shines like paradise—gold streaks like the sand of an island atoll in the intoxicating blue of ocean. One gazes at me, its turquoise beautiful as hope. A lionfish, scion of some ancient Oriental dragon dynasty, lurks in menacing splendor, on a dark ledge. It blooms with "wings" and pokes out its long elegant spikes and venomous spines. A trumpetfish, Janus-faced, has a tail that pretends to be a head—oh, and its nose is like that of a duck-billed platypus. The Napoleon fish, the enormous giant wrasse, pomps overhead like a barrage balloon.

Streams of fish, tinkly like a honky-tonk piano, jingle past in a second and are gone. Fish swim sideways, flatwise, to look at you, or gulp up at you from a vase sponge. Hundreds, maybe thousands, of pyramid butterfly fish fall around me like petals, skyfuls of fish. There's a teardrop butterfly fish, yellow and white with a bold black dot on its side, a big fat minim on a lighthearted score. There's a flapping, bothered pufferfish, bloated and out of breath: seven boxy fish swim together in a bloc, a flat-sided dull-trumpet march-past, and the fabulous clown triggerfish hoves in, dotty-belly and all. Two bickering fish peck at the coral like hens quarreling over seed. The smooth flutemouth hangs in the air, motionless, innocent, butter wouldn't melt. A moorish idol streams a defiant pennant of a fin, and nearby damselfish live in certain anemones. (A "damselfish" really ought to come with a "dulcimerfish," but I don't think there's any such thing. Pity.)

A blue-finned fish swims curious out of the coral, like a midnight blue promise from a trombone. A batfish, yellow-gold and round as a penny, shines like a huge and weightless sovereign in a blue fairy-tale street. A yellowfin parrotfish has psychedelic scales of diamonds, and a bannerfish boldly goes, brilliant and exulting, like a risqué thought and an exclamation mark. Gulping under a rock is a black-spotted moray eel, with a mad look in its eye, and near it the stealthy Iago-intelligence of the yellow-margined moray eel. Then the syncopated yellow dots blue dots yellow dots of the blue-spotted ribbontail ray. Stingrays flutter like flattened rats on the sea bottom while one, with bulging eyes, ledge-lurks. Then, all satire and ire, the fire dartfish zooms past, its body all the colors of flame from the pale yellow at its head to the dark orange embers at its tail. Angelfish look as if they invented iridescence and sweep along, their fins trailing the glory of it. Black fish skulk in ashy gray coral like punks in a pub in the afternoon.

The coral world, thousands of years old, is a phantasmagoria of the spiny, the prickly, the feathery and spirally; fiddle-headed, pronged, whorled, tubular, spotted, dotted, spiky, gauzy, gossamery and crusted. It is home to the hiders and lurkers, those wearing their sperm on their sleeves, or their eggs on their hairy legs (the female lobster). It is the home of the falsettos, the pretenders, the deceivers, fakes and mimics, the transvestite and transsexual fish. Slipper shells (*Crepidula fornicata*) begin life as males and switch to females as they mature. Scorpionfish, bream, snapper, bass and some anemone fish are all born male but become female.

Fish are masters and mistresses of disguise: the ghost pipefish, in a mandarin costume of mustard with red squirls, is camouflaged to look like a drifting piece of seagrass seen against feather stars. The scorpion fish is very hard to see because of its ragtime camouflage of color and texture, and its edges are smudged as if it had been designed after too many spliffs and the designer had attempted to erase it in the morning. Many fish have a large dark dot, a "false eye," to confuse predators. There are prey fish that evolved to resemble predators, and the comet fish, which, if threatened, will dive nose first into a hole, leaving its tail sticking out. But the tail is rounded with a large eyespot and looks like a moray eel. *Eat my shorts.*

At certain times, great pulses of coral spawn are ejaculated in a giant reef orgasm: the seas are cloudy with sperm, frothy with reproductive juices, thick with sex. (A trunkfish with rowdy blue stripes twanging around its belly sneezes out jets of sperm and egg into the sex-soup.) Swim in it too long and you're surprised you haven't been impregnated yourself, by a dozen clownfish and a white-tipped shark at the very least.

And then there's the tender lovemaking of the blue crab. The male, larger than the female, crouches over her, holding her tight. This triggers her to begin to release herself from her shell. Very slowly—very, *very* slowly—the female lets go of her shell; the patient and protective male fans her to make sure she has enough oxygen. After three days or so, her shell gradually slips off, the male helps her shift out of it, then the female turns over onto her back . . . And there, dear reader, we shall leave them. Or take the courtship of the banded pipefish. Every morning, the female joins her mate and they twine themselves together, two thin threads of fish, and they dance, wrapped, enraptured, proud as swans, in a simple dance of devotion of every I for Thee, in a duet of delight every dawn. I would be a pipefish if I could.

Mating seahorses greet each other belly to belly and brighten with color, and the male squid's tentacles flush red as he mates. Hammerhead sharks have to stop swimming when they mate so they fall helplessly through the water. The "sea tiger"—actually a blue and yellow slug—first tries to eat its mate, then has sex. Each is both male and female, and they mate extruding a penis. A turquoise one.

The Victorian Henry Lee, whom Jacques Cousteau calls "the Boswell of the octopus," writes of octopus courtship, and you are expected to use your imagination here to fill in the gaps Lee is too coy to expound. One limb of the male octopus becomes swollen and from it extends "a slender elongated filament. When its owner offers his hand in marriage to a lady octopus she accepts, *and keeps it, and walks away with it.*" Get that. The barnacle, while we're on the subject, organizes its housing needs according to the length of its member. Most barnacles are hermaphrodite but they can cross-fertilize with a long penis that can be extended from one barnacle to another, so they settle near other barnacles, ideally no farther away than the length of a barnacle penis.

Diving at night you might see the ocellated lionfish if you're lucky, with a butterfly tail, wings of a bird, striped like a zebra, eight inches of pure dragon and looking more ready to fly than to swim. I felt a magical disorientation in the dark for I had no left or right or sense of depth, knowing only whether I was upside down or not. There's a Japanese slipper lobster, eight inches long, creature of a coral boudoir, purple-eyed, each rimmed with pink like embroidery. The blue glints, will-o'-the-wisps, led me down and I willingly sank, somersaulting away from the wall of the reef, away, down, toward the dark abyss.

As I resurfaced, stars were shining and lightning flashed on the horizon. Thirty night-feeding fish burrowed down suddenly as they saw the first light of dawn. The faint yellow sun dappled the water and a white-tipped shark swam past and in this half light, in this half second, all I could see was the tail fin in the blue-gray depths, like the Cheshire Cat's smile. Much maligned is the shark: more people are killed by donkeys than by sharks. But they are feared, perhaps because their tracking ability gives the impression that they have an eerie sixth sense and in a way they do, because they are sensitive to sounds on a very low wavelength, which is exactly the noise emitted by moving muscles. They can also detect weak electrical signals in water, generated by muscle movement.

The whales and dolphins mind all this. They envisage it in sound, know these creatures, remember routes and coastlines, they know it, are aware of coral and turtle, otter and fish. They notice it, sing of it, tell of its water-wildness. They enmind it: from echolocation they can draw mental maps and their minds contain the songlines of the oceans. They enmind it too, because they fill it with meaning, message and thought. All the oceans rock with their song—the ocean is created in their minds and in turn their minds, through sound waves and vibration, suffuse the oceans in a wild mindscape.

UNDERWATER MIND

For the human mind, the crossing from air down into water has powerful effects. Unable to smell, losing accustomed gravity and losing our air hearing, it is surprisingly difficult to carry memory across the border. When I stayed on Sulawesi, I was very conscious of its immediate past, for barely six months before, Christians and Muslims had massacred each other. Underwater, though, it could have been a million miles away.

Underwater, writes Cousteau, "one forgets the sun. One forgets a lot." All the petty, dry concerns are left to the squabbling gulls. The air world is hard to recall on the instant of merging in the saltwater world we knew before. It is enigmatic that memory can meet amnesia here, how completely and instantly we forget the world of air, our corrugated corner of earth and our dry lives, but seem to remember, opaquely, as if memory coursed through our salty veins, that this ocean was once our home.

The water's apparent silence is its first sublimity, and the tranquillity of the underwater world makes your psyche respond on the instant. This kind of quiet is the madeleine that instantly dissolves ages and centuries to the primordial past we have never quite forgotten. No ancestry, no history, just the mind, finally, come home to the eternal now. Silence first. Then sound. You hear as if with your body. There are melodies here, there is music in the mind that even breathing hesitates to interrupt. Diving for the first time is like hearing music for the first time: not a piece of music but the entire category "music."

Oceans are full of creatures chasing one another, to kill for hunger. But it's hard to imagine a clownfish taking a machete to a damselfish because one preferred a coral of crescent formation and the other knelt, fishwise, dipping at an altar of crossed coral branches.

Underwater, little intrudes from the dry world. Things seem to stop at the sea-light ceiling of the water surface, the dancing light like moonlight shining upward onto pale liquid gold. This ceiling seems a boundary not only between water and air but between different ways of thought.

The Latin adjective *altus* means both "high" and "deep"—and "deep-seated" (of feelings) and "ancient." The noun *altum* means the deep, the sea, and height too. It seems appropriate that the human mind, ascending too high, too fast, up mountains is subject to altitude sickness, and this is mirrored underwater by the "nitrogen narcosis" of diving too deep and coming up too fast. The bends.

Underwater, mind belongs. Our earliest perceptions as both creatures and individual fetus are of gentle, thrilling waters. All mind began here: memory, perception, fear and desire. Ocean is full of wild mind. It melts the separation of mind and body and loosens the distinction between self and world. I'm searching for a word. Ocean dissolves the arbitrary dry idea of mankind's island mind. But these words irk me a little—*dissolve* is the best but it is not right, the word is too Latinate, too remindful of salinity and science when I want a word with less history, more pure past. I want, perhaps, a word from an Aboriginal Australian language that would carry a meaning of an element touching mind, rain reaching out to psyche or water speaking to dream. I know there is Ocean in Uluru, and not because of a devious dualism pretending to state by contrast, or even some ancient Chinese wisdom that each extreme carries its opposite within it, but rather because I suspect that mindful memory may have survived there, all the forty thousand years of culture and all the millennia before, from when our clumsy bodies first lugged themselves out of the water onto dry strange shores.

It seems to me that the difference between air and water is more absolute than a matter of breath: after all, there's oxygen in both. The absolute difference is a matter of mind. You have a sense, underwater, of diffused mind, participation that doesn't restrict or deny individual mind but enhances it, because no mind can believe itself dry-islanded down here. Descartes' thought is not a thought that could have been thought underwater. Underwater our heads are immersed, we are connected far more directly and intimately to everything else. Dolphins "know" the minds of people underwater. They recognize depression and seem to feel for its victims. Fish in shoals feel that quicksilver shiver of fear when one has seen a predator and their fear passes like electrical currents through water.

The abovewater world makes pedestrians of us all but underwater the mind swims to a freedom before words, before the worlds of Rome or Byzantium. All the kings of England are a clutter of insignificance compared with giant kelp. Milton just another mean old man compared with the whale. Money, mortgages and the stock exchange are laughable litter, which the oceans wisely ignore. Casts of mind gather here. Curiosity, quick and clean, is here, but not intrusion. Quizzicalness, certainty, doubt and fear but not spite or cruelty. Hunting but not humiliation.

As I dive deeper, the ocean's twilight keens my senses. I feel the need for sharper ears and eyes, my body feels a nascent itch, just a hint of the enormous need that deep-sea creatures have for eyes that would become larger if they could, straining to see. My skin quivers with sensitivity; it prickles like the tiny pinprick beginnings of a longing for quills and fins and antennae. And I long to be able to smell underwater.

There is a nation of Aboriginal people on Mornington Island in the Gulf of Carpentaria in northern Australia who are known as the Dolphin People. Their shamans know how to whistle to bring dolphins close to the shore, whistling more animatedly, then stopping. The shamans then say they begin to speak to the dolphins, mind to mind. The Inuit say they "like the way whales think." For myself, the more I learned about cetaceans, the deeper my respect—and the more brittle the contradiction seemed between my devotion to whale mind and my admiration for the Inuit way of life, including whale hunting. The only resolution is the logic of the land: the hunger of ice.

Cetaceans demonstrate a capacity for abstract conceptions; they have emotional intelligence, and the sheer complexity of humpback whale song suggests memory, thought and profound intelligence. But the intelligence we can see may be only a part of the whole: Edward O. Wilson comments, "Perhaps the Sperm Whale is really a genius in disguise; the possibility cannot be totally discounted." Karl-Erik Fichtelius and Sverre Sjölander write, "The inborn biological, morphological, and physiological prerequisites for human language are a well-developed brain, something to talk about, and something to talk with. A comparison between dolphin and man in accordance with this list shows that on every point where we have adequate information, dolphins are superior to human beings."

They may have invented puns and bathos, zeugma and jokes. They may have a thousand terms for different types of spins and different reasons to spin. Humpbacks may applaud new songs or may be singing parts of a song cycle a thousand years old. They may have verbs we don't. They may be attempting to make up new terms now for things they have never needed to think before. *Exploitation*, perhaps. Or *extinction* or *finity*, which has nothing to do with dorsalness or pectorality. They may have a very particular term that means "feeling-nostalgia-for-the-ancient-Greeks-with-their-lovely-lilting-language-and-respect-for-us." They may have named emotions that we have not yet identified: transcendent and transparent surges of happiness, or being engulfed in sea-sorrow-fear. They may have named our various human languages onomatopoeically. Since we know they can distinguish between different materials, they may have terms for wood, metal and glass, and for harpoon, bomb and gun. They may have a term for commercial whalers and a name for a particular Inuit hunter and a name for his favorite inlet of his favorite hunting bay. They may have mapped the world in songlines with a certain segue for the horn of Africa and particular clicks for the bays of Raasay. They may have learned our Morse Code and their teenagers may use it to tease the adults by pretending to be as dumb as some of us.

Orca whales have "dialects" and "languages"—the differences can be as slight as the difference between a Lancashire accent and Yorkshire, or as large as that between the English language and Japanese. A whale can sing a particular song to another particular whale and they could theoretically express emotion, news, opinion and memories.

Whales may, for all we know, discuss the melting of the glaciers. In Delphinese (Heathcote Williams' term for dolphin language) there may be terms for wilderness and for freedom and new words for prison, which they have only needed since their capture in dolphinariums. How many terms do they have for water? Currents? Waves?

A SOUNDSCAPE THE SIZE OF THE WORLD

Sound is noise. But as a verb, *to sound* means "to fathom the depth of the seas." Meanwhile *to be sound* is "to be whole," of sound body and mind, healthy, intact. In the beginning the condition of sea was sound and unsounded. In sound, music and ocean meet: with each wave's rise and fall, the rise of a tide and its fall, the ocean breathes, each breath like the arc of a phrase of Ravel's *Jeux d'Eaux*. According to Hindu creation mythology, Vishnu slept in the ocean and breathed regular breaths, which brought Time into being. Sound followed, the foundation of world: time and sound together created music.

Before words, music. Before tool, sound. Before *Fiat*, song.

Male humpback whales only sing during the mating season and males are thought to stop singing when they mate. Each song cycle may be ten to thirty minutes long but the entire performance may last for hours or days. The songs are like fugues, divided into themes, and a new theme is introduced every couple of years. The call of the finback whale carries over twelve hundred miles underwater and it is suggested that it could carry as far as twenty-five thousand miles—the circumference of the earth. There are in effect "channels" of sound, formed by thermoclines, where the speed of sound is at a minimum and where sound tends to remain. Within such a "deep sound channel," low-frequency sound waves can travel hundreds or thousands of miles before dissipating. Whales, particularly finbacks, use this channel, broadcasting their mysterious music across the world. The viola d'amore has a set of "sympathetic strings,"

which can't be played but which sound in response to notes produced by the
bowed strings. It is as if the whale has played the ocean like a viola d'amore,
finding its fabulous resonance so the seas resound in sympathetic song.

Dolphins—blipping, clicking, chirping, rattling and barking—may be
able to communicate their thoughts more precisely than we know. In the
company of humans, a dolphin will alter the frequencies of its voice, concentrating on the sound range humans can hear and, says Heathcote Williams,
in his breathtaking hymn to cetaceans, they try to imitate the sound of human speech. They "listen" to one another's bodies as well as their calls, to
know how another dolphin feels. They are aware of menstrual cycles in
women. They lament and express frustration and joy. They live in an oceanic
synesthesia where emotion is almost tangible, where movement is audible,
song is felt, electric signals can be heard and dolphins can "see" in sound. The
supposed "silence" of the seas is a human untruth, told and believed because
we can be so deaf to its music.

The calls of dolphins and whales, their squeaks and mews and deep moans,
fill a range of sound far beyond the reach of human ears. If ultraviolet rays are
light rays known to exist but invisible to the human eye, then this dolphin
song is ultraviolet sound. Unfathomable to us. It is deep—*altus*—farther than
the fathom of our hearing, and it is high—*altus*—beyond the topmost reach
of our ears. The "infrared" lowings too low, the "ultraviolet" whistlings too high.

The whales were there before us. We do not speak their language and
should not presume that their messages are frivolous or resemble "infant"
"babbling," as one commentator alleged, which is like announcing that whale
song has no meaning because the whales do not speak proper seventeenth-
century Castilian.

Pods of whales sing, jamming away for a lifetime, singing the truest blues,
the mind of the ocean sung in ultramarine jazz, a true rhapsody in blue, in
turquoise, a rhapsody in azure. A humpback's song can be funny, quick as a
joke, followed by the low, full strings of a cello, long notes of infinite sadness,
searching, longing and then a sound like the plucked strings of a ddubble
bbass, then a fluting and a trumpet of grace notes, whistles, whirrs and purrs.
A bassoon, the bark of an elephant and a creak, a tweaked high note and a low
contented growl, then the sound waltzes up, a sound-shape the same as the
curl of a wave. Then a foghorn, a sweet whistlesong and a satisfied snore.

Bowheads can sing an ethereal glissade of squeaks and giant mews, fast and high like a radio being tuned: they can chirp and chatter, croak and caw like birds in jungles, chirruping, chissicking, squawking like parrots then cooing, with the reassurance of dove and motherlove, a haunting siren, whistling, querying. They have a spinning music, threads of turquoise, threads of gold. They can sing a round, a catch of melody repeated, spun up to the skies and spiraling down again, then spinning up and out, then inward and down, whirring and purling in a gyre of sound. All music, all water is here, the beautiful shape of water in a whirlpool, a gyre of waterful sound, spinning up beyond our highest hearing, spiraling down below to the depths of ocean sound.

When writers have wished to describe wilderness positively, they have often concentrated on its silence: de Tocqueville, in the American wilds, spoke of "a silence so deep, a stillness so complete, that the soul is invaded by a kind of religious terror." Thomas Cole, in his 1835 *Essay on American Scenery*, describes how "the silent energy of nature stirred the soul to its inmost depths."

Wilderness, in a negative sense, has often been described in terms of noise. In America, Nathaniel Hawthorne called wild country "howling," filled with the "savage yell," and for decades, Puritans referred to the "howling wilderness."

Similarly, when ocean wildernesses are portrayed negatively, the oceans are noisy: the seas

Burst into chaos with tremendous roar
. . . Wild as the winds, across the howling waste
Of mighty waters
    —*James Thomson, in* The Seasons *(1726–30)*

As King Lear becomes more wild in his mind, he is:

As mad as the vex'd sea; singing aloud.

And when people wish to portray ocean wilderness positively, the seas are silent: Herman Melville in *Moby Dick* describes a night "when all the waves rolled by like scrolls of silver; and, by their soft, suffusing seethings, made what seemed a silvery silence, not a solitude." Frank T. Bullen, in *Idylls of the Sea*, writes, "The very silence . . . was sweet."

But all this misses the point. The seas are never silent, for though the surface may be calm, its wild true music is almost entirely expressed below. The sea's surface-songs, the roars of wind and breakers, are the least interesting of its sounds. For centuries, people seem to have heard the crashes at the surface but missed the music of the underwater, rather like going to a concert and only listening to the coughs in the audience, the scrape of the chairs as the musicians sit down, the dull thuds and clicks as the orchestra unpacks its instruments. And missing the Mahler. We have for too long ascribed meaninglessness to things whose meaning eludes us and there is a whole world of acoustics, beyond our hearing and beyond our understanding but not beyond our grasp to injure, for modernity, deaf to the sea's music, has imposed a cacophony.

Mid-frequency sonar is known to cause mass beachings. British, American and other NATO members are testing a submarine-detection system that employs Low Frequency Active Sonar, which reaches 240 decibels. They aim to use it across 80 percent of the oceans within a few years. Even when the sonar's source is hundreds of miles away, LFAS changes the song pattern of the whale; the tremolos and whirrings, skirlings, chucklings and gyres of sound are twisted. Since they sing to one another for fun, for messages, for suggestive remarks in a croon, or information about food in a zipping ping, the effect on their breeding and socializing is not known—cannot be known—to us. We the idiot-thunderers are, in the words of Heathcote Williams, parasites

Who view the whale only as an industrial resource,
And eat through their musical society like deaf maggots.

Perhaps, if we listened, we would be able to hear some of the blue whale's anthemic basso profundo, lowing across miles and miles, now mewing, now moaning, a deep requiem for the singing oceans it used to know. Perhaps we would hear a cetacean Schumann driven mad, humming tunelessly to himself, a whale with eardrums exploded, a deaf Beethoven roaring with frustration. A Debussy moaning in pain, forced to listen to pneumatic drills and jackhammers at twenty times their volume.

Bernie Krause, advocate of wild soundscapes, has spent years recording the "biophony" of the world. In 1968, he comments, he could record fifteen hours of nature's sound and about one hour would be free of human mechanical noise. By 2001, it took nearly two thousand hours of recording to obtain one hour of natural sound. The main cause is habitat loss and the second cause is the increase of human mechanical noise. James Watt, secretary of the Interior under Reagan, commented, "To most people noise and power go hand in hand." And he promoted the idea. Loudly. Watt's protégé, Gale Norton, a later secretary of the Interior, thought that it would be a good idea to "recognize a homesteading right to pollute or make noise in an area." Where a wild soundscape is damaged by engine noise, animals are emotionally affected: in one study a biologist from Montana State University showed that stress enzyme levels in elks and wolves rose and fell in direct correlation with the rise and fall of levels of noise from snowmobiles.

Canadian composer and author R. Murray Schafer, working on the ideas of soundscape and acoustic ecology, notes the connection between loud noise and macho power: the louder the sound, the more virile the person feels. (Which may perhaps not come as a surprise to women.)

Like wilderness, women have often been described by men in terms of sound. When men have wished to express disapproval of her wildness, woman is described as noisy, she is a gossip, a chatterbox, she must be clamped with the scold's bridle, and at sea there are "sirens." Approval, by contrast, attaches to the silent woman, as to the silent oceans. The perfect woman is the Virgin Mary, hardly known for her speech making: she is blue, serene and silent as a calm, flat sea. "My gracious silence, hail!" is how Coriolanus speaks to Virgilia. The worst women are those who have opinions, who speak their minds volubly. Katherine in *The Taming of the Shrew*, is explicitly compared to a wild and stormy ocean who

Began to scold and raise up such a storm
That mortal ears might hardly endure the din.

Petruchio insists he will marry her

were she as rough
As are the swelling Adriatic seas.

Petruchio's "taming school" exists "to tame a shrew and charm her chattering tongue," and Katherine's worst characteristic to men's ears is her refusal to be silent. She is wild, as the play repeats, and her taming is equated with her silence.

The Taming of the Shrew was probably written around 1592. In 1558, John Knox, the Scottish Protestant reformer, published his full-volume airwave-ruler: "THE FIRST BLAST OF THE TRUMPET AGAINST THE MONSTROUS REGIMENT OF WOMEN." If a woman presumed to rise above a man, she must be "repressed and bridled," Knox wrote. The patriarch would rather blast the trumpet than hear women, would rather be the voice shouting in the wilderness than listening to it.

Other societies have heard nature's wild pauses and open silences. Luther Standing Bear described the childhood of the Lakota peoples in the 1870s, saying that children were taught "to listen intently when all seemingly was quiet." A Soso man, Modupe, speaking of his childhood in what was then French Guinea, said, "We learned that silences as well as sounds are significant in the forest and how to listen to the silences. . . . Deeply felt silences might be said to be the core of our Kofon religion." Vernon Harper of the Northern Cree has said, "In the Cree teachings, 'The Listening' means more than anything else to us. The Cree Indian people learn how to listen to the environment, to the wind, to the rocks. We learn how to listen to everything." Barry Lopez recalls asking a man in Anaktuvuk Pass what he did when he visited a new place. The answer: "I listen."

AND DEATH ALSO RISES

The oceans are almost as old as the earth itself. Oceanos is the genesis of all, says Homer in the *Iliad*. It washes forward over will be, washes back over was, and washes now over is, brimming with beginningness. In the mythology of island cultures, the sea is very frequently accepted as a preexistent fact, needing no explanation.

The earliest birth and the ultimate death meet here. All life, the arthropod and seaweed, comes first from the ocean and runs through endless metamorphoses to the passionflower and you. And through other endless metamorphoses, through soil and river water, via the bodies of many animals, the remains of much that once lived returns to the ocean, washes out into the sea as pale flakes of almost-sucked-out life and falls, marine snow in the ocean winter, marrow sucked from bone till only dust remains, sinking to the sea bottom.

Many cultures—and individuals—feel the oceans have a resonant frequency with death. The Viking boats of the dead were pushed out to sea. Fishermen and sailors have often believed that a flood tide meant life and strength, an ebb tide weakness and death. Walt Whitman describes an old sailor's death: "he went out with the tide and the sunset." Many people find the ocean is consoling in its bleak anthem, which refuses to lie. Death *is*.

But the wild magic of it is this, that fertility springs up from there. Right at the lowest turn of the wheel, in the most profound copulation, death and life, opposite lovers in a common seabed, roll, for from the seabed, life rolls up again, each unfurling spring, as the winter's cold waters sink and the warmer waters of the seabed roll up. The tiny, infinitesimal flecks of ex-death slip up with the streams of rising warm waters to be a peck of life for plankton, and the seas thrive, spinning a new season to life. For the sea in winter, curled up tight, taut, is compressed energy, the fiddlehead of a fern or your hot concentrated testicles in my laughing hand, ready to burst with life. From the depths comes a surge of beginning, quickening from adagio to andante and a jubilant giocoso, joking, poor old Michael Finnegan-begin-agin, the round of it all, the beginning rolled up in the end, roll up, roll up to see the amazing rolling ocean.

There is a widespread perception of the fertility of water. "Offspring" is a water metaphor for children. According to Pliny, drinking from the "offspring-giving Nile" aided Egyptian women to conceive more than three babies at once. The Aboriginal Rainbow Snake was associated with both water and fertility. Esther Managku of the Kunwinjku people in Australia tells of the Yawk Yawk, or the "Baby Dreaming," in Kudjekbingj country: little spirits live in the waters and she intercedes with them for young women who want to become pregnant. Tethys, wife of Oceanus, by legend the mother of the Nile and the other great rivers, was mother of three thousand daughters, the Oceanides. All life was born from the ocean and this is our inheritance. Seventeenth-century poet Thomas Traherne wrote, "You never enjoy the world aright, till the sea itself floweth in your veins." It already does—70.8 percent of the Earth's surface is ocean and the same proportion pertains in the human body.

The individual human life, too, begins in its own small ocean, the amniotic sac, breathing through "gills," nine months underwater in the mothering ocean. Then the waters burst, we come bobbing out, marooned, bedraggled, to cry salty drops of water at the dry strange shore where we have been jettisoned. The elderly, often drawn to retire by the seaside, are like mature rivers having run their slow full course back to the sea. I stand between offspring and old river. There is no generation gap. We all flow the same way, from the same waters to the same waters. I have my mother's hands, and mine are older now than hers as I first remember them. The present is older than the memory, as one wave can overtake an earlier one. Chilly, I skip a stone over the water. I'm effing freezing, let's go home. (We are already there.)

MOTHERSEA

W hat it is like to be a woman, the irreconcilable difference of it—that sense of living one's deepest life underwater, that dark involvement with blood and birth and death," wrote Joan Didion.

The wildernesses of waters, rivers and oceans are linked to the female. In many cultures, probably most, women are associated with what is "wet" and men with what is "dry." (This association is demeaned today, so that the playground slang for girls or effeminate boys is "drippy," "soppy" and "wet.") In Chinese thought, fire is yang, male, active, phallic and conscious. Water is yin, female, passive and unconscious. Freud and Jung, too, through analysis of folktale and ancient literature, concluded similarly: water is fertilizing, a place of regeneration; it represents what is potential and female.

For the Incas, the sea was Mamacocha, mothersea. In India, wherever rivers have been dammed, there has been a huge resistance. Why? Because everywhere, they say, "This is our mother"—every river the mother.

The relationship between men and the water wilderness is often sexual. The search for the source of the Nile was called the "romance" of the Nile. With intensely sexual overtones, Kipling writes:

Who hath desired the Sea?
His Sea as she slackens or thrills.

La mer is *la mère*, the mothering ocean in French. *El mar*, the sea, is masculine in Spanish, but as Hemingway notes, *la mar* "is what people call her in Spanish when they love her." Swinburne, in "The Triumph of Time," writes:

I will go back to the great sweet mother,
Mother and lover of men, the sea.
I will go down to her, I and none other,
Close with her, kiss her and mix her with me.

When the sea is "well behaved," she is patronizingly approved, for the good yachting sea and the good yachting wife are alike calm but breezy, helpful and sunny. Mermaids and Venus arising from the waves are also well-tamed women, tresses like wavelets (not stormy waves), pretty as a seashell, with scalloped frills of dresses, curtsying to men.

"Three things have been difficult to tame: the oceans, fools and women. We may soon be able to tame the ocean; fools and women will take a little longer," according to Nixon's vice president Spiro Agnew. Both women and the sea are tamed to be exploited. Petruchio's overt motive for taming wild Katherine is simple financial expedience: "I come to wive it wealthily in Padua." Another character describes her similarly to her father:

'Twas a commodity lay fretting by you,
'Twill bring you gain, or perish on the seas.

Shakespeare was writing of the taming of a wild woman just when wild seas were being routinely tamed by maritime empires for financial exploitation.

The (male) Doge of Venice married the (female) sea every year, and if you look at a painting of this by Canaletto, what you see is not marriage but domination, for the sea is sumptuously tamed, the ripples on the surface as ornately ordered as the brickwork of the Doge's palace. The sea has been Virgin Mary'd—a pretty creature of silenced superfluity.

It is rare to find water wilderness addressed as "he," though there are a handful of examples, the Old Man of the Sea, for instance, or Emerson, in *English Traits*, writing, "The sea is masculine, the type of active strength," while in *Moby Dick*, Melville writes of the "strong, troubled, murderous thinkings of the masculine sea." John Fowles in *Shipwreck* offers both genders: "The sea's moods and uses sex it. It is the great creatrix, feeder, womb and vagina, place of pleasure; the gentlest thing on earth, the most maternal; the most seductive whore, and handsomely the most faithless." Yet it is also male: "a giant bull . . . the patriarch who cuts that green stripling, man, down to size." But obviously it is Fowles who has sexed the sea, because he considers deceit a female characteristic and strength a male quality.

Male writers may have used the sea as an image to demean women, to caricature us, perhaps to compliment us, or even to understand us. Some women may dislike drawing parallels between women and nature; for them it has a hint of biological determinism. For me, I seize the affinity. This is not fatalism but the sheer freedom of the seas. This is real liberation, to know the wild boundlessness of the oceans within, played out in the oceans of this blue world. No one can catch flowing water. It goes where it wills. You cannot tell the sea when to swell. We are not captives of the image but liberated beyond the confines of our lives when we see our reflection in salt water.

I know I am oceanic. I fathom it in other women too. I know we can speak at the shoreline and feel in our depths. I know we are pervasive. I know we have a capacity for empathy with others as if the seawater within us flows out through our permeable nature, not recognizing the boundaries of our own skin. We flow easily into other minds. Even our voices are like waves, the pitch of our voices alters over a month, low-voiced at the menstrual edge, high-voiced at the ovulatory. We hold experiences and memory as water holds the scent of every trickling brook it's passed through (that clue the salmon smell). We dissolve, they say, into tears, as if that salty dissolution were a weakness. I cry easily, letting the inner sea out, with women or with ocean-minded men, and it is not weakness but expression; the sea expresses itself this way. And in our feral state we smell of the sea and we taste of the sea.

If I were a man, I might also feel a kinship with the seas—and if I did, I'd relish it. But I can only speak from my own waters, from my own tides, from my own life. I know my mother's mothering was like the sea and she flooded beyond the bounds of her separate self into me and my brothers, and I know that her love was a flowing water that knew no dry borders, for she was not like the sea, but she *was* the sea, as she carried us our nine months each, and in our childhoods her motherlove was open silverwater for us three fish to swim in.

Maybe what women still know through our biology—what we cannot help but know—is what modernity refuses to men; an undeniable resonance with the elemental sea. We are tidal in our moods and wombs, the high waters and low waters of mind and body. We are flux, salty blood, tears, tides, waves, ebbs and flows.

A HAZARD TO SHIPPING

The Hereford *mappa mundi* (from about A.D. 1300) shows an island marked *Hic sirenae habundant*. Here be sirens. Seductive females and voracious whirlpools are part of the sexual portrayal of the seas. Scylla, nymph made monster, sings alluringly from a rock and calls sailors to their destruction. Charybdis the whirlpool is slipperily vaginal; she "sucked down the salt sea water" and "when she swallowed the salt water down, the whole interior of her vortex was exposed," writes Homer.

At sea, the female is given two roles, at two extremes: one is the loyal waiting wife to whom the sailor is spliced, the other is the siren-voiced ocean spirit. Sailors, it is said, often go to sea to escape being tamed by the Wife on land, while they themselves try to tame and control the Wild Woman, the sea. (The ship, addressed as "she," is the perfect female to the misogynist mind: obedient, silent, never answers back.) The *Odyssey* reveals the archetype of the two poles of womanhood: Penelope is the sailor's wife at home, grieving and weaving, weaving and grieving, while at sea, "with the music of their song the Sirens cast their spell" over the seamen. (And you can spell that how you like.)

Although European culture creates two poles of womanhood—wild Kate versus the Virgin Mary, the Sirens versus Penelope—in fact the deeper truth is that every woman is both, moving from wild and stormy to peaceful and calm. Semonides of Amorgos (in the seventh century B.C.) wrote that the gods made one type of woman out of the sea. "She laughs a lot, and any stranger, seeing her, would say: 'This is certainly the best wife in the world, and the prettiest.' But the next day she won't let you near her for snapping. The summer sea might be calm and beautiful but without warning it will rage and storm. This kind of woman is exactly like the sea."

When Western culture wants to make parallels between women's wildness and waters' wildness, more than anything it is the alterings of the sea's "moods" that are noted: now tranquil, now ogreish and stormy. To be female is to be tidal, to move from the cape of ovulatory tranquillity to the sea of menstrual storms.

Hemingway's Old Man makes explicit a menstrual analogy between women and the sea: "If she did wild or wicked things it was because she could not help them. The moon affects her as it does a woman, he thought."

The Kogi people of the Sierra Nevada de Santa Marta in Colombia understand the menstruous sea. "In the beginning was blackness, only the sea. The sea was the mother. She was when she was. She was memory and possibility," they say, as reported to Alan Ereira in his television documentary "From the Heart of the World." "The great mother: she is not a distant god, she is the mind inside nature. The mother 'spun her thoughts' and she spun nine worlds. The mother bled. She had her period. She was fertile and the world was fertile." To the Kogi, the image of the loom is the central image of creation, and the earth is an immense loom on which the sun weaves the fabric of life.

This image of spinning and weaving, the back and forth of the tide, is a quintessential female image, back and forth in menstrual tides, we are the loom of the moon, the loom of the womb, each of us Penelope, each the Siren, in the Odyssey of our own lives. James Joyce in *Ulysses* writes of the loom and the female sea: "Under the upswelling tide he saw the writhing weeds lift languidly and sway reluctant arms, hising up their petticoats, in whispering water swaying and upturning coy silver fronds. Day by day: night by night: lifted, flooded and let fall. . . . To no end gathered: vainly then released, forth flowing, wending back: loom of the moon."

We and the seas are wild and wildly alike. Of Cleopatra, they said, "You cannot call her winds and waters sighs and tears." Mary Wollstonecraft wrote in her *Letters*, "For years I have endeavoured to calm an impetuous tide—labouring to make my feelings take an orderly course—It was striving against the stream."

Oceanic storms rule me and many women. We are forces of chaos, changeable as the seas, surprising, capricious, fickle, delphickle, our wisdom is as oracular and unbelieved as Cassandra cascading her wet blood-wisdom by dry ears. We are fluid and fluego, fluego and fluid, roaring our absolute disregard for bounds like the seas, which overmasculine minds desire to control, with quadrants and longitude and the terse "masculine" language of shipping—the uniform, sparse commands. But nothing can stop our oceans within becoming periodically turbulent, hurling a typhoon; woe betide a ship crossing us now: *We are a hazard to shipping.*

THE LOWER DEPTHS

The Bajo people were happy to admit that the oceans depths were frightening to them, though they said it was important not to show your fear of those depths. If you are looking for a terrifying water wilderness, it is always to the depths you must turn.

Cavernous jaws wrapped with virtually transparent gray gauzy skin, a shroud around a gaping grave. (The pale round-mouths.)

Teeth like spikes in a medieval torture chamber. (The saber-toothed viperfish.)

The image of malice, a tiny, mad eyeball with furious stare, its eyes gleaming in the dark. (The hairy anglerfish, which has also been called the sea devil.)

There is an aesthetic here. Humans find land predators such as lions frightening, but they are not necessarily ugly. To the human mind, the deep-sea creatures embody ugliness. They are hideous. They represent aspects of human ideas of hell: one creature named the "vampire squid from hell" can turn itself inside out. Other names for angler fish include the triple-wart sea devil and common black devilfish. In the depths are the blind, rasping round mouths of creatures that live on corpse flesh, sucking, groping and sawing. The creatures of the deep suggest decay, they seem ghoulish, their gray ghostliness seems a deformity of life. The eel-like "hagfish" rips flesh off other creatures, twisting its body into a knot to get better torsion. The deep-sea squid has one big eye and one little one—it is thought to hang around, motionless in the depths, its large eye looking up and its small eye looking down. Like ghosts they are associated both with darkness and with weird kinds of light. The *Opisthoproctus* has luminous bacteria in its anal gland. They—and the depths they haunt—seem to represent the lower depths of the mind, our subconscious fears made flesh and living beneath us. With suggestions of incubi, small male anglerfish bite into the much larger female's belly until the two become fused and her circulation takes over for both, so he is a permanently attached sperm supply. There are deep-sea creatures that look like half-slaughtered, gashed ghosts vengeful and near to death, but ready to devour.

The iconography of hell seems based on terror and revulsion at these creatures, as if in the subconscious of our species persist memories of these shocking and starving nightmares from the abyss: teeth and trickery, ghost and shroud, the glaring eye in the dark.

Shallow water has played a vital part in the evolution of life. The abyss, though, is forbidding to life because of the immense pressure, cold and dark. Even when there was life in the deeps, it only evolved slowly and creatures remained the same here for millennia. Six-gilled sharks have existed unchanged for 150 million years, living in waters as deep as 2,500 meters (8,202 feet).

The rhythms of life and light lie always above, for neither time nor tide reach down here. No season, no sun, no pull of moon, no change. The Challenger Deep in the Pacific's Mariana Trench descends over eleven kilometers (seven miles). As you descend, the symphonies and soloists of reef grow quiet: you go deeper down into the depths of silence. The trenches of the abyss are dark not with the darkness of night but the thicker, deeper dark where there has never been light, though just occasionally there are darks of extra shadows, deeper thicknesses. Very little moves in the hollow, chill waters, a wilderness of *devastasis*, a perpetual state of unmoving, unchanging vast water. The human eye may clutch at the deep-sea creatures as if they will relieve us of this pitiless torque of dark but they don't, for they seem to embody the spirit of the deep even more than the darkness does. In the abyss are the inevitable final throes of death, all the throws of life's dice, the rose and lice and lilac and peewit finally sink, slow, the last meaning sucked out a mile above, now devoured, final and sunk.

About half the world is ocean depths, miles down black, as if the world above represented the light half and the world below the dark, as if half was awake and half was asleep. Asleep and troubled with nightmares.

As you first dip underwater you see the lovely lightwater of the surface, shimmering liquid curtains of bright shadow, drifting in currents, skeins of fluent light, struations of shining floodlight. Light fades as you sink. The rays of reds are gone by two or three hundred feet, the rainbow reduced. In the twilight zone, creatures are silver and gray, opalescent and pale. Deeper, the light is pearly, misty, a glint trickling through water. After the greens give out and by a thousand feet down, there are only blues and violets—the bluelight brilliant, intense and cold. If the water is clear there may be violet rays still a thousand feet farther. And ultraviolet, though we cannot see it, the ultraviolet, which reaches deepest of all.

Curling opaque light courses downward, then dims into near darkness. All color is bled out, and only remains remain, earbone of whale and tooth of shark, bleached bone and leached color. A gleam of light tickles the water one last time and is gone. At the limit of where the light can reach, though, for a twentieth part of the day, the pure, straight longest rays of the midday sun at its height penetrate—though even this can only make of the dark a violet-black, bruised twilight.

In this dark, like the darkness of space, there is a kind of starlight, as many creatures flash with bioluminescence. (Perhaps half of all fish of the dark waters are luminescent.) The mind longs for light where there is none, it catches at any glinting zigzag, any streaming iridescence. The "Dumbo" octopus peacefully floats like a plump, pearly-pale aubade for a dawn that has never yet broken in the depths. The almost totally transparent deep-sea amphipod Cystisoma is like a glassy arpeggio, each visible outline of leg, tail or antenna a note with a blue silence in between. Almost nothing is visible.

But pause a moment. Think the other way. Instead of imagining losing colors into blackness, imagine how it might be to see colors arising, lifting out of the dark, imagine what it would be like to first see color in darkness, that rapturous hour when turquoise first sang itself out, to the waters' pure amazement.

Blue, lowest of colors, is everywhere. Two blues are water-related words, navy and ultramarine ("from beyond the sea"). Fish come in all shades of blue, powder blue, lapis lazuli, indigo (lustrous and low) or the serenade of pure azure, sapphire fish flashing across a reef like violins across the arc of an afternoon. You can almost hear the blue, a vivid vibrancy, a ringing blue. Blue is the last color to be named in many societies, according to anthropologists—perhaps because it is remembered from the deepest memories of evolution, a remembered blue that thrills along the veins with a timbre of its own, a pitch where color is sound and sound color, where low light shines. Blue has the intensity of the pitch of grief or love, blue fathoms the past as no other color. Blue is the color of the eternal in European color symbolism, the blue ocean is Emily Dickinson's "deep Eternity."

Blue is the color of barrenness too, the open sea far from land is a lifeless blue in contrast to the lively, leafy greens of the coasts. As all the deepest visible colors are blue, so the lowest of feelings are blue. Humans know a rainbow of emotions, from the livid reds of anger, the exultation of oranges in the sun, yellows of happiness in candlelight, greens of woodlands, allotment-contentment, down to the pale blues of yearning or nostalgia, the deeper blues of sadness, getting the blues.

And then there's the ultraviolet, the color invisible to others but which one knows in oneself, the anguish of depression, ultraviolent, lowest of all feelings, most barren and close to death. That waste of life, that wasteland of the mind.

Where there are no maps.

MAPS

A Dutch anthropologist in Sulawesi told me of the glee with which the Bugis people seized on maps, immediately grasping their symbolic import. A central aim for the Bugis people is to get the human world as far from nature as possible, he explained, living by the Word of the Qur'an, not by feeling or "natural" intuition. Nature was equated with disorder and people with order. So, he said, when Dutch cartographers first came to make maps, it struck the Bugis as a really civilized thing to do, to turn the horrible mess of nature into a symbolic paper description.

Maps seem to control wild nature as clocks appear to control wild time. In the early years of the European so-called "discovery" of the world, sixteenth-century technicians' work often straddled both clockmaking and mapmaking. (Kaspar Brunner was master of ordnance and clockmaker.) Ever since Harrison's chronometer, the ability to "master" wild time and the consequent precise calculation of longitude, unfenced time was boxed into hours and minutes, and oceans and lands were ruled and fenced into lines and grids.

"Wilderness" became identified with the blank spaces on the maps, as Marlow, Conrad's narrator of *Heart of Darkness*, remarks: "Now when I was a little chap I had a passion for maps. I would . . . lose myself in all the glories of exploration. At that time there were many blank spaces on the earth." By the time he grew up, one such place "had ceased to be a blank space of delightful mystery—a white patch for a boy to dream gloriously over. It had become a place of darkness." The white spaces are virginal and their "blankness" is a hollow, to be filled in by men. In cartography these blanks are sometimes known as "sleeping beauties"—the sexual suggestion is of passive, unconscious and female land, which needs to be woken by the active male will, the kiss of the cartographer-prince, the stroke of his pen. In Conrad's work, "wild" land, like woman, is flung to the poles of meaning. She is either virgin or vamp, either the white patch for a boy to dream over (hmm) or the sinful whoreheart of darkness. Further, the blank spaces were terra incognita—"unknown"—to the mapping nations. Once "known," they lost their virginity, just as a man can "have knowledge" of a woman in the biblical sense.

When the Spanish came upon the Galápagos Islands in the sixteenth century, they called them Las Islas Encantades. You could translate this as "enchanted" isles, but a truer translation is "bewitched"—to men who believed in literal witchcraft. These islands, in their feminine wiles, wildly resistant to mapmakers' demands, refused to stay put. Bewildered, some mariners became convinced they were floating islands, and only much later did people realize that idiosyncratic sea currents and frequent mists, rather than female witchery, caused these islands to be so hard to pin down.

More recently, the identification of "wilderness" with the blank spaces on the map has been dear to wilderness protectors. Aldo Leopold's cry "Of what avail are forty freedoms without a blank space on the map" has been taken up by others arguing that wilderness areas should not be mapped; that managers of wildernesses should print no maps for the area; that visitors should be discouraged from carrying old maps of the area with them. It is as if the identification of woman with land still persists, and as explorers of old wanted to "penetrate" wilderness as sexual conquest, today some men feel a chivalrous urge to protect the fragile maidenland from those who would fuck (with) her.

Of all areas on earth, the oceans are still the least mapped. More is known about the surface of Mars than about most of the sea floor, and the deeps are almost completely unmapped. Ten square kilometers of deep-sea floor have been mapped, while 300 million have not. More people have been to space than to the bottom of the ocean, and only five submersibles in the world can get down to the abyssal plains.

Sea maps (sometimes called Neptunes, as land maps were Atlases) were really coastal maps, and for generations, losing sight of land could be terrifying. Conrad in *Falk* writes of the stricken ship drifting down into Antarctica, "They had drifted south out of men's knowledge." The earliest European sailing directions to the Americas were "south, till the butter melts, then west."

"It's not down on any map. True places never are," wrote Melville in *Moby Dick*. There is a tricky relationship between map and truth. The most any map can offer is a truth, but the conventional maps of the West pretend they are the truth, that monotruth so dear to monotheistic cultures. Ordnance Survey, the way, the truth and the map, a universalized, uniform way of representing the diverse earth.

Around the world, though, there are thousands of maps: maps of the mind, maps that the sun makes on a loom of light, maps in the mind of humpback whales, moral maps and maps to heaven.

In the States, world maps show North America at the center of the world, while the British go one better, not only organizing world maps with Britain in the middle of the world but also with noon running slap bang straight through Greenwich. From Greenwich, both empires of land and empires of time were ruled. Like the British, the Anaguta of the Jos Plateau in northern Nigeria think they live at noon at the center of the earth. "Time flows past the permanent central position . . . they live at a place called noon, at the center of the world, the only place where space and time intersect," according to Stanley Diamond in his *Anaguta Cosmography*. Unlike the Anaguta, though, the British went full steam ahead to impose their noon, their monotime, on all the diverse and wild times of the world, and to impose their monomap on all the diverse and wild lands.

The Kogi people feel themselves to live in the heart of their world in a place that is mapped to a perfect integrity, coherent and ordered at all levels. Their maps are geographical, anatomical, sexual, cosmological and spiritual. Their way of thinking gives meaning, via mappedness, to everything. Gerardo Reichel-Dolmatoff describes their mapped-mindedness in *The Loom of Life: A Kogi Principle of Integration*. The human body is identified with certain topographical features of the Sierra Nevada and these features mark the outlines of a loom. "A loom—any loom—thus becomes a map of both land and human body" and the expression "the part where one does the weaving" has an overt sexual connotation. Spinning and weaving represent moral maps too, the rules of Kogi life: responsibility, cooperation, nonaggression, truthfulness, obedience and sobriety.

Maps of land, for Aboriginal Australians, can be made in bark painting or body painting, which become performative maps. They represent the land's primordial nature and rarely refer to literal boundaries. No European settlement or road is included on them, for that is not the land's truth.

Some indigenous people have begun to map their sacred sites in an effort to protect them, but this "cultural mapping" can backfire. The Mirrar people of Australia, who long opposed the Jabiluka uranium mine on their lands, were not particularly keen to carry out cultural mapping, revealing their sacred sites. Perhaps because if you name one place as sacred, then (to a dualist-minded Western company) you're calling another place profane. And therefore a good spot for a uranium mine. Perhaps it is wiser to avoid being too specific about where sacredness begins and ends. Because it doesn't exactly begin and end. And even if it did, why tell Rio Tinto?

Hugh Brody, in *Maps and Dreams*, describes Native American people of northeast British Columbia who map not only their hunting areas but also the trails to heaven, and these maps are revealed to hunters in their dreams. He is told, "You may laugh at these maps of the trails to heaven, but they were done by the good men who had the heaven dream, who wanted to tell the truth. They worked hard on their truth." He is shown such a map, a moosehide bundle, and he is told, "Up here is heaven; this is the trail that must be followed; here is a wrong direction." A corner of the map was missing and Brody is told the reason: "Someone had died who would not easily find his way to heaven, so the owner of the map had cut a piece of it and buried it with the body. With the aid of even a fragment . . . the dead man would probably find the correct trail."

Early European maps were spiritual maps, representing how important was Christ to their view of the world. The Ebstorf map, thought to have been completed around 1250, shows the Word of god made Map. Christ's head is at the top of the world, his feet at the bottom, his hands embrace its sides. At the heart of the map is Jerusalem, and upward (eastward) toward the risen sun and the Risen Son of god lies the Garden of Eden, the Four Rivers of Paradise. The map represents the mind of the times, makes literal its moral compass. The point of the map was not so much to make acquaintance with this world but to relate this world to the hereafter. It was a map of the trail to heaven, if you will.

In Thailand, up until the mid-nineteenth century, two types of map existed. One, like the Ebstorf map, was cosmography, another map to heaven, in this case a representation of the Buddhist worldview, its heavens, hells and earths. Thai life was (and is) marked by a striking contrast between its sacred and profane aspects, and the second type of map was the pragmatic diagram map for warfare and coastal shipping. Similarly, while Western nations had their sacred maps, the *mappae mundi*, they also had their profane ones, the *portolani*—realistic maps showing coastal information and trade routes.

Cultures choose what to make prominent on their maps according to what they value. Gerard Mercator, born Gerhard Kremer, Latinized his happily apt name from the Flemish. *Mercator*, means "merchant," the class for whom he scribed his map. Maps of trade lay the land out before you, for you to exploit as you will. *Treasure Island* begins with a map locating the treasure, just as survey maps pinpoint the treasure of minerals and oils.

The most readily obtainable maps today are tourist maps and road maps. In terms of available information, our map of the world is as peculiar as the Ebstorf map, the Tourist replacing Christ, straddling their power across the world, Ibiza the Jerusalem, Koh Samui the palm-fringed Paradise with near-naked Eves: how to get to heaven on the cheap.

Maps are representations of power and also a means to power: for commerce, for tourism, for mining, for invading sovereign countries and for stating the extent of empire and the seats of power. Maps will show government buildings but never mark the place in a city where people go to protest. The first "road maps" were made in the mid-thirteenth century, and made in connection with the Crusades. For today's so-called "crusade" against the "axis of evil," the U.S. Army bulk-ordered maps of Iraq before the first invasion of 1991. It was a country pinned down before it was attacked. "Give me a map," growled Marlowe's Tamburlaine.

> Give me a map; then let me see how much
> Is left for me to conquer all the world.

In the Roman Empire, maps were owned and used only by state authorities and the possession of a map by an individual was considered a criminal offense. For hundreds of years, governments have used maps and boundaries to deny, restrict or erase land rights to indigenous people. Sure-yani Poroso showed me two maps of Bolivia, one from before 1920, with Leco territory marked on it, the other a few years later. In the latter, his people's land has been "disappeared"—wiped off the map. "My people looked at these two maps and they started crying," he said, and he could not speak. He had tears running down his cheeks, and he continued, "My people wept seeing these maps; they didn't know how to read and write but they understood this."

Maps have cropped up in many conversations I've had with indigenous people—any maps I have brought with me are pored over and they have always wanted to show me theirs. They unfold them, trace them with their fingers—maps always arouse interest and enthusiasm. Westerners look at a map with purpose in mind, wanting the map as a tool for a journey or as a representation of ownership. Indigenous people look differently. A map evokes the land, and this evocation delights them; they look at a map longingly as you might gaze closely at a portrait of a friend, in recognition, to compare your memory with its representation, in impurposive love.

Orthographic maps take the visual position of the ultraobjective, the so-called "eye of god"—a projection onto a surface at an infinite distance, an uninvolved, unreciprocal stare. Modern maps pretend to be the highest authority, perfect in accuracy. Conceptually, the map is the edict of power, the declarative statement, neither dialogue nor question, policing the wild, putting all the world behind bars. Interestingly, the inventor of coordinate geometry, which led to the possibility of accurate mapmaking, the objective representation split from subjective coinvolvement, was none other than Descartes.

One of the greatest powers that mapmakers have is their power to name. Feminist language specialist Dale Spender thinks that the division of power in naming is so fundamental and universal that she describes the world as composed of "The Namers" and "The Named." To name is to tame, or at least to partially "catch" a place. In the English language, a good description or accurate portrait "captures" its subject. Naming in language is a way to take captive what is conceptually wild, and perhaps no language expresses this better than Saami, where the same words are used for both "learning a language" and "looking to see if there is anything caught in the snare."

In the days of European expansion, the invaders dominated the lands they saw by naming them, frequently with their related gods of Finance and Christianity. Colonial Africa (from around 1880 to 1960) was littered with names according to their monetary value to Europeans, the Gold Coast, Côte d'Ivoire; or according to their ownership, the British Cameroons, the French Sudan; or after European individuals such as Lake Albert and Victoria Falls, so the Namers could look at a map and see themselves reflected there. Science, too, maps the moon, naming its craters after astronomers, and is thus able to look at the moon and see itself reflected back: Copernicus, Tycho and Kepler.

Names are given to express power in all forms: language power, colonial power, spiritual power, royal power, financial power, explorer power (Baffin Island), academic power (the Astronomical Society Islands in Nunavut) and cultural power (the Musicians Seamounts, north of Hawaii, include Bach Ridge, Beethoven Ridge, Mount Mozart, Gluck Seamount and Puccini Seamount.)

Rarely, though, has biscuit power been celebrated in the nomenclature of nations. But as James Hamilton-Paterson describes, an area of the Atlantic seabed to the west of Spain celebrates British biscuits. There is the Peake Deep (which a captain modestly named after his own good self) and a later expedition found a second Deep, which they called "Freane." Two ridges nearby were named Huntley Ridge and Palmer Ridge. And, last and sweetly least, Crumb Seamount.

Australian wilderness artist John Wolseley, keenly aware of the colonialist timbre of much Australian art, speaks of subverting the strategies of surveyors and mapmakers. He is always out on the land, and always refuses to walk in straight lines. Wandering, he is an antimapper, in tune with the antiauthoritarian Lettristes and Situationists, in their "drifting" and "psychogeography." The art of drifting was an antimapping experience and the idea was to wander, to meander around a city, at every moment being alive to whatever drew you. You were in thrall to the spirit of place, rather than having place under your thumb, on a map, on a plan. The material gained from psychogeography was used for "emotional maps" of areas, the opposite of the eye-of-god objectivity to which mapmakers aspired.

Modern maps have an odd characteristic. They never show wildness. They cannot show it, for they are implacably opposed to it. Maps are cages in which to imprison wild land. Maps put wildness in chains of measurement, corral it till its wildness dies. No shark lurks, no wild boar crashes in the undergrowth. Cartography hunts down wildness, tracking nature in the crosshairs of the grid, shooting it like an animal and pinning the parched dried skin up on the wall; the map is the ultimate hunting trophy. The only things that can "grow" on most maps are human constructions: towns, buildings and roads. To look at a series of maps of one place over the years is to see nature as static background, but to watch Edifice grow, its only tendrils are tarmac, its only saplings concrete, its only leaves made of brick.

Early maps purported to give information about strange phantasmagoric animals, the denizens of the wilderness, the creatures of a scary ocean, two-legged dragons, dog-headed people, weird beasties, amalgamations of several different animals, which showed the devilish nature of disorder. "Wild" people, too, were vilified on maps—the giant twice as large as a man, whom they called *patagon*, the Bigfoot of Patagonia, dehumanized in order to justify an attack. One of the most famous mapmakers was "Sir John Mandeville," published by the ineffably named Wynkyn de Worde. He described geese with two heads, thirty-foot-tall giants, ants as big as dogs. His "travels" were enormously influential—and entirely invented—and he has been roundly censured for being a fraud. But this isn't the point. The denunciations presuppose that what was sought was literal truth. The opposite is the case. When any people go to war, their governors give them propaganda to make the enemy hateful, and these maps were a kind of early propaganda against the enemy, wilderness. For all propaganda must first make the enemy frightening, hideous, bestial and unnatural: the body of a unicorn, the paw of a weasel, the tail of an anchovy: wild nature was to be feared first, then defeated.

There is a perfectness to maps. Land is perfected, over, finished, and there is no life left in it. But wildness slips away, swims through the net of the map. The wild world is simply too wonderfully four-dimensional to be caught. Waterwild, especially, is unmappable and flows through the grasping fingers of mapmakers. You may net the world in grids of latitude, but you will never net the water. Tides may be described on a map by the line of dryness, but ebb they will and flow they will. Rivers are drawn in a thin dry line, but flood they will, still. And when they want to.

Furthermore, water wildernesses are mapped in minds other than our own. Green turtles can find their way across 1,500 miles of ocean to reach the tiny island of Ascension (just 7 miles wide) to lay their eggs at the same turtle rookery where they themselves hatched out. No human knows how they do this. Humpback whales have maps in mind and may be informed by sun and moon and tides, by hydrothermal vents, coral reefs and the underwater mountain ranges. Perhaps the map in its mind may be music, composed of pure sound, the memory of echolocation. Whales navigate through sound, they express themselves in sound, they think with musical meaning and remember in song: it seems to me more likely than not that their maps are nothing less than songlines that they can follow from the Arctic to the Galápagos Islands.

PARADISO GIOCOSO

Whales are serious about play, in deliberate delphic delight, in a porpoiseful paradise, having a whale of a time. Cetaceans play with feathers and flotsam, twigs and jetsam, turtle-teasing, buoyant and bubble-blowing. Play is at the height of their culture and they make the entire Pacific ring to their paradise tune. "Eden saw play," the hymn says; actually Eden *was* play, for "Eden" was the Hebrew word for delight.

The ancient Greeks believed that Ocean is where the earth ended and heaven began and the whales knew that too. They had no need to search for paradise in the past or the future or on any island—dolphins could recognize an Eden when they echolocated one. The geographer Posidonius wrote that the ocean "stretched to infinity." Whales, who presumably knew that the Earth was round a long time before humans, ascertained that fact, knew it was finite in area, but infinite in beauty and paradisality. It is also our paradise lost, this place we crawled out of to begin our dry existence on earth, as if Genesis and Darwin were both right, and there is a paradise from which we are now too evolved ever to return.

Or can we? "Back to nature? Farewell to civilization? It is one thing to dream of it and another to do it. I tried it. Tried to return to nature. Crushed my watch between two stones and let my hair and beard grow wild. . . . I tried to enter the wilderness empty-handed and barefoot, as a man at one with nature." Thus Thor Heyerdahl in *Fatu-Hiva*, on his glorious, youthful attempt to seize paradise like a watermelon in both hands and cram his lovely smiling face full of it.

The idea of wilderness has a complex history. It has negative connotations of chaos; savage, frightening and deadly nature beyond the safety of human walls. But it has also suggested a heaven on earth. "Wilderness" has been seen as both the paradise *and* the snake. Wilderness has been sited on both sides of the wall.

When wilderness has been associated with paradise, it is often seen not in the present but the past—a place still existing from the dawn of the world. In a British expedition to Australia in 1801, the naval officer Matthew Flinders took his ship to Kangaroo Island off the southern coast. It was a place, he remarked, where the Golden Age still seemed to endure. Thomas Livingstone Mitchell, a Scot who made four expeditions to New South Wales between 1831 and 1846, writes that the land "lay before me with all its features new and untouched as they fell from the hands of the Creator . . . it was indeed a sort of paradise to me."

Columbus, who famously confused West with East, was in absolutely no doubt about one thing: he had discovered paradise, he had found "the original abode of our first parents, the primitive seat of human innocence and bliss, the Garden of Eden." He stated that the Earth is not round but is "in the shape of a pear which is round everywhere except where the stalk is, there it is higher: or it is like a very round ball, on one part of which is placed something like a woman's breast and this nipple part is the highest and closest to heaven." He reported that he was "sailing gently up it" but (becoming *slightly* overliteral) "do not expect that any man can get to the nipple, for that is Paradise itself, from which we are barred."

UTOPIA

The oceans are a theater of desire, where sailors have strained for the sight of the coastline of Utopia, from the crazed Columbus's nipple of paradise to the lost Atlantis, Insulae Fortunatae, the Isles of Bliss, the Isles of the Blessed, these misted coastlines of the mind, touching past and future but never present, almost visible behind as nostalgia, almost visible ahead as longing, which are never-quite-but-almost seen, a partial glimpse, a shadowy outline through a frayed cloud, a smudged shore, never sure, nearly found but never quite. When the sites of these fantasy places are explored and no fantasy found, the fantasy is never lost but softly, silently shifts to another place, always, ever, just out of reach. Those who make literal searches for them never find them, for these places *are* not, yet they are: they are a psychological state, the thirsty longing for sweet contentment; the open-hearted hope that knows no grid reference. And doesn't want one.

With the increasingly exact mapping of the real world, the irreal longings moved off the maps altogether into literature, the most famous early example being Thomas More's *Utopia* of 1516.

Of all the utopias and dystopias written over the years, there are two that demonstrate the most polarized attitudes to wildness. The first is Francis Bacon's *New Atlantis*, published in 1627. The second is Yevgeny Zamyatin's *We*, written in 1920. *New Atlantis* describes a supposed utopia, perfect because wildness has been controlled to death. *We* shows a dystopia where wildness is the only possible salvation. *New Atlantis*, the work of a woman-hating mind, is the apotheosis of control, where everything is ordered and nothing allowed its own wild will: it is a manifesto against the wild. In *We*, wildness is personified in a woman and wildness represents the only possible opposition to the deadly overcontrol of the state.

In *New Atlantis*, the narrator begins in the South Seas. His ship is blown off course by the wind—nature, from the start, is self-willed and hated by those who wish to control both her courses and their own. The crew find themselves "in the midst of the greatest wilderness of waters in the world," where they abandon hope and think they will die. Wilderness is set up as the counterpoint, the deadly chaos in contrast to the perfect island state, which the crew find on the island of engineers.

The engineers have knowledge of other cultures, and have a statue in honor of Columbus. Also honored from European culture are "the inventor of ships" and "your monk that was the inventor of ordnance and of gunpowder." This supposedly ideal society has invented a hideous arsenal of explosives and weaponry—including something much like napalm, something "stronger and more violent" than any invented in Bacon's own time.

Time, wild and slippery, has been caged here, in many different clocks, and wild chance is not welcome in their experiments. Nothing is left wild: even plants must conform to a rigid order. All things, all people, all behaviors are ruled and clockworked. Nature's wildness is controlled in an astonishing passage prescient of genetic engineering where Bacon describes how self-willed nature and self-willed time are both subjected to the will of man. By their engineering, they make "trees and flowers to come earlier or later than their seasons; and to come up and bear more speedily than by their natural course they do. We make them also by art greater much than their nature."

The word *u-topia* means "a no-place." Bacon intends this as a "eu-topia," a good place, because all is perfected. Nature has been engineered out of evolution, so there is no more chance, no more self-willed nature, no more uproar in the wild margin. Bacon's island is a dry and rigid place surrounded by the flowing, wild seas. Like so many alleged eutopias, it is as awful as any dystopia, because what is perfect is finished, over, unchanging, absolute and fixed. What is perfect is dead.

But wildness and life lean toward the changeable, mutable and imperfect.

Imperfect Eve, first to fall, gives us life in the dark, wet, wild. Evolution is never perfect, never perfected, never finished.

Zamyatin's *We* describes a future totalitarian world, where wildness is the enemy of the state. (The book was the inspiration for Orwell's *1984*, and it is a far richer, far more interesting, though far less known work.) The state, called The One State, has perfected all life until there's almost no juice left in it. The One State is an entirely artificial, erected civilization, a world of edifice and wall. The book's narrator, who, like everyone, has no name but only a number (D503), describes for the reader both his own world and the world of the "ancients"—our own world. In The One State, a key to controlling people is controlling their time, and everyone's hours are clockworked to the Tables of Hourly Commandments. The "greatest of all the monuments of ancient literature" is the "Time-Tables of All the Railroads"—Zamyatin having an unerring ear for that fascistic compulsion to tame wild time.

In the time of "the ancients," the sky was "still untamed," but under The One State, the sky is overcast with special technology to disperse light evenly and keep out weather. All the "wild world" is "long since exiled beyond the Green Wall" and there, we gradually understand, is wildness, in all its anarchic, roaring green life, walled out. Walls themselves are iconic in The One State: "Man ceased to be a wild animal only when he had built his first wall." It is a world that controls its environment completely—harnessing and taming the sea's wildness: "From a feral beast spattering foam we have made a domestic animal."

When Zamyatin wants to describe the wildness on the other side of the Green Wall, he leans to metaphors of wild water. "Out of the unencompassable ocean of greenery on the other side of the Wall a raging billow of roots, flowers, boughs, leaves came surging toward me; it reared up on end, was on the verge of sweeping over me . . . the irrational, hideous world of trees, birds, animals." The book's messenger of wildness is a woman, E330: sensual, illicit, and independent-minded, and the narrator's potential savior.

E330 plays the piano, and is told to play Scriabin, in order to demonstrate the state's disapproval of the ancients, because the music illustrates the "wild, spasmodic, motley" of "that wild epoch" with its suggestion of "a wild, careering, scorching-searing sun . . . how self-willed the music of the ancients." She plays with such ferocious passion that it has the opposite effect—it kindles a

wild love in the narrator, not just for her but for all she represents, vivid, sexual, colorful, thriving wild life. He follows her to the Green Wall, imagining
that it has been demolished and the water-wild has flooded in, hoping that
"everything that had been beyond it had rushed in like a tidal wave." But The
One State cannot allow this most subversive of transgressions. The wilderness beyond the Green Wall has a counterpart in the human mind: imagination, or fantasy, so The One State invents a medical operation to remove
fantasy from the brain: a fantasiectomy. With this operation, The One State
blares, "You are perfect; you are on a par with machines." Francis Bacon would
have applauded.

CALIGULA TO THE SEAS

In the Bajo village, I talked to one old man, Saurin Pontoh, snoozing and
smoking after lunch. There are spirits in the deeps, he said—and spirits in
the shallows. They are sometimes frightening and sometimes not but, he
warned, if people at sea see something strange (a head of a person, for example, in the sea, which would actually be the sign of the spirit), they must not
gasp or show shock, for that is forbidden; the spirit is like a human, so you
should not be surprised to see it sometimes in human form.

One of the things that angers the sea, he said, is throwing useful things
(he names cigarettes and food) into the sea without ceremony. The Bajo people fear the anger of the sea spirits, which can create storms, though there are
certain rituals that can be performed on the open sea to stop a storm. But,
said Saurin, it's a secret. He doesn't like to tell people what it is. He described
in outline how he would go to the front of the canoe with his paddle, moving the paddle from side to side, like a shield rebuffing arrows, until the
storm is fended off. He showed me his traditional goggles, which were glass
lenses, bonded to wooden frames with a rubber strap. These goggles were
in use well before modern kinds, for the Bajo people realized long ago that
with goggles you could see better underwater. He regularly dives twenty meters underwater. Tying stones to themselves, sea gypsies can sink deep and
stay underwater long enough to forage for food, including sea slugs and fish.

To the Bajo people, the sea represents relationships of respect, and is a place of knowledge and understanding. The sea to the Bajo is "alive" with character and morality, and they take the wild untamed freedom of the open seas as a birthright—"We prize freedom," they said. Far from being an empty wasteland, the seas are full, wild with storm spirits, now playful, now potent.

Meanwhile the seas were getting choppy. The weather was turning jumpy and so was the boatman. The journey back to the small quiet island where I was staying was almost two hours. We left, and as we did the wind picked up, the waves far too high for comfort; all of us were worried, the boatman most of all, as the motor cut out repeatedly, leaving the boat tossing like a tin can, useless litter among the sucking waves.

Like many sea-sensitive peoples, the Bajo have a special respect for dolphins. To the ancient Greeks, dolphins were companions of the gods, and indeed the gods sometimes manifested themselves as dolphins. Apollo, god of music, sometimes transformed himself into a dolphin, and as Heathcote Williams points out, the Delphic oracle was named after wisdom of the dolphin kind. To dream of dolphins was a good omen, while to kill a dolphin was as bad as killing a person. The Bajo people (who, like indigenous people the world over, are keen hunters) say they never kill a dolphin, because it is "good" and "likes to help people." They don't kill whales either, because they're "lovely"—a reason surprisingly emotional for any hunter-gatherer people. Whales and dolphins are intelligent, say the Bajo: they lead people to fish. They help people who are injured in the water, jumping high so that another boat out on the seas will notice and come over. Dolphins will also push injured people toward a boat or will indicate to a person to hold on to a fin, and then the dolphin will swim to a boat.

Millennia ago, marine creatures crawled out of the ocean to live on land. And then, millennia ago, some moved from the land back to the waters again. Lucian, in *Dialogues of the Sea Gods*, describes a conversation between Poseidon and the Dolphin, who says, "Don't be surprised, Poseidon, that we're kind to men. We were men ourselves before we became fishes." The kindness of dolphins to humans is well recorded, if unfathomable, considering the unkindness of our kind to them. The Chukchi people of Chukotka have tales in which whales and dolphins are described as relatives of mankind. (The kind, wild ones.)

But where wildness shimmered and sang through dolphins and calling

198 WILD An Elemental Journey

whales, modernity is imposing a wasteland: bleak, toxic and silent. Highly sensitive to temperature, coral can "bleach," lose its colored algae and die, making it painfully sensitive to climate change. Entire reefs become ice-ghosts of white skeleton in the blue—of their coral are bones made—as the coral, which can be several hundreds or thousands of years old, carves its own last lines of an underwater tragedy. Remote reefs have been used for nuclear experiments and for dumping waste. Agrichemicals and industrial toxins are shunted out to coral reefs, poisoning them. Modernity behaves like Caligula doing battle against the oceans—Caligula, who, after a storm had sunk a thousand ships, announced that he would take his revenge: "I have a quarrel with Neptune." Insane and violent, Caligula sent his archers and cavalry into battle against the sea, and rode forward himself, cutting at the waves with his sword as the infantry hacked at the waters.

Commercial whaling involves "bombing" whales with explosives that detonate within the body of the whale. Other whales are grief-struck by these deaths, which they do not understand. And the deaths come in such numbers that whales are stunned by them, so the orphaned few haunt the empty oceans still calling for the rest, the ghost whales whose songs they still remember. So there are virtually no more Greenland whales. Humpback, fin and sei whales nearly became extinct. (The Antarctic blue was reduced from a quarter of a million to a few thousand. People made golf bags from the penises of the blue whale.) Of the dolphins, the snubfins, bottle-nosed, melon-heads, spinners, spotted and piebald, the Irrawaddy, the hourglass have been killed in their millions. Giant gill netters throw shrouds of nets over miles of ocean, killing dolphins as casual collateral damage. The dolphins, their jaws ripped off, their beaks broken, are washed up onto shores in mute reproach. The intelligence and sensitivity of dolphins were turned into weapons as the U.S. and former Soviet navies trained dolphins for military use as "guard dolphins." The Soviet navy reportedly sent dolphins on "suicide bombing" missions with explosives strapped to their bodies, to blow up enemy submarines. It is also alleged that dolphins trained by the U.S. Navy carried small explosive charges under their necks, which could be detonated if the dolphins chose to "desert."

But there is wonder still in the seas, still glory, still wildness, ultramarine and minded, a kind of mind we need.

Maybe—and we do not know this—whales and dolphins have an idea of their evolution and ours. Maybe—and we do not know this—they have a theory of those distant changes formed not on the basis of time but of water, those most-evolved being the most marine-minded. Maybe they think that they are the world's most intricately sophisticated creatures, choosing to move back into the water, a judgment based on music and how sound carries farthest and most ecstatically. Maybe for them there's no hierarchy of future over past. Maybe quite the contrary. Maybe the past seemed a wise place. Maybe they have songs for yesterday—their brains are theoretically able to hold such a concept—but no song for tomorrow, because they extrapolate from their present into their extinction. Maybe they have another idea of "maybe" not to do with event or being but to do with sound: maysound, mayhear, maysong, maymusic, in the tentative, suggestive, optative acoustic of potential. Maybe. We do not know.

We do not know their wild ocean minds, cognizant of the waters we returned to late and understand little. Where still, the dolphin, its legato smile beguiling, yodels as it swims, desirous, velvet and smiling over an easy sea.

Wild Fire

OUT BUSH

All children, black or white, born in the hospital in Alice Springs are of the Caterpillar Dreaming. This creates relationships between people; so Anjou, a three-year-old white child, was thus the "baby grub" of a local Arrernte woman, Magdalene.

Magdalene was so old that her granddaughters were grandmothers now. When I met her, she was perched on her veranda, an ancient wisp of blindness, more spirit than substance, ashy with years. A fine filigree of lines, necklaces of time, traced light arcs around her throat. She walked with great difficulty. Her eyes were sealed shut with trachoma and were sunken, dusty in their sockets, with the blue-purple bloom of plums. She touched people to know them, holding Anjou's mother's hand for ages, stroking it, feeling it, murmuring quietly.

Lareena's hand was a fragile, sensitive hand, white and young. Magdalene's old black hand was wrinkled and soft, crumpled as tissue paper, light as a feather, full of knowledge and story. Touch was the only language they shared and both had eloquent hands, Lareena's querying and delicate, Magdalene's sadder and more knowing. As old as the last century, she grew up in the deserts before the whites came. She wouldn't talk about old times, though, for as she said haltingly to Rod, Anjou's father, "It make me too sorry." Her language surrounded her mistily, she spoke softly. She knew very little English and was fluent with no words except a rapid "fuckingcunt"—a phrase she used often and mellowly, more like a gentle "bugger."

When we had arrived at Magdalene's community and got out of the truck, twenty hungry cats had poured into it like monkeys in a Hindu temple. There were shacks of corrugated iron and rusty upended vehicles everywhere. A small boy with a rubber dinosaur was chasing his smaller brother, who was crying. The dinosaur was taken away from the first boy, whereupon he cried too. Half an oil drum was used as a firepit and the ashes were still warm. Someone relit the fire, tossing a handful of gum leaves onto it, to light cigarettes.

While we were visiting Magdalene, I got talking with some of her relatives. Why don't you come out bush with us? they asked. "Just the ladies," they said. So we would.

A couple of children happily squabbled, both wanting to eat a kangaroo tail. "Best bit," said Ernie Williams. He was an old and knowledgeable Arrernte man. I asked him about the land, about wildness. He didn't say anything for ages, then answered slowly. His voice was not bitter, but his words were a reproach. "Always we were roaming around, before the white people came." He paused, stared ahead of him. "Roaming, roaming, roaming."

When we left the community, the first sign we saw was a huge sign on the perimeter wire fencing of the airport, saying NO TRESPASSING. One Aboriginal man, Jackie Margoungoun, commented, "For we, for sistergirl, I can't go back on my land—it was an Aboriginal sacred site but the government made it their sacred site, leased it to cattle stations. We're going to find weself in jail for trespassing on our own lands." And two bodies were slumped by the road, blind drunk at 11 A.M.

So the "ladies trip" happened. All of us—Agnes, in her sixties, her daughter Jane, a cousin Sandra, Lareena and I, with Anjou and Nikita (Agnes's three-year-old granddaughter), piled into the truck a few days later and went out bush.

Jane, in the front seat of the Land Rover, picked out animals no one else could see. We surprised a kangaroo by the roadside, the kangaroo, that creature of zany proportions, its sweet delicate head like a fawn, and its front paws helpless-looking. Then *ker-pow* it scooted off with its tail thwacking out a giant's stomp, fee fi fo fum, it thudded away like an animated space hopper, several meters in one bounce. Sand spurted up like a cartoonist's scrawls to signify speed as it skedaddled away but, running too fast, it fell over, in a cloud of dust and embarrassment.

"This grandma country," said Agnes, and she introduced me to the land as if to a living person. There was an etiquette to this, because strangers need permission to enter someone's country—they should be brought there by someone who belongs. The belonger may introduce the stranger in words, or go to a water hole and pour water on the stranger, or rub a little underarm sweat on them.

After several hours, we reached their outstation, three large houses in a compound. No one wanted to be indoors and we sat on the wide low veranda. Agnes lit a fire to cook supper. Jane and Sandra played a game of solitaire and indoors a smoke alarm kept going off. "When we're out here, out bush," said Jane, "we don't feel lonely. We look after the land by coming back."

I asked them about white people claiming to be the "first to cross" the desert here. They laughed in scorn. "White people don't know anything. It's all lies that white people were the first to cross the desert." People could live in this desert because they could find water at soakages or from the roots of trees or follow finches to water.

Inside the house, little Nikita pissed in the middle of the floor, and little Anjou loudly pointed it out. In the loo, there were hundreds of small dead moths. Old clothes hung over the barbed-wire fence. There was solar-powered water heating but the tap was broken, so hot water constantly poured into the sand. Inside there was a gas cooker that no one would use. "Might explode," said Agnes.

Half asleep in my swag, I heard hooves in the night. There were sheets of corrugated iron from a fallen shed that banged against one another as if being kicked by a frightened colt. Shooting stars—there were many—dropped in the dark pool of night.

At dawn, the mosquitoes were whining. Two were spinning, dazed, mating. A willy wagtail swooped down to my swag, perched, gulped at the mosquitoes and caught a last unlucky moth of the night. Budgerigars flew an emerald streak in the rising sun.

I found the compound a depressing place. On the ground there were bones and hooves, a blunt ax blade and a tomahawk and a bucket full of empty beer bottles. There was an empty drum of plain flour, a 3 kg barrel of

Bushells tea, empty oil drums, broken shoes and the rags of trousers. The wire fencing around the compound clicked as it cooled with a metallic, prison-like clang. There were sardine cans, a broken plastic laundry basket, Coke cans and medicine bottles, hankies, an old asthma inhaler, a kangaroo spine and a burnt can of Victoria beer. Halfway up a tree hung a kid's bike. Inside the house, the fridge door was open—the fridge didn't work anyway. Moldy bones dripped water onto newspaper and there was a smell of warming rotten meat, swollen and gassy under popping cellophane.

Agnes seemed to pay no attention whatsoever to the compound and all this government-issue stuff. All her concentration and conversation was about the land. We walked through dry creek beds, lit by the bluish radiance of eucalyptus, and Agnes told me stories of the land: this was Carpet Snake Dreaming. There was a spring in a valley and the valleysides were carved by the Carpet Snake. "When it crawled down here?" I asked. Agnes threw me a look and shook her head. "Of course not. It crawled *up* here. Can't you see how the land is dented?"

Agnes's expression, when she was talking about the land, was lit up and shining with love and memory. Trachoma had sealed one of her eyes shut and the other was closing. In a few years she wouldn't be able to see this land. She would only have memory, but even the past had been damaged. She told me about the special rocks near here, which were the "eggs of the Carpet Snake" but which had been stolen. "We can't get our treasures back from museums, and then the land loses its power and energy. You lose sacred things and you lose memory. It makes me sad."

This land was storied with its Dreamtime life, and as a body has scars, marks of distinctive biography, so the landscape was storied with its specific geobiography. To Aboriginal eyes, the land is alive, jumping with vitality. In these desert places, everything jumps. The sky jumps up at dawn, a kangaroo jumps, the colors of sand jump, green shoots and fire jump, a new child (a little gunduburrie) jumps in the womb, dot paintings jump to the eye, the Milky Way jumps up into the sky and the rain jumps down. Land is sown with the seeds of verbs, jumping up out of the earth.

The god of Genesis created only through the single command, *Fiat*, but the Ancestors created the land with a variety of Totemic Actions: Urinating, Crawling, Scratching, Firelighting, Sweeping, Menstruating, Giving Birth,

Arguing, Making Love, and the land retains the vivid vitality of these lively acts. In the Dreamtime, Ancestors poured spirit and significance into all things. Unlike the biblical creation, the Aboriginal genesis is egalitarian: Dingo, Emu, Termite and Carpet Snake are all creators. The Honey Ant bounces belly to belly with mankind. Wallaby wisdom is not inferior to yours or mine. Carpet Snake has Dreaming, as has Spinifex Hopping-Mouse, Flying Ant or Wild Yam. (Wild Yam and the great I Am, Jehovah and Vegetable on equal terms at last.)

We went out in the Land Rover, looking for witchetty grubs, keeping a weather eye open for wild bull camels, which can get aggressive if you're between them and water. Using a crowbar as a digging stick, the women knocked on the ground at the roots of bushes, trying to hear a certain hollowish sound. An "empty sound root," said Sandra, was what you wanted, for that meant the *tyape* (pronounced chapa) could be inside. She yanked up a root— "Might be *tyape*, might be not"—and snapped the root in two. If there was a bulge, and a sawdusty end ("grub been through eating wood"), then it was inside. Some grubs were small, just half an inch long. Others, fat and yellow, could be up to two inches long. If they clung to the root with their claws you could knock the root against the digging stick and they would fall out. Or you could poke them out with a thin hook of a plant stem. Sandra did this, and pulled a face: "I busted im. I didn't wait."

Agnes found far more grubs than Sandra, so Agnes surreptitiously added some of her own to Sandra's pile, and Sandra quietly borrowed a few more, so in the end they had the same. No one would be made to feel "shame" by having fewer.

We went back to the Land Rover and Agnes tossed a fat grub to Jane in the front seat then dropped the rest of her collection into a Diet Coke bottle, and back at the compound we toasted the grubs on the warm ashes of the previous night's fire. They were cooked after a couple of minutes, then you squeezed the head off and ate the body. It tasted like fried egg and roasted sweet corn.

Little Nikita, with her sun-cracked cheeks, her hair sun-dyed to bronze-blond, had a brilliant smile and a roaring smoker's laugh. She knew scant English, though as she played a game with Anjou she came out with a raucous "motherfucker." Swearwords are the wild weeds of language—wiry and gleeful, flourishing on the edges of horticulture, for there, on the boundary, rejected language growls robust as weeds, like demented nettles sniggering with brambles and thistles making mischief with the grass. All over the world, when people have learned English not from horticulture-dictionaries but from common English speakers, it's the swearwords that are learned first.

As we left, after a few days out bush, Agnes said quietly, "We love our land, pass it down generations. People used to be free, go anywhere. But white people came and took our lands." (Ernest Giles, a white explorer who called Aboriginal people "Troglodytes," referred to them as "intruders.")

Farther along the road, Sandra commented, "Bin rainin round here. Little bit." To me, there was no visible sign. Agnes pointed at a track and said, "Camel. Fresh camel. Went that way. Might be last night."

Our trip had a miserable end. Lareena and I dropped the women back at their community. There were drunk people on the veranda of Agnes's house, dogs and dogshit everywhere else. Agnes and Jane were angry at the sight and Agnes—who for days had been so gently happy—began furiously shouting at a man and disappeared indoors. I didn't see her again. Jane's expression, which had been so quick and observant out bush, was dull and careless here. Sandra, pointed and funny out bush, became crossly resigned here. Another quarrel flared up as we left, one old woman angrily gesturing at a younger man, shouting at him in a stream of Arrernte, punctuated frequently with "fuckingarsehole."

A COMPASS IN THE HEAD

An Arrernte friend came to visit Rod in his house in Alice Springs. Rod showed him a painting he'd done of land that the two had visited together. The Arrernte man couldn't recognize it. "But you were there with me," said Rod, surprised and a little disappointed. The guy squinted at it, troubled. Suddenly his face cleared: "Ah, you've got it on the wrong wall, that's why I didn't recognize it." If the painting related to a site west of the house, he expected it to be on the west wall. Rod moved the picture to the appropriate wall and his friend nodded enthusiastically. "Yes, yes of course I know it."

Even indoors, Aboriginal people have an unerring sense of direction, a skill people need to live in the deserts. In Alice, I briefly met the painter Marlee Napurrula. She was a large woman with a strong physical presence: talking of Haasts Bluff, where she is from, or Sydney, where her paintings are sent for exhibition, she oriented herself to exactly the right direction, hurled her arms at the walls to gesture to places, as if her elbows were boomerangs and the walls weren't there.

For Europeans, one of the frightening things about any wilderness is that you can lose your direction. Here, Aboriginal people practice directions from childhood, using terms for north, south, east, west, for objects, people and places. You could ask someone to move a pot on the fire farther to the north, tell a child where to look for a cup, "west a little, that's too far, east a bit." Blind people can also be given directions: "Go south a bit, there's your blanket." In the Great Sandy Desert, some blind Aboriginal people developed such a good sense of hearing that they could clap as they walked and "hear" their way, in a kind of echolocation.

People needed to remember routes through the land to reach, for example, a water source from the direction of a certain tree, taking a bearing, perhaps, between the angle formed by two particular branches or remembering exactly how many riverbeds you must cross on a particular journey. Aboriginal people describe poking a sharp splinter through the hard skin on the finger, so they could remember exactly how many sandhills they had to cross on a particular route. The pain would remind them, and it would be worth it, for if they needed to find water this information could be a matter of life and death.

SONGLINES

You can know where you are through music, along songlines. A songline will describe, for instance, the Possum Ancestor, traveling from three big rocks and over a creek bed. The line of the story will describe the lie of the land, and people can even travel across country they've never seen, provided they know the song, for it will guide them like a map. Thus wild land is negotiated by song.

In Central and South Australian music, one songline will keep to one melodic form, so if a stranger arrived, unable to speak the local language, they would know from the music what songline they were on.

The songlines don't sing *about* nature, they sing nature itself, voicing crevasse and rock, tree and dune. The land is vivid with melody, it proliferates with story. This music is not the indoor music of chamber orchestra, bar, score and metronome but uncaged song that has burst through the bars, scorched the score paper, and its only metronome is the rhythm of footfall and the measure of rock.

I spent an evening with a Katyetye woman, Alison Ross, and her husband Jackie Margoungoun, talking about the country. The land, to them, is talkative, ringing out its messages. "The language is on every bird, on every tree. That's an elder of the tongue of Aboriginal people," said Alison.

People talk of the reciprocal relationship between themselves and land as if it is a resonant frequency, so the land sings, people resonate with it, and it makes them feel rung to a sung pitch. That sound is sung by humans, and is in turn picked up by the land, which "hears" human pitch and resonates to it in turn, in a round of song where each voice echoes the one before.

Song, for Aboriginal people, is a treasured possession, giving meaning to land and to individual life. It is a map, a mnemonic, a way of thinking and a form of order. The songlines and the story they contain are also a part of "Law," for stories illustrate morality and are like parables, knitted into the land itself, telling people how they should act.

There is something similar among the Western Apache: stories are frequently moral, detailing a wrongdoing and a comeuppance, and each story is tied very precisely to one place—a hill, for example—so whenever you look at that hill, you remember the story that took place there and its moral. One young woman commented that the site of one story "stalked" her every day. The morality is permanent, because it is located in the land.

Songs are also medicine. I met a painter and story-doctor in Alice, Margaret-Kemarre Turner. She judges which story to "prescribe" for someone's situation. "I give right story for right thing. And I never misplace story." (Stories do heal: it's how good novels and all folktales work; it's the consolation of empathy between individuals.) "All of this land, everything in it, is medicine," says an old Shoshone woman of the Nevada desert. To Western eyes, medicine, law, land and song are entirely separate, but to many indigenous people they are aspects of a single ordered entity, call it harmony or health or law. They cocreate this deep order inherent in nature, through ritual, through song.

Aboriginal people say that the continuation of ritual and ceremony contributes to the well-being—happiness, even—of the land, and this in turn makes people happy. In the Ngarinman language, used by the Yarralin people, there is a word, *punyu*, which means happy, strong, healthy, knowledgeable and socially responsible: it is the state of being fully alive. The term is used for land as much as for people and for the Dreaming as much as for either, for all of these are necessary to the fullness of life.

Jackie Margoungoun described a song he could follow from Doomadjee to Mataranka, a distance of about 385 miles, or 620 kilometers, and also one he could follow from Katherine to Borraloola, and from Borraloola to the Queensland border. "Only three people left can follow that song," he said. "The Church stopped the ceremonies so people couldn't practice them and they were forgotten. Four or five songs are gone now and no one can ever find them again."

And when the songlines are silenced, a conceptual wasteland is all that remains.

"LAND OUR HEART. SOUL. COUNTRY."

Often when I asked Aboriginal people about land, they answered about family. "This mother country . . . granny country." Land needs visiting the way grandparents do, and if people have any money, they often spend it on a four-wheel drive to get out and visit the land. The country "brought them up," someone tells me—an ineluctably familial relationship.

Pintupi people speak of land as something that is held, as an intimate act of care, as a parent holds a child and is responsible for it. But which the parent and which the child? Both are both. Margaret-Kemarre Turner describes to me the reciprocal relationship: "Going to a place keeps it alive and keeps you alive too. . . . You've got to honor the land. Nurture the country, because the country will always nurture you."

Sometimes the relationship between people and land has sexual overtones: the Ancestors were fecund, procreating everywhere, and the sexual intimacy between men and women is mirrored by the intercourse of the elements. In songs from Goulburn Island, the playful erotic fertility between the young men and women at the billabong is linked to the monsoonal fertility of nature, and as the Lightning Snakes are "writhing in the sky, copulating, twist-ing and turning among the clouds," a flash of lightning "gleams on the cabbage palms, and on the shining semen among the leaves."

Certain trees or rocks or water holes are incarnations of totemic ances-tors, so if this tree is cut down or that waterhole polluted, people grieve as if a relative had died. "People have committed suicide when their Dreamtime sacred sites have been mined," says Jackie Margoungoun. "A lot of people had to die with pain inside and couldn't show it, crying for their sacred places. A lot of people who passed away, passed away from sorrowness."

People say the land can feel a similar distress, and environmental anthro-pologist Veronica Strang, in *Uncommon Ground*, describes being told how, when the "owner" of one place died, a lagoon went dry with grief. "When his father died, Emu waterhole dried out . . . the place died with him. . . . If the young people don't come back to this country, the country will feel that 'Oh well, look like no one don't own me now,' so this country will just sort of die away."

People express the land, they narrate its lines and shapes, they sing its spirits, give voice to its inaudible essences, they tell its history. "We are the tongue on the body of the land," says a Yolngu woman.

Aboriginal people do not see themselves as owning land as property. Rather than landowners, they are landknowers, for owning means possessing knowledge, story and ceremony. ("Ownership is not a given, but an accom-plishment," writes anthropologist Fred Myers.) Aboriginal people, before the arrival of the whites, never took other people's territories precisely because other people's land was *meaningless* to them, in direct contrast to whites who could see no meaning in the land and used their ignorance as an excuse for land theft. (To reflect the presumptuous ignorance of the British, Aboriginal man Burnum Burnum planted the Aboriginal flag at Dover in 1988 and de-clared, "I, Burnum Burnum, being a nobleman of ancient Australia, do hereby take possession of England on behalf of the Aboriginal people.")

I asked Margaret-Kemarre Turner if there were terms in Arrernte that approximate to *wasteland* or *desert*. There is "the-place-where-nobody-has-walked," or "where-there's-no-water." But, she says, "there is no land that is empty in the eyes of Aboriginal people. The desert is not empty." When Aboriginal people spoke to me of deserts, what was all-important was the reason for desertedness. Linguist Myfany Turpin suggests that in the Kaytetye language there are words for country that is "desert," with no water courses, so people would visit there only with great caution, and the Kaytetye word *alpawe* is "a country that has little to offer." Little but not nothing.

There are terms for places deserted because someone has died: *arrkwe-tyetye*. Alison Ross comments of this, "We are moving away from this place for a while because someone has passed away, but we will return after the green grass has covered this place." There is also the word *ahaylenge*, defined as "no name." This term is used out of respect, instead of naming a place where a recently deceased person is from. Meanwhile another term for desert, *akngenpe*, means that people have not hunted there recently, and it is a positive reason to go there.

Chinese words for desert translate as sandy, lonely places, and similarly in English *desert* comes from *desertum*, forsaken or left: wilderness is often associated with an unhappy psychological state of being abandoned or alone. Aboriginal people of the deserts countenance no such desertedness. A wise man of Aboriginal cultures would traditionally spend a long time alone in the deserts, meditating, finding what Yolngu people call "*mind* medicine," which Wandjuk Marika, Aboriginal painter and musician, describes this way: "So the spirit of the earth, the feeling of the earth, it's come to you and then you feel free, well and strong."

In Alice, I walked along Lhere Mpwertne, or the Todd River, where Aboriginal people often gather. In one housing block, built for Aboriginal people, there is a big notice, prissy and patronizing as a primary school noticeboard: "Territory Tidy Town Camp. Special Effort Award . . ."

For thousands of years, Aboriginal people have camped in the Todd River bed. Now signs lined the river: NO CAMPING (the NO was scratched out on sign after sign) and NO DRINKING. (Underneath one such sign was a maroon wine box of Stanley premium tawny port, a two-liter cask, 16.5% alcohol.) At the bottle shop by the dried-up Todd River, there was parched dryness in people's eyes, a dangerous thirst, the wasteland of alcoholism. Here the desert had come and people's spirits ran dry till nothing but thirst remained.

To Margaret-Kemarre Turner, living in urban situations is a kind of wasteland for Aboriginal people. People should live out on their land till they die there, she says, so that the spirit will stay there and a child can be born with that spirit. "The body goes back to the land like planting six hundred seeds. The cycle never ends. It goes down down down down down down." Life curls down through the generations, natural and factual as seed fall. You couldn't put a seed in a concrete box and expect it to sprout, nor can that happen to the human seed-spirit, which dies in concrete towns and needs the land to yo-yo itself back into new life.

Every community has its stories of accident and revenge—often involving alcohol. In one place a teenager shot another teenager. Although it was entirely accidental, the teenager was sentenced by white law to six or seven years in jail. In revenge for the death, the bereaved family took the youngest son of the other family and murdered him with an iron spike. In another incident, a man accidentally rolled a truck and the crash killed someone. The driver was "sung"—killed with a spell.

Only three generations ago, people lived out in the wild and free country, with its Law, its Songlines, its Way. Now, a whole society seems gaunt, staring, lost, caged and alcoholic, maddened by a cultural death they didn't deserve, crazed by walls they never built and furious with a thirst not theirs, lost in a psychological wasteland.

While I was in Alice, I met the painter Michael Nelson Jagamarra and talked about land. "White people don't understand our land, our Dreaming. Every creek has a meaning. Every rock. Riverbed."

"Is there any such thing as wasteland to you?"

"Nooh. No. Land our heart. Soul. Country." He said this with a grievous passion, as if the words on his lips and the look in his eyes could together recreate country. He was drunk, his arm around me, flirting with me outrageously. (Peggy, his sister, was sitting on the floor close by, painting the Rainbow Snake. "Really, really bloody dangerous, I can tell you," said Jagamarra. "I had that Dreaming from my grandmother.")

I asked him what he felt when he was out on the land and he immediately took an enormous deep breath. "You feel that you can *breathe* and you're alive and you see that the big country can talk to you while you're dreaming. This happen. The wind blow and hear the ancestors and talk for you." He paused and smiled gently, his flirtation turned to utter pity for me. "Not for you, for black people. For the spirit we got in our life and in our heart." He suddenly shouted out, "This is our fucking land, this is our earth, this is our land. Our bloody land. White people got to know." His face was jerky with emotion. "We should make white people understand. And we can only read and write by painting." He looked suddenly drained and sad.

ART, THE WELL OF THE DESERT

Art demonstrates land rights. Galarrwuy Yunupingu, a senior Arnhem Land bark painter, says, "We paint to show the rest of the world that we own this country, and that the land owns us. Our painting is a political act." Fifty percent of Aboriginal people call themselves artists.

I've seen two pictures of the Great Sandy Desert. The first is a European map, expressing a dull, almost featureless, almost colorless, monotonous terrain. The second is the same land seen by Aboriginal artists. The picture is full of color, life, movement and story. There is no desertedness, no vacancy, no emptiness, no blank, no wasteland, no *terra nullius*.

Aboriginal art listens to the land and makes its latent expression audible, not giving it voice but crafting the precise word aloud that the land is already quietly speaking, giving it utterance in perfected expression. Art is the greatest well of the desert; brimming with meaning, fluent as water, it springs up from the land. The paintings overflow all containers, spill out of all frames and course like rivers.

Aboriginal artists never see Nothing, they know no blank. Paintings are full of story, full of dot, full of designs, compressed light. "There was never any use of space for its own sake," said the late Geoffrey Bardon, early champion of Aboriginal art to the white world. The first piece of Aboriginal art done "publicly" was the painting of the Honey Ant Dreaming on the walls of the school where Bardon taught. Later, white authorities ordered that it should be painted over—whited out. The blank gaze of whites preferred a blank, meaningless, white wall.

BELOWNESS

In Aboriginal art, dot patterns are used not only to reveal (an animal, for example, in the shade) but also to hide something below the surface, to conceal the most sacred element of a painting from the uninitiated. Aboriginal art cultivates the difference between the "outside" story, apparent and open to everyone, and the "inside" story, known only to those of sufficient standing.

Bill Neidjie says of the outside story:

Anyone can listen, kid, no matter who
But that "inside" story you can't say.

"We pay too much attention to the surface of the earth. It presents itself so obviously to our eyes. We forget the layers above and below," says artist John Wolseley. "You people try and dig little bit more deep you been diggin only white soil try and find the black soil inside," says Aboriginal author Paddy Roe.

The Dreaming is inside the land, latent as a dream lies latent in sleep. Here, deep underneath, is the spirit and the beauty, says Margaret-Kemarre Turner, "only seen by Aboriginal eyes."

Most of Uluru, two-thirds of it, lies underground. It illustrates to me a quality of belowness in the central deserts—a sense of incipience and inheld energy. The Underneath of things can seem stronger than their surface. Inside masses into view before outside statement. Meaning is luminous and happens on the outside of event. In other environments, you have to intuit the within, learn the skeleton by inference: here land seems exoskeletal; it wears its bones on the outside. This is what you see most perfectly expressed in Aboriginal "X-ray art."

Aboriginal people talk of the land as if it is a body merely and recently clothed with the supermarket, golf course, airport or town, as if in time the body could and would shuck off these flimsy shifts and be naked again. As if "Adelaide" were as inconsequential as pajama bottoms and a street just a scarf to be lightly tossed aside in the breeze. You may think you tame the land with concrete and pavements, but its wildness persists, primal and feral, below.

Below, too, there is an immanent world of "spirit business," which I heard about on the slant, a scrap of paper from a diary blowing in a garden, a paragraph of tension, a look askance, a brief recollection. It is as if the land has veins under the skin, hot with the blood of revenge and power.

The land has been bought and sold by whites but the spirit of the land has never given itself to white culture, say Aboriginal people. The spirit runs below, beneath and within. The white writer and activist Dave Foreman describes being in Sydney with an Aboriginal man who asks him what he sees. A city, pavement, buildings, comes the reply. The Aboriginal man says, "We still see the land. Beneath the concrete we know where the forest grows, where the kangaroos graze. We see where the Platypus digs her den, where the streams flow. That city there . . . it's just a scab. The land remains alive beneath it."

In Alice, Dog Rock (a sacred site associated with Dog Dreaming) is between Pinky's Pizza Shop and the main highway out of town. The Dog Rock will endure because it has its spirit below, say local people. "The town grew up dancing and still the dancing is there under the town," wrote Aboriginal author Wenten Rubuntja.

"A HIDEOUS BLANK"

In Alice, there is a Burke Street and a Wills Terrace and Sturt Terrace and the Stuart Town Jail, all honoring white explorers, John McDouall Stuart, Robert O'Hara Burke, William John Wills and Charles Sturt, "discovering" the land.

Aboriginal writer Herb Wharton, in *Unbranded*, described an Aboriginal child learning the white lie: "At school he learned of the discovery of this great land by white sailors. A wide uncharted unmapped land. At night he listened to the tales around the smoky fires. . . . The stories told in stars, rivers, hills and sky. These stories not in the history book told how the land was charted, mapped and known to a race of people for thousands of years. . . . Fifty thousand years of footprints were stamped upon the earth long before white explorers came."

I asked how people felt when the whites rolled up and declared that central Australia was a desert wilderness, *terra nullius*. "We all thought it was a lot of crap," came the blunt reply from one man. "It was already people's home. Our people's home."

A "hideous blank" was how the *Argus* newspaper of Melbourne described the central deserts in the mid-nineteenth century. "The same dreary, dreadful, dismal desert," writes John McDouall Stuart. Barron Field (whose very name seems a pun on his observations), author and friend of Coleridge's and Wordsworth's, found Australian land "monotonous" and wrote, "No tree, to my taste can be beautiful that is not deciduous. . . . I can . . . hold no fellowship with Australian foliage." John Forrest in 1874 called the Australian deserts "a barren worthless desert." Explorer Daniel Brock said, "The country is horrible . . . a Climax of Desolation—no trees, no shrubs, all bleak, barren undulating sand. Miserable! Horrible!" In 1868 the Royal Geographical Society described Western Australia as half a million square miles of unknown: "the greatest absolute blank on the face of the globe apart from the Poles."

Such blankness could only come about when one people invaded land they didn't understand and couldn't read: the explorers colonized the land by ignoring its meaning, colonialism being the power to impose one's ignorance on the land. The land was a hideous blank, to *les blancs*, the white men. Theirs the blank stare, theirs the blind eyes, the dead eye glaring. Charles Sturt was literally almost blinded, as a result of his journeys in the "Simpson" desert. The whites named one set of mountains Ophthalmia Range—reflecting the inflammation of their eyes but not their mental blindness. Meanwhile in a painful legacy of the blank blindness of the whites, today many Aboriginal people are blinded by trachoma, a disease thought to have been brought by the whites. The metaphorical blindness of the blank white gaze is now transferred, in a poetic injustice.

"The real voyage of discovery consists not in seeking new landscapes but in having new eyes," wrote Marcel Proust.

NAMING AND TAMING

The white explorers wrote their emotions on the land: Mount Dreadful, Mount Misery, Mount Desolation, Mount Despair, Useless Loop, Lake Disappointment, Cape Catastrophe, Thirsty Sound, Possession Island. By naming, they conceptually settled the land, which otherwise bore such writhy names as Urrinka-willartji, which means "the teats of the Dingo bitch Dreaming." They colonized this new piece of empire with names like Victoria Springs and Great Victoria Desert. In the northern "Simpson" Desert there is actually a set of hills called "Adam Range," as the Europeans ostentatiously established their god-given dominion of this world, an Adamic self-portrait.

He (it usually is he) who names, tames. There is a convention that when a wild horse is broken in, the breaker is given the honor of naming it. The "wild" land of Australia would be broken in.

Thomas Mitchell, appointed surveyor-general of New South Wales in 1827, attempted to find and preserve Aboriginal names for places. It was worthy enough as an ambition, but it has been suggested that many of the names Mitchell was given turned out to be variations of "I don't understand you," so he dutifully transcribed the terms of incomprehension; a truer representation of the colonial mind than any "correct" place names could ever be. (Similarly, in Mexico, Yucatán allegedly means "What?" or "What are you saying?" as people responded to the Spanish invaders.)

Australia is full of English place names: Iffley, Highbury and, with superb suburbanismo, Croydon. When I visited Uluru, an English woman near me was staring at the rock for ages, then turned triumphantly to her guide. "I've been trying to relate this to parts of England. You know, this could be Cornwall." *This could be Cornwall.* And there she had it—grasped it in her fist as if it were a soggy pasty. Thomas Browne, in *Religio Medici* (1643), writes, "All places, all airs make unto me one country; I am in England, everywhere, and under any meridian."

Naming is an act of domination over wild lands. If I call one place the "Simpson Desert" I master it, superscribing layers of meaning (European, colonial, financial) but I fail to describe wind, color, creature, bones, spinifex, geology or sunrise. Naming makes boundaries, so the "Simpson" Desert is not the "Gibson" Desert and both are opposite of the sea. But landscape does not acknowledge such boundaries. Land merges, melts and fades, moves from plain to mountain to plain again. In the long view, even desert is not the opposite of sea but her daughter—for the sands of the desert are formed of seashells.

WHITE MAN'S RUBBISH

W *aste* was a word used frequently for desert wildernesses, with its connotations of rubbish, pollution and degraded land. Peter Warburton, nineteenth-century explorer in Western Australia, wrote, "We had great expectations of this place, but distance had deceived us—the hill is rubbish, and we obtained no hopeful view from it." Some white Australians still refer to areas of land as "rubbish country." The land was self-willed, free and full of meaning but when the whites came they saw a wasteland, barren and unstoried. There were stories there, but the whites were deaf to them. The land was riotously alive, but the white gaze was blind to the life of it.

"We never see 'nothing' looking at the land. Might see snake tracks, might be food. Kangaroo and goanna, witchetty grub and yam and seed and sweet potato and bush banana and wild orange and wild passionfruit and wild tomato," said the ladies on the ladies' trip. The land is not empty but full of knowledge, story, goodness and energy, they say.

The word *waste* is related to the Italian word *guasto*, meaning "ravage, damage, injury." The wasteland that the whites feared was in fact one they created themselves, by putting cattle on fragile desert lands, which were thus severely damaged—laid waste—by overgrazing. In October 2002, a whirlwind in the central deserts, almost biblical in its proportions, became a giant dust storm and ten million tons of topsoil were swept out to the oceans. Just as Aboriginal people were not allowed to sing their songlines and Aboriginal children in white schools were forbidden from speaking their own languages, so in the Aboriginal deserts, land was not allowed to speak its own language, not allowed to hum its long, dry phrases with the grace notes of frilled lizard and wallaby, but was made cattle country, the land forced to speak a banal version of English, lit by no idiosyncratic verb, with no specific adjective to spark it into flame.

Whites destroyed and *destoryed* in a physical devastation of land and a devastation of meaning, by removing or exterminating the people who knew the story and sang it. In 1788, there were an estimated 750,000 Aboriginal people. The European invasion caused the death of some 600,000 of them.

A bora ring is an ancient place of ritual significance to Aboriginal people. Aboriginal poet Oodgeroo Noonuccal describes one now:

Notice of estate agent reads: "Rubbish May Be Tipped Here."
Now it half covers the traces of the old bora ring.

Britain exploded atom bombs at Emu in 1953 and at Maralinga in 1956 and 1957 and carried out tests with bombs containing plutonium at Maralinga between 1960 and 1963. Plutonium, with its half-life of thousands of years, haunts the desert, poisoning people and animals. To the British, writes Dorothy Johnston in her novel *Maralinga, My Love*, Australia is "a rubbish dump, a bit of desert to do what they like with."

"The government treats us like rubbish, just like pieces of rubbish flying up and down in the wind," says Mogetse, a Bushman from the Kalahari Desert, speaking of their forced removal from their own lands by the Botswanan government.

"We're whiteman's rubbish," writes Athol Fugard in his play *Boesman and Lena*. "That's why he's so mad with us. He can't get rid of his rubbish. He throws it away, we pick it up. Wear it. Sleep in it. Eat it. We're made of it now. His rubbish is people." And like the alcoholic Boesman, the Bushmen stagger drunkenly around the shanty reservations, alcohol the only thing strong enough to obliterate the pain and the humiliation of the hunter who is now the prey.

Bushmen described themselves as *zhu twa si*, "the harmless people." Non-Bushmen are *zo si*, or animals without hooves, because non-Bushmen were angry, dangerous—wild—like lions and hyenas. Although the Central Kalahari Game Reserve was one of the very few parks in Africa that explicitly granted rights to the indigenous people of that area, the Bushmen have been removed.

In the early eighties, a diamond deposit was found on Bushman lands. A few years later, the government announced the Bushmen would be "relocated"—nothing to do with the diamonds, of course. A formal evaluation of the mine was finished in 1996, and the enforced evictions began in May 1997. A coincidence. Clearly.

The government sent thug-officials to brutalize and torture the Bushmen, tying them up, refusing them food and water. And in February 2002, the government cut off their water supplies, emptying their water tanks into the sand. And evicted them in earnest. Thirty thousand years or more brought to an end.

It's a tale of two maps. One, made in March 2001, before the main evictions, shows diamond concessions on Bushmen's land. There are small incursions at the edges but most of the land is free. Then, see a map of November 2002, and virtually the whole area is swiped by concessions. Only one tiny area at the northwest corner has not been earmarked.

The American magazine *Mother Jones* reported, "Many observers ... believe that there was an ulterior motive to the government resettlements: vast diamond deposits under the Kalahari sand."

De Beers and BHP Billiton, the world's biggest, fattest mining companies, the corporate faces of greed, sit fatly on their concessions, licking their lips, the consumer consuming all. And in a grotesque image-reversal, during the time of these evictions, the *Telegraph* magazine ran a story by Tessa Thomas about the San Bushmen and the Kalahari. The article calls them "primitive hunter-gatherers" and virtually the entire story is an excited gabble about how the Bushmen knew a plant that could suppress appetite. Great news for slimmers! "After two weeks the volunteers had each lost a kilo," her article pants delightedly.

LAND RIGHTS

In many parts of the world, indigenous people have lost their land for the idea of "wilderness." In South Africa, the forces of apartheid and conservation joined together to throw black people off the land to create wilderness parks for whites. Bernhard Grzimek, the so-called father of conservation in East Africa, announced that the Serengeti was a "primordial wilderness" and no native peoples were allowed to live there, though it had been their home for thousands of years. Wildlife preservationist Joy Adamson described the Samburu as "squatters"—on land once theirs.

Baird Callicott, American philosophy professor, comments, "Wilderness is a legacy of American puritanism. It played a crucial role in masking colonial genocide and ethnic cleansing. It is a powerful conceptual tool of colonialism." Yellowstone, the world's first national park, was created by expelling the Shoshone and others from their own lands. Yosemite, Crater Lake, the Grand Canyon, Rocky Mountain and others had all been land belonging to Native Americans, who were excluded or removed. The Chinese government has announced that part of northwest Tibet will be declared a "wilderness"— only possible in the wake of the mass murder of Tibetans.

TERRA NULLIUS

What is the difference between somewhere and anotherwhere? Can you have an unwhere? Is wilderness the strange slippage between here, there and nowhere? When the whites came to the Australian deserts, absence was all they saw, an echo of a nullity, an alibi land of nothing, a nowhere that annihilated their idea of somewhere. They could not see what was there, only what wasn't. Those who knew nothing of this land declared it had nothing to know. Since power determines what is considered to *be* knowledge, they called it *terra nullius* and said it belonged to no one, and there was nothing there, calling part of the land Nullarbor Plain, because they looked for their trees and found them absent. Aware only of what wasn't there, they created a Sartrean geography where "nothingness haunts being." (*Terra Nullius* could only have been seen by *Mens Vacuus*.)

Captain Cook, claiming Australia for Britain, relied on John Locke's definition of property thus: "As much Land as a Man Tills, Plants, Improves, Cultivates, and can use the Product of, so much is his Property." If people did not work the land or build visible forms of government, the lands were *terra nullius*. (Recently reading Homer's *Odyssey*, I was taken aback to see the Lockean idea prefigured: the Cyclopes are described as "fierce, uncivilized people" because their crops were "unsown and untilled," and because they had "no assemblies for the making of laws" nor "any settled customs.")

This prejudice is still going strong. At their national convention in 1991, Australia's Young Liberals voted to withdraw support for Aboriginal Land Rights because Aboriginal people "did not possess any concept of private ownership of land." No property had therefore been taken from them. Further, they did not deserve support for land rights because they "did not attempt to convert the land into property through improvement, exploitation or settlement." To an Aboriginal sensibility, free land should not be tamed. Land is self-willed and does not need to work its passage. "The Dreamtime didn't tell us to *work*," says Jackie Margoungoun disgustedly.

For many Aboriginal people, the vision can be reversed: they say that the white towns and cities are a kind of *terra nullius*, without meaning, without story, without totemic ancestors, without spirit.

Muta, a man of the Murinbata people, commented to anthropologist W. E. H. Stanner:

White man got no dreaming,
Him go 'nother way . . .
Him got road belong himself.

HEADHUNTERS

No wilderness is complete without headhunters and savages. Let me tell you about some of them. In Australia, there was a sport called "Lobbing the Distance." White settlers would bury live Aboriginal children up to their necks in sand and see who could kick off the heads of the children to the far-thest distance from its body, as Kevin Gilbert, Aboriginal writer from Wirad-juri country, describes it. "Another pastime was to cut the throats of Black women and men and let them run in terrified flapping circles and, when they collapsed, throw the bodies while still alive upon the fire." He reports how Aboriginal people were herded into swamps and "dispersed" with guns and clubs, "whereupon these pioneering, head-hunting whites cut off a large num-ber of the people's heads, boiled them down in buckets and sent 45 of the skulls and other bones off to Britain."

In nineteenth-century Queensland, one settler kept the ears of Aboriginal massacre victims nailed to his walls.

There are records of poisoned flour being given to Aboriginal people as a common occurrence; in one case Christmas pudding was given to them laced with strychnine. A Queensland government report of the nineteenth century describes how "the niggers [were given] . . . something really startling to keep them quiet . . . the rations contained about as much strychnine as anything and not one of the mob escaped."

Explorer John McDouall Stuart, planting his flag in the center of Australia in 1860, wrote, "And may it be a sign to the natives that the dawn of liberty, civilisation, and Christianity is about to break upon them." (As if.)

One Police Constable Willshire, writing in 1896, stationed in Bilinara Country near Victoria River Downs, described an attack against "a mob of natives . . . they scattered in all directions . . . throwing occasional spears, and yelling at us. It's no use mincing matters—the Martini-Henry carbines at this critical moment were talking English in the silent majesty of those great eternal rocks."

The first governor of South Australia, John Hindmarsh, was to say, "Black men: We wish to make you happy. But you cannot be happy unless you imitate white men. Build huts, wear clothes, work and be useful. . . . Love God. . . . Love white men. Love other tribes of black men. Learn to speak English."

The same kind of English is still being spoken: in June 2003, the Aboriginal Tent Embassy in Canberra was firebombed. Founded in 1972 on "Invasion Day," the anniversary of Captain Cook's "discovery" of Australia, it represented the Aboriginal Nations' fight for sovereignty.

Aboriginal people were classified by whites as either "wild" and "nomadic" or "domesticated blacks." Aboriginal Yarralin people talk of "wild" people too and to them *wild* connotes selfishness, people who lack self-control, who are antisocial, ignorant or irresponsible, aggressive, often drunk and violent. It was an apt term for the whites.

And if you thought Britain's racist ideas about desert people disappeared long ago, let me refer you to some choice remarks made by a feted *Guardian* journalist, Geoffrey Moorhouse, in *The Fearful Void* (1974). He attempts a journey in the Sahara that local people know is so dangerous as to be idiotic. He is then apparently surprised that only total idiots and the desperately poor will accompany him. Moorhouse's journey was done so that he could collect fame and fortune back home. His companions risk their lives for virtually no reward. He refers to local people as "these primitive human beings . . . who slithered deviously from one apparent fiction to another."

"I would have felt sorry for myself in civilized company," he writes. He predictably calls the Sahara "this savage wilderness" and "a blankness." (Wondering to himself about the appeal of the desert, the answer is its "suggestion of virginity." Snore.)

Of course Aboriginal people were not the only desert people who had to be "civilized." In the sixteenth century, European settlers in southern Africa called the Bushmen "vermin" and hunted them for sport. Some 100,000 Bushmen are thought to have been exterminated or dispossessed in South Africa. In Botswana, the Bushmen who lived in the deserts were termed "wild," while the sedentarized and schooled San were called "tame" Bushmen. Today's Botswanan government refers to the San Bushmen as needing to become "civilized" and states that tourists will not want to see "primitive" people.

A MAN CAN ONLY BE FREE IN THE DESERT

A man can only be free in the desert.
—ARAB PROVERB

I went to central Australia for the openness of the deserts. But the most striking thing about Alice is the Wall. Metal walls, brick walls, wooden walls, corrugated iron walls, cement walls: Alice is a walled city. Many of them are huge, seven feet high, with chicken wire at the top. These walls speak in a language Aboriginal people understand, a language of suspicion, of racism, of exclusion, a presumption of theft and trespass.

One Warlpiri man explained that he did not like walls because they made it hard for him to see, hear or smell what was going on around him. "A house is just like a big jail," says another. *Fence*, cunning word, means not only boundary but also the keeper of stolen goods, and settlers, stealing the land, fenced it before they did anything else. Many white names for places depend on measurement of walls and fences: "Five Mile Paddock" and "Eight Mile Yard." Naming a place by measurement makes land conceptually homogeneous. For Aboriginal people, this is nonsense: every part of land is distinct in quality—and most Aboriginal languages contain no words for numbers beyond three.

To the Western mind, fences were not only functional but also significant, representing both possession and aesthetics: a fenced land looked controlled and therefore beautiful. Further, a boundary gives meaning, because a distinction (a border) marks the difference between two things or concepts. From the Aboriginal point of view, these boundaries rupture meaning, for meaning is layered, associative; one thing wants to merge with another in order to achieve its fullest meaning. Anthropologist Michael Jackson explores these ideas, adding that to Aboriginal people, ownership grows downward, profoundly, in depth of knowledge, so the deeper your knowledge of a place, the more you "owned" it, while to the white mind, ownership extends superficially and lengthwise: the longer the fence, the greater the ownership.

The white settlers brought walls to a wild land and prisons to people who had only known freedom. The whole of Australia was a prison for the transported criminals, and from 1860 onward, Aboriginal people were interned in reserves where whites would control who they married, their employment, their movements, barring them from one place, forcibly moving them to another. The white authorities could search people, read their mail, confiscate property, remove children to dormitories, order floggings and expel individuals to places far from their families. One Aboriginal man remembers his grandmother only as a "face behind the wire" of the "native settlement" where she lived her life as a guiltless prisoner.

Aboriginal woman Rita Huggins, in the book of her life written by her niece, describes how when she was young, before the Second World War, troopers came out to where she and her family were living in the bush and rounded them all up into a cattle truck and took them away to a reservation. One old lady broke away from the others and screamed, "'Don't take my gunduburries! Don't take my gunduburries!' She was stopped and held by the officials who wanted to keep 'wild bush Blacks' on these reserves." Meanwhile, of course, "the whiteman could roam free."

With poetic justice, some of the imprisoning Europeans felt themselves imprisoned in turn. Members of Sturt's expedition, attempting to reach the center of Australia, were to describe their sense of being imprisoned by thirst in the desert, unable to leave the one place where they had found water. "We are thus completely imprisoned . . . our confinement . . . our ruinous detention . . . we were locked up," and he asks for a "release from prison . . . the idea of detention in that horrid desert was worse than death itself."

Prison is the opposite of desert wilderness but in a savage paradox some of the most frequently imprisoned people in the world are nomads and the people of the deserts. In southern Africa, British administrators disliked the fact that the Bushmen "tended to move about too freely." The resettlement camps where they live today they call "places of death" and Bushmen represent a disproportionate part of the prison population in all the countries where they live.

The reserves for Native Americans were effectively prisons in the nineteenth century. In 1865, orders were given to kill any Navajo person found off the reservation without a pass. Chief Satanta, a Kiowa chief, was to say, "I have heard that you intend to settle us on a reservation. . . . I don't want to settle. I love to roam over the prairies. There I feel free and happy, but when we settle down we grow pale and die." And Chief Ten Bears of the Comanche said, "I was born upon the prairie, where the wind blew free and there was nothing to break the light of the sun. I was born where there were no enclosures and where everything drew a free breath. I want to die there and not within walls."

"Openness of all openness. Desert, where the voice, profane or sacred, human or divine, encounters silence in order to become word," wrote Egyptian-Jewish poet Edmond Jabès.

Gypsies, or Roma, of Europe are proportionally the most imprisoned sector of the population of countries where they live. Sixty percent of male inmates in Hungarian prisons are Gypsies, twelve times the national average.

A report in the late 1980s showed that in Roebourne, in Western Australia, every Aboriginal man, woman and child was arrested on average three times a year. The 1991 Royal Commission into Aboriginal deaths in custody stated that Aboriginal people were twenty times more likely to be arrested and were twenty-three times more likely to die in prison than whites. And 63 percent of their arrests were for minor offenses.

Aboriginal writer Mudrooroo, in his novel *Wildcat Screaming*, describes the sense of going stir-crazy in a prison, unfree and spied on, but then suggests that even outside the prison, he is still in the white man's jail, "where the sky is the division roof; the houses are the cells, and the streets the exercise yards, all lit up at night just like here, so that the screws, the coppers, can keep an eye on you." It is only by imagining the "dark thoughtfulness of the bush" that there is freedom. He imagines being with his uncle by a fire, and his uncle saying, "The bush 'lives in you. It calls you if you let it.' And then he goes quiet and we sit along that fire and a sense of freedom comes over me."

THE LAW OF THE WILD

Not the law, but the land sets the limit. Desert is the name it wears upon the maps," writes Mary Austin, early-twentieth-century American writer.

Outlaws, not bound by law, inhabit the badlands and the wilds. Savage nature and the beast within acknowledge no law. And wilderness is lawless and chaotic. Allegedly. The ancient Greeks feared the wildness of nature and came up with the notion of "barbarian" nature, beneath or beyond order. Hobbes' *Leviathan* (1651) argued that nature is a state of chaos and that humans too were inherently violent and disorderly.

Plato refers to the "wild beast in us," which "will go to any lengths of shamelessness and folly." Every time Plato mentions evil, he uses nature to portray it: black horses, wolves, lions, hawks, asses and pigs.

Philosopher Mary Midgley, in *Beast and Man*, describes how Western societies have considered beasts to be lawless and savage, yet studies of animal behavior show the reverse: that animals lead highly ordered, "lawful" lives. Take the wolf. They are, writes Midgley, "by human standards, paragons of steadiness and good conduct. They pair for life, they are faithful and affectionate spouses and parents, they show great loyalty to their pack and great courage and persistence in the face of difficulties, they carefully respect one another's territory, keep their dens clean, and extremely seldom kill anything that they do not need for dinner." In folkloric terms, the wolf is used as an emblem for lawless cruelty, in contrast to humans. The truth, argues Midgley, is rather the reverse. People used to flay wolves alive in medieval France. Do wolves ever flay people alive? Do wolves flay wolves alive? Humans are more cruel to one another and to animals than any other creature, but humans have projected onto animals their own savagery.

For much of the world, for most of history, Nature *was* Law—it was the way people organized morality. For indigenous people, Law is in the land and nature is anything but lawless; rather there is a profound core of order within wild nature. "I am the Way," said Jesus. By contrast, all nature-based philosophies have seen that in *Wildness* was Way. American anarchist Murray Bookchin comments that the term *Way* is universal to all early communities, meaning ethics, rituals, a sensibility and lifeways, as well as universal meaning, an eternal order that rules everything: the sun, the moon, plants and animals, all of nature.

This universal law, or Way, is Asha in Zoroastrian thought; Maat for ancient Egyptians, R'ta in Vedic India, Dharma for Hindus and Buddhists, and Tao in ancient China. For the ancient Greeks, Themis was goddess of law, the law of nature as distinct from human law (and when Themis is disregarded, Nemesis brings retribution). The deep law of nature was Maligait for the Inuit, it was Wouncage, the old way, for the Oglala Lakota and the Dreaming for Aboriginal people. They are all expressions of a profound Law beneath everything, a Way of being. Wildness, nature, freedom and law are all part of this Way, not in opposition to it. Wildness—complex, free, beautiful and only apparently chaotic—is part of a larger, deeper order.

"The Law is in the ground," say Aboriginal people. Anthropologist Deborah Bird Rose quotes a Yarralin man: "Everything come up out of ground—language, people, emu, kangaroo, grass. That's Law. Missionary just trying to bust everything up. They fuck em up right through." For Aboriginal people, the land and song, intimately connected, are both profoundly ordered. Song is universal harmony and order, for humanity and the land. The songlines are Law. The poet Oodgeroo Noonuccal comments that the white race is peculiar, and peculiarly unhappy in its relation to law; in leaving nature's law and making "civilized" laws instead.

Koyaanisqatsi is the Hopi term for chaos, a world out of kilter, inharmonious and unhealthy, out of balance, a crazy life, life disintegrating—a state that calls for another way of living. This was the murderous disorder the whites brought.

The purpose of indigenous law throughout the world is essentially to ensure that the natural world remains the same. In contemporary Euro-American law, however, exterminating life on earth is legal. Genocide may be officially outlawed, but acts that kill or threaten to exterminate other creatures or destroy the very climate of the earth are not thought to be crimes at all.

DESERT DAYS

There was a sign in a roadhouse near Alice. FOOTWEAR COMPULSORY. Who doesn't wear shoes?

It was one of the first things I noticed here. Aboriginal people don't. But they know how to read these signs, like the one in a café saying DRESS STANDARDS APPLY. Only white people eat there. I was shocked by Alice: it felt the way South Africa used to feel. Where people seem to walk down glass corridors of invisible but certain segregation. Where white people confide their racism in you, confident that if you are white you will share it, and where, knowing this, black people don't want to look at you if you are white.

I was glad to leave.

I met up with Rob, a landscape painter and my friend for twenty years, and together we traveled to the Arrernte Desert.

It was the worst drought for a century in Australia. Signs by the roads indicating "Fire Danger Today" pointed to orange, "Very High." We drove through a dust storm and a ball of dust rolled across the road in a thick turbulent and choking yellowy gray, reducing visibility suddenly.

Paddy melons like large grapefruit lined the road. A wedge-tail eagle clawed a dead kangaroo, shiny and swollen in the sun. Huge long-legged grass seeds cartwheeled across the road like five-legged stilt walkers. There were gidgee trees—a kind of acacia that can smell of cat's piss in damp weather. A shaggy emu trotted away from us, its feathered behind dolloping after.

Tires and Coke bottles littered the road, and everywhere were green cans of Victoria beer, suggesting a party, a shag, a smack in the face or a warm tight hug. Among gum trees and mulga bushes, an upside-down car was rusting away. The bullsand was tricky to drive through and it would be easy to lose control of the steering and hit a tree or ricochet against a ridge of sand and turn the vehicle. Telegraph wires strolled across the landscape in step with the road, and a red line of hills glowed on the horizon, while burnt trees scraped the sky. In the trees hung nests of the itchy grub, like swollen haunches of skinned meat, pinky brown and smooth. If you touch it you won't forget about it for days.

We stayed for several days in the MacDonnell Ranges, camping near a dry creek, lined with river red gums, kind as grandmothers with their soft wood and rumpled folds of bark. You could read the past in the trees: a reckless helter-skelter of driftwood flung six feet up in the air told of a flash flood.

The MacDonnell Ranges were once as high as the Himalayas, jutting nine kilometers into the sky, 310 million years ago, but erosion has worn them down so all that's left are their hunched stubs, a thousand meters above the plain. Rocks have their rhythms: from the earth's crust they crack in the heat, explode and cascade upward into the sky, then, cooling, they gradually grind down, rows of giant molars in the jaws of millennia.

A spiny-cheeked honeyeater sounded a high *gok* like a glockenspiel and I sat in a gum tree in the riverbed and watched two zebra finches, with their red beaks and stripy zebra tails, make fluttery, rapid birdlove on a branch of a dead gum tree. A crow laughed mockingly in the distance. Nearby, a spinifex pigeon strutted by with its sleek Mohawk.

Every day we would walk and Rob would set up his easel to paint the ranges. I would walk on, one day climbing to the mouth of a huge gorge, through charred rocks, tawny outcrops and crags of burnt honey. A bushfire had run through here, so severe that the rock had melted to shininess. The rhythm of fire and life seemed suddenly clear. Plants and trees grow, dry out, go hollow, become tinder and then are swept up in a flash fire. Tree trunks are scorched and in the hottest places the rocks blacken and crack with heat. Nothing remains but ashes. But from the ashes, life arises, fresh, young green shoots.

Toward the top, the wind picked up exultingly. And at the neck of the gorge I looked right over the range to see miles and miles of rockscape beyond. I was utterly alone, the sun burning the rocks and me, and I had to take my clothes off, with the drum of the sun almost audible on the stones, raising the temperature, and I felt the insistence of heat, the demand of the drum and, feeling the heat of the rocks and the dust humming in my thighs, I licked my fingers and had an incandescent orgasm. An imperative of the land.

When I got back to Rob, he had almost finished a painting of jutting rocks in a land of purple and orange. It was glorious to me. But the painting seemed incomplete to Rob, and he asked me to sit for him, on a rock in the middle ground. An eagle flew curious over Rob's head as he painted.

In the honey-scented evenings, we would come back to our camp, our trousers streaked with charcoal from walking through burnt-out bush and our clothes matted with seeds. Seeds are some of the world's best nomads; they would walk across Australia if they could. Light and long-legged, with a lick of breeze, they would roll across miles, footloose roamers. Each seed has a story, how it came here, how it will leave, seeds that disperse by barbs, arrows, wings, downiness, featheriness, furriness, fluffiness, prickliness, helicopter wings and parachutes. There are clingers, blowers, harpooners and spikers, gliders, firecrackers and spring-loaded exploders, and seeds that hitchhike, each hook a thumb for our passing socks.

We heard brumbies galloping in the night across the desert. In the early morning, birdsong seemed to rise directly out of the land. Dawn was at about six and sunrise about seven. Light was let out, heat set free and birdsong let off the leash of night. Rob caught sight of a camel, stepping out of the trees, stopping as it saw us, and the sun exaggerated the camel's niches, the baroque flurry of flesh under its chin. The camel is ornate, a creature of a festooned world. Brought to Australia by Afghans, it seems to me to carry still the trappings of tapestries and souks and bazaars, the camel for whom hauteur is de rigueur. Stepping in the sand, it left soft pocks of bowl prints. And archly walked away.

We traveled on into the Arrernte Desert, where the sand ridges were like wrinkles on old, old skin. We both wanted to camp for a week or more on a sand ridge right out in the desert.

"There is no desert but was once a name," writes Jabès. You won't find the Arrernte Desert on most maps. In 1939, it was named the Simpson Desert, after one Mr. A. A. Simpson, president of the Geographical Society, by C. T. Madigan, who led the Simpson Desert Expedition, financed by Simpson. ("We say money is the whitefella Dreaming," says a Warlpiri man.) Madigan was to claim that Aboriginal people did not go there, despite Aboriginal people telling him that they did, and openly deriding his idea of it being an "unknown area." Arrernte people lived in the western part, Karanguru the east, Wangkamadla people lived east and north, while Wangkangurru people lived in the central and southern parts.

The dunes of the Arrernte Desert can reach the height of a three-story house and can run two hundred kilometers in length. There are more than a thousand of them, over 56,000 square miles. The dunes slouch their way northward across the desert, inchingly slowly, though in some years they may move several meters. Australia's central deserts are worlds of dunes; swale to crest, rhymed by the wind, the dunes spin in a counterclockwise spiral, as if one wind once wrote one signature on this one land.

It was a world of mirages, shimmerings and glares, of salt pans, bull dust, spinifex and mulga scrub. Little crimson chats skimmed by acacia trees and a lizard out in the open kept one eye on the sky for fear of hawks. On a sand ridge there was an intact camel skeleton, pure white bones in the sand, lying just as it died, under the last tree's shade it could reach. Another tree had the corpse of a camel underneath it. (If you knocked on it, it sounded like a drum. The bones were breaking through at the knee, shoulder and sternum, its eyes were pecked out and its hump, its fat reserve, was torn open and eaten.)

A reed, with shushing grassy stalks, bent over by the wind, described concentric circles in the sand around it. These things have a double impermanence, written by the wind, on the sand, the echo of a whisper. Occasionally, a willy-willy would skirmish over the sand.

Astonishingly, there are frogs in the Australian deserts, which survive the rainless time by holding a bladderful of water and burrowing three feet below the surface, where they hold in their moisture and "aestivate," a reversed hibernation—this is a summer-slumber, lasting up to three years—and they are woken by floods or rains if the water is sufficient to penetrate this far down. Then they scramble to the surface, feed and breed. In the Northern Territory, Aboriginal people hunt frogs as a water source. They are found by stamping on the ground and listening for a distant croak. Hear that and you can dig out a frog.

The king brown snake is here, one of the most venomous in Australia, and the spinifex hopping-mouse, which looks like a miniature kangaroo, hardly ever drinks, eats dry seeds and kips with nine or ten others in a burrow during the day. There are geckos, with large eyes for night vision—and they clean their eyes with their tongues. And there is the stumpy-tailed lizard, which looks like it has a head at both ends of its body.

Small birds, light as confetti, tickle the brittle spinifex, sprinkling tiny footprints around the bushes. The variegated fairy wren, sultan of spinifex, ripples its song loudly from the best bush in its territory.

Finches fly fast, chasing one another, *peeeuw peeeuw peeeuw*. And a wedge-tail eagle soars on thermals hunting rabbits. A swallow, or perhaps it's a swift, bothered by my presence, tizzicks on the ridge. But when the stealthy shadow of a bird of prey—a brown falcon or an Australian kestrel—palls over the sand ridge, silence falls in its wake and the birds don't even squeak their fear.

One plant sends out strong, stringy shoots, which reanchor into the ground some ten feet from the parent plant, so taut and tough you can pluck them like a guitar string. Sandhill canegrass is angled like swastikas.

I came across a dead Thorny Devil lizard, dry, crisp and crackly to the touch, its desiccated limbs and claws scratching at the sun, scraping the sky for more life, its mouth open for a last suck of moisture. This lizard, *Moloch horridus*, struts into a tiny moist patch in the sand and absorbs water feet first— the body gradually darkens with liquid sponged up till it reaches the mouth. In life, it feeds exclusively on black ants—the ants that feed on it now in death. (Ants, paparazzi of determined curiosity, never seem to feel the heat.)

The wind was welcome, cooling you and blowing away the flies. Whenever the wind died down, tiny birds in dry thickets would chirp up. (There are cinnamon quail-thrushes here and the rufous whistler, the rare Eyrean grasswren and the orange chat.) On the dune, for miles, there was no human footprint and for days we walked carefully, near the bushes, leaving the sand in smooth sheets. At the crest of the sand ridge there was a scooped-out hollow like the impress of a giant lute and the wind swept the shifting sand till it surged in orange with a pulse of light and hissed as it stirred over itself.

The Yolngu people call the dawn of the dawn the "time before morning"— the time when the tree of life can communicate between the world of spirit and the world of Earth. In the Kukatja language there is a dawn-before-the-dawn, *rakarra-rakarra*, or dawn-dawn, when the eucalpytus exhales its ultra-fine mist of perfumed oil, the satin bowerbirds and lyrebirds recall the light and the kookaburra laughs at the sun.

The very early mornings were needlingly cold; the water in our kettle turned to ice one night. The moment the sun had any warmth in it, the flies began their infuriating crawl, up your nose, into your ears, over your lips, into your mouth, doggedly clambering into the corners of your eyes. They droned with a dull and horrible persistence. They hunched themselves into your nostrils, they swarmed in their hundreds, stupid squadrons of dumb nuisance. The only two things that made them desist were wind and sunset. That was all.

The sands in the morning were apricot and saffron. A couple of hours later they turned deep terra-cotta while a young ghost gum shimmered silver. By noon, the sky was electric blue, highly charged, and the sand under it like a hot song sung without audience. At noon there is no nuance, no secret, no lean of perhaps. No potential waits, all is actual, no metaphor, only glare: the burning sun asks nothing, implacable and stark hour.

The tones of color in the sands were like tones of music, for in the bright midday the sand's high notes of straws and yellows sang out, while toward late afternoon the lower notes sounded, of orange and cinnamon and cayenne pepper, and in the evening, when the fiery day had burned out, the deepest tones of burnt toffee, burnt sienna, burnt umber and burnt plum hummed and hummed with the sun's low warm and reddest rays. Orange was mixed with purple and magenta in a shy and surprising consonance.

One afternoon I was looking at the work of Aboriginal desert artist Pansy Napangati, particularly her painting *Old Man at Ilpilli*. The painting has colors of straw, orange, ocher, black, tawny, pink, yellow, purple, dark blue and white. I took a pinch of sand, poured it onto the white page of my notebook and separated the grains, matching them to her work, and there they all were: grinning orange, soft ocher, slow-breathing purple, and a navy blue grain as blue as night elbowing day out of the way. When I got home, in a slug-and-conker green Welsh valley, and was looking at the book again, I saw how some grains had crept into the spine of the book between pages of paintings. From the other side of the world, these grains of sand spoke a world of cinnamon and sand-light. Desert art has a deep relationship with light. Brilliance and brightness are transformative and the power of the land is evoked by radiance through dot paintings or cross-hatchings.

In the evening, twilight cracked like an ax between day and night. You cannot avoid duality in the deserts. Day and night. Sun and shade. Fire and water. Heat and cold. Black sky and star. The myriad stars in the desert are dots of sharp staccato light, reckless in their generosity.

Landscapes such as these, sculpted by wind, are called aeolian, and the wind creates slopes of sand—and the slopes in turn affect how the wind, air and sand blow in vortices. Words will carry for miles here—any sound will.

"Fear Allah like a sandstorm" is a Bedouin saying. In a sandstorm in a desert you can lose all sense of place or direction and sometimes only the song of the sand will guide you, or the touch of the ground. The Bedouin can work out where they are, and their direction, even in sandstorms, by feeling the stones on the ground. The pitted surfaces always face north, because that is the direction from which the shemal wind blows.

The Sahara (as many deserts) is feared for its fierce winds, which, beginning with a booming and rumbling in the distance, will blow shrieking curtains of sand. Sandstorms have buried caravans, oases and cities and if people are caught in them they can lose their way and die of thirst. But the Sahara plays a wild trick on the unsuspecting. More people drown there than die of thirst. For when it rains, flash floods are created in wadis, riverbeds and creek beds.

For me, the most poignant story of someone who drowned in the Sahara was Isabelle Eberhardt, a writer half-Russian, half-French; she dressed as a young Arab man in north Africa at the end of the nineteenth century. Depressive, passionate and alcoholic, she was drawn to the Sahara as if to quench an emotional thirst "steeping her wild, besotted mind in the intoxicating expanse of the desert." She asked "for burial right here in these white sands gilded at dawn and dusk by that great and greedy scarlet sun." And she got her wish. In the Sahara, aged just twenty-seven, she drowned in a flash flood at Aïn Sefra.

Deserts can drive you mad, what the French Foreign Legion called *le Cafard*—desert madness, a feeling of severe depression that can make people crazy. (And the Bedouin spoke of djinns in the desert and claimed that if one faced a djinn, it disappeared.) These immensities panic some people. They make me calm.

Here there was only myself and Rob; each of us a hermit during the days, we would go our separate ways, often walking far away from each other, and then returning in the evenings to chat and cook.

A full moon rose as the sun set. We lit our evening fire, cooked and ate, then Rob cleaned his brushes and burned his oily, paint-filled rags. Warm by the fire, we shared a big bar of chocolate, while the resins of the wood hissed, and Rob said quietly, "Probably no one's stayed here so long or loved this place so much for a hundred years."

"MY EY DAZELS MY TONG BURN"

We were there in the Australian winter with gallons of water. But these same deserts can be killing in the heat. When Charles Sturt was in the central deserts in 1845, he wrote of his expedition's suffering because of the heat: "The blasts of heat were so terrific, that I wondered the very grass did not take fire." The mercury in his thermometer burst the bulb, and the dogs lost the skin off the soles of their feet. Because of the heat "the lead dropped out of our pencils. . . . Our hair as well as the wool on the sheep, ceased to grow, and our nails had become brittle as glass."

One man who died in the central Australian deserts left this last note: "My ey Dazels my tong burn."

Aboriginal people had a trick to search for water: take meat, salt it heavily, and feed it to crows. The salt would make the birds thirsty and they would fly toward water. People survived in the deserts through knowing exactly where water sources were to be found. The wells are all storied: full of Dreaming event, to make the routes to them more easily memorized.

A camel survives in deserts because it excretes very little water in its shit, piss, breath and sweat. Thirst makes plants thrifty with water, and in the deserts, plants cusp themselves, and live on mist. Cunning for water, they are like the canny poor who must think in farthings in a world of millionaires. Hoarding the dew, the ruby saltbush curls its whorled gray leaves into itself. People of the deserts know how to collect the dew from plants.

In the Atacama Desert of Chile, there are said to be places where it has never rained. The Turkana people of northwest Kenya call one desert area "Beyond Urine," because you can't take enough water and must be prepared to drink your own. Not for nothing has the Kalahari Desert been described on maps as a "thirstland," but (before the evictions) the Bushmen had survived here, using sip wells, sucking water up through a hollow reed from deep under the sand. Also, they would blow out the contents of an ostrich egg through a tiny hole, then fill the egg with water and bury it underground as a cache for dry times. The Bushmen lived following the lightning, for lightning means rain, greenery and game.

For the Samburu people, south and east of Turkana land in Kenya, the word for rain, *Nkai*, is also the word for their god. That is how rain is treasured in the deserts. In parts of the Sahara—for example, the Sand Sea in Egypt—rain only falls once in forty years or so.

Wilfred Thesiger crossed the part of the Arabian peninsula known as the Empty Quarter in 1946 and was to say at the end that "the reward had been a drink of clean, tasteless water. I was content with that." He tells of how the Bedouin survive. "If people are truly desperate they push a stick down a camel's throat and drink the vomit."

In the Uighur Autonomous Region of China is the Taklamakan Desert, the name given various translations from the Uighur language, including "Desert of Death" and "You go in but you don't come out." In the Gobi Desert, temperatures can reach 40 degrees C in the summer and minus 40 degrees C in winter. Its potential deadliness for humans is reflected in the myth of its creation: a Mongolian chief and sorcerer was pursued by the Chinese army and as he fled, he cried out "black words," so the landscape withered and died in his wake and nothing was left for the Chinese but waste.

The sun is the founding fire of all life, lighting quiet green candles of chlorophyll the world over, but in the deserts the sun is a foundry fire that even iron cannot fight. It devours dew; it evaporates the blood in your veins, leaving a viscous treacle in your body. (The opposite of the lizard, whose blood thickens in the cold, so it is sluggish in the early morning but in the hot noon sun it scampers, frilly with movement.) The heat turns your tongue to a dry slab of swollen leather and your mind is dulled too, words bulge stupidly, painfully, against your temples, each "thought" is a bruise, purple and ugly, shoving at your head. With a splitting headache, dizzy and immobilized with fatigue, all you can do is moan. I know thus far: I had heatstroke once, in a Greek heat wave, in a canyon, at noon.

In the midday sun, this landscape is a forge for the smelting of cliffs, a furnace for the cracking of rocks. A screaming, iron heat, boulder-splitting, it cleaves crevasses and chimneys. The sky has a blue to delight you in the early morning but by noon it becomes a burning, blinding blue, heartlessly, crazingly cerulean. A brilliant, cruel, killing blue, implacable as a sheet of stainless steel hammered right across the sky.

Your mouth is nothing but a motor, moaning for—for what? In theory, water and shade are what you need, but you feel beyond water, beyond shade, moaning maybe for time, for an hour to pass or three, for night to come, for darkness, not to have your head sway, for the movement is excruciating. Dying of dehydration begins with fatigue and fever, then dizziness, slurred speech and paralysis. The skin cracks, delirium sets in, the thickened blood cannot cool the body, and you die. And maybe, at the end, dying of thirst and heatstroke in a desert, your final wish would not be for water but for quiet death coming welcome as coolness, lovely as liquidity, the need for water abstracted and rethought, Buddha-like, into the quelling of desire for it, and in that moment, maybe water metamorphoses into death. And you would drink at death, thirsting for it. Maybe you would die with your thirst satisfied.

A SAND ALGEBRA

The wind draws dented diamonds in the sand, patterns subetched by gravity. Math has long been important to Middle Eastern cultures (*al-gebra* is an Arabic word and *al-gorithm* is partly based on the name of an Arab mathematician) and in the deserts you see why. Omar Khayyam, poet of deserts, wrote a treatise on algebra and used the Arabic term *shay* to mean the "unknown" in an equation. Translated into Spanish, the term was spelled *xay*, then abbreviated to *x*. The unknown, like terra incognita, this is *numerus incognitus*, desert space of mathematics.

On the dune, I'm struck by the math of the desert, how sand is blown up into an ever steeper gradient, how it reaches its peak, a dark shadowline keeling away sharply from a bright rim of sand. Sand is a trapeze artist, taking gravity right up to the line, in a show of brinksmanship. Sand builds until the slope attains a critical value. Once that slope is reached, sand avalanches occur. The slip. The critical moment at which the sand can no longer pile up but must fall, and falls sheer, under a fragile cutaway lip, down into its angle of repose, only to find the wind once again begins to increase the tension of its angle. There is trigonometry in the triangles of slide and arithmetic everywhere. With patience you could find the endless math of sand soaring to the limitless while the curve of the exponential spirals out to the galaxies.

In the math of sand, I can understand the appeal of the absolute in number and how there seems absolute truth in a desert. Through the math of the desert you can feel the lure of infinity, the origin of the idea of an infinite god, and the idea of eternity. (In the Namib Desert, there is a plant that can live for up to a thousand years, the *Welwitschia mirabilis*.)

ETERNITY IN THE SANDS

Water represents time—the words *tide* and *time* are etymologically related—and rivers are metaphors for time all over the world. Here in the dry deserts, time seems to evaporate, the temporary is baked away, what is left is the eternal. People have construed "timelessness" in deserts and the Desert Fathers drew their idea of eternity from the desert sands. Deserts tell of vast pasts, the sand from shells of millennia ago, and in Australian deserts, Aboriginal people know the eternity of the Dreamtime.

Aboriginal writer Ruby Langford describes her first visit to Uluru in *Don't Take Your Love to Town*: "It made me think of our tribal beginnings and this to me was like the beginning of our time and culture. Time was suddenly shortened to include all of history in the present, and it was stretched to a way of seeing the earth that was thousands of years old." This is a culture that wasn't frightened of ages, but made a waking dream of eternity and dwelt in it.

Deserts can seem both eternal and ever-changing: 750 million years ago, much of Australia lay under ice. The desert was once rainforest, which was once sea. (Geology speaks to ancient wisdom: "This too will pass.")

Some of the rocks of central Australia are nearly two billion years old. Here is sheer age, where the open reaches of time are like an unending wilderness of the fourth dimension. A deserted-world existed before mind was there to name it or to care, before a word for wind or anyone to mark a year. A stretch of time vast as the Gobi Desert, in comparison to which our age is one grain of sand winking in miniature, ruby and turquoise, blood and song, and contained within that grain, the first tottering steps of an alphabet, Byzantium, Omar Khayyam, chess, the Yanomami and all of architecture. Gone by twilight.

For eternity reaches into the future as well as the past and the desert wind will sandpaper out the last record of us without enmity or pity or grief. For these words and the minds that think them will not last the night. The desert's wilderness suggests the time when even evolution is over. Wind as it was in the beginning, and sand and gas, light and dark, omega to origin, a second time, after the end as before the beginning, or even the idea of "beginning" or "end."

In that wasteland, waste post waste, there will not be the mercy of finality or the grief of memory. All the words for the Sahara and the atom bomb gone, all the ways to describe winds in the Gobi forgotten, in the Kalahari the last click song sung, the will of the wind alone will be done, after earth and heaven, after even their idea, are empty of meaning and cease. Again.

THE NEWSPAPERS OF THE DESERT

Although the sands of the desert suggest eternity, the tracks that crisscross the dunes suggest currency, *the now*. And although the math of sand suggests infinity and the absolute, tracks, by contrast, suggest the necessity of story, the complication of the absolute, that something is truly infinite only by being infinitely complex.

There were tracks of a nonchalant lizard, swinging its tail. The track of the drunkenly named legless lizard. The track of a dragon lizard delighted me because I could see the line of its tail and on either side the lovely feathery prints of its tiny claws. Sand will stay loyal to a lizard's claw or a pissing man, or the pock of the hop of a spinifex hopping mouse.

One small beetle's track zipped up the side of the dune, and told its story days or even weeks after the beetle had gone. It came up this sheltered valley, two feet wide, and it detoured around this spiky burr, crawled under this stick; here it changed its mind about which direction to go in, or perhaps saw a fly, cornered sharply and headed for a spinifex bush. Another beetle scuffed up this way, but something pounced, indenting the sand. No more beetle tracks. I wanted to tread lightly here, not to stamp out these smaller stories.

Tracks represent way-wending minds, they illustrate curiosity or nerves, lust, hunger or boisterousness. Intricate stories all, each creature's story bound to all the others.

In the desert, you are in fact sitting in the middle of a text, with lines, history, reference and narratives that remain until the wind wipes the slate clean, erases the pencil marks on the page, and then the tribes of tiny scribes of beetle and bird begin to write again.

The stories of Dreaming tracks are congruent with the precise lie of the land. One story tells of the Two Brothers: one was exhausted from too much sex and the story says you could see in the ground the impression of his penis, dragging along the land.

Tracks can lie too. People used to steal horses from cattle stations, then shoe the horses backwards and ride away, so it looked as if they came from the place they were actually going to. Aboriginal people, wishing for their tracks not to be seen, would wear emu-feather boots, which would softly sweep out the sign of their passing. In the language of tracks, only humans have learned fiction and lies. Other creatures use nonfiction only, tell their truths: here where a creature scampered out of its burrow, there where tiny shovel marks in the sand show how a small animal with half-inch-long paws sprayed sand behind it as it buried itself. A long winding track under the sand shows where the mole cricket has tunneled its underground way.

A lovely cock-of-the-walk bird strutted along the top of the sand ridge as I walked one morning. An Australian kestrel flew up into the sole tree for miles, with its keen sweeping beak and talons, its body a toolkit, neat and perfect as a Swiss Army knife, then soared up and over the dune. I followed it up and read the kestrel's earlier story. First I saw the tracks of a small rabbit. Then I saw the sudden jolted sand where the kestrel had divebombed the rabbit out of a clear blue sky, there the sand was buckled by claws and beak and battle. Twelve feet farther down lay the fur and skeleton of the rabbit.

Tracks have a texture of time—were they made just now, yesterday or after a recent rain? Tracks tell what walked where and when, why and how. They are the newspapers of the desert, in first edition in the very early hours of the morning, as creatures find it safer and cooler to move around at night.

Aboriginal people read the complexity of tracks: which particular camel had passed a certain way, sometimes knowing it individually by the shape of its print, and they can tell from a human footprint whether the person was carrying a heavy load.

The Gikwe Bushmen can deduce from an antelope track not only its size, sex and build but also its *mood*. "When you track an animal, you must become the animal," they say. Tracking a cheetah, for instance, they say, "We put on the cheetah mind and follow him."

Tracks need not be visible and there is a whole world of tracks written in the intimate signature of scent. English has no word for being deaf-of-the-nose, because we don't even know what we miss by not being able to sniff out the tales and tracks of smell. Maybe here rabbit's urine twangs near a salt-bush, or there a mouse has emitted a puff of fear by the spinifex. Maybe a scent-hint still hangs near a thorn, dusky musk lingering, furry with desire, spicing a low branch with gamy loin-smell of a female kangaroo. Maybe the gall of a rejected male kangaroo still sulks by the acacia, and a lizard's ant-breath oils the air around its favorite siesta rock. And the ants secrete their own squeaking smells, faint pheromones by which they communicate. Water-scent, too, lilting lightly in the still dry air, trickles a tiny track to those able to follow it.

MIRAGES

Vision is strange in deserts, because there is no middle distance, so figures walking toward you stretch in heat's elastic, becoming the Giacometti figures of elongated legs and torsos.

One day, I saw an astonishing sight—a clear blue lake in the distance. Seeing a mirage, you know how easily you could be driven crazy by them if you needed water. The deception is complete: a perfect reflection of your hope. I clearly saw not only the lake but also the far shore, with red cliffs dipping down. Do animals too see mirages? Is that why you sometimes see animals, dead of thirst, miles from shade?

People die every year crossing the Sahara because they follow mirages and seeing what looks like an oasis, they go miles off course, in a fatal drift. Most mirages I saw were of water but one afternoon there was a mirage on the horizon as if blue flame, several miles long, were rolling in at us, a strange and deadly sky-blue wildfire.

The white explorers loathed these mirages, but arrived with mirages of their own. Charles Sturt came to central Australia with a heavy wooden whaleboat because he was obsessed by the idea that central Australia had an inland sea. (It did, yes, but some 350 million years previously.) Later, the boat was found, carried—ironically—by a flood some twenty miles down a creek where it had been abandoned.

A DESERT CAPRICE: PHALLUS TO THE FORE

A mirage was a very type of feminine wile to the explorers' eyes. There was witchery in this: the land would "bewitch" the explorers with the mirage, which made her (falsely) appear lifeful, waterful and young.

But even without such bewitching, the land was female to the explorers because it was inconstant, unpredictable, unfixed. (All attributes long associated with women.) Rainfall was erratic. Rivers would suddenly flow and suddenly cease. The land was fickle in its waters and the explorers saw it as unreliable, deceitful as a woman, changeable as the moon and capricious. The editor of John McDouall Stuart's *Journals* wrote of the "caprices of Lake Torrens, at one time a vast inland sea, at another a dry desert of stones." Charles Sturt writes of Australian rivers that he could not "trust" them; "they are deceptive all of them." And the male explorers called various places Mount Deception and Mount Delusion.

For the whites, exploration was a pinnacle of masculinity and many explorers were fanatical about crossing the land *in straight lines.* Phallus to the fore. Ernest Giles writes, "For several years . . . I had desired to be the first to penetrate into this unknown region where, for a thousand miles in a straight line, no white man's foot had ever wandered. . . . On that expedition [1872] I explored a line of nearly 700 miles of previously unknown country, in a straight line from my starting point." The mirage is the inverse opposite of the explorers' straight line. The mirage is something you can see but doesn't exist. The straight line is something you can't see but does exist, later, on a map. The mirage (to their eyes) female and treacherous: the straight line male, trustworthy and moral too, bringing to the land the biblical injunction to keep on the straight and narrow.

In Australia, the male explorers were obsessed with planting a phallic flagpole in the central hole of Australia's desert. Edward Eyre, leaving Adelaide in 1840 to try to reach the center, gave up at "Mount Hopeless"—a mount named for a failed erection. John McDouall Stuart did plant his phlagpole in a place he mounted and named: Central Mount Stuart.

Why do male explorers always have to "mount" expeditions? I only ask.

Recently, Nicholas Luard wrote a book about the Kalahari Desert that begins with one of his companions on the way to the airport leaping out of a cab and giving a female stranger a "nipple squeeze" before they leave: sexual assault is just an amusingly macho pastime for these desert explorers. Sturt wrote of the explorer's duty "to penetrate" the land and writes of "penetrating the deserts." Morton Cohen in 1960 was to write of Rider Haggard's *King Solomon's Mines*, "There was no heroine, nor should there have been one; penetrating Africa was strictly a man's job." It is believed he wrote it without irony. C. T. Madigan wrote of his journey in the "Simpson" Desert in a book which he dedicated, hilariously,

TO MY WIFE

WHO HAS DONE SO MUCH AT HOME

The Arabic word for *desert, badieh,* is feminine, as is the word for *desert waste, barrieh.* (And, purely for fun, a search on the Internet for *barrieh* will reveal a sponsored link to "pedal operated feminine hygiene units." We'll be coming back to that.)

"Wilderness" is a strange concept that has been treated as both Paradise and Hell, a place of Purity and of Pollution, the Great Mother and the place of Corruption. It is seen as "virgin": an idea that compels some to violent plunder and equally compels others to a passionate protection. The Genesis of all, it is also seen as the place of downfall. It is cloacal, a hideous drain, a waste place for waste products, and yet it is also the place of orgasmic ecstasy. The only thing that has equivalent cultural paradoxes and polar reactions is Woman. Wilderness is at once Muse and Devourer, Inspiration and *Vagina Dentata.* It is something men must conquer and subdue because they hate it, or it is something men love because it makes them feel most virile.

Wilderness is the cunt writ large.

And both woman and wilderness can be seen as a "no man's land"— a wasteland without meaning. Otto Weininger, a philosopher who influenced the Nazi movement, wrote in *Sex and Character* in 1906, "Women have no existence and no essence; they are not, they are nothing. Mankind occurs as male or female, as something or nothing. . . . The meaning of woman is to be meaningless." This is how explorers in Australia saw the central deserts: a meaningless land of lacking.

Images of land as a virgin to be impregnated by the settlers' seed are ubiquitous in European explorer literature and likewise images of land as a wild, libidinous female that needs to be tamed. In Australia, a third female type was brought into play, the hag, with her shriveled-up breasts, dried-up womb, unseeded, unhusbanded and barren. (One place was named by the whites "Mount Barren.")

To me, these deserts are anything but barren. They have an explosive fertility like Hakea seeds, which need fire to germinate, for only such heat will crack their seedcases. There also seems an incipient sexuality here, hot as flame. Light dances right next to darkness on the cusp of brilliance, the hot breeze tantalizes just below certainty, the hot land is like the inheld breath— something in suspension—the core temperature within you rises to the hot shimmering sands. A gasp . . . No wonder the Desert Fathers had lustful thoughts. It's just a pity they didn't enjoy them.

THE DESERT FATHERS

For the third-century Desert Fathers, god was pure and man was potentially so: desert and woman were impure. Spending time in the desert was done in part to overcome the lascivious thoughts of fork-tongued fornicators that would tempt the saints there. (For the Israelites, the desert was seen as the place of sexual temptation.) St. Jerome, who spent five years in the desert, "in that vast solitude parched with the fires of the sun," describes "watching the maidens in their dances: my face haggard with fasting, my mind burnt with desire in my frigid body, and the fires of lust alone leaped."

"The body of a woman is fire," says another. We women are of ourselves evil unless we renounce our womanhood. The sayings of the Desert Fathers include a description of a "harlot and actress" visiting a bishop. "My lord," she says, "I am a sea of wickedness and an abyss of evil. I ask to be baptised." She became a monk and eunuch, "Brother" Pelagius, and shut herself up in a cell.

(It did make me idly wonder whether this was the origin of those timeless jokes: "As the actress said to the bishop . . .")

One of the oldest summaries of the Desert Rule for the Desert Fathers contains an old man's answer to the question of what kind of man a monk should be: "So far as in me is, alone to the alone." (The Desert Fathers, funnily enough, found that their retreats became so popular that the deserts became positively overcrowded, much to the chagrin of the firstcomers.) The word *hermit* is derived from the Greek *eremites*, which is from *eremia*, which means "desert," formed on *eremos*, "solitary, or deserted," and the vaunted individualism of the solo hero in the desert wildernesses follows directly in this tradition. T. E. Lawrence and Wilfred Thesiger both wrapped their solitudes around themselves in the desert. This solitariness became part of the Western idea of wilderness, the lone traveler in an "empty" land, and the American definition of *wilderness* calls it a place where "man does not remain"—which was only possible after the white settlers had exterminated so many Native Americans.

THE DEVIL IN THE DESERT

When Europeans invaded Australia, they came with an ancient prejudice that deserts were an allegory of sin. Henry Halloran in 1853 wrote of a "cloven waste of gaunt and hungry sand." (Cloven, of course, like the devil's hooves.) In the New Testament, Matthew 4 describes it as the lair of the devil. The first of the Desert Fathers, St. Anthony, reported a devil shouting at him, "This is our place! What are you doing here? Get out!" The Desert Fathers hated nature—St. Anthony was angry with the sun for disturbing him in his prayers. So intense was their loathing that the "Stylites" lived their lives standing on a column to get away from the sinful stuff. (One, Daniel, went up a column at age thirty-three and stayed there till he died in 493, at age eighty-three. His feet were first inflamed, then worn away by microbes feeding on his wounds and his hair was crawling with lice.) The anchorites, according to John Cassian (d. 435), were keen to fight the devils of the desert, "in the freedom of the vast wilderness."

In the Christian tradition, if you deviate from the "path" of virtue into the trackless wastes, you are in the wilderness of evil. Terms for sin and evil were taken from the natural world: the snake, the apple, to sow wild oats, the cloven hoof, the primrose path, brutality, the mark of the Beast, the beast within. Terms for sinners were also terms taken from nature: a black sheep, bad egg, dog, jailbird, cur, hound, skunk, swine, rat, viper, serpent, cockatrice, basilisk, reptile, tiger, hellhound, hellcat, bitch—as if both wildness and beasts were of themselves devilish. By contrast, the words for virtue do not lean to nature but to the off-ground sky world: saintly, heaven-born, angelic, seraphic, godlike. (At this point a Christian apologist will be interrupting, "But what about St. Francis of Assisi?" His attitudes to nature were such a rarity in the Church that he came close to being labeled a heretic.)

The Old Testament god used the desert as punishment, sending plagues of locusts, famine and the deadly desert wind. Deuteronomy 28 threatens "the earth that is under thee shall be iron. The Lord shall make the rain of thy land powder and dust." If his chosen people sinned against him, he would drive them back into the desert wastes. The deserts of nomads contrasted with both the Garden of Eden and the agricultural land flowing with milk and honey.

For Judeo-Christianity, god is disembodied, inorganic and estranged from earth. He is supernatural, abstract and associated with desert. God became as "blank as the desert air," in George Steiner's words. The god was associated with desert but certainly not identified with it. The desert itself could suggest the character of Yahweh, his omniscience reflected in the all-seeing eye of the sun glaring down, while the dualism of god versus devil was reflected in the desert's dualism of night and day, water and thirst. The numberless grains of sand were like the infinite god, everlasting as deserts are endless. He is a fiery god, not a watery one, associated with the parched landscapes and the burning sun, which, like their god, gives life and blasts it to nothing; his breath is hot and dreadful, the khamsin, fatal wind. Perhaps the Israelites were far more influenced by nature than they knew; for maybe it was the desert itself that created the type of god the Israelites thought they found there. Not so much "God created man in his own image" but rather the *land* created *god* in *its* own image. Stark, ruthless, eternal, unforgiving, burning with hell's fire at noon.

And cruel. Psalm 102 places affliction in the desert: "I am like a pelican of the wilderness: I am like an owl of the desert. . . . I am withered like grass. . . . My days are consumed like smoke, and bones are burned as an hearth."

The term *wilderness* appears 245 times in the Old Testament, 35 times in the New. There are also hundreds of instances of *desert* and *waste* meaning essentially the same as *wilderness*. Deuteronomy 32 refers to this "howling waste of a wilderness." John the Baptist was "the voice crying in the wilderness" and Christ was tempted by the Devil in the wilderness for forty days and nights. Cotton Mather was to use the biblical imagery of the desert wilderness explicitly: the Puritans were, he said, "this little Israel now going into a wilderness."

The Desert Fathers represented the introverted violence of fire, but the extroverted violence wasn't far behind: the witches and heretics burnt at the stake, the fires of the Inquisition, the Crusades in the desert lands.

PURITY AND THE SCAPESCAPE

For the Israelites, bodily functions were the main source of impurity—the body's primitive animality was a pollution per se. *Inter faeces et urinam nascimur*, as St. Augustine was to put it. "We are born between the shit and the piss." Purity came from separating body from soul.

"The goat shall bear all their iniquities upon him to a solitary land . . . the wilderness." Thus the scapegoat appeared in the Old Testament, bearing the sins of the tribe. All ritually polluted things were to be thrown outside the camp into the wilderness, the desert. (Recall here the Arabic word for "desert waste," *barrieh*, now the name for a brand of pedal-operated feminine hygiene units.) Gradually, then, the wilderness became identified with the pollution, the landscape itself the scapegoat. Not a scape*goat* but a scape*scape*. Going to the desert was purifying, not because the desert was pure but rather because it was purifying to triumph over the evil that the desert represented.

By contrast, to the Bedouin, writes Murray Bookchin, the desert was *itself* a source of purification and of freedom. Chief Luther Standing Bear wrote that "when the dust blew, the Lakotas said the air was being cleaned for them, for when the wind subsided the days seemed brighter and clearer. . . . The Lakota thought of air much the same way as the white man does of water— something cleansing, something to bathe in." T. E. Lawrence said that he was drawn to the desert because "it is clean." (Even death in the desert seems "clean," because what is left, very soon after death, is pure shining white bones.)

The desert is the landscape of fire and in fire is purity. In the desert, every- thing irrelevant is burned away. Stark and ultimate, only skeleton remains, absolute and utter: all irrelevance gone, only truth is left. "The desert teaches by taking away," writes William Langewiesche in *Sahara Unveiled*.

Pollution, of course, has two meanings. One is the religious notion of defiling something sacred, the other is the idea of contaminating an environ- ment. As far as wildernesses today are concerned, "pollution"—in an en- vironmental sense—is a crucial idea, with activists fighting against air pollution, or water or light or sound pollution. There is also a current anxiety over the "purity," or "pristineness," of wild lands and a belief that pure nature is polluted by contact with humans. It's seductive but dangerous, because it ig- nores the fact that almost all land all over the world has been influenced by people and because it suggests that we humans are not a part of nature, that we are both literally and spiritually a pollution. Our mere presence is re- garded as an impurity and some wilderness enthusiasts zealously want to keep the "stain" of people out of the "purity" of wildernesses in a quasireligious frame of mind.

ON FIRE

Aboriginal people are technicians of fire. People know plants that catch fire easily, plants that will burn even when wet, those that don't burn, those that will burn slowly (useful for overnight fires), those that burn with a lot of smoke and can be used to drive away insects, those that have a bright flame and make good torches. People also know "whose" fire has run through par- ticular country, because only people with a particular relationship to land have the right to fire it. Fire communicates, too. A woman from the Great Sandy Desert, quoted in *Yarrtji*, comments, "We bin lighting fire for grandmother, she might come. . . . That fire like telephone. People know for fire. We bin watchem. They coming up."

People use fire to "tidy" the country, to "keep it clean," and to give greenness a chance to flare up again from the land. To use fire knowledgeably is part of culture and people have long used "fire-farming" in desert areas, for regrowth. When they have lost control over land and cannot burn off the scrub as it needs, they call the land "dirty" and "wild" and they worry that the land will burn out of control in the lawless havoc of "hot" bushfires.

The act of firelighting, gently, firmly, repeatedly rubbing a stick in a groove of dry wood, filled with dry grass and dry kangaroo dung, sends pulses of warmth through the wood, which then flickers, glows with warmth, flushes with a spark and creates a cascade of small flame. (Relief. A deep breath. Laughter. A cigarette.) From this act, fire is born, like a small and tender seedling hardly out of piphood; the young flame, thin and cool, needs tending, care, feeding and protection.

Fire, like us, has its ages.

After the young fire comes rascal fire, in its hot adolescence, tall and rangy; arsonist fire; antic flame fucking all the tinder in sight, pants-down, leg-over, hot-humping branches, heaving and leaving the moment it has burnt its way. With a restless, energetic, explosive hunger for new wood, it streaks across thickets, licks its tongue of flame over unburnt scrub and, at the moment of its frenzied eruption, abandons it charred, burnt-out but glinting black with knowledge.

Then comes the slower fire, a thoughtful, mature thinker-fire, studying more carefully what to burn off: yes, the brash, littering tickertape of brittle dry undergrowth but not the trees and stands of plants. This is the socially useful fire of middle age: the one Aboriginal people encourage to burn the land.

And finally there is elder-fire, soft, generous and warm, lingering for days in one place, the stooped, comfort-fire of hearthside and home, memory-fire, whose every flickering low flame has a story, tells it in an ashy voice, gray-featherlighted and orange-thoughted.

One of the paradoxes of fire, and perhaps in the deserts its deepest truth, is its unexpected affinity with water. After a fire, bright shoots spring up as if rain had freshly fallen. Both rain and fire rip through the land suddenly, rain like wildfire and fire like wild rain. Fire floods over country, a golden, over-flowing, orange river bursting the banks in a torrent of flame.

In deserts, wind is an accomplice to fire, and the dry earth. In fact all the elements conspire with fire: water by its reticence. Fire is always about to happen—that is part of the "latency" of this land, the tension of its pent-up energy.

By legend, the phoenix flaps its wings in a nest of spices and a fire arises, in which the phoenix is reborn. Here, the phoenix *does* arise from the fire: from fire comes new life. This image concentrates the energy of flight and fire, alchemically melting everything to its essence; all the elements are present in the story. The element of earth is portrayed in turmeric and clove; the element of air in the brilliant wings and a gust of wind; the element of fire, incandescent and outboasting—for a moment—the jeweled bird till the miracle. From the charred and blackened ground comes bright green life, shining. Then comes water, concentrated to its most perfect expression: life flashes up in a green silk fountain of cool leaf.

Like us, fire needs to breathe, feed, dance and reproduce: it is wildly alive, utterly free yet obedient to laws—too much water will kill it, insufficient food will starve it. Fire has its moods, its contentments of glowing embers, its weird greenfire, and we have its burning passions, lust's flames and rage's incandescence. We too, a combination of oxygen and carbon, burn lively into ashes. We too destroy, create, change, transform.

We take the Promethean role, and sometimes we play Prometheus as thug, burning holes in the ozone layer with the stub of his fag, not only thief but arsonist. Sometimes we play him tender as candlelight, in our lovely capacity for illumination.

Fire is the ur-energy of art. (No art comes from the fireless, congenitally tepid, lukewarm heart.) Those whose words, unsaid, would scald them, or those whose eyes burn to paint what they've seen on the far side of the manifest, or whose ears are incandescent with the cadence of music they were the first to hear—all artists know fire, have burnt with it and have been burnt by it. Woden, or Odin, god of ecstatic poetry and magic, controlled fire. The Finnish epic the *Kalevala* describes the relation of poet to world and to word:

> *Of what use are we singers . . .*
> *If no fire spurts from our mouths . . .*
> *. . . and no smoke after our words?*

Fire is a verb, too, to fire the land, to fire clay, while to fire something with love is to intensify it. One Aboriginal artist, Clifford Possum Tjapaltjarri, painted *Sun Dreaming* (1972), which was painted, according to Geoffrey Bardon, "in exultation and happiness, using the incandescence of the sun as a metaphor for love."

Fire in the Australian deserts seems to come up from the land: fire creates landscape. "That's in the song, how the sparks jumped across the country. The fire burnt from Atnwengerrp right up to Hamilton Downs, then the spark jumped to Kings Canyon. These hills here are burnt from the fire," wrote Wenten Rubuntja, whose own surname means fire.

And we too have the nomadic urge to run like wildfire.

NOMADS ALL

Great is all townsmen's dread of the Beduw, as if they were the demons of this wild waste earth," writes author and traveler C. M. Doughty in 1888, describing these "land-loping Beduw." "The settled folk in Arabian country are always envious haters of the nomads that encompass them, in their oases islands, with the danger of the desert." Settlers have always wanted to tamp down the inhabitants of the writhy wild. The hostility can run both ways: when the Kel Tamashek (Tuareg) of the Sahara use the word *haritin*—"culti-vator"—the term is tinged with contempt.

Leading environmentalist George Monbiot, in *No Man's Land*, writes of the conflict between roamers and the settled, suggesting that restlessness is fundamental to our nature, for in the savannas of Africa, where humankind evolved, we needed certain characteristics in order to travel; two-leggedness, complex brains, sight as a primary sense. And "with them came emotions—our great capacity for anger, fear, excitement, curiosity and wonder . . . these emotions, while once they kept us alive, now they torment us."

Although it appears that it is the roamers who move and the estated who stay in one place, in the long run the opposite is true. Nomads and hunter-gatherers dwell in one area of land though they move freely within it, while the most ferocious horde of marauders are those Europeans who have swept over the world, stealing whole continents.

Wealthy, European men of estate—heterosexual, Christian and adult—have long marked one characteristic in their Other: the poor, the non-European races, women, homosexuals, Gypsies, Jews, hunter-gatherers, the supposed insane and children. Along the strata of power (sex, class, race, religion, sexual orientation, mental norm) there is a common factor: a hatred of *nomadism*.

A woman who is sexually free is termed a "tramp." Prostitutes are "street-walkers" and a "loose" woman is unfixed, liable to movement. (Such a woman is one for whom "man is a visitor and does not remain," as the famous U.S. legal definition of wilderness in 1964 states.)

To women, mainly, are accorded the derogatory verbs "gadding about" or "gallivanting." "Flirt"—which the *Oxford English Dictionary* tells us is said of women more than men—also combines movement with sexual license. The word *flirt* is a fickle, inconstant person, "a woman of giddy flighty character." *Flighty*, says the *OED*, is used "usually of a girl." Women are flighty, like birds (and *bird, chick, duck, hen* are all nouns used of women). Birds have long been a symbol of freedom of movement and the word *flirt* is used of winged creatures—birds "flirt" their feathers and it means taking short quick flights. People can flirt a bird feather or fan (both traditionally women's costume), moving them suddenly and swiftly. In all these terms, it is the wild *mobility* of women's behavior that is criticized. The derogatory phrase "to run off with someone" is more often used of women than men.

The worst of all flighty women were witches, the broomstick flitters, flying wild, flying high, nomads of the night. Women were accused of witchcraft for allegedly killing cattle and crops—the accusation always made by settlers against nomads. In *The Crucible* the Reverend Hale asks one of the girls, "Does someone afflict you, child? . . . Perhaps some bird invisible to others comes to you— . . . Is there some figure bids you fly?" *Flight*, quintessential freedom of movement, is devilish and wild. (Being "be-*wild*-ered"—a term used several times in the play—portrays someone straying or wandering in a sinful sense.)

Women's physical movement was "hobbled" in hobble skirts, we were "stayed" in stays, and in China, women's footloose freedoms were notoriously footbound. Women's very bodies are nomadic in their courses as we are always in flow, a woman's body is a Gypsy, ever moving on, in a state of flux.

Women's conversation "rambles." We don't get to "the point." We don't

"think straight." We make excursions off the subject, digress, think circu-
itously, and our free linguistic nomadism infuriates the overmasculine mind.

"Wild women" in *Brewer's Dictionary of Phrase and Fable* (1978—first published in the nineteenth century) are those who "go in for women's rights"—
these wild women are "runagates" who would "stump the country." (My grandmother was a Pankhurst, and I would love to think she was loosely related
to the runagate Pankhursts who stumped the country.)

All over Europe, another class of nomads was hated by the established
Christian Church and often mistrusted by the settled classes: the wandering
players, the traveling circus with clowns in their nomadic tents, the touring
theater, the jugglers and acrobats, the troupes of commedia dell'arte, the wandering minstrels, the jongleurs, whose music and dance contained elements of
rascalry and mischief making, the serious joker, the gleeman who, more than
musician, was also jester, player and trickster.

Vagrant, vagabond and *tramp* are all pejorative terms used of the very poor
and all have nomadic overtones. *Drifter* is a term of abuse. In modern America, "transients" are treated like dirt. The word *vagabond* in its early usage was
simply nomadic, not living in one particular place. It acquired its negative
meaning when it began to be used of an idle waster, someone possibly criminal.

In Britain, in 1494, the "Vagabonds and Beggars Act" was passed, which
insisted that vagabonds and beggars should be forced to stay in their own territory, and if they roamed, they should be set in the stocks for three days. In
1547, branding and slavery were imposed as the punishment for persistent
vagrancy.

The purpose of the Poor Laws was to control the poor, to shackle them to
one place. In 1662, the preamble to a new act of Parliament read as follows:
"By reason of some defect in the law, poor people are not restrained from going from one parish to another . . ."

The acknowledged hatred for the nomadic poor was expressed in the poet
Edmund Spenser's lines in 1591:

Wildly to wander . . .
Withouten pasport or good warrantye,
For feare least we like rogues should be reputed

Adults speak disapprovingly of "wayward" children and of teenagers being "led astray." Anyone or anything "out of hand" is unwelcome. *Err, transgress* and *stray* express moral disapproval.

Insane people are called "unsettled," "disturbed" and "unstable"—their mental mobility is considered a sickness. They are "all over the place" and their thinking is "erratic"—they are "deranged" and "deviant," their minds are "wandering," and they may well be "out of their heads." And the response is to confine them, just when they need their freedom most.

Most culture heroes travel: the Aboriginal Ancestors, Odysseus, Beowulf, Don Quixote. Arguably, leaving one's community to travel is a necessity for full development. Yet from the late nineteenth century, Western society turned a need into a pathology and people with a compulsion to flight were diagnosed as suffering "hysterical fugue." In 1893, a French study was published of Jewish "neuropathic travelers"—the figure of the Wandering Jew, medicalized. The Wandering Jew was supposedly condemned to wander the world till the Second Coming, and the anti-Semitism of the Nazis came in part from the fact that Jews were stateless, were a wandering people. The Nazis, with their rootedness of Blood and Soil, could wander about as *Wandervögel* but did so as an estated people, picnicking on their own lands. Nomadism, by contrast, was repugnant to them. The two other groups most persecuted by the Nazis shared the same—loathed—nomadic quality: the Gypsies and homosexuals, who were wanderers across sexual bounds. Homosexuals "transgress," they are sexual nomads who go "cruising." In pantomime, sex-change parts were known as "travesti"—crossing the borders of sex-appropriate dress and giving rise to the morally loaded term *travesty*.

The Nazis murdered up to half a million Gypsies, but treated with relative lenience any Gypsies who could demonstrate that they had lived settled for over two years. Gypsies in France were also known as "truands"—the wild, free and hated opposite of the schooled uniform majority. Their life was "O lungo drom"—the long road—in the Romany language. In the eighteenth century in Germany, signs were erected showing Gypsies being flogged and hanged, they were hunted and killed like wild animals, and one estate owner in the Rhineland in 1835 lists creatures he "bagged" while out hunting, including "Gypsy woman and suckling babe." Just being a Gypsy was a hanging offense in several European countries. Throughout Europe, Gypsies still face being beaten to death by racists and often live in poverty. In Britain, about 67 percent of traditional travelers' sites were closed between 1986 and 1993. In 1994, the Criminal Justice and Public Order Act effectively destroyed Gypsy nomadism, removing the duty for local councils to provide sites for travelers.

In 1554, a British law said that people calling themselves Aegyptians were in fact "false vagabonds" and were condemned to death. These "false vagabonds" are today's "bogus asylum-seekers," imprisoned in detention centers. The modern media's metaphors for refugees almost always use terms from wild and *moving* nature, "tidal waves" and "floods," "flows," "streams" and "surges," as the tabloids give a pernicious new voice to an ancient violent hatred.

When European settlers invaded other lands, it was the nomads they loathed the most. In 1910 in Canada, the French missionary Father Le Clercq commented that the "wandering and vagabond life" must be brought to an end, and a place "suitable for the cultivation of the soil" found so that he could "render the savages sedentary, settle them down, and civilize them among us." By 1927, in southern Africa, it was illegal to carry a Bushman bow and "vagrancy" was a crime. (The etymology of *vagrant* is from *vagor* in Latin, "to wander, to roam free.")

In the mid-nineteenth century, in Australia, Kooris were criminalized under the "Vagrant" Act: not having material possessions, Kooris were automatically defined as rogues and vagabonds. They were also caught under new trespassing laws.

In 1888, the *Illustrated London News* reported that Aborigines were "wandering, restless, half-starved, lazy, dirty naked savages, homeless and miserably depraved." The Aboriginal "on Walkabout" was and still is mocked by white Australians, though the wisdom of that practice is profound. (So nomadic are Aboriginal people that even their languages can be nomadic—many Aboriginal people are named after an animal or plant, but when someone dies, it is forbidden to use their name, so the name for that object is changed and thus language walks on, to a new lexical camp, returning perhaps only years later.)

Also in 1888, the "Aborigines' Protection Association" stated that any parents who "roamed the country" should have their children stolen from them by the mission.

Everywhere that Christian missionaries established their mission stations, they have first forced local people to settle, and then they have turned
their attention to the object of their greatest hatred: the shape-shifters of the
Amazon or the Arctic, the shamans of the world, nomads even in the spirit
world. Their nomadism took the form of transformation, trance-formation—
through dance, fasting or drugs—and the spiritual experience was in direct
conflict with the fenced mission stations; the shamanic nomadism was ecstatic, standing outside the walls of the ordinary: these outlaws of god, beyond
the fence of *fiat*, vaunted the reckless, adventuring human spirit. Potential
shamans were characterized sometimes by illness, physical or mental, and by
their emotionality, mood-nomads, mercurial, sometimes refusing food, sometimes greedy for it, sometimes sleepless, sometimes full of sleep and dreams,
and they were typified by a need to "wander," restless in their minds.

Thus hundreds of years of hostility from the Establishment against all
forms of nomadism, and the nomads are losing ground at every turn. In fact,
so successful have the Settled Classes been, and so complacent are they in
their success, that they can now afford to co-opt the last vestiges of nomadism
in the form of package tourism, and invent that laughable self-contradiction,
that apotheosis of turgidity the static caravan.

But the lure of wild and nomadic freedom has never left us, any of us. It is
in our lungs, breathing in freedom, in our eyes, hungry for horizons, and in
our feet, itching for the open road. Put your boots on.

Old boots are thought to bring good luck, but old boots are good luck of
themselves, as all walkers know. Boots that have folded and softened and bent
to your foot: boot and foot in a cozy, comfortable marriage. (Old boots were
traditionally tied to the wedding car of newlyweds, to suggest that on the long
walk of life, it's good to have that easy familiar necessity.) Boots keep their
history, but even more so do the feet of nomads, skin cracked like claypans in
the desert, journeys ground into the soles, feet cross-hatched with the tracks
they have followed on the ground; the land has written itself into people's feet
as the feet in turn have written pathways and tracks on the land.

James Joyce wrote in *Portrait of the Artist*, "There was a lust for wandering
in his feet that burned to set out for the ends of the earth. On! On! his heart
seemed to cry. . . . He was alone. He was unheeded, happy and near to the

wild heart of life. He was alone and young and wilful and wildhearted, alone amid a waste of wild air."

Thoreau writes, "I fear chiefly lest my expression may not be extra-vagant enough—may not wander far enough beyond the narrow limits of my daily experience. . . . Extra vagance! It depends on how you are yarded. . . . I desire to speak somewhere *without* bounds; like a man in a waking moment, to men in their waking moments."

To wander is the Taoist code word for becoming ecstatic, and roamers, farfarers and wayfarers know the intoxication. The Sufi have a tradition of "aimless wandering"—the aim of aimlessness is psychological purification, practicing "sacred drift."

Isabelle Eberhardt was almost annihilated by destitution, and in this situation, she violently embraced a life that in fact she had little choice but to follow. "Vagrancy is deliverance, and life on the open road is the essence of freedom." Her defiance is a peal of bells for nomadism, "to be free and without ties, a nomad camped in life's great desert." "Now more than ever do I realise that I will never be content with a sedentary life, and that I will always be haunted by thoughts of a sun-drenched *elsewhere*."

Nomadism is like an original fire in our wild minds; we stole it from the gods, and we made it into our own, leaping to new places, quickening to motion, curious and light as flame. The keen urge has never left us to take a flitting tent and fling it under the stars, then swing on, on at dawn, on an elemental journey. That is how to burn most brightly. That is how to catch like wildfire.

Before the white people came, we were roaming, roaming, roaming, Ernie Williams had said at the start of my journey, and as he had spoken those words—sung them, almost—their rhythm evoked their meaning, and the words were regular and endlessly repeated, the strides of a nomad, roaming, roaming, roaming, and I couldn't forget them—the words left footprints in my mind. The whites exiled Aboriginal people from the land, but they were themselves exiled, as modernity is exiled from the nomadism we are still heir to. For its call has never lost its power; wanderlust is with us still, the desire for the open road, to be Gypsy, tramp and bird of passage; we are wayfarers all.

Walk. The drum begins. Follow it. Follow the drums of thunder. Follow the sun. Follow the stars at night as they lean their long slant down the far side of the sky. Follow the lightning and the open road. Follow your compulsion. Follow your calling. Follow anything except orders and habit. Follow the fire-fare-forward of life itself. Go where you will, burn your bridges if you must, leave the paving stones smoldering and singe the gate as you leave, leave an incendiary device by The Wall, and scorch your way across the land. I dare you.

All children, but only a few adults, are wise enough to know they must run away and join the circus, the Traveling Circus, the really Big Top, where the sun itself is the ringmaster and the circus tent the whole round of the world, and every day the fervid performance, free and for everyone. And all you have to do to get an entrance ticket is come with your boots on.

The troubadour and minstrel knew it; the gleeman and the band on tour; the gleeful, romping nomadism of the traveling singers. Watching them leave, on the road again, the settled seethe with restive envy. For the settled, in their suburbs, steeped in that stagnant and tepid sink, time is sluggish with routine: a bleary sunrise and a blearier sunset. There, the past is framed in a fixed photographic grin, and the future is tamed with a pension plan. Nothing in nature is suburban. Nothing wild is phlegmatic and complacent. Nothing compares to the grotesque infantilism of the suburbs, sucking the dummy of the supermarket and every week squirting out the waste into giant plastic nappies, the bulging trash bags by the closed gate. In the suburbs, the alertness of all wild creatures is degraded into neurotic curtain-twitching. The curiosity of all animals degenerated into bingeing on Sky News. Queasily obedient, here life is just a dull lull, tethered to a bungalow, an index-linked nap between two sleeps.

Active in an environment, people may be serene. Passive and inert, people feel a cage-rage so pervasive that they do not recognize its cause: our exile. We, though we know it or not, long for the open road, the path yearning on, swinging past, lean and agile, full tilt to the horizon. Not knowing if the wind will whip you or soft sun stroke your face, but walking on in trust, a kind of faith, not that some overweening god will show you the way, but that the way itself will show you the way. And all you need to do is put your boots on and walk. But walk you must.

We were made this way: our feet are winged as Mercury. Our spirits are forged with the fire of nomadism. Highly alert, our eyes are alive to paths and cannot resist following lines on the land. We were made to walk through our lives wildly awake: our minds mobile, quick, changeable. We all are mercurial, our minds as winged as our feet, receiving signals and responding, volatile by nature; sunshine and showers, storms and dog days, we are various as the wild weather on the way and wet with it.

New horizons for the eyes liberate the mind and to be a nomad in one's mind is in our gift: to move and learn, to be a student always, to discover new lands, leaving behind some rock of certainty, to wonder without doxy, letting the mind wander till it surprises itself. The mind, let loose, is a walking, asking, searching thing, an *extra-vagrant* of mental journeys, questioning, questioning, whose root, of course, is to seek, to go on a quest.

Out on the road, with your senses wide open, you have to wake at dawn, because you follow the sun, which rises and reaches its way across the sky. The rhythm of day is the rhythm of fire, the tiny flame, dawn of the dawn, birds rubbing their beaks together to make a spark of morning, the roaring teenage fire of noon, the mature fire of afternoon, and on, on, the sun walks on, to the low hearth fire of evening, grandfather fire and grandmother ash.

Out on the road, you can see time as a nomad, always moving on, now running wild, now dawdling, now stripping every leaf from the tree, now swollen with desire, its restless, endless turnings, time winding around the hills of worlds we don't yet know, time spiraling the vortices, hurling up the mountain ranges and grinding them down.

Being on the road has an inherent quality of song. It feels so natural to sing as you walk, in wanderlust, lustful, full-throated, belting out melodies at the hills. Sing up the sun. In your walking you sing your path. Nomadism's rhythm is the sun. Nomadism's melody is the songline. On the leaning way, the slanting way, the canting way, music echoes the lilt of the land. The singer is chanting, canting the descant part, till the way is steeped in song, enchanted, sung, the singer chants the way and walks the song, and the way and the song and the singer are one. *On!*

Wild Air

ON THE BARE MOUNTAIN

Here is desolation. There is no path. Too few people ever cross the summit of this mountain to leave a trail. There were small cairns below us, waymarkers, but up here there are no cairns and no stones to make them with. Only mist, mud and sparse, short tree ferns and tussock grasses. At the peak, there is no peak, just miles of cold swamp with clouds clinging like cold ghosts in colorless exhalation. It is a shapeless, slouching summit that makes me long for an alpine triangle of snow and rock, so the narrative of your climb can rope itself to the contours of a mountain. Here, there is only a claggy swamp for miles.

Josef, my guide, says you have to climb the peak in complete silence, for if people sing or speak, the spirit of the mountain may kill them, sending thunder and freezing rain. There is one voice here, the wind, which would wrench the breath from your mouth and shudder the roots of a stumpy dwarf bamboo.

I'm badly affected by altitude and here, at over 3,600 meters, I feel dizzy and disoriented. My head aches and I'm exhausted. The wind is a sour shriek in my ears. Even though it is overcast, I wear my sunglasses because my eyes ache with the whiteness. Theo, one of the guides, holds my hand. I feel desperate to descend and I walk as fast as I can, plunging straight into thick mud pools.

Geert, an athletic young anthropology graduate from Eastern Europe, seems entirely unaffected by altitude.

On the days walking up to this point, the four guides have fostered me and villaged me (daughter, sister, mother). They have learned the length of my stride, which bogs I can jump and which we must detour. Without my quite realizing it, they have watched me closely—lovingly, in fact—so they would know when I need help. It is now.

At the beginning of our journey, I was proud. I can do it myself, I learn to say, in the local Lani and Dani languages, as well as Indonesian, the lingua franca here. I've climbed many mountains in my life and I've always carried my own gear. Not here. Many days ago, Theo waltzed off with my rucksack and laughingly refused to give it back. I accepted and was more able to write notes along the way. As the path wound higher, I had to accept help more— the logs and roots that make up the path were slippery like glass poles greased with pig fat and water, and they are sometimes set on uphill slopes for over fifty feet. For me, it's an almost impossible balancing act. Sometimes the logs are so rotten they are bendy, or spongey with moss.

I'm dragging on the air like a smoker denied a fag and every three steps I want to sit down and cry. I lean into Theo's shoulder, hook my arm through his and accept that no, I can't do it myself. I stare at my boots and I keep barging on, for a while. Then I look around and feel the chilling fear of wilderness. The skull gleams pale under the skin. I have utterly lost my sense of direction and I have no idea how Josef is finding the way. He doesn't use a compass and the clouds are too low to give him any view of landscape. The swamp looks, to me, absolutely indistinguishable in all directions.

For some time, I walk with my eyes shut, trying to stop the horizons' sickening spinning, and so that I can hear better my own urgent and simple advice to myself: *Do not stop: keep walking.* I lean heavily on Theo, lurching, climbing, climbing, wading through thick bog up over my knees, climbing, climbing. *Do not cry, do not stop, do not slow the others, drink water, walk fast, do not stop.*

At odd intervals, pale sticks have been hammered into the ground. Each stick, says Josef quietly, is where someone has died: Lani people, probably lost, dying of exposure. In the hours of our crossing the summit, I count up to six. Then up to twelve. There were a few more after that, but I'd stopped counting. Here is a theater of death, like a Greek tragedy, where the action has already taken place, each person a player staggering alone on stage. Only the mountain your audience, and the wind heckling your last words.

At one point the guides light a fire to propitiate the mountain spirits. The smoke drives off the mists, which must have shrouded the dying, up here. The cold mists move stealthily, sideways, creeping along the ground, and the smoke billows lustily upward into the skies.

The grave sticks look like a parody of waymarkers. Follow them, and you would go around in killing circles, wandering, maddened, lost, until you collapsed and joined this crazy circus of the dead.

The bodies are gone, but the sticks are eloquent of people's last moments, angrily keeping a last little bit of precious life locked up in their chests until death, treasure-hunter, thief, finally picks the lock. Did they die silent? Or howling into the night for help beyond hearing, a forsaken, jagged voice screaming to the wind? *Eloi.* Death sniggers. God didn't come for Jesus, why the hell should he come for you?

More than anything, these searing gaunt sticks nailed on the sky suggest the implacability of death. Not cruel, but absolutely ineluctable. Though the living, hot and angry, may rail against it—the insurrectionary bereaved here struck the fierce gash of their grief as they drove the stick into the earth—yet death and the mountain shrug in cold austerity.

In the silence, you can hear the dead, says Stefanus, another Papuan friend. Here, I feel I'm not breathing in oxygen but silence. My mind is silent even to itself. There is no pure synonym for silence. If there were, the two would speak, each vying to be voiced. There is no true synonym for death either, only sickly euphemisms. If there were, they would have a debate too lively for their own meaning. But *silence* and *death* are each the last word on their own subject, which is why the most appropriate metaphor for death is silence and for silence death.

As sound is sucked out in silence, so personalities are bleached away. In this stark white light, color and significance bleed away. What matters on mountaintops is brutally practical. The right route. Daylight. Water. Sugar. All the things that make life worth living—cartoons and conversation, herbs, cider, kindness, puppies, fiddlers and the idling geniality of valley life—are utterly insignificant here.

Air matters, but the words that can breathe meaning into that air do not matter. Words, lovely butterflies, too fragile to survive up here, are of no use. My boots, though, are of use, my emergency bivvy bag, my matches wrapped in a knotted condom for waterproofing—all these matter, but words, like coins, have no currency here. My feet matter but not my emotions. Thoughts come to me only in cold, stark realizations. My leg muscles matter more than my mind.

Everything is pared down to blunt necessity. I have been hollowed out, here: the knife that scraped the shape of these mountains has carved me too and the mountain's cold sweat is mine. Rain clogs my clothes. My nose is a drainpipe and my hair is greasy with rain. My socks are sodden, my boots are heavy with wet mud, and my trousers, wetly wrinkled, cling to my skin. The clouds lean down on the land.

Then, suddenly, we reach the top of a cliff face, the mountain wall, and the descent begins. It is in parts a steep vertical climb, and I reach for handholds and footholds on cold, wet, slippery rock. After about two hours my legs are aching. Geert has found the descent far harder than I have, and is a long way behind. By five, we have been walking and climbing for ten hours. My legs are trembling violently and I wonder if they will just give way beneath me. That would be a disaster. On most of the descent, there isn't even a platform or ledge wide enough to lie down. No one could carry another person down here without risking a fall that could be fatal. At best, there are rotten runged ladders pegged into rocks, but these are treacherous.

We go on, and I climb down slowly, in pain. The sky darkens. Then the darkness darkens more, then it blackens. And then it rains, in huge ropes of water plunging out of the sky. It doesn't get lighter, even after the rain, for evening is closing in fast, as we finish the almost-vertical part of the descent. But we still have miles to go before we reach anywhere we could make a camp. Josef and I wait for Geert and another guide, Mathias—I have a flashlight but I don't know whether they have one, and it's dangerous to walk in the dark.

Geert and Mathias eventually catch up to us. Geert has only a very weak flashlight, which lights nothing. He doesn't thank us for waiting. (Why should he? He'd do the same for us.) But now I'm worried, for the pathways here, like most paths in the Papuan Highlands, are slippery logs over "ground" that is not ground at all but a mass of loose leaves, old mold, crumbly vegetation that can simply disappear underfoot. You can walk for an hour without touching stable earth, and at each step you must duck under branches or over them, balancing precariously around thick knots of trunks. At every step, any one of us could break a leg. For Geert or myself it would be nasty but not disastrous, because we would eventually get a message out via radio or a runner, and we both have insurance to cover an air ambulance. For the guides, though, a broken leg could mean months of agony, and they wouldn't be able to work or hunt.

After an hour or so of walking in the dark, we saw embers in the distance. I thought it meant we'd reached camp. It was Seth, one of the Papuans, who was ahead of us on the path but had turned back to come to find us, bringing burning bushes as torchlight for us to see our way. He tore branches off trees as we went, setting them on fire too. Finally, after another hour carrying a blazing torch, we came to a hut. Hallelujah, said Josef, and meant it. I collapsed by the fire and pulled off my boots. My socks were red with blood, for my gaiters had come unloosed from my boots and their metal loops had dug into my ankles, cutting open wounds, holes in the flesh an inch across. I hadn't noticed, simply because the rest of me was in so much greater pain.

In Papua New Guinea, people use the birds as a clock: wanting to meet someone at dusk, a person might say, "I'll see you when the bird of paradise sings." Here, in the circular hut, with a smoke-blackened roof, and a fire in the center, a stream nearby and frogs croaking, I fell asleep with the mountain bird of paradise—the "quintessence of beauty," according to naturalist Alfred Russell Wallace—singing its last song of the day and the guides singing, gently, around the fire, singing the story of that day, singing the mountain.

A RUCK IN THE MAP

There is a ruck in the map of the world. Just above Australia, there is a huge island in the shape of a cassowary bird, which comprises Papua New Guinea in the east and West Papua. Papua New Guinea seems to have entered the imagination of the world, but not the western half of the island. It is as if in the minds of most people, there is a fold in the map, and lost, swallowed up in the ruck, is an entire country.

When I talked of my plans to go to West Papua, I found few who knew it existed, and fewer still who knew anything about it. One friend of mine, a left-wing expert in international politics, first confused it with Papua New Guinea, then couldn't remember who had invaded it. (Indonesia, with international connivance.)

Few Papuans speak English; few can travel to raise awareness about their situation. Few foreigners visit West Papua; few journalists come here; very few editors want to commission reports about it. It causes barely a footnote in the great text of international media comment.

I sought out maps in the best map shop in the U.K. Nothing. There are no good maps of the country. I went to the map section in the British Library and asked the staff for maps of West Papua. Papua New Guinea? they asked. *West* Papua. They shook their heads. Never heard of it. Irian Jaya? I say, using the name Indonesia put on the country. They still shake their heads. I ask for U.S. Air Force flight maps for Indonesia, and pore over the maps for days.

The ancient Greeks called the mountains *agrapha*, "unwritten places." They were originally so-called for the most dismal of reasons—they were places not included in tax ledgers—but the term now has a wild, free resonance to it: mountains untrapped by texts, unmapped, undescribed, uncaught. There are few unwritten mountains now, but the Highlands of West Papua are the exceptions. "Relief Data Incomplete," say the maps, on the huge white expanses of unmapped land. "MEF indeterminable." The maximum elevation in feet is unknown.

As I waited in Jakarta's dark and almost empty airport, long after midnight, for a flight to Jayapura, the capital of West Papua, I felt very alone and very scared. Not of the wilderness of the mountains, not of the disease yaws, which eats away your face, not of tales of leech wounds infested with maggots, and certainly not of going somewhere off the map, but scared of the brutal Indonesian military. Indonesia refuses visas to writers and journalists, so I had gone on a tourist visa. If I had been discovered doing work clearly outside tourism and talking to people about wild land, freedom and independence, I could have been imprisoned or shot, as other foreign journalists have been. Of all the journeys I have ever taken, this was the one that frightened me the most.

From Jayapura, I was headed for Wamena, the main town in the Highlands. But the military had chartered every civilian flight to Wamena for a week—fearing "unrest," they said. So I went in a cargo plane, finding myself sitting between a cocky Korean missionary, intent on making Papuan people take off their penis gourds and wear "proper" clothes, and Geert. He and I had met by chance. We both happened to be waiting at the same time at the central police station for a permit to travel to Wamena. We both wanted to trek for days or weeks through mountain villages. To do this, we'd hire guides, which would be very expensive for either of us alone. So we decided to go together.

I knew Papuan human rights activists in Wamena, and at a restaurant in town they introduced me to a mountain guide, Josef. He became my guide, translator and more than anything my friend.

One of the Lani tribe, Josef was one of the gentlest men I've ever known. He came to the restaurant (run by Indonesian transmigrants, as almost all businesses are) and waited awkwardly in the doorway, but didn't enter. It took a second to see why. He is the black man in apartheid South Africa who will be kicked out of a white bar. He is the Tibetan, exiled in Lhasa. The Papuan in the Indonesian military dictatorship. The only way he could come in is if I told the owners he was my guest.

He sat silently with us. We were speaking in English and after a while I said quietly to him, in my scratchy Indonesian, "You can understand what we're saying?" "Oh yes, don't worry, I understand completely," he replied in fluent English. Afterward, I asked him about his life. Did he have children? Shadows fell. "I have two daughters," he said. "And I had a son who died two weeks ago." He smiled sadly at my pity. "He was weak. He was ill. He died." A simple story. After the death, a Lani custom took place. His wife's relatives came to his house and took away everything he owned: he was left with no spoon, no cooking pot, no chair. It is supposed to symbolize that if you can't even look after your own child, you can't look after anything. I gasped at this cruel aesthetic, making a consonance out of the dissonance of death. He was pleased to be coming with me, he said: he could earn enough money from our journey to buy himself the spoons, the pots and the chairs. I asked (awkward, Western) if his wife needs him for, ummm, emotional support. Again the sad smile. He shook his head. I had the impression that in her grief she blamed him. I didn't ask more. "My daughters miss me when I'm away," he said later. "When I come back, they wrap themselves around my legs and won't let go."

Josef asked three other guys to come too: Theo and Mathias, young, funny and devoted to one another, and the older and more reserved Izaak. (To protect the people I was with, most names in this chapter have been changed.) A local villager, Seth, joined us, after our party had stayed a night at his village. He came partly just for the hell of it, for he, like me, reveled in the company of the guides. I suspected that there was another reason: it seemed that his village was too hot for him and I guessed that he had been caught in an illicit affair. He ducked out at dawn to join us as we left, and when we were several hours up the path, two young boys caught up with us, sent to give Seth a message to go home. He shook his head with a slightly scorched smile: guilty and amused at the same time.

The first village we came to was in the middle of a pig feast. The pig is the most important material and cultural commodity Papuan people have. Pigs are used to buy wives, to celebrate the election of a chief, to honor guests. So important are they that a motherless piglet may suckle at a human breast. A woman would walk with a *noken*—a large string bag hanging down her back, held by a headband worn around the forehead—filled with yams and other vegetables, the odd baby and a piglet tossed in together.

The whole village was gathered around an open fire. The schoolteacher and the women bossily cooked and clucked at the children. One little girl was in a grass skirt and another in a scruffy T-shirt with a bobble hat saying WEST PAPUA. Several of the men wore the red beret so beloved by Dani tribesmen and some wore feather crowns. I was invited to sit with the older men and found myself looking straight through the large hole in one man's nose at a tuft of fur on the end of another man's penis gourd, as someone said a Christian grace before eating. "*Wa*," said the men to me—this word I was to hear a thousand times. It means hello, yes, thank you, I agree, good-bye, I understand, nice one, well done. You can't go wrong with *wa*.

There was a lot of shouting about how the meat should be shared out and I accidentally trod on a bunch of damp leaves on the ground—a plate for food. Everyone was smoking. Many people keep tobacco wrapped in a pandanus leaf, others tuck it into their penis gourds as if into a handy pocket, and one man kept his in a tin of Tokyo City pomade, lavender-scented.

The men told me about the mountain spirits and one pointed to a nearby tree: "That tree has a spirit. It provides food and pigs, so we do a special ceremony for the tree and kill a pig for it." And, they said, they wanted to talk about independence.

In one hut, there was a poster on a wall of children of many different races. "Don't separate us: we are all together," it says in Indonesian. It's crude propaganda from the Indonesian government, which fears the independence movements in many provinces: Aceh and West Papua, following East Timor.

We left and walked on, past a small market where two paths crossed, and women sold handfuls of pandanus nuts or five small oranges in a pyramid, or fans of bananas, kept cool under a wet leaf. We crossed the Baliem River, passing through acres of small tilled fields and tiny, neat gardens producing corn and sweet potatoes, beans and bananas. Low stone walls laced the land with ordered precision and wild strawberries grew here. On a hilltop there was a flash of sunlight on a machete blade where someone was cutting wood. The Baliem Valley lies in the middle of the mountain range, a mile to a mile and a half above sea level, sixty kilometers long and not known to outsiders until 1938.

Theo and Mathias mucked around with each other, fighting like puppies, and the austere Izaak pretended to be annoyed, but let his guard slip and laughed with them. They would sometimes greet each other, saying "*namalogo*" and falling about laughing. This is a greeting term specific to old women, so it is like a macho seventeen-year-old guy saying in a quavery voice, "Hello, dearie"—it has them in stitches.

Streamers of clouds lined the valley bottoms and mixed with smoke from cooking fires. On the path, we passed men with bows and arrows, out hunting birds, and boys with small penis gourds, and women with their fingers cut off. When someone died, it was traditional that young girls, sometimes three or four years old, relatives of the deceased, had a finger hacked off. I saw many older women whose left hands were just fistfuls of stumps and sometimes their right hands were mutilated too. (People still do this, but if the police hear about it, they get fined a pig.) Women have said that they could "feel" these amputated fingers: it was as if the spirits of the dead can still be felt even though they can't be seen. Often young boys were expected to join in and the upper part of their ear was sliced off in mourning.

Death here is seen as aberrant. It does not simply happen: someone caused it. Death comes, the hardwood arrow in the jugular vein, because someone pulled the bowstring taut. Death is a ferocious severance; it maims the living, the crash of the piano lid on the pianist's hands, a discordant blow. And, after death, grief. Grief is not pretty. Grief is grotesque and will not politely police itself to be nice. It is the gargoyle, contorting your face, it is a savage fury.

We walked on in a twilight of cloud, passing small girls with a *noken* on their heads, an old woman loyally followed by a piglet. In the skies, the mountain bird of paradise. An old man on his own was cooking sweet potatoes in a burnt-out tree stump.

At night in the villages, we went to one of the "men's houses"—there are sometimes several in each village. (As a visitor, and a writer, I was treated as an honorary man.) Much to the consternation of the Christian missionaries in the area, men from the tribes of the central Highlands—including Dani, Lani and Yali—detest the idea of sleeping with their wives. The men sleep in the men's house, where they stay up late around the fire, smoking and talking. It's as cozy as a well-loved local bar. The women don't have any equivalent women's house, but each sleeps in her own house with her pigs and children.

The men's house (*pilai*, pronounced *pee-lai*, in Dani) has a humming intensity, both exciting and comforting. You stoop to enter the low door, and inside it's a slow place of smoke and long, indrawn tokes of tobacco, a place of sleep, conversation and history. With thick walls and a fire in the middle, it has a temperature that is always constant; it is cooler in the day and warmer at night. The ceilings shine, blackened by smoke and bright with years of pig grease. One man was roasting pandanus nuts at the fire, moving them around with his dexterous toes. Every once in a while, someone would take a blowpipe and gently blow air into the embers.

The hut is quiet and small, perhaps twelve feet across, and circular, so it is easy to hear everyone speak. Since few men wear anything but penis gourds, they are clothed here in their speech alone, and without the distractions and cues of clothing, it is easy to get the fathom of people: the wise, the silly, the joker, the kind.

There are two places in the world where I have felt immediately at home, with an instant sense of belonging: in the houses of shamans and in these men's houses. Apparently alien to me, they seemed utterly familiar, people taking their places like worn-down seats in a favorite pub, and they reminded me of low-lit long evenings smoking in student rooms, quiet conversations around campfires long into the night, where all that matters is firelight and friendship. The long penis gourd comes into its own, here, as a rhetorical device, as a man might tap his gourd with a fingernail, calling your attention, then dramatically drawing a breath and waggling it to one side to make his emphatic point. There is no costume on earth more glorious, exuberant, proud, with more sheer chutzpah than a Dani man's penis gourd—particularly if it's decorated with a bird of paradise feather, pluming at the tip.

In the evening, I needed a toilet. The bushes weren't a good solution, since every time I nipped out I was followed by a yodeling line of curious children with their miniature bows and arrows, stalking me, giggling. And I just wasn't going to change a tampon applauded by an audience of under-tens. There was a drop-toilet, though, with a rickety fence, offering a little privacy. And, fumbling in the dark, I dropped an unused tampon in the loo. As any woman who has traveled much will know, this is a major misfortune. I was traveling as light as possible and had calculated exactly how much of everything I would need. Nothing was spare. I needed the little fella. So I shone my torch down and saw it had landed not in the shit but on a dry ledge. I took a breath, leaned in and picked it out. (The next morning in full daylight I returned to the toilet and saw something that froze me in fear: there, unseen by me the previous night, curling happily in the toilet pit, was a large snake.)

In one men's house, I'd heard they were keeping cultural objects from four different villages in the area. They were safeguarding them from the missionaries, who were organizing ritual bonfires of all amulets and sacred objects. "We don't want Christians here, because we want to keep our own customs," said one man. I wanted to talk to them and they agreed in principle to let me and Geert into the men's house, but before we went in there was a long animated discussion between the men and Josef. I wondered if it was a debate about allowing a woman in, or about what to tell us and what to hold back. In fact it was a discussion about how much to charge us. Everything in life is an exchange, and it seemed fair enough to me that they should get money if that was what they wanted. Geert was clearly cross and began to make disparaging remarks: "You must not sell what is sacred," he said. "It is not spiritual to do this." Fortunately he spoke no Indonesian, so no one except me and Josef understood him.

The men's house was warm, the floor covered in clean straw, and the walls were hung with pig bones, dozens of smoke-blackened pig jawbones and pig tails, kept from ceremonies for the spirits or a wedding. For seven generations, they said, they had kept the bones of pigs and kept the stories and customs. "My father promised me the culture. As long as people stay here, we won't lose it," said a man.

Spare penis gourds hung between slats in the walls and necklaces of cowrie shells, which were once currency, and there were carefully wrapped pouches of pandanus leaves for keeping tobacco. There were fire-rubbing sticks too— you twirl the stick in a hollow of wood until friction lights the sawdust and tiny dry pieces of tinder—and there were pig-killing arrows and amulets of protection.

The headman was puffing a huge rolled tobacco leaf in the darkness. His skin was wizened, and he had tufts of fur and cowrie shells around his neck. "We let you come in because you're writing about us," he said. "We'd never let Indonesians in."

I asked about the mountains, they answered about independence.

We left the house after a time and walked on, over the crest of a hill, where five men sat selling nuts. A woman was digging sweet potato in her garden, with an umbrella made of pandanus leaf wrapped at her back. By the river, another woman was washing sweet potatoes. She had a *noken* dangling down her back, and suddenly the *noken* bumpily moved and a baby inside cried. There is a whole world in a *noken*. Far below us now, the river was running white in crests over rocks. I walked with Josef and we were walking in cloud. We passed a whole family, parents, kids and pigs, coming the other way on the path. White trumpet flowers surrounded one village, planted for protection against spirits. Josef showed me a medicine leaf that, he says, stings like a nettle. "We use it for headache relief," he said. If it stings, how does that help? "It distracts you from the original pain." (Of course.) The guides above us were softly crooning and fluting like birds to one another, picking a flower or leaf to tuck into their hair. As we climbed, through rivers, up rivers, across them, on suspension bridges made of rattan, or across fungal old logs, I would give my notebooks to Josef because my footing was so unsure. I slipped and fell many times in the muddy ocher clay.

The mud of West Papua is an element all of its own. Mud has its own music, the gurgle and sloop, glug and grunt. It sounds like a hundred frogs croaking fatly and then like a soggy fart, mud sucking, squelching and plopping. We walked sometimes for hours at a stretch on the muddy logs, roots and poles that formed the pathway, and every step was slimy with algae and rain.

We passed a woman wearing the rags of a T-shirt. Her breasts hung out of the holes. This didn't concern her. It's considered immodest, though, for a woman to have her back uncovered. She had a digging stick with her and was looking for frogs and shrubs. We passed a group of people, some women and girls in skirts of tree bark. Whenever we passed people in traditional dress, Geert wanted to photograph them. The kids were always keen and would run to be in his picture, but Geert shooed away anyone dressed in shorts or T-shirts. This reality would spoil the pristine picture he wanted to present.

Most people ask for a small fee, 1000 rupiah, or about five pence, to be photographed. Geert was cross about this. It's all give-and-take, I said—we want to take a photo, and they want an exchange. Then one person asked for 500 rupiahs and Geert beamed at him. "This is better. They are not so spoiled here," he said. I walked ahead, fast, to be with Josef.

A dripping curtain of creepers fell from giant groundsel and there were strangler figs and stilt-rooted pandanus trees and lichen. There were frogs, the size of your little fingernail, one of the many things here still unknown to Western science.

Josef showed me leaves that were good for wrapping babies when you tuck them in your *noken*, and which plants are used to make the *noken*. Then he stopped and pointed to a small clearing. "Remember the family we passed on the path? Here's where they stayed last night." I could see absolutely no sign. He showed me one tiny straw twig: part of the special bamboo strip used to create friction to light a fire. He showed me gourds growing that would be used for penis gourds—as they grow, stones are tied to the gourds to stretch them into the long, thin shape required. And he told me of a crackdown by the Indonesian military, which meant that he had had to flee his home in town and take to the mountains to hide.

Part of the path ran high above the river. The path was very narrow and the drop was very steep. "Stop," said Josef. He told me to listen to the calling of a particular bird. It was the spirit bird whistling, and "you stop because it's telling you there's some news, good or bad. It's communicating, giving you a message." (Similarly, the Vogelkop bowerbird is called the "knowing bird" by mountain people of the Arfak Mountains of West Papua.) The news was that Geert had fallen off the path and tumbled down the valleyside, clutching at saplings. He caught us up a few minutes later, panting and scratched. The guides had saved his life, he said, yanking him back.

On one of our nights in a village along the way, Josef and I got talking with the villagers about the world. The sun and moon came from this village, they said with cosmic cultural self-esteem. "Here we are rich in sun." Do you know white people have been to the moon? I asked. "Yes," they replied, "and we know they've been to the sun too." They were a little put out about this. "Dani people could do it too, if we had the technology." To Lani people, the moon is male because it comes out at night, like a man hunting. The sun is female because it shines during the day, like a woman working in daylight.

Again, when I asked people about land, they answered about freedom, *merdeka*, independence. Independence from Indonesia is the furious fire in every Papuan heart. We talked for ages and they asked if I could get them guns and ammunition. I can't. One young man suddenly picked up his bow and arrows and gave them to me as a present. Take these, he said, they are for you, for supporting us, for understanding us. The arrows were beautifully carved and each different. One, spear-shaped, was for killing a pig. Another, with two serrated prongs, was for killing a large bird. Some were for killing fish or small birds. One with three edges, notched so it could not easily be removed, was for use against humans in tribal wars.

I was so touched I felt choked. It was, as Josef said later, a very big gift. And it binds me, as all good gifts do, to the giver, to this village and to *merdeka*. Later, back home, I sent the best gift I could think of for him: a really good Swiss Army knife.

COINSPIRING AIR

The inner—what is it?

If not intensified sky

—RAINER MARIA RILKE

Air is a sacred element for many cultures. Air is unmistakably what animates us: when the breath ceases, the spirit is gone.

Many ancient languages see a direct connection between soul or spirit and breath. *Anima* (Latin) means both "breath" and "soul," and is derived from the Greek word *anemos*, "wind." *Psyche* (Greek) likewise means "breath" and "soul." *Neshamah* in Hebrew means both "soul" and "breath." *Atman* (Sanskrit) means, too, "breath" and "soul." The Chinese concept of *Ch'i* means "breath" and also the "vital universal energy in air."

Meanwhile *spiritus* (Latin) means "breath" and "spirit." *Pneuma* (Greek) similarly means "breath" and "spirit." *Ruach* (Hebrew) means "breath," "spirit" and "wind." God, at the creation, is identified with the wind moving over the waters. ("Wild air, world-mothering air"—Gerard Manley Hopkins.)

In Inuktitut, the word *Sila* can mean "air," sometimes "oxygen," but it goes deeper, as George Kappianaq, an elder of Igloolik, comments: *sila* is connected to soul, for the soul leaving the body leaves the gravitation of the earth, which can be interpreted as departing from *Sila*, the force of life. *Sila* can also mean "weather," "wind" or "outside." *Sila* is a hard word to translate. It can also mean "wisdom." To be "full of Sila" is to be wise, *Silatujuq*, while to be foolish is to be without *Sila*: *Silaittuq*.

The Inuktitut word *anerca* means "soul," and both the terms "to make poetry" and "to breathe" are derived from *anerca*. The hunter, shaman and poet Orpingalik, a Netsilik Inuit man, said to Knud Rasmussen, "Songs are thoughts, sung out with the breath when people are moved by great forces and ordinary speech no longer suffices."

David Abram, in his remarkable book *The Spell of the Sensuous*, writes of the relationship between air, breath, spirit and soul. "Nothing is more common to the diverse indigenous cultures of the earth than a recognition of the air, the wind, and the breath, as aspects of a singularly sacred power." Air's obvious links to speech—"spoken words are structured breath"—lends to air "a deep association with linguistic meaning and with thought" and "many indigenous peoples construe awareness, or 'mind,' not as a power that resides inside their heads, but rather as a quality that they themselves *are inside of*," and this power is sacred. Jung also argued that the psyche is not in mankind, but rather that mankind exists in the psyche. Edmund Carpenter writes, "Thought, to the Eskimo, isn't a product of mind, but the forces outside of man. Yet thought can't exist without man. True, the universe must speak first, make itself known to man, affect him, move him. But he alone can release it from its chaotic state." In Inuit thought, *Sila* is foremost—breath created before anything else.

Among the Creek Indians (in the Southeast of the United States), the creator god is the "Master of Breath." For Lakota people, the most sacred aspect of Wakan Tanka (the Great Spirit or Great Mysterious) is "The Enveloping Sky." "*Woniya wakan*—the holy air . . . spirit, life, breath, renewal—it means all that," says Lakota man John Fire Lame Deer. The winds are sacred, the messengers of the gods.

The Navajo concept *nilch'i*, called the Holy Wind, means the winds and air, and atmosphere in general, and it grants awareness and speech. The four Winds (of their four sacred mountains) are also called the four Words. We are only able to speak by articulating breath, and by extension, say Navajo people, wind has the power of language. An elder comments, "It is only by means of Wind that we talk. It exists at the tip of our tongues." The four sacred mountains would express themselves through the Wind-Words, and the winds have long been considered messengers. Air, then, is associated with language and is considered holy and full of mind.

It is as if human language and the world's air exist in a delicate exchange. We draw knowledge from it—something is "in the air," immanent, as if air is aware. For the air's gentle collective unconscious glints with meaning, glistens a moment in the psyche and is exhaled through voiced air, back into the listening air, a reciprocal inspiration. ("Charlie Parker was my delight / He breathed in air, he breathed out light."—Adrian Mitchell.)

We get vitality from air, physically inhaling a living brilliance, and we exhale the vitality of spirit in music or words. The word *inspire* connotes both respiration and inspiration, breath and soul. Before written language, words were expressed only through expiration—in air mind was made manifest. Bright, electric and wild, air—wide as sky in waiting potential—was the medium of mind, and this must have been the most rapturous delight our species has ever known, as we leapt into language and realized that we could make the outer air ring with the sound of our inner minds, psyche and world mutually (and literally) co-inspired. The soul, distilled to its most potent, is embodied in speech and song. *Om* was the "seed syllable" that created the world in Hindu and Buddhist thought, and in the Dani language the soul is *etai-eken*, which means literally "seed of singing." The work of missionaries in West Papua focuses heavily on literacy, and this campaign profoundly alters people's relationship with the wild world, for as the written word begins to shout its commands, the voices of wild nature fall silent and the immanent and lovely co-inspiration of mind and mountain is gagged.

SONGLINES OF THE HILLS

In the Highlands of West Papua, the guides said, "We sing to the mountain." They sang as they built a fire at lunchtime, they sang cozy in the men's huts at night. When we were far from any village, camped on the mountainsides, warm around a fire, they sang for hours, singing up the world. Sometimes I shyly joined in. There was a basic melody kept up by one singer, and the others extemporized around it, picking a few notes within the key and singing them in a slightly syncopated rhythm. Their shared song was a round, running around the circle of the fire, the circle of toes and wet socks, the circle of smoky wooden walls until the whole song resonated inside your chest, only interrupted as someone broke away from the fireside for a piss, or to cadge a cigarette, or just laughed aloud for pleasure.

Song, in West Papua, can be far more than entertainment. It has also played a political role. In 1978, the musician Arnold Ap formed a band called Mambesak. Using music from many Papuan tribes and cultures, the band played songs of freedom. The music was adored and played in radio stations in towns and on "boom boxes" in the smallest villages. To the Indonesian military, Ap's iconic status was a serious threat and he was arrested in November 1983, imprisoned without charge for sixty-six days, then taken to a beach and machine-gunned to death.

West Papua is resonant with songlines. The guides sang the routes of paths around mountains and sang the stories of how people came to be here. They sang about our trip, describing where we stopped, people falling over, funny remarks and good, big fires. ("Our destination was very hard but we made it, over mountains and swamps, with the girls in grass skirts." "Our destination was very hard, and our feet got very cold, but we made it over the mountain and the swamp.") Improvising long and funny poems in blank verse is a skill they share with many Papuans.

Anthropologist Steven Feld describes the acoustic world of the Kaluli people of Papua New Guinea, and their songlines.

> Tok means "path," "road," or "gate," but as it is used in song, the sense is more that of "map." The device refers to the way that a song, from start to finish, projects not merely a description of places, but a journey. The song is successful when listeners are totally suspended into a journeying mood, experiencing the passage of song and poetic time as the passage of a journey. . . . Constructing a song as a path, or tok, sets the listeners on a journey during which they simultaneously experience a progression of lands and places and a progression of deeply felt sentiments associated with them. . . . All songs are sung from the point of view of movement through lands. The composer's craft is not to tell people about places but to suspend them into those places. Singing a place is not a descriptive act but rather one that "impregnates" identity into place, tree, water, and sound names.

The Kogi people of Colombia also have songlines, subtle songs of the spirit world. Alan Ereira describes it thus: "The song leads along a path in 'aluna'—the spiritual world—in the maze of memory and possibility to a point in the real world."

In the meantime, back in the real world in West Papua, Geert and I were on the point of strangling each other.

CANNIBALS AND QUARRELS

He insisted on calling conversations "investigations." I said I wasn't study-ing people, I was talking with them. He criticized me for expressing my point of view to them. I said it was patronizing not to. He wore a Christian cross and called himself a Christian and said he wanted to study people "pure" in order to make pronouncements about their pristine way of life. I said that such purity was an anthropological fiction, and that Papuans had been treated to cultural genocide by Christian missionaries.

More than anything, he criticized me for not conversing in an orderly way. "Unless you first ask them about their kinship system, you will understand nothing. *Nothing*." I said I wanted to hear what they wanted to say, not drag them into some dreary prescription of academia. In conversation after con-versation in the villages, the men would gather to talk to me about *merdeka*, freedom. The conversations would be long, animated and emotional. And then, after a while, Geert would lean forward to conduct his "investigations." He would take a deep breath, cast his eye over the men and say in a low, urgent voice, "*What is the kinship system in this village?*"

At first, Josef, translating, was completely stumped. So Geert spelled it out. "If the man owns the field and the man dies, does the field belong to his wife or to his children? If to the children, is it to the son and daughter or only to the son?" And so on. And on. Believe me it went on. Josef would valiantly translate. People's faces around the fire would lose all their elasticity. A couple of men made an early escape. One tried to answer in an offhand way. Another said it really wasn't important. Geert would try again, several times, in fact, in each village. The Papuans hadn't heard of "kinship systems" but they knew monumental boredom when they met it. At the conclusion of one such inves-tigation, there was only one man left and he was fast asleep.

We arrived in one village on a Saturday. My ankles were now open wounds, each day being rubbed wider open. They were painful and they were also infected and festering because "walking" in West Papua means wad-ing through bogs time after time. I needed a layover day, to try to keep my ankles dry and clean long enough for a scab to form. I had also fallen, and had a twelve-inch-long bruise, my leg swollen as if I had a thick sock in my pocket.

It was a Christianized village, and the following day out of curiosity I went to the church service. The rectangular church building was odd in an architecture of roundhouses and it had glass windows with neat yellow curtains. Out on the church steps, there were piles of flip-flops and slippers, so I took off my boots before I went in. There was a blackboard and a clock. The church was divided into the men's half and the women's. Always, on this trip, I had been treated as an honorary man, and was ushered into the social space of men, so I asked Josef if I could sit with him. Fine. Women, traveling, can often find that they are welcomed as a woman by women *and* as a man by men. Men journeying do not have the same double access. So it was here.

Geert, not having noticed the piles of shoes outside, came into the church loudly stamping his boots. And sat with the women. They shifted away from him, visibly uncomfortable. He didn't care. As the service got under way, he took out his camera and began taking pictures of them. They shot him angry looks, pulled their scarves over their faces, shielded their eyes with their hands, tutted and hissed at him.

The pastor, his eyes shut tight, stood in the pulpit lunging his arms forward over the congregation. The priest had been—as all his village had been until three decades ago—a cannibal.

When I had been in the capital, Jayapura, I had found myself at loose ends one Sunday, and I had gone to an American fundamentalist service; I explained I was writing about wilderness and that I wanted to talk to some missionaries. One of them had told me about their early travails here. Her eyes blue and round as a child's, she told me, "Our first two were martyred by the Yali people several years ago." What happened? I asked. The carriers didn't want to go on; the missionaries had insisted, so the carriers had killed them. "They were *eaten*," she said in an appalled whisper.

Oh, I said, trying to be diplomatic. Did that put you off a bit? Silly question. Missionaries came flocking here after that, she said. "It spurred people on to come here because of the darkness that these people were obviously living in."

Did you tell them, I asked sweetly, absolutely determined to quote Flanders and Swann, did you tell them that *Eating People Is Wrong?*

She missed the reference, but apparently told Papuans that many things were wrong with them. Wearing penis gourds. Thinking mountains were sacred. Keeping their religious objects. A convert passes in the garden, wearing a bright white blouse. (Oh, and you can always tell the color of the soul from the whiteness of the shirt.)

And now, here I was with the Yali cannibals. We talked to the priest in the evening. Geert was sitting with his eyes closed and his face set rigid. People kept glancing nervously at him. Was he angry? His Christian cross glinted in the firelight. Was he also a priest? they wondered. He roused himself. Did you eat people because you were hungry? he asked. They looked at him as if he was very stupid. Of course not, they said. "You must establish this first," he informed me. "You must have *order* in studying them."

They explained the principle: the fat of humans makes you stronger to fight against enemies and fat is good for plants, children and animals, especially pigs. During one war, fought against people from the next valley, a hundred people were killed, and when a person was killed, the body was shared among the others in the villages.

What happened with the missionaries? I asked. The story flooded out. Missionaries had invaded their village. The Yali people were terrified and ran away into the forests. The missionaries chased them, as if hunting them, and the Yali people fled again, frightened, farther into the forests. A third time the missionaries came after them, and this time the Yali people couldn't take it anymore, got their bows and arrows and shot them. And then ate them. It seemed quite reasonable to me.

The priest had been eight or nine at the time and everyone was a cannibal then. (The whole village has since turned Christian, and they no longer eat anyone except Jesus, and him only on Sundays.) What did it taste like? I asked. Geert sighed loudly. "You do *not* ask that question," he said, as if he knew the conversational etiquette of cannibalism. "It tastes a bit like beef," the priest is quite happy to tell me. "And," he went on, "when we killed and cut up the missionaries to eat, one missionary was too fat and didn't taste good so we used him as firelighters." For the record, I did try not to laugh.

After a while, the priest said he wanted to tell me something else. "Independence," he said. "Freedom. *Merdeka*. We need it. We want it. It is our right." He asked me for any more information about his country's political situation.

He was, he said, just a villager with no way of getting news except by word of mouth. I tried to sum up what I knew about what was going on around West Papua. And then I told him about the Ploughshares women in Britain, protesters who smashed up Hawk jets bound for Indonesia, where they would almost certainly be used to bomb villages in East Timor and West Papua. (The women's defense was that they had committed one crime, damage to property, in order to stop a greater crime, genocide, from taking place.) The priest slapped his thighs and grinned, pleased as punch.

When we left the following day, I was still exhausted. Every step made me wince in pain, and as the wounds on my ankles were rubbed rawer again, I had smarting tears in my eyes. We climbed again, hour after hour, higher and higher, until it seemed the journey was endless, as if the summit would never come. I felt as if I was walking in a dream where your legs don't work and the air is thick sludge. Josef walked with me and Theo held my hand and I leaned on him, a hurt dance as we swapped hands in midair to negotiate a tricky bit. The other guides, with all the camping gear, were walking with Geert. Don't go too far ahead, I said to him. I'm having trouble, and I don't want any of us to have to walk in the dark to catch up.

I've walked and climbed a fair bit, but I've never known terrain as tough as this. It was a salve to my pride that biologist and writer Tim Flannery also reports being "reduced, through sheer exhaustion, to crawling up some impossibly steep mossy slopes. Finally, I lay on the side of the trail, defeated." Heinrich Harrer, no slouch either, was to remark, "My expedition to the Papuans involved more hardship than any of my other expeditions. . . . I have never returned from an expedition so physically battered. . . . On more than one occasion we had to negotiate absolutely vertical gnarled root faces. My bones are still aching and I must confess that this was the most difficult jungle passage I had yet met. New Guinea is notorious for having the wildest jungle landscape anywhere in the world."

Geert and three guides went on far ahead. Josef and Theo were going at my pace and I was walking more and more slowly. My head ached with altitude, my legs were bruised, and my ankles were stabbing with pain. The afternoon wore on. Here, for the first and only time in my life, I gave up. Suddenly, feeling utterly hopeless, with hot tears in my eyes, I sank down in the mud in the middle of the path, and gulped, "*Tidak bisa.*" I can't do it. Can't do it anymore. That was it. I couldn't go on.

Theo smiled encouragingly and just said gently, "Oh, *tidak bisa,*" and the kindness in his face made me burst into tears. I didn't care. I'd lost all my pride. I crumpled like a child. Josef came up, with surprise, worry, sympathy—and a plan. He and I could walk back to the nearest airstrip and there might be a plane in one week's time, which might have a seat. Or not. Suddenly he and I looked at each other and laughed out loud. That option was rubbish.

"But don't worry," he said brightly. "I told the guides to stop about two hours up the path."

"Your hours or mine?"

"Yours," he said. "I'm translating all the hours into your speed, don't worry. I knew the little mother was exhausted so I told them not to go on past a rock cave they know. We'll stop there for the night."

"I'm sorry," I blurted out, smiling and crying, which was a big improvement. And so we went on. Two hours later, just as Josef had said, we reached a large rock, almost a cave, a great place for a campsite and the place where Josef had told the other guides to stop. But they were not there. Josef was the nearest to angry I had ever seen. Then one of the guides appeared. Geert, he said, had forced them to walk on.

Now I was really finished. I had screwed up all my strength for the path thus far. We would now have to walk for an unguessable length of time and it was getting dark. The guides with Geert had all the food and water, the tarp and tent and all the camp equipment. We had waited for Geert, that day long ago when he was having trouble, and was a long way behind us on the track, because it was the right thing to do. It hadn't occurred to me he would not do the same for us.

This is how mountains get dangerous at a stroke. I was hungry and exhausted and we were all very cold because we were all going at my pace. Night fell, and we had to walk for several hours in darkness. Every slippery step could mean a twisted ankle or broken bones, every slashed branch by the path edge was a spear that could slice into your eyeball.

Finally, at about nine in the evening, we reached the others. Geert was in a petulant temper, and remarked crossly that "the guides wouldn't walk enough today. Only five hours." He tapped his watch. "I counted," he said. Nothing on earth was going to infuriate me more than Geert tapping his watch, criticizing the guides. I've written a whole book on the politics of time, and this gesture, this nasty example of European cultural domination, sets my teeth on edge. I tried to say evenly, "Don't ever, ever force people to walk in the dark—" But then I noticed something else.

The guides were putting the tarpaulin up over the tent. *Why?* I asked. Because Geert has complained that the tent is not waterproof, they said.

Way back in Wamena, when we were preparing our gear before this trek, I had talked to Josef about tents. A tent, he said, for you and Geert. And a tarp for us. I said no: I wouldn't walk with a "first class" for us and "second class" for them. We'd eat the same and sleep the same and I'd pay any difference. "It's okay, Jay," said Josef. "We *prefer* the tarp. It's more adaptable than a tent and it's what we want. And you can't light a fire in a tent." So we left it like that.

Then, on this night, Geert had decided that because the tent let in a few droplets of water, he needed both the tent and the tarp. I was pale with anger. "So it is acceptable to you that you have two coverings and they have none?" I asked him. He nodded. "That they sleep like animals with no shelter?" "Yes," he said, succinctly.

"Okay, fine," I said, and I dragged my sleeping bag and mat out of the tent and dropped them at Josef's feet. "I will sleep outside with all of you."

Josef groaned. "You can't do that, you'll get wet and cold," he said. Exactly, I said. And so will you. You have to have the tarp. I knew that my being wet and cold would worry Josef. I also knew that a woman offering to sleep in the same place as the men would give them the willies. I was right. Under the threat of sleeping near a woman, they simply couldn't move the tarp fast enough.

Then we agreed that since Geert wanted to walk fast, he should go on ahead with two of the guides and we would never have to see each other again. He was as pleased as I was and at dawn they left. It was a beautiful morning for the rest of us: a morning of rainbows, orchids and time. In the relief that followed his exit, the guides sang louder than they had ever sung before; they yodeled and croaked and hooted, found a blind for shooting birds—with arrows, for there are no guns in the villages. We stopped to look at the orangey-brown cuscus droppings, and the guides showed me a secret cave where Yali people had left stones wrapped in leaves "for the spirits." And they sang the song of yesterday: "The little mother found it very hard yesterday, but she did it, she *did* it." They were proud of me, and I felt tearful when they translated the words.

WILD MOUNTAIN LUST

In most high-profile mountain expeditions, the motives and language speak of *superismo*, the peak of Everest the place for tawdry nationalism to flap out its paltry politics, the climbers' obsession with getting to the top, no matter the cost.

Rare are the antiexpeditions, such as that of 1971, when three Norwegians went to Gauri Shankar in the Himalayas, one of Nepal's most sacred mountains. There, Nils Faarlund, Sigmund Kvaløy and Arne Naess climbed only on the slopes and their aim was not to summit, because the summit was holy. Rare too are the commentators who express a wish for any mountain to be left unclimbed. In the *Evening News*, reporting in 1920 on the expedition to climb Everest, were these lines: "Some of the last mystery of the world will pass when the last secret place in it, the naked peak of Everest, shall be trodden by those trespassers." There is poetry in mountaineering, but among the grandeur and the mystery of mountaineering is a muddy pragmatism. A nineteenth-century writer, describing an attempted climb in the Lake District in 1818, notes, "I should, I think, [have got] to the summit, but unfortunately I was damped by slipping one leg into a squashy hole." John Keats, here, sounding more like *Just William*, insisting on his unblemished heroism even as he admits the smallness of the obstacle that defeated him.

Mountaineering literature is full of men "conquering" mountains or "laying siege" to them. An account of the 1924 British expedition to Everest (during which George Mallory died) was called "The Fight for Everest," and a newspaper obituary for Mallory described him as one of the "assailants" of the mountains. A recent TV documentary on Everest spoke of the "assault" and "conquest" of the mountain—the squalid and juvenile language of attack.

In 1953, Ronald William Clark was writing of Alpine summits "beaten into submission" by British climbers. Heinrich Harrer, climbing in West Papua, writes, "We came to a high pass which we promptly named 'Assault Pass.'"

H. B. George, describing mountain journeys at the turn of the nineteenth century, wrote that the desire "to explore the earth and subdue it" had "made England the great colonizer of the world, and has led individual Englishmen to penetrate the wildest recesses of every continent."

Military might, imperialism, nationalism and masculinity (penetrate, penetrate) were fused, and this kind of mountaineering appealed to German Nazis: in the 1930s the Third Reich encouraged the so-called "Nazi Tigers," young mountaineers.

Philip Temple, who accompanied Harrer, describes an expedition making "a more penetrating attack" and he writes of the "Carstenz" Mountains of West Papua, where the Freeport mine is now, "unconquered, their virgin state was forgotten until . . . 1935." In both these quotes, he combines sexual metaphor (penetration and virginity) with metaphors of assault (attack and conquering), as so many writers do in the Western canon. (His nasty image is now a reality, as the women of those mountains are raped and tortured for protesting against the mine.)

Plenty of indigenous people also see mountains as female, but this gendered attitude suggests a mothering deity, a protective stance both from the mountain and from the people. Ecological writer Dolores LaChapelle, in *Earth Wisdom*, describes Paleolithic statues that combine the veneration of mountain as mother and the observation that the mother is mountain to the child. The statues were carved from the child's point of view, hills of breasts, ridges of hips, high buttocks and, of course, *mons veneris*. ("By landscape reminded once of his mother's figure." —W. H. Auden.)

Europeans seem to be peculiar in seeing mountains as a female to be sexually assaulted. Rare in the European tradition is the male writer who reads femaleness into mountains and does so with love—Ruskin considered mountains female in nature, referring to Mont Blanc as "Mount Beloved." And rare too the male writer who reads a transcendent transsexuality into the act of climbing: Penny Rimbaud, drummer and lyricist of the anarcho-punk band Crass, writes in his extraordinary poem "HOW?" of the artist's superb reach as a kind of lovemaking with the mountains of the soul. The artist is watched by the dull stare of the conformists of the mind's lowlands, "who were happy to be the voice, but not the word, happy to be the piper, but not the tune" and who "on seeing the mountains rise chose not to scale the shattered scree ... who chose not to see the crag-clinging goat nor hear the clank of steel on rock nor even imagine that there might be a way to reach those cloud-scurrying heights, or who merely decried those who fought the shadow, not seeing that that fight was a form of glorious lovemaking, that that slow, tentative reach might lead to greater heights wherein that greater love might be consolidated."

Women, when they climb, can share something of his view: a wild mountain lust.

When I was sixteen, I climbed Mont Blanc with an ageing *alpinistre*, whose wife had insisted he stop climbing and open a small chalet in the French Alps. I spent that summer waitressing at his chalet, and when he invited me to climb with him, I couldn't get my boots on fast enough.

A thousand people have died climbing Mont Blanc, which I hadn't known at the time but which wouldn't have affected me if I had. I was too young to think I was mortal and too ecstatic for mountains to care. In this ecstasy women feel—surely—a sexual shimmer.

In 1838, Henriette d'Angeville was the second woman known to have climbed Mont Blanc. When she planned her trip, she was frustrated by weeks of bad weather, which prevented what she termed her "wedding" to her "frozen lover," the "delicious hour when I could lie on his summit. Oh! when will it come?" Passion here, whose heat would melt the ice that gives the mountain its name. Her yearning for union was sexual; mine was a kind of transsensual union—a metamorphosis that merged myself and the mountain.

I remember little about the climb now. I remember it was tough, I remember feeling as if I were a giant, in my seven-league boots, one boot in Italy, one in France, and I remember a feeling of dazzling glamour, brightness dancing outside me, brightness dancing within me. I gasped at a rush of ice on my cheeks. The air was singing in my ears eight octaves higher than human hearing. My cuffs and scarf were covered with frozen diamonds and I swept up a handful of crushed stars in my hand and in sheer glee hurled them back at the sky. There was ice in my hair and sun in my eyes so bright that snow shone inside me and when I spoke there were no words but only the voice of the wind, and I laughed aloud at my own translucence. So immersed, so unimportant, so careless of myself did I feel that the mountain was all that mattered and it included me in its massif—an elation so enormous that I was utterly lost and happy to be so: so minimal myself, so mountainous.

TELL ME ABOUT THE SAVAGES

As I write this, back home, an e-mail comes, telling me that the Indonesian army has just launched another attack on Wamena. Three dead. My mind jumps to Josef. I worry for him, partly because he is politically engaged and reckless for his own life, and partly because I felt so close to him. Then, I think bluntly, what does it matter *which* Josef? One more one whose life has come to nought, nudging 99,999 dead to 100,000, the figure Amnesty International puts on the death toll in the genocide here. Every Papuan I met, priests, children, grandmothers, in towns and in the mountains, wanted independence. And many of these, Papua's one million population, were prepared to die for it.

I have a photograph in my hand. Several boyish Indonesian soldiers, one shy, one grinning, pose, holding up for the camera the trophy of a hunt, as you would an animal's carcass. It is a dead Papuan leader, Yustinus Murib, killed in November 2003. He is naked, and their fists clutch handfuls of his hair to yank his corpse up to the camera.

Indonesia was land-hungry and wanted West Papua for its acres and for its wealth of natural resources, and in 1962, it invaded and began the mass murder ignored by most of the world, occurring as it did in that strange ruck in the map. Tribal people's villages were bombed and napalmed. Women were raped and men tortured. The colonial power, the Netherlands, had tried to give West Papua independence. America had had other ideas. For geopolitical reasons, the United States wanted Indonesia to take the country—"a few thousand miles of cannibal land" was how Robert Komer, J. F. Kennedy's CIA adviser was to describe it. And under the inauspices of the United Nations, there was a referendum of a thousand-odd Papuans, who were taught to mouth the words "I want Indonesia." One man who refused to say the line was shot. The rest were threatened with a similar fate, or with having their tongues cut out. So the chapter began. Even before Indonesia invaded West Papua, Indonesia was in talks with the U.S. mining company Freeport. Quid pro quo. Freeport could have mining rights and the United States, sugar daddy, would see that Indonesia could invade in peace.

And still it continues. It suits America and Britain very well, as Indonesia continues to give them license to steal resources, but there's another thing: the genocide is irresistibly lucrative for the corporations and companies in the arms trade. In 2002, U.K. arms sales to Indonesia reached £41 million. That's about a quid from every adult. Every bloody one of us.

I was told of an incident in Sarmi where the military said they wanted to "tame" the Papuans. So they tortured and killed a man, roasted him and forced his wife and child to eat him. I met a man who was imprisoned for raising the Morning Star, the flag of West Papua. He was beaten almost to death. Children have been raped by Indonesian soldiers. And when I passed the compounds of the Indonesian military, they were goose-stepping around the parade ground, the storm troopers of this corporate holocaust.

Papuans have a new fear of the sugar daddy now, for when America declares its phony "war on terror," Indonesia pipes up, saying it has "terrorists" at large. The tribes of the Highlands, wanting only their freedom, armed only with bows and arrows and a shining kind of courage, are translated from victims to perpetrators of savagery.

And the rest of the world does nothing. It is as if the Papuans fall on the far side of a Wallace line of cultural perception. They are seen as somehow not fully human, as not deserving life, let alone dignity.

The traditional way of life for Papuan tribes involved fierce and harsh warfare: "We burnt houses, slashed banana trees, tore the aprons off women and raped them, axed big pigs, broke down fences, fired houses . . . Eyes were put out and legs were lamed," reports one Papuan man, quoted in *Man on Earth*. Josef refers to one tribe that still practices cannibalism. (Has he been there himself? "No, I couldn't go among them because I smell of soap.")

He comments that warfare was part of a man's identity. If you didn't kill someone you wouldn't get a wife. ("And there is now great prestige in killing Indonesians.")

But tribal wars, a "wild, fierce festival," in Peter Matthiessen's words, were fought with equal weapons and were evenly matched: the warfare was of limited duration, very small-scale, and there were—after a fashion—rules of engagement. What the Indonesians have unleashed is a war where the slaughter never stops, where one side uses bows and arrows and the other the most sophisticated weaponry in the world.

In the European imagination, there have long been two types of people who live in the wilderness. One is exemplified by the innocent gentle Arawaks (the Noble Savage, the dwellers in earthly paradise), while the other, their enemies, are the Caribs, from which the word *cannibal* derives. (Often, it seems, such stories are exaggerated for effect, or invented for a gullible audience, or told to besmirch the reputation of a neighboring tribe.)

Europeans have been fixated by cannibals and headhunters, buzzing with a self-delighting frisson of horror. Frankly, I've never really understood why headhunting and cannibalism give people the heebie-jeebies in the way they do. It seems that these practices are often done with purpose, for ritual reasons (an understanding, for instance, that life springs from death) or out of cultural self-preservation and, importantly, done in a limited way: limited by the temporary insanity of bereavement, or limited by small-scale tribal war.

Sure-yani Poroso told me of the ritual headshrinking practiced by his tribe in Bolivia. "We recorded our history in trophies of shrunk heads and drums made from the skin of fat Incas. It was to teach children to defend our culture, because we used them to illustrate how different people had killed Leco people. When an Inca was killed, if he was fat, we would cut and peel off his skin and cure it and use it as the skin for a drum. With Wari people, for example, we would practice headshrinking because Wari people killed and assaulted our culture, killed our women and children."

The head would be washed in herbs and cut open at the back and the bones would be removed. They would fill the head with sand, sew it back up, sewing the mouth shut, then cover it with parsley juice and tobacco juice, then wrap it in tobacco leaves and put it in a rock oven. The heat dried out all the liquid and the blood, and then the head would shrink. Then they would take the head out, cut it open again and refill it with sand a second time and put it back in the oven, so it would shrink down further. A third time, they would take it out and refill it with sand and put it in the oven. By the time it was finished, he said, it was the size of a large baked potato, and people would keep it in the smoke of a fire, where it would last 100 or 150 years.

"The Catholic Church prohibited head-shrinking," said Sure-yani, "and called us savages for doing this. But we were not savages. It was a part of our history to do this. And we shrunk the heads of our enemies, of those who had tried to destroy us—we had good reasons for killing them. The real savages are those who kill without reason, the rubber barons in the past, the capitalism of today." (And the recruiting sergeants for today's genocidal corporations are called what? Headhunters.)

It wasn't for ritual or self-defense that the European invaders of North America ordered Native Americans to be murdered. General Jeffrey Amherst wrote in a letter to a subordinate in 1732, "You will do well to try to inoculate the Indians by means of blankets in which smallpox patients have slept, as well as by every other method that can serve to extirpate this execrable race. I should be very glad if your scheme of hunting them down by dogs could take effect." Tell me about the savages.

An eyewitness account by one of the Europeans, reported in *Bury My Heart at Wounded Knee*, details what happened when the troops attacked a Cheyenne camp: "The squaws offered no resistance. Every one I saw dead was scalped. I saw one squaw cut open with an unborn child, as I thought, lying by her side. Captain Soule afterwards told me that such was the fact. I saw the body of White Antelope with the privates cut off, and I heard a soldier say he was going to make a tobacco pouch out of them." Another eyewitness says, "I also heard of numerous instances in which men had cut out the private parts of females and stretched them over the saddle-bows and wore them over their hats."

I've spent a delightful weekend with cannibals, and the descendant of headshrinkers is a good friend of mine. But nowhere have I come across any savagery equal to modern American warfare, dropping cluster bombs designed to discharge within the body, causing agonizing death, particularly among children. In 1954, the American air force informed the rest of the mil-

itary of a plan to attack the Soviet bloc with hydrogen bombs. Said one par-
ticipant, "Virtually all of Russia would be nothing but a smoking, radiating
ruin at the end of two hours."

No headhunters in history have ever caused an inferno so that "bodies
were stuck in the hardened black mass of their own fat, which had melted and
run out onto the floor. . . . Many had shrunk to the size of dwarves; others
had blown up like balloons. . . . Their skulls had burst at the temples where
the brain pushed out, and their intestines bulged out under their ribs." Fifty
thousand dead. A night in Hamburg 1943, reported by Sven Lindqvist.

In Iraq, American forces used earthmovers to bury thousands of Iraqi
soldiers—some still alive—in more than seventy miles of trenches. Tell me
about the savages.

Meanwhile, what of headhunters in the wilderness of Papua New Guinea?
In 1877, Luigi Maria D'Albertis journeyed up the Fly River, writing in his
journal, "What an advantage it would be for the natives to appreciate us, and
to understand how many benefits they might derive from our acquaintance!
But no, they come with the intention of killing us, perhaps that they may
adorn their houses with our heads." The local people do no such thing, but
a crew member goes ashore, shoots a local person and cuts off his head.
D'Albertis pickles the head in spirits, and hopes that by his doing so the local
people "will learn to moderate their desires for the heads of strangers."

There is a similar reversal of victimhood in a nasty little episode from the
1990s in which an adventurer hunted out a tiny tribe of previously uncontacted people in order to get material for a book. Let's be very clear about this:
indigenous peoples have died in the millions from sicknesses that are often
no more than a minor cold for the outsiders who invade their territories. The
author is aware of this phenomenon and even reports his knowledge of it,
yet still pursues his adventure, knowingly risking the deaths of those he
"contacted," as the euphemism has it.

The writer speaks to various people (who do not appear to have any
knowledge of the tribe) who describe them as cannibals, and they do so with
a kind of comic-book racism that would be merely risible if it weren't used by
governments around the world as a justification for exterminating tribespeople. Writing of his short stay with the tribe, the author uses animal images to

describe them, and portrays them as vengeful, bloodthirsty, frightening and threatening, yet he can give no example of his fear having any basis in reality. Far from being threatening to the author, the villagers are terrified, and flee from him, hiding in the forests. The tribespeople are no longer cannibals, but this is no hindrance to the author's portrayal: he treats the reader to his lurid fantasy of one of the tribesmen drooling over human flesh.

Throughout the book, the author makes himself out to be the potential victim, but the truth is surely the reverse. He chose to force himself on the tribe, while they had no choice. He risked their lives. He intruded on their society aiding in the undermining of the tribe's traditional power structure and culture by addressing as leader not the traditional chief but the government appointee, basing his visit at the house of the nonlocal Christian priest, and giving a talk in the Christian Church in this traditionally animist village. The author, a Christian, brings with him Christian guides, and the book is littered with his prayers for deliverance. But whose deliverance from whose evil? During his brief visit, some villagers die and the author comes to be regarded by the tribe as a murderer. Still they offer him no violence, and yet still he portrays them in bloodcurdling terms as if he is about to be killed by them.

One god-botherer on an apparently selfish mission is bad enough, but what is worse is the influence a book like this might have in encouraging unthinking bigots to go on similar "adventures" while further contributing to Western society's distorted views of indigenous people. In my opinion, in a just world any uninvited intrusion into any uncontacted culture should be seen as a human rights issue, and this book should never have been published. But we do not live in such a world. Not only was the book published, it was lauded by reviewers, making themselves moral accomplices to his invasion, gullibly hiccupping their ignorance. It was a testament to the profound racism shown in our society toward indigenous people that reviewers couldn't see what they were reading. If, for the sake of a good story, the author had risked even inadvertently infecting a village in Hampshire with the AIDS virus, it would have been judged reckless by many people. He does something equally risky to a village of isolated indigenous people and is given fawning tributes. Tell me about the savages.

FIRE ON THE MOUNTAIN

In the villages I stayed in, the early mornings were delicate, quiet hours. As the sun rose, it would drive the clouds off the mountains and in each thatched hut, small and round like a beehive, people would light fires, so that from the outside it looked as if each hut made its own smoke like a mountain making its own cloud. Early morning smokers' coughs would break out across the village.

The villages were remote from the control of the Indonesians and the villagers were defended from the soldiers by the land itself. The "main road" into one village involved climbing a large, sloping rock face, very slippery, with only tiny cracks for fingerholds and toeholds. It was pouring rain, and I was cold. It took me about half an hour to cross perhaps fifty meters of rock, which fell away sheer below.

For days into weeks, we walked on. Out on the pathways Mathias and Theo were hooting at each other, gleefully, laughingly. As we picked our way on rocks down one river, my ankles were biting with pain, and I stopped and sat on a rock. A couple of men passed, wearing only their gourds, so their backsides were at eye level. Near-nakedness had come to seem quite normal to me. One lunchtime we tried to light a fire, but it didn't catch because the wood was too wet. Theo, bored, climbed a few feet up a tree and fell asleep. The others kept trying, to no avail. Suddenly, to everyone's surprise, not the wood but the tree caught fire—with Theo in it. The sparks flittered from its crackling twigs. Theo woke up and roared with surprise. Mathias knew he was going to fall about laughing, so as a precaution he lay down first. Then he howled with laughter. It was hardly dangerous. Theo jumped down the far side and came up to me looking sheepish. Mathias's giggles were infectious and I had tears of laughter in my eyes.

That evening—the last night—we had a proper fire. The tarp was thrown up over two tree ferns and secured with guy ropes; ferns and straw were scattered on the ground and loads of firewood were cut to last through the night. The guides stuck forked branches in the ground, balancing a long thin branch between them as a washing line, and I tried to get my socks if not dry at least less wet. The squat trunks of tree ferns lined the firepit like huge spliffs. And the guides sang the mountain, sang our journey, sang and sang, and I sang with them, the lovely part-songs and gentle harmonies.

The word *companion* means literally those who eat bread together. (*Panis*, in Latin, means "bread.") There should be a similar word *comignion* from *ignis*, "fire"—the friend who shares your last cigarette or sits at your hearth long after midnight. And then we could also have an adjective *comignionable*—old men nodding together over a pipe, scruffy and happy. Papuan people are comignionable in the extreme, forever lighting fires, while everyone, even small children, smokes like a chimney.

On the last day I was struggling (again). Toward the end, we crossed a bridge over the Baliem River. On this river, there is a village called Kelika. Here, in 1977, helicopters landed and Indonesian soldiers rounded up Papuan village leaders and lined them up on the airstrip. One by one they were asked if they supported Indonesia or West Papua. If they said West Papua, they were shot. Some ten thousand people are thought to have been killed answering that question. They say the Baliem River ran red with blood.

We passed a man carrying a pig with its feet tied together and its snout tied shut with blue string. There was a bushfire on both sides of the path. There was no other way, so we ran, the fire burning to the left and right. It wasn't dangerous, though it scorched us as we went, but I felt past caring, in a deep, almost passive exhaustion. When the path reached the river, we jumped in to cool off and, getting out, Josef told me the end of the path was very close; it would be about one hour until we reached a road where we could catch a bus back to Wamena. The last half hour. The last twenty minutes. The last five. The end. I had never looked with love at a wheeled vehicle before.

WHY CLIMB?

Why are mountains so alluring? Whether it's trekking in mountain ranges or scaling single peaks, why do it? When your exhaustion makes you sob like a child, why climb? When you're forced off a summit because the wind is hurling rocks and the cold has viced your fingers' flesh onto their own cold bones, why climb? When you could injure yourself for life for one piece of sky, why climb?

For a sense of perspective, literal and metaphoric. Mountains cut the crap, they clear confusion, and their sudden clarity can make me laugh out loud.

For the tense triangulation of mountain, moment and you: the route you choose is the line of your will, your summiting is your will's realization. On the way, you doggedly climb, through ice to the stars, every climber an Inca for the sun.

For the wild silence in the mountains, silence that creates a waking, alert vitality—nothing dozes up here, no humming of innumerable bees, no clonk of cowbells, no squeaky gate. The silence speaks of potential danger and this wild silence gives wings to mind.

For the raw rock and unassimilated ice, for its undomesticated otherness, essential and brilliant, as wild mountains keep fealty to geological time and to unfingered sky.

For the eternity up there: Byron wrote of the Alps which "throned Eternity in icy halls." Yet on mountains, the moment is critical. All climbers know the crucial point of *this* step, and *that* choice, the weather right *now*.

For the joy of the unnecessary, the game of it: French *alpinistre* Lionel Terray called his memoir *Conquistadors of the Useless*.

For its sexual nature: the foothills the foreplay, the summit the climax and the cocreated "*estupendo*" gasped at the summit, the sheer relief, the laughter.

For the pleasure of the descent into the ordinary, for reentering the domestic life of the valleys, the pint, the pub, the fireplace, the kitten.

For having within you, afterward, all the mountains you have ever climbed.

For the poetry of it: the most romantic signature in the world is surely that of the late King of Nepal's brother, who would sign himself simply *Himalaya*. (The sheer poetry of mountains infuses even the stories of mapping: the Himalayas were secretly mapped by British-sponsored Indian cartographers, called "Pandits," who walked the mountains in disguise as pilgrims with notebooks tucked inside their prayer wheels and rosaries containing one hundred beads instead of 108, to help them count their steps and measure distance. In their staffs, they kept thermometers so they could measure altitude by the boiling point of water.)

But above all, it seems people climb for the glee of freedom. *More sky! More sky!* To be able to walk away from things. Vertically.

MERDEKA. ELEUTHERIA. SAOIRSE. AZAADI. AZADI.
RANGWANG. WOLNOŠČ. FREIHEIT. LIRI. SVOBODA.
VRIJHEID. ÖZGÜRLÜK. VABADUS. LIBERTADEA. LA
LIBERTAD. LA LIBERTÉ. LIBERTAS. LIBERTATE.
FREEDOM.

These words for freedom make the very air ring as they are spoken out. Of all elements, air is most associated with freedom—the airscape is escape, "free as the wind," the wind "bloweth where it listeth." There is a Norwegian term *Friluftsliv* (literally "free-air-life"), which combines an exuberance for the unenclosed life, for you cannot trap the air or net the sky. And mountains, of all landscapes, seem the freest. One peak of Kilimanjaro is called Uhuru, meaning Freedom, and it suits all mountains. Mountains are associated with the freest things we know: air, wind, the flight of birds and the wings of mind, for thoughts have a quality of glide, up here, and the human mind needs mountains as a mirror for its flight. Joseph Beuys once said that a mountain "taken as inner psychology . . . represents a high pitch of consciousness."

In the Middle Ages, only artists and birds were considered truly free. The free flight of birds was impossibly out of reach for feudal peasants, tied to the land. Flight has become literal now, but its meanings have become more complex as humankind has flown to outer space. But even as we achieved the ambition of a new Icarus in soaring flight right out of the sky and into the wilderness of space, so the myth was strangely made manifest, and came true in the most unexpected but most apt way of all. The wax of the *mind* melted. Astronauts saw Earth as never before. The human psyche turned soft, liquid and lovely, yearning for home. That was the slipping back, the wise mind fully itself only on Earth and falling, falling like Icarus falling, in love with home. A second and more knowing time, a second and more knowing love.

In the thirteenth and fourteenth centuries, there was a rebel philosophy, the Brethren of the Free Spirit, expounding nakedness, sensual pleasure and hedonism. By following natural instincts and urges, they believed they were acting out divinity. They have been linked to the Catholic mystic anarchist Heinrich Suso, who described a vision he had in 1330 of a spirit:

suso: What is your name?

spirit: I am called Nameless Wildness.

suso: Where does your insight lead to?

spirit: Into untrammelled freedom.

suso: What do you call untrammelled freedom?

spirit: When a man lives according to all his caprices without distin-
guishing between God and himself and without before or after.

Without before or after? It was a succinct summing up of a sense of moment,
an utter and divine spontaneity that they believed in passionately. They considered that every action of theirs was performed not in ordinary time but in
eternity. What they recognized has been all but lost to modernity: a wild idea
of time that demands a sense of being right at the edge of the moment, just at
the point where the moment meets the eternal, as Eastern religions know.
This conjunction of the moment with the eternal is not a paradox but an exquisite fulfillment, for it is only through the one that you can reach the other.
And in this momentous now is the freedom of uncountable choices: spontaneity, caprice and absolute freedom of wild time.

The church deemed the Brethren heretics and they were tried by the
Inquisition for making love too freely and for believing that humans could
be divine.

"Once I moved about like the wind. Now I surrender to you and that is
all," said Goyathlay (Geronimo), an Apache chief, surrendering to the whites
in 1886. The joint loss of land and freedom was what finally destroyed the
Native Americans. In 1967, Clyde Warrior of the Ponca people wrote, "our
old people felt rich because they were free. They were rich in things of the
spirit, but if there is one thing that characterizes Indian life today it is poverty
of the spirit. . . . We are poor in spirit because we are not free." The demon-
strations against racial segregation on buses were called Freedom Rides, but
the word is now perverted. The "freedom" of endless war that Bush seeks to
impose on the world, the "freedom" of genocidal imperialism of this nation,
which imprisons more of its own citizens than any other. Bush has taken this,
my favorite word, and turned it into the F word. And "freedom fries" make
me spit.

Women's history has long been a demand for freedom as if for the very air we breathe.

"Leave me the heart that now I bear,
And give me liberty!"
gasped Emily Brontë.

The Japanese Women's Movement was founded in the 1880s, and one early feminist called for women's horizons to be "as large and free as the world itself." Result? She was jailed for a week. Mary Wollstonecraft spoke of breathing "the sharp invigorating air of freedom."

In Greek, there is an expression "Madness goes to the mountains." Nijinsky, half-mad, went to the mountains, so his spirit could be free, deviant, walking the idiot path, idiosyncratic—that word that is etymologically first cousin to *idiot*. Freedom demands that you go your own way though the world calls you mad for it.

Freedom is passionate—the word *passion* includes in its root an ability to suffer. Following a passionate freedom can mean loneliness, penury, humiliation, for we live in a world where the caged hate the free. Do you have the courage for it? For its pyrotechnics and its raw unforgiving, for its gambling, the peak or crevasse? Ace or two? If you want to play it safe, you should never have come up here, for this is the freedom of rebels and outcasts, the mad and manic and misunderstood, the misfits and artists, anarchists and poets, the metaphysically alone, the suicidal comics and all those who sat at the back of the classroom, tipped back their chairs and blew smoke rings to lasso the teacher who tried to tame them.

Freedom is absolutist. "I so love freedom," wrote Montaigne, "that if someone forbade me access to the remotest corner of the Indies I should feel myself a little hemmed in."

Sensible habits and good road safety skills will keep you alive till eighty. So what? If you didn't know freedom, you never lived, never knew that thrilling whisper, turning blood to quicksilver, reflecting sheer fear and pleasure—to be most alive is to be most free is to be most wild.

The spirit of Dionysus, that god of wildness, was also called Eleuthereus:

freedom. "A wilderness is rich with liberty," wrote Wordsworth. Freedom means to light out for somewhere, like Huck Finn, rafting down the river, shining, fluent and free before he is dammed by adulthood. For a delight in freedom is something we are taught to scorn and to outgrow, till our innate freedom is dulled and dimmed, deadened and demeaned by detail and deadline and caution and clocks.

But roaring underneath all this, still, freedom growls in the dusk. Freedom is because life is. The soaring buzzard in the freedom of its wings, choosing its moment to plunge, bundling down on the mouse, the song thrush choosing a tune for this configuration of cloud, gnat and jeweled stream. And when the arpeggio lifts on an in-breath to a melody, the jazz saxophonist—winging it like the eagle adjusting its wingtip feathers to the current of the air, winging it in an improvised riff—catches airs of melody and adjusts by a semitone at the fingertips the angle of the song.

Raw freedom hurls you terror and wonder, writes its ruthless poems in your life. Freedom, uncathedralable, would piss on St. Paul's and despise any orthodoxy, for freedom knows the transcendent road sweeps lonely to the summit, no map, no guide, no god at your heels.

Freedom is not the opposite of Necessity but itself an absolute and implacable demand, an electric and sudden necessity. Freedom is an intrinsic part of wildness. Wildness must obey Freedom: an apparent paradox but the only one that leaves the human spirit truly intact. There is no compromise. Freedom is not polite. It doesn't knock or telephone first. It slams its hand down on your desk and says *Dance*—as the mad fiddler, his fingers bleeding on the strings, plays an elegy at the speed of a reckless waltz till the sky breaks down in tears. Do not give me diamonds. They are too domestic. Give me only freedom.

The Kapauku people of the West Papuan Highlands so value personal independence that "they believe that such freedom of action and absence of compulsion is essential not only to man's well being but to his very existence," writes anthropologist Leopold Pospisil. A person deprived of freedom will die, they think, so they do not use jail, captivity or slavery. The Kapauku believe "that the essence of life is a free cooperation of the body and the soul. Any interference in this cooperation endangers the life of the individual. The soul (mind), when unable to control freely the actions of the body, becomes displeased, and tries to sever its relationship, thus ultimately causing the death of the individual."

In West Papua, freedom is a necessity that people die for. "We are born with freedom," said Thom Beanal, the current Papuan leader, to me. "Outsiders may intimidate us but we know we were born with freedom." Another man commented, "Freedom is one of the rights from god. It's like love; nothing will stop it."

Ask about sweet potatoes and men will tell you about freedom, *merdeka*. Mention pigs and they will talk to you about independence. (And if you know anything about Papuans, you will know how dear to them is the wriggly, squiggly piglet and the grunting sow.)

Merdeka is broadly defined by Papuans. Comments anthropologist Eben Kirksey, "It is variously a desire for divine salvation, equitable development, environmental sustainability and political independence." *Merdeka* seems to me to have an element of almost supernatural release from the chains of injustice and all forms of slavery. Freedom would come like a flash of lightning, righteousness would shine sudden as a second coming and strike out as loudly as bells in the night, the chimes of freedom, which Bob Dylan could have written with West Papua in mind: the storm at midnight that sets free the oppressed.

REBEL ANGELS

Josef offered to take me to an OPM stronghold in the forest. (OPM stands for Organisasi Papua Merdeka, the "Free Papua Movement," the freedom fighters.) I leapt at the chance. To get there, we had to take a road past a police post. I had permission from the Indonesian authorities to be in only a handful of places. I was certainly not allowed to be here. I wore sunglasses and a hat and light scarves around my face, and as we passed the police post, Josef gestured to me to lie down on the van floor. The police didn't notice me and waved us through.

At the village near the stronghold, there was a small roadside market. Josef quietly talked to someone he recognized, telling him why we were there. That man introduced us to another, who turned out to be senior in the command structure at the compound. He took both my hands in his, smiled broadly and told me he had had a dream that a special guest would arrive today. "That was *you*," he beamed. So he had gone to the market to meet me.

We walked for an hour, through fields and woods, and I had no idea what to expect. Some OPM leaders have kidnapped Westerners—this was not my fear because I trusted Josef's judgment implicitly, but I still felt unable to picture the situation. Thousands of ragged Papuans waiting for the word? Stockpiles of weaponry? The disillusioned infighting of those permanently denied power? In West Papua, they say everyone is a member of the OPM: every man, woman and child, in their hearts. But I didn't know what the OPM soldiers would be like.

Close to the compound, the Morning Star flag was fluttering bravely in the breeze, and we were stopped a short distance from the entrance while someone went ahead to announce us. The compound was built within a high wooden palisade and at the entrance when we walked through was a small, tidy porter's lodge, with a visitors' book. And then I saw, on the far side, two lines of men armed with bows and arrows, all saluting us. We were meant to walk between these rows and I felt very disconcerted—and undeservedly honored. Should I salute back? I ended up vaguely stroking my forehead, half a "hot" gesture, half a salute, feeling wholly foolish.

We were ushered into a small wooden hall, to meet the commander. Josef introduced me, and when he had finished, the commander, his lieutenant (who had met us at the market) and a senior man each spoke, quietly, ceremonially, welcoming us. I suddenly saw the character of the place. There was an atmosphere of purity and serenity: it was calm and ordered and the gentle smiling chief was more a minister than a military leader. Far from visiting a gang of desperadoes, this was like being in church. The commander was a poised, charismatic young man who shone with faith—their first strength, he said, is god, and their last strength prayer. And they prayed for money to buy weapons—bring me my bow of burning gold, bring me my arrows of desire— because all they had was wooden bows and arrows and the spiritual shield of faith with which to fight for Papua's green and pleasant land.

Where now what the Indonesians offensively call the "Wild Gang Terrorists" of the OPM? Other OPM strongholds may well have a wildness that could be their salvation, a ferocity to wreak their own redemption. But in this jungle fortress, what were they doing? Praying. Preparing themselves spiritually for the fight. "All night we spend working for independence," they said, and it reminded me instantly of the wise virgins keeping their lamps trimmed.

It was as sweet and hopeless as honey for a stab wound. The commander, in word and expression, looked untarnished, as if nothing had ever corroded his vision and as if he was ready not so much to foment rebellion as to fling wide open the gates to a haloed Jesus, when the OPM oppressed would become the OPM triumphant.

They lived by their dreams, as I had seen when the lieutenant approached us in the marketplace. A dreamlike quality permeated all their conversation and a time of dreams washed over their days of reality. "One day" they will fight, "one day" they will drive the Indonesians out, "one day" they will rise up, and "one day" Christ will rise again—these days merged in a dreamtime future, longed-for and prayed-for. They were living, they believed, in the last days, the last days of Indonesian occupation and the last days before the Second Coming.

It wasn't only Jesus they waited for. They also waited, watched and prayed for the United Nations, which, they said, *must* support them because it is un-just not to do so. If the UN knew that Papuans unanimously sought inde-pendence, it would help them, they believed, as the UN did in East Timor. They speak with shining belief of the members of the European Parliament who know the situation and must therefore act, because it would be wrong not to do so. And they put their faith in Western journalists to come here and write about their situation, because it is their duty to do so. They beg me to write so that journalists will come and tell the world about their situation. Their faith hurts me. The Western media *does* know—and it ignores them. A BBC film crew, led by one Bruce Parry, went to West Papua recently and broadcast sixty minutes of prime-time "tribalistic" guff using Papuans as exotica for reality TV and failed entirely to mention Indonesia's savage slaughter. Papuans would have wept bitterly at this betrayal. If this corporate-driven genocide doesn't make the headlines, then what the fuck is the point of an international media?

They put their faith in their own leaders too, and tell me, heartbrokenly, the story of Obet Tabuni, one of the founders of the OPM, who was killed by the Indonesian military, who then cut out his heart and kept it, in effortlessly eloquent savagery. The Papuan leader Theys Eluay was assassinated in No-vember 2001. His heart had been ripped out by the Indonesians and the rest of his body was returned to the people. They did not send back the heart.

They have faith in nature, which, they say, is political—nature has taken sides and joined the OPM. The rainforest kills Indonesian soldiers, they say, a beautiful "she-demon" in the forest invites Indonesian soldiers to sleep with her. They try to, she vanishes, they die. "Every animal, plant and stone is a member of the OPM," says Viktor Kaisiepo, a Papuan leader in exile in the Netherlands. Mosquitoes deliberately target Indonesians, snakes poison them, leeches suck their blood, wasps sting them and trees fall to crush them. They are "Natural Commandos," *Komando Alam*.

Eben Kirksey writes of these ideas of nature or *Alam*: quite apart from inspiring the Papuan resistance, the idea of *Alam* "has instilled fear into troops that the untamed interior of West Papua is a dangerous place inhabited by guerrillas with supernatural powers." *Alam*, he says, is defined as "world" or "realm," "nature" or "environment" or "knowledge." Kirksey comments that Papuans build on the definition of *alam* as knowledge "to encompass the variety of forms of indigenous magic. . . . *Alam* in this sense is used as a weapon of Papuan freedom fighters."

The one group of people in whom they have no faith whatsoever is the Christian missionaries. The missionaries do not care about Papuan freedom and independence, said the commander, because the missionaries support the murderous Indonesian government who, in turn, supports the missionaries. (I was to meet dozens of missionaries in West Papua, and only one thought that the Papuans should be free in their own land.)

The older man was quiet for most of the meeting, and after a while, I spoke to him directly to ask about his life. "You don't see many people my age," he began. "Because so many people my age have been killed." He spoke of 1977, when the Indonesian military bombed many of the Highland villages in retaliation for their demand for independence. "Most of my friends were killed," he said simply. "Our last promise to you is that we will fight for our freedom though we die for it." "*Wa*," came a quiet voice. "*Wa, wa*," came the agreement around the room. The commander asked everyone to pray before we left.

And die they do. Some months after I visited, the village was attacked by the Indonesian army. Soldiers shot people and seized one man, slashed his face and body with a razor, poured gasoline over him and set him on fire.

And die they must, they say, for freedom. The Morning Star symbolizes Papuan freedom, and at one flag-raising protest, the military opened fire, killing several people, including one man who died hugging the flagpole. In Sorong, in July 2002, there was a flag-raising ceremony. Four hundred soldiers opened fire on the crowd, killing an unknown number. In Biak hundreds were shot for raising the flag; in Wamena the same story. At flag raisings, says an OPM representative, "people do not care if they get shot anymore. It seems like freedom is already in their hands."

Cry freedom and the Morning Star—as a man defiantly raises the flag and is shot dead. The scene has been played out a hundred times—a symbol, the flag, for an abstraction, freedom, apparently so futile a gesture but actually more precious than life in the theater of the human soul. Bow and arrow in his right hand and the Morning Star in his left, he stares out death down the barrel of a British gun. And he laughs at the bullet, free beyond fear of death. He juxtaposes freedom with oppression, the soaring star-bound gesture and the sullen bully who guns him down. Unshielded, nearly naked and needing no uniform other than his humanity, he lights the tip of his arrow, which blazes vivid and true into the air. The audience never pays for the masterpiece. But every author of every masterpiece has paid an intolerable price. And here, this author of this gestural masterpiece leaves the theater; paying the debt he incurred, he contemptuously buys the ticket as he leaves, throwing his own dead body like loose change at the box office clerk.

CRY FREEDOM!

The capital city of Jayapura is surrounded by hilltops. On one is a cross, on another the antennae of an Indonesian TV transmitter, on another a red neon sign of an oil company, on another the Indonesian army base and another the Indonesian police base. Between them—the missionaries, the media, the corporations, the military and the police—they have this country in chains.

But not the mountains.

When Papuan people have resisted the occupation, they have fled to the hills for safety, and though the Indonesians have burnt the forests and bombed the villages, the mountains are still the site of freedom, for the Indonesians cannot control them.

Mountains are the quintessential site of political freedom, home of freedom fighters, independence movements and political outlaws—all over the world.

On north Sulawesi, freedom fighters against the Dutch fled to the volcano Gunung Klabat. The Kelimutu volcano on Flores, near East Timor, was adopted as a symbol of the East Timorese Independence movement. In the Chinese *Water-Margin* novel, the bandits' "liberated area" on a mountain of Liang Shan P'o "would expand to become a region, a province, the nucleus of a force to topple the throne of heaven," writes Eric Hobsbawm in *Bandits*. Japanese Zen master Dōgen Kigen, in *Mountains and Waters Sutra*, 1240, wrote, "The imperial power has no authority over the wise people in the mountains."

The island of Dominica is very mountainous, and for this reason became a stronghold for indigenous people escaping the colonization that took place in all the surrounding islands. The Algerian war of liberation began in the mountain wilderness of the Aurès. The Kurdish liberation movement made its home in the mountains. In Afghanistan there is a Pashtun saying: "Be tame in the city and rebellious in the mountains." In the late 1950s, young Cubans went to the Escambray Mountains and were later joined by Fidel Castro's fighters; from there they fought the Batista dictatorship. And today, of course, the Zapatista freedom fighters operate from the mountains of Chiapas.

Romanticism understood well the relationship between mountains and freedom fighters. Wordsworth applauded the French Revolution and in "National Independence and Liberty" described the two voices, of sea and of mountains: "They were thy chosen music, Liberty!" Shelley, supporter of republican liberty, saw freedom in the mountains, the "chainless winds" in his poem "Mont Blanc." Salvator Rosa, early Romantic painter, was said to have spent time as a child with the outlaws in the mountains of Abruzzi, and painted wild mountains with the figures of "*banditti*." Byron, watching the mountains at Marathon, dreamed that Greece might be free. ("Great things are done when men and mountains meet.")

The Greek mountains have long been the site of resistance; the *klephtes*— literally "robbers"—were freedom fighters who fought from the hills, resisting the Turks who had overrun Greece. It was from the mountains that, in the Second World War, Greeks organized one of Europe's biggest resistance movements. Later, Communists opposed to Anglo-American domination would take to the hills.

The Pyrenees have long been a refuge for political and religious dissent:

after 1968, hundreds of disillusioned French protesters went to the mountains. The "Haiduk" heroes, the guerrilla-bandits of Hungary and the Balkans, were dissident peasants, seeking freedom in the mountains, whose role was fundamentally political—catalysts of the growing demand for national liberation.

"The gentry use the pen, we the gun; they are the lords of the land, we of the mountain," says an old bandit from Roccamandolfi, quoted in Hobsbawm's *Bandits*. Hobsbawm also describes the merging of freedom fighters with social bandits—the word is from the Italian *bandito*, someone who is banned, outside the law. The state may regard them as criminals but the people consider them heroes, "champions, avengers, fighters for justice": Robin Hood figures, fighting for justice, outlaws who are outside laws they don't respect but who have a strong code of honor and an egalitarian political streak.

Rebels, outcasts, outlaws and freedom fighters—and all those in sympathy with them—know that wild lands matter as a last stronghold for opposition: wilderness is the objective correlative for all those who demand political freedom. In the wilds, we cannot be controlled or policed or pacified. In the wilds is our political autonomy. *Cry freedom* in all the mountains that have ever heard the rebel yell and suburbia, malleable clay to fascism, can go to hell.

PARADISE FOUND

When Westerners first flew over the Baliem Valley in 1938, they perceived it as a paradise. In 1944, two American war correspondents described it as a "Shangri-la"—the same image used by James Hilton, portraying it in his novel *Lost Horizon*. (And in the seventy-odd years after Europeans flew over it, these perverters of paradise have ensured that it has been bombed and brutalized.)

Paradise has long been considered an opposite of wilderness; thus a desert wilderness is opposite of the oasis of the desert city, and the paradise within the monastery walls is opposed to the forest wilds. The word *paradise* is from the Persian *apiri-daeza*, a walled orchard.

When I trekked in the Baliem Valley, I was struck by the neat, well-tended gardens. Walking for weeks, I would always see, somewhere, specks of men in the high fields, in red berets and ocher penis gourds, cutting a new field into a slope or repairing a stone wall, or a woman in a grass skirt weeding a field, her breasts folding over a suckling child, with a digging stick in her hand and a *noken* hanging down her back, her stick prizing up a root. Pallets of fresh vegetables lined the paths, full of corn, sweet potatoes, beans and bananas, taro, yams and cassava, wild strawberries and gourds, the larder-litany of plenty, variety and ladenness. All's well and full.

In the Christian tradition, landscape is read in religious terms. The Garden is equated with paradise both at the beginning of time (the Garden of Eden) and at the end of time (the unearthly heavenly paradise). The present, though, is not seen as paradise but as the place of fallen nature, and Christianity stares at it with fear and loathing, for the earth is wild, untamed. The *Oxford English Dictionary* lists a rare archaic use of *wilderness* to describe this present world and *earthly life*, by contrast to the future life in heaven: paradise in the past and in the future but today the wilderness. (Jam yesterday and jam tomorrow, but never jam today.)

In Canada, one of the incoming French priests, Father Biard, in 1616, considered the land a wilderness and thus satanic, but thought it could be converted (like a sinner) into god's own lawn. "All of this region . . . through Satan's malevolence which reigns there, is a horrible wilderness," but the French ambition was "to make a Garden out of the wilderness." The effortlessly perceptive Montaigne was to remark that we call wilderness anything that is not *our* idea of a garden.

In forcing an opposition between the Garden and the Wilderness, there is a conflict of wills. Wilderness expresses its own will, the will of its nature. A garden, on the other hand, expresses the will of the gardener (or, in the case of the Garden of Eden, the will of the god). The starkest European example of the expression of human will is the formal gardens of stately homes, the strict, clipped foliage, the military lines of trees. The gardens reflected the political will of the ruling classes, while the wild weeds of the peasantry were on the far side of the ha-ha, where nature's will held wild sway. Interestingly, just when formal gardens held greatest sway, there was protest against them with Metaphysical poet Andrew Marvell, in 1681, seeing a vitality on the wild side, describing the fields outside the garden wall,

Where willing Nature does to all dispense
A wild and fragrant innocence

But within garden walls was a "dead and standing pool of air," where nature is "stupefied."

But I would argue that gardens are not an opposite of wildness and that paradise is not in conflict with wilderness. The truest gardening weaves the way of the wild within it—the will of nature and the will of humans not in battle but in cooperation. The most beautiful gardens are not expressions of hatred for wilderness; rather, they are a cultivated wild, deeply cultured.

The gentle georgics of the well-dug garden have a tender poetic: tilled and well tended, the work of thoughtful hands, picking the right place to plant and the right time to harvest. It is one of the sweetest expressions of humanity, wild nature nurtured by hard work, a place where culture is enrooted with cultivation and care.

Europeans have long been fond of claiming that a paradise from which mankind was expelled is a universal truth. But anthropologist Hugh Brody, in *The Other Side of Eden*, refutes this utterly: "Genesis is not a universal truth about the human condition. Inuit children do not grow up with the curses of exile. . . . Everything about the hunter-gatherer system is founded on the conviction that home is already Eden, and exile must be avoided." Heaven is under our feet, wrote Thoreau; paradise can be here and now—in fact now is the only possible time to ransack paradise and suck up its juices. We are not exiled from the garden of Eden but living in it still. Paradise is not in the past or future but only in the present, this Earth an untamed heaven, a wild paradise garden.

THE ANARCHIC WILL

Wild landscapes—self-willed land—defy human will. The Chinese word for wild nature translates as "Self-thus," which Gary Snyder glosses as "nature-not-programmed—generating its own rules from within." An-archic, something that rules itself, willful. Wildness has intensity and vitality. Will is a force. A wild creature is not subject to any will except its own.

Anthropologist Gillian Gillison writes of the Gimi people of the Eastern Highlands of Papua New Guinea, "The idea of 'the wild' is central in Gimi thought." To the Gimi people, there is a sense of profound order in wild nature. "Things in the wild exist in their original, eternal and in that sense perfect form. The stated aim of men's initiation rites is to achieve the 'ideal type' in nature," she writes. "The Gimi wilderness is an exalted domain where the male spirit, incarnate in birds and marsupials, acts out its secret desires away from the inhibiting presence of women." But women, too, are occasionally associated with wilderness. "Stories tell of the '*kore badaha*,' literally 'wild/spirit women' who temporarily escape domesticity." One flees her husband and acquires stupendous powers in the forests and is known as "Sir Woman."

In the same book (*Nature, Culture and Gender*), Marilyn Strathern describes how, for the Hagen people of Papua New Guinea, certain kinds of spirits are wild and inhabit forests or uninhabited lands. Some spirits are uncooperative and capricious, ready to attack. People too can be wild because of insanity or because they act antisocially, being greedy or irresponsible, and women, they say, are more prone to behaving wildly. Wildness, for the Hagen people, is seen as the source of life and of creativity, and magic belongs to the "wild" domain. (And in a dusty secondhand bookshop in Hay-on-Wye, I once found an old English-Malay dictionary. *Jalang*, it said, meant "wild: of buffaloes, cats and disorderly women.")

Women have expressed their will with mountains in mind: Henriette D'Angeville, on climbing Mont Blanc in 1838, carved her motto in the ice: *Vouloir, c'est pouvoir*. (To will it is to achieve it.) And Emily Brontë wrote:

> *I'll walk where my own nature would be leading—*
> *Where the wild wind blows on the mountainside.*

Nietzsche, in *Beyond Good and Evil*, writes, "A living being wants above all else to release its strength; life itself is the will to power." The strong-willed will overrule the weak. Women, unsurprisingly, come off badly. "Women should be kept, provided for, protected, indulged like delicate, strangely wild, and often pleasant domestic animals."

When wild animals are domesticated, the results include the following: Docility. Submissiveness. Reduced mobility. Reduced hardiness. Infantilization. It reads like a description of ideal Victorian womanhood.

"Man is born free, and everywhere is in chains"—Jean-Jacques Rousseau, his fabulous, famous declaration ringing out down the years. And woman? No such luck. Rousseau writes of girls that "they should also be early subjected to restraint. . . . They must be subject, all their lives, to the most constant and severe restraint, which is that of decorum: it is, therefore, necessary to accustom them early to such confinement, that it may not afterwards cost them too dear; and to the suppression of their caprices, that they may the more readily submit to the will of others." (*Emile*.)

In *The Taming of the Shrew*, Katherine is self-willed: she is called a wildcat, and she is wild in the sense of being proud, free, unsubmissive, unbowed. When Hortensio attempts, early in the play, to teach Katherine the lute, he "bow'd her hand to teach her fingering." Katherine is gloriously rebellious to this attempt, smashing the lute over his head, but she cannot hold her own against Petruchio. Her will is to be broken by his—"And will you, nill you, I will marry you" is the sinister phrase on Petruchio's lips. Her will is of no account, nor her consent.

By the end of the play, her vaunting, fencing, boisterous self has been killed, demonstrated by the single most devastating image of the play: Katherine offers to place her hand—her previously unbowed hand—under the foot of her husband so he can crush it if he wills. No source has been found for this gesture: it seems to have been Shakespeare's invention. Shakespeare, though, knew what he was doing, for as a writer he knew what it would mean to have your hand crushed—it is the crushing of your own free expression. Katherine's willful voice, wild as hell, is crushed. To me one of the most anguished of Shakespeare's tragedies, it is listed in the misogynist canon as a comedy.

The earliest myths of Christian culture suggested that wildness was the sign of the devil's will; chaos and confusion being attributes of Satan, the "great Anarch." God's word, by contrast, will bring order and rule. Milton, in *Paradise Lost*, writes,

Confusion heard his voice, and wilde uproar
Stood rul'd, stood vast infinitude confined.

All nature would be tamed by the will of the good shepherd, the wild lion lying down with the lamb, and all human nature made docile, submissive and
infantilized by the will of the father in heaven, in a piece of odious domesti-
cation, so that the shepherd could control his obedient bleating flock of
woolly stupidity.

This was the taming of the soul, of the self-willed human spirit. Tamed
creatures are dolt-minded and dumb, insipid and bland. They are coarse in
thought and need, only wanting to eat, to shit and to obey. Wild creatures,
though, have a quality of fineness: subtler, keener-minded, electric-thoughted,
clever and intense, sniffing the scent, sensitive, highly reactive. Untamed,
our ears are taut with receptivity, tuned to every note on every instrument,
any language of any creature. While the untamed have ears for poetry—
all kinds of poetic voices—the tame are trained only to hear the voice of
their tamer, having ears only for command. The tamed know only the
plumpness of convenienced asexuality: wild creatures smolder in the groin,
thighs slippery with juice, raw hormones, pheromones glowing in the dark.
But the Christian god will never win, for still, still proudly anarchic, in thunder and cunt, cock and lightning, the raw core of our human spirit is still
untamed, full of will, eloquent, complex, kinetic and fleetly wild.

A NOD TO THE GODS

The mountain is where you go to get a dream, they say, in the Papuan
Highlands. One man describes to me a "dream-shrine" on the mountain,
about three hours from his village, where people will spend a night, hoping to
net a dream: a dream to guide them, or a dream of the future. On waking,
they tell their dream to no one until it comes true.

In dreams, mind runs wild every night. Nothing constrains dreams, they
obey no rules of physics, they are untamed by time, unconfined by any place.
In their free irreality, they are precious to our wild minds. "Sleep hath its own
world / And a wide realm of wild reality," wrote Byron.

I have always dreamt more strongly the higher I have climbed, and my mountain dreams have stayed with me for years. People often report vivid dreams at high altitudes. It is as if mountains had an intangible but valuable mineral resource: *oneiros* (dream). As if the air has less oxygen for respiration but more dream for inspiration, and here in West Papua you should mine a mountain only for dreams. Nothing else.

"Wilderness is where people maintain and develop relationships with the ancestors," says Neles Tebay, a Papuan priest and journalist. It is also a place where people go for guidance, listening to messages, for "the birds speak symbolic or allegorical language." In the mountains, there are taboo places of sacred intensity, and in certain places sex is forbidden, or spitting in a river, or defecating, or touching trees with tools.

Everywhere out in the mountains, people light fires, to propitiate the spirits. The firesmoke drives off the mists, and the smoke seems the opposite of mist. Smoke suggests shelter, protection and home: mists suggest exposure, vulnerability and wilderness. One is the cozy hearth, the other the bleak heath. One suggests human creation, cooked food and culture: the other suggests the inexorable rawness of nature. Smoke represents warmth, community and the living, while mists suggest cold, isolation and the dead. Although mountains are sacred, they are not places to linger in. When Christian missionaries first arrived here, local people were shown the missionary pictures of "heaven" and "hell." One place was a spooky land with pallid and chilly-looking white men, floating eerily in a cold mist on mountaintops. The other a warm and cozy place, with good, big fires, always lit, and filled with friendly dark faces. Without a second thought, they plumped for hell.

To Papuans, the mountains were vibrant with spirits, invisible pulses of power that could be dangerous, sapping people with sickness or making people crazy. (It seems likely to me that altitude sickness has been long interpreted as a spiritual rather than a medical matter.)

Everywhere in West Papua, people tell me that the mountain spirits, if angered, can send thunder and hard rain, which only a skillful rainmaker can prevent. I met one rainmaker in his hut, surrounded by feather crowns, bows and arrows and tins of pilchards. Old, talkative, toothless and blind, he told me how he could stay a storm for a couple of hours: his words could hold back the clouds and his anger could halt the rain. There are no gods close to the village, I'm told, but away up in the hills, where the mountain is wild, there are gods—suggesting that sacredness persists only in wildness. The rainmaker tells me that the mountain spirit gave writhy vigor to people, pigs and plants, but now that the Christian missionaries have come, people and pigs don't have the strength they used to. The mountain gods are unpredictable, sometimes healing illnesses and granting requests, but they can also be tricksters, mischievously making things disappear and reappear. The high and wild lands are associated with high and wild emotions: fear, anger and awe, and with wild weather. As the rainmaker speaks, he seems to suggest that the mountains are highly charged, as if the wildness of the mountain spirit is a necessary force without which life itself grows pale and weak.

The mountains were traditionally places of diversity. But things have changed since the Christian missionaries arrived: "The spirit is gone now," said Josef, sadly. "Before we became Christians, we thought the mountain was wild because there were many gods, so different places were sacred. Now it is not wild because there is only one god." Monotheism itself tames wildness, huge as the mottled gray sky, falling like a tombstone and crushing the plurality of the spirits of the land. Mountains, now, are no longer the place to find a dream, but are the places of commandment—Mount Sinai, or the Sermon on the Mount—and a commandment is the opposite of a dream.

All over the world, mountains have been considered sacred—it seems to be a human constant. In Papua New Guinea, people thought that spirits came from Mount Sunavi. Gunung Agung, in Bali, is the center of the Balinese universe, the mountain peaks are the lands of the gods, and people orient themselves to them, sleeping with their heads toward the mountains.

Mount Apo is sacred to the Lumad people in the Philippines, and is home to the creator of their world, who told the Lumad people, "Guard this place, never let anyone destroy or desecrate this place. . . . Never give the mountain."

In Nepal, some years ago, I climbed the Annapurna circuit, trekking for days up through small villages, past temples on hilltops and prayer walls, inset with prayer wheels, which you spin for a safe journey. I climbed over the Thorung La Pass, at 5,416 meters, in a weird agony of exhaustion, altitude sickness and dysentery. Every step took all my willpower and my head felt as if someone was hammering nails into my temples, and I had to hurl myself at the snowy slope, staggering often, while the endless ascent was punctuated by having to stop to vomit time and again, applauded by the jeering laughter of a crow. But at the top, these things seemed to disperse, in a sudden respite. At the pass, prayer flags streamed, torn ragged by the winds but still eloquent, for they made fluent a sense of the sacred. The very thinness of the air here seemed to yearn into the ultimate element of Hindu and Buddhist thought; above earth, air, fire and water there is ether, the fifth (quintus) element, the quint-essence. It is as if the soul has gradually left behind all things of the trudging world, all things of weight; wood, water and wet wool, and is spun to a thinner but more perfect silk, rare in a rarefied atmosphere. I had a sense of one's spirit wanting freedom from the body, an ecstasy in the aerial world.

And then, right at the top, a boisterous—and extremely cold—young man wearing nothing but a Ramones T-shirt and a pair of shorts threw his hands to the sky shouting, "I defy you, ye gods!" It was a superb and sudden *coup de théâtre*. But it wouldn't have worked if he hadn't felt at some level that there were gods there to defy. ("The only Zen you find on the tops of mountains is the Zen you bring up there," said Robert M. Pirsig.)

Nepali, Tibetan and Indian mythologies honor the Himalayas: these mountains are collectively the home of the greatest gods. Individual mountains are spiritually significant, and Kangchenjunga, for instance, near Darjeeling, has long been worshipped as a guardian spirit. Local people felt their well-being depended on the good humor of this god, for he could destroy crops and villages with storms, floods and avalanches. Mount Kailash in Tibet is so sacred that you do not climb it but walk around it.

People living near Mount Njelele, in Zimbabwe, say that to walk around the whole mountain would mean gaining all divine knowledge. So it is prohibited. The Ik people of northern Uganda regarded Mount Morungole as sacred and, it is reported, couldn't bear to live out of sight of their mountain.

Chomolungma, according to Tibetans, is "Mother Goddess of the World" and is known in Nepal as Sagarmatha, "Goddess of the Sky"; Tseringma, the Sherpas call it, "Mother of Long Life." Stripped of its identity as female deity, it was given the name of a male functionary, the surveyor-general of India, George Everest. From goddess to bureaucrat at a stroke of a pen.

In Tibet, every year tens of thousands of pilgrims circle the holy mountain Kawagebo. Meanwhile the Chinese phrase for "to go on a pilgrimage" literally means "to pay one's respects to the mountain." From the fifth century B.C., Chinese Taoists saw divinity in wilderness. The mountain, T'ai Shan, was divine, the chief of the "Five Sacred Peaks," and both Taoists and Buddhists built temples in the mountains.

In Mongolia, an old Torgut man who loved to meditate on mountains said, "Wisdom one learns among men, but the higher qualities of the soul one acquires in the mountains."

In the Japanese Shinto religion, the whole of Mount Fuji is a shrine. After Mount Fuji the second most sacred mountain in Japan is Ontake, which has a Shinto shrine on top. Shintoism deified mountains and other wilderness areas. Shintoism and Taoism identified wildness with what was divine, in polar contrast to Christianity, which identified wildness and wilderness with the devil.

Kuo Hsi, eleventh-century Chinese landscape painter and writer, described the spiritual necessity of wild mountains: "The din of the dusty world and the locked-in-ness of human habitations are what human nature habitually abhors; while, on the contrary, haze, mist, and the haunting spirits of the mountains are what human nature seeks, and yet can rarely find."

I have never felt so keenly the "din of the dusty world" falling away beneath me as when I climbed Kilimanjaro. Below, the world of chat, commerce and shops. Above, light and ice. Part of the meaning of the word *sacred* is something set apart, and no mountain seems to stand out so much from its surrounds, a world above the petty, pedestrian plains. At the equator, on Africa's hot and dusty plains, a vast snowscape, alone and soaring to the sky. (The glacier is melting with global warming, and local people have traditionally said that if Kilimanjaro ever loses its snow, terrible things will happen.)

It takes several days to climb Kilimanjaro, but only the last part is hard. You have to leave the final camp in the middle of the night, in order to cross scree, which is jelled by ice at night, but which, under the morning sun, unfreezes and is hard to cross. The moon was nearly full and there was a snow mist, so the light was ghostly. For a moment only, the mist rolled away, and we walked in starlight. I felt weird with altitude. My head ached, as ever. I was vomiting frequently, as ever. I walked with a thick streak of vomit on my coat collar, walking the ceaseless trudge on a changeless path through the endless night.

I made a list of the things I wanted to do when we stopped for a minute.

Number one, wipe the sick off my coat. Number two, blow my nose to get the sick out of my nostrils. Number three, eat Kendal mint cake. Number four, drink water. The trouble was that this short and humble list seemed impossible, with my hands encased in mittens and my mind clumsy with altitude. Polar bears don't have the paws to play chess, I kept thinking. I went over my list again. It wasn't important to wipe off the sick. It was important to eat something. Drink first, then eat? It was too cold to take my gloves off, and I couldn't unwrap the mint cake. So I tore it open with my teeth and smashed it on a rock to break it into pieces. Then, as the gray dawn broke, I began to think the snowy boulders and ice fields were houses, tents, pianos. Then they looked like pillows and duvets and I longed to sink into them, curl up and sleep, for they looked cozy and warm. These were not safe thoughts, and another part of my mind—strict, cold and utterly rational—stepped in, telling off my fantasizing mind.

Then we reached the sheerness, the high snowfields, the peak, the sculpted whiteness, the brilliant and entire ice. Every climb is a spiritual transformation, a little death-and-rebirth story, for you see in the mountains how fragile is your life.

Local people around Kilimanjaro told me that a few generations previously, in times of drought, they would go to the mountain, sacrifice sheep and pray for rain. For the Samburu people in Kenya, god lives high on Mount Nyiru. The Meru people consider Mount Kenya to be sacred and they go to the mountain to pray. Kenyan Nobel Prize winner Wangari Maathai says, "According to my mother, God lives on Mount Kenya. But people are told that the mountain which is important now is Mount Zion. Because my mother's wisdom was not written in a book, it was trivialized. When the missionaries came, they said 'God doesn't live in the mountains; He lives in heaven'. So people began to view nature as a commodity to be exploited."

All over North America, mountains are sacred to Native Americans. For the Lakota, the Black Hills are sacred, and one of these peaks was the site of the vicious dispossession of Lakota lands. It was the burial place of ancestors, and the Great Spirit, Wakan Tanka, was immanent in the mountain. Lakota man Leonard Peltier (imprisoned for a crime he did not commit) describes "the four white presidential faces that desecrate the face of the holy mountain they call Mount Rushmore."

Navajo sacred space is bounded by four sacred mountains, and Mount Graham in Arizona is a sacred mountain for the Apache and home to the spirit dancers. The Vatican has planned to sponsor a telescope to be located there, an act that the Apache say is a "desecration." (How Galileo would have laughed at the Vatican's reversal of roles in this clash between astronomy and the sacred.)

In the Andes, people who are descended from the Incas, such as the Runa people of Peru, call mountains *Apu,* meaning "lord, ancestor, a protecting god with power over the destiny of those who live nearby." For the Andean Laymi people, the peaks are sacred: places of influential, protective guardians, and yet home to spirits that can be malevolent. They are the source of both life and illness. The Aymara term for grandfather or ancestor is also used for mountain deities. These spirits are a source of fertility (which is often associated with wildness in Laymi ritual) and they are also known as a wild fount of creativity, and are said to bestow musical tunes, sometimes through dreams, to men who leave musical instruments at their abodes.

To the Kogi, their mountains are a sacred mimesis of the world, from the snow peaks down through forests and the lowlands. They believe the whole planet depends on what happens in the Sierra Nevada. They, as its inhabitants, are responsible for ensuring the earth is in balance. The mountaintops are the "Land of the Mother" and every mountain peak has a Mamo, a Kogi high priest, an Earth doctor charged with keeping the land healthy, in harmony. The peaks, they say, are like temples, and the high Sierra is where wisdom resides, so that one day it can be retaught to the rest of humanity.

The Mamos act as physicians of the Earth, but they are also metaphysicians of the mountains: they have thought the mountains, laying layers of subtle metaphor and association, making these true mountains of the mind. Every part of life is linked to the mountains and all is congruent: meaning and mountain, deity and the peaks, consciousness and light. Guardians of these mountains, they are guardians of mind—ours as well as theirs, and they act as the conscience of the world.

Over the last century, the Kogi have watched the white races, whom they call the Younger Brothers, fell 85 percent of the forests of the Sierra, where jaguars and howler monkeys live, together with many species that exist nowhere else. The Kogi say, "The Younger Brother didn't listen; didn't understand. He was sent away over the sea: given knowledge of machines and sent away."

They resent intrusion, and have not wanted to communicate with outsiders, but they broke this custom to talk to Alan Ereira. "Up to now, we have ignored the Younger Brother. . . . But now we can no longer look after the world alone. The Younger Brother is doing too much damage. We are the Elder Brothers, with knowledge of all things, material and spiritual. We know what you have done. You have sold the clouds."

The highest peaks—their most sacred places—are now the source of their terror. For on these, they believe, all fertility depends. Yet the snow is retreating rapidly, leaving yellow lands that should be green. When these lands die, they say, everything that depends on them will die. The mountains, the heart of the world, are withered, their fertility is sapped, and the sacred peaks are cracked.

The European view of mountains has gone through enormous permutations and paradoxes. Matthew 4 describes Satan taking Jesus to a mountain as the site of temptation. The Bible describes the "voice crying in the wilderness," where "every valley shall be exalted and every mountain and hill shall be made low: and the crooked shall be made straight, and the rough places plain." The voice *in* the wilderness cries for the end *of* wilderness. Heinmot Tooyalaket, or Chief Joseph of the Nez Percé, in the 1870s, said of his own people and the Europeans, "We were contented to let things remain as the Great Spirit Chief made them. They were not; and would change the rivers and mountains if they did not suit them."

But the biblical attitude is complex. In the Old Testament, hills and mountains often represent positive qualities. Psalm 121: "I will lift up mine eyes unto the hills, from whence cometh my help." Psalm 36: "Thy righteousness is like the great mountains." The early Israelites designated god "El Shaddai"—God, the One of the Mountains. In Judaic, Christian and Muslim traditions, many sudden epiphanies and transfigurations take place on mountains. Mountains became haunts of Christian hermits, living the higher life of the spirit, above the mundane world below.

Petrarch, ostensibly describing his climb up Mount Ventoux in 1336, is

held to mark a crucial turning point in Christian sensibilities toward mountains, because he used this experience to demonstrate the transcendence of
soul over body and the unimportance of nature. At the summit he allegedly
opened Augustine's *Confessions* at random and read the warning not to take
joy in natural scenery. Petrarch was angry with himself that he "should still be
admiring earthly things who might long ago have learned . . . that nothing is
wonderful but the soul."

What all cultures seem to have recognized is that mountains are potent
places of spirit, and in the European mind this became associated not with
the good but with the bad and the ugly.

Michael Drayton's "Poly-Olbion" (1612–22) is a long poem describing the
geography of England. He refers to the "Divels-Arse" in the Peak district and
describes the Peaks as "the pourtratures of Hell." John Evelyn in the 1640s described the Alps as "strange, horrid and fearful crags."

Marjorie Hope Nicolson, in her fascinating book on mountains, *Mountain
Gloom and Mountain Glory*, describes how some classical authors wrote of
mountains as "*verruca*" and "*ulcera*." She quotes Joshua Poole's book *English
Parnassus; or, A Help to English Poesie*, which was a book of advice to aspiring
poets. In the 1677 edition, most adjectives recommended for mountains are
negative: "insolent, surly, ambitious, barren, sky-threatening, supercilious,
desert, inhospitable, freezing, infruitful, crump-shouldered, unfrequented,
forsaken, melancholy, pathless." They were "Earth's Dugs, Risings, Tumors,
Blisters, Warts."

In the seventeenth century, mountains were described as "Nature's *pudenda*,"
and this, together with the "dugs" and "warts" seems to suggest witchery in the
peaks. With a similarly witchy suggestion, to Andrew Marvell, mountains
were "hook-shoulder'd" and an "excrescence," and they were, interestingly,
"unjust." In 1671, the Christian theologian Thomas Burnet found mountains
so horrible that he decided they were not created at the Creation.

Between the middle of the seventeenth century and the end of the eighteenth, notes Nicolson, English attitudes toward mountain landscapes un-
derwent a complete transformation. By the end of that period, mountains
were considered not only beautiful but also spiritually uplifting. Ruskin declared, "Mountains are the beginning and end of all natural scenery," and he
saw mountains as the generative, life-giving heart of life.

Through the work of artists, poets and writers, including Burke's well-chronicled theories of the sublime, mountains were an integral part of romanticism and early environmentalism. Thoreau, on climbing Mount Katahdin, described his fearful awe: "Nature was here something savage and awful, though beautiful. . . . This was that Earth of which we have heard, made out of Chaos and Old Night . . . the home, this, of Necessity and Fate." And Aldo Leopold was to advise, "Think like a mountain."

I spent time climbing with a friend in the Pindos Mountains of northern Greece—arguably one of the last mountain wildernesses of Europe and certainly one of the least known. Maps are hard to come by and few people come here, not least because of the wild dogs, which have attacked and killed people. We were chased by a pack of them, circling us, snarling. We threw rocks at them to drive them away, to no avail, and I ended up climbing a tree to escape them, holding my mosquito repellent in my hand, ready to spray it in their eyes if they got their jaws on my feet.

We walked higher and higher. We met a couple of Vlach shepherds and shared our coffee and salami with them, and though we could not understand each other, we took a mutual delight in finding that our word *juniper* is, in the Vlach language, *dzínepe*. We went on up, passing only the occasional shepherd in the high pastures. We would gesture our route and they would lean on their staffs and look at us as if we were absolutely crazy. On the paths, there were hundreds of small Greek Orthodox shrines by the wayside, with little Glaxo bottles of oil, votive candles and ten-drachma coins, with icons tucked inside. But as we climbed higher than the paths, right up into the peaks where the fog is a careless trick to throw you off course, where lightning bursts inside your head and the rain falls hard, it was the old gods I nodded to. In the huge bowl of sky, we slept nights on the bare mountain in a cave shelter. Zeus still seems to rattle around here, where the gray boulders look like thunder and the thunder bangs like rocks and Vulcan still keeps his forge furious in the clouds and every fire is a Promethean defiance. This is the stamping ground of the gods of Olympus, all of them, feral divinities of fury and compulsive lust, petulant and bold, who growl, seduce, hurl bolts of lightning and would shatter the peaks with their fucking: proud and frivolous both, one eye on grandeur and the other on the short skirt, who would speak words of silver velvet and then cadge a light off the stars. These mountains need these gods.

"NO TOBACCO, NO HALLELUJAH"

But with the advent of Christianity, the old gods were driven from the mountains. From Greece to West Papua, the story is the same.

Wilderness was what the missionaries sought—sought not to preserve it but to destroy it. In West Papua, they pray for "untouched," "interior" places to be "opened up" with airstrips and mission stations.

"We have given them the Ten Commandments," said a missionary to me, brusquely. "That would certainly have a taming effect on any culture." To them, the Papuans lived like wild animals. Des Oatridge, an SIL missionary in Papua New Guinea, has called people's traditional lifeways "animal-like behavior." After conversion, ruminated a pastor from Ohio to me, "they would no longer be"—he hesitated—"I hate to use the word *savages*, but, you know, *savages*," and another missionary added for good measure that people were "controlled by evil spirits." Commented another, "They are about as natural as you can get: they have no concept of God" (which is a pretty fair illustration of the opposition between their god and nature).

Near Jayapura, the missionaries live in all-white private compounds, with all the appliances and gadgets of suburban America. They eat American food in restaurants with Teletubbies tablecloths and worship in all-white church services. The missionaries' ignorance of the land they lived in was shocking. One woman, who had recently lived for a year in Dani tribal lands, couldn't remember the name "Dani." None could pronounce one of the major towns in West Papua. And they insisted on calling the country "Irian"—the Indonesian name, which Papuans loathe.

The missionary from Nebraska said that the Papuans were obviously living in a "spiritual darkness that is a wilderness." She nodded and blinked. "Just our presence there sheds light to the people," she said, self-effacingly.

I heard this line about light and darkness everywhere I went. In the Bible, darkness connotes misery, ignorance, wickedness and the grave. It also suggests things that are "unclean." Its contemporary use suggests an insidious racism: black faces and black ways are of the darkness, while white faces and white ways are of the light.

In one tiny village in the remote Highlands, I stopped to look at a huge sculpture. It was a memorial to the missionaries who first came here, a hideously ugly hubris-for-Christ. A giant white man, ten or twelve feet tall, towers domineeringly over figures of crouching Yali people, portrayed as child-size in the sculpture. The missionary blesses them and there is a quote from Ephesians 5: "For once you were darkness but now you are light." There is a slab of concrete with footprints stamped in when the mixture was wet; the missionaries' feet, stamped forever, recalling, or so the missionaries hope, Isaiah 52: "How beautiful upon the mountains are the feet of him who brings good tidings." And the date too is stamped: 24/3/1961. The stamp of the feet, together with the stamp of the date, has an eerie effect, a kind of B.C. and A.D. established, the moment when Christ's gospel came here and wilderness was banished, the moment when this new god stamped the numinous life out of the mountain. Wildness and wild time gone at a stroke. Henceforth people would no longer live in their own time but in the time of the invaders. In many villages, "A.D." begins when missionaries have insisted on a ceremonial "fetish burning," where people burn all their traditional sacred objects. From that point, the village will call itself Christian, and for many villagers that is the only date they know. One man told me that some people now regret the burnings and "are sorry that they don't have any culture left—and now they need it."

I know this fundamentalist mindset well. For a few years as a teenager I was one of them. I know the roaring certainty of their god and I heard enough from the ministers, deaf shouters of marvelous rank incuriosity, their prejudiced beliefs about other cultures living in darkness under the spell of the evil witch doctor. I know that their religion is more Paulianity than Christianity, and I know how Paul and his disciples were blinded and never recovered their sight. I had the reverse insight. Walking blindly down the straight and narrow, I found myself gradually, painfully, able to see: only a little, but after such blindness how beautiful is sight.

It was a world where thought was not free—no mere girl was allowed to question the pastor. He was the shepherd, I was the sheep, and the job of the sheep is to eat green grass, grow white wool and stay inside the pasture fence. Wherever sky was, God was, till I hid in bed, read Marx under the blankets by torchlight, won courage from it and took *Das Kapital* to Bible camp. (V. bad.)

The elders came to my house and the pastor told me I would never find happiness again. I would go to the worst level of hell, reserved for the apostate. I was seventeen and terrified. I read *Jane Eyre* that night for the ninth time, knowing what I had was pure, free, howling loneliness. I had lost the warm and easy life and I would never find it again. The pastor was right. I didn't find happiness. But I found defiance and self-will. I lost a bigoted suburban god who cared about kitchen units and blessed his believers with wads of cash. I lost a walled city but found a wildness and freedom. I never regretted it. I lost the narrow-minded way but found the broad expanses of desert, ocean, mountain and sky. Walking very alone, I was god-forsaking, not god-forsaken, and I found midnight, ice and fear and ferocious necessity, a frightened, unsure Eve un-adamant trying to name the world for myself without Adam's god to tutor my tongue.

When the missionaries came to West Papua, they brought an enormous amount of cowrie shells, currency in the Highlands. In fact they flooded the market, and destabilized the economic system, causing a crash in the value of the cowrie shell. And the huge numbers of steel axes that they brought were to knock the bottom quite out of the stone ax market. The missionaries came from the sky in helicopters full of goods that Papuans had never seen. The astonishing arrival of goods from the air (one plane, searching for survivors of a previous plane crash, dropped tents, guns, beer, eggs and bacon and "a set of scanties for Corporal Hastings") triggered a wave of cargo cults, including one group who fervently believed that a bicycle pump thrust in the ground would result in the emergence of goods. In 1971, pilots reported that some villages had built large copies of helicopter landing pads, in the hope of encouraging the goods from the sky to drop there.

Why on earth did Papuan villagers adopt this foreign religion? I put this to the Papuan pastor from the Yali village that had eaten the missionaries. He looked at me as if it was the daftest question he could imagine. "Because the missionaries brought metal axes and knives and mirrors," he said. People identified this new god with goods and became Christians to get the goods. Papuan tribes have long been noted for their own kind of capitalism, unusual among indigenous people. In a now-famous incident, Leopold Pospisil reports, many Kapauku villagers were happily attending church services, after which the missionary would distribute tobacco and other "desirable" things. Then the missionary's tobacco supply dwindled, and for several weeks he could not get a shipment. Church attendance dropped dramatically. Confused, the priest went to talk to the headman, who merely shrugged and said epigrammatically, "No tobacco, no hallelujah."

With the arrival of Christianity in West Papua, the mountains were stripped of mystery and magic; what had been numinous became mere matter. Minable matter. When I spoke to the aged rainmaker about the missionaries and mines, he said, "I'm really angry about that. When villages become Christian, they want mines, and it's not good to mine the mountain. Here, we don't want mines; the power of the mountain spirit keeps the soil, plants and animals healthy."

In the Highlands, I talked to people in two villages, just a couple of miles apart and comparable in all regards, except that one village had become Christian and the other had not. In the animist village, the mountains were sacred and they would not mine them. In the other, Christianity had desacralized the land. "Before we became Christians we believed in the mountain gods, and we wouldn't allow mining. Now if someone wants to mine it, we'd allow it," they said.

SIL missionaries preach submission to the state. Any state. Even a genocidal one. Mission airstrips are used by the Indonesian government, with the full blessing of the missionaries. I asked one SIL missionary for a comment on the way Indonesian authorities treat Papuans. She refused to condemn it.

In West Papua, the missionaries tacitly support not only the murderous Indonesian authorities, but also the corporations. One told me plumply how they helped an oil company to build a runway, that the oil companies want missionaries in their area "to keep the situation stable" and that the missionaries happily oblige. The Christian Missionary Alliance, Papuans tell me, prays for the success of Freeport, this mine that has the worst record for human rights abuses of any in the world.

Some Papuans have declared missionaries one of the four greatest threats to ecological and cultural survival.

CLIFFS OF FALL

arrived in Timika, the town that services the Freeport mine, with letters of
introduction to various people, including Papuan human rights workers
and some in the Papuan freedom movement, the OPM. One was a pastor, a
thickset man who spoke in a hushed and fierce whisper, his eyes shining *vive
la résistance*. Hunched forward to talk, he glittered with outrage. Injustice had
not broken him but flinted him, and his words and eyes struck sparks from
the very air.

He lived in fear of the bullet in the back, hour by hour, but the courage
needed to live like this had made the man a mountain. He had helped coordinate the destruction of pipelines, cables and roads of the mine that is de-
stroying the Grasberg mountain. (The second-generation pastors, Papuans
"trained up" by the Catholic missionaries, are possibly the only good result of
missionary activity here.)

I spent an evening with Thom Beanal, Papuan leader and president of the
Papuan Presidium Council. He is successor to the assassinated Theys Eluay.
Was he frightened of assassination? I asked. He smiled. "I am, quite literally,
next in the firing line." A month before I visited, eight masked men had come
to this compound, asking for his house. They wore black masks and long-
sleeved shirts. Fortunately, everyone they spoke to was quick-witted enough
to give them very clear directions—to entirely nonexistent places. Beanal is a
broad-smiling bear of a man and his old wife skips through the room, barefoot and betel-spitting, grinning. Papuans, he says, take from the land what
they need. To Beanal, the most astonishing thing about Indonesians, Americans and Europeans is their greed. "It seems like they consume everything,"
he says. It is a greed without limits. "They are proud of this and think they
are clever but we know they are not."

I spent some time walking alone around town, hating every minute. The
atmosphere was uneasy. Everyone seemed on edge, aggressive and over-alert.
In spite of the wealth of the mine, this town is poor. The mine makes a profit
of a million dollars a day: local Papuan people, the owners of the land, spend
their days standing in the poisoned river picking over rubbish.

I was harassed and pestered by Indonesians, and men would shout banal tourist-English nonsense—*hey missis, fine fine, how are you, hey you, lady, good morning*—while their eyes were cold with intense dislike. Indonesians know perfectly well that white people here, if they are not missionaries or Freeport operatives, are very likely to oppose the Indonesian occupation.

One morning at seven, there was a sharp knock at my door and a woman's voice. I opened it and in bounced Manika, with Tupperware boxes full of breakfast, a broad smile and a quip for everything. Manika, a local human rights worker, brave, funny, clever and mischievous, would be my guide to the strange world of the Freeport mine.

We went in a Jeep belonging to the organization she worked for. It looked as if it had seen some bumpy roads and mud slides in its time, and there were small holes in the windshield. Stones? I asked, thinking they could be bullet holes. "Yes." She laughed. "The small ones were all stones. But the big one was a bullet from the army." She told me the story. Local people had organized a protest against the mine, and children raised the Papuan flag in church. The army had attacked the congregation, and a woman was shot and bleeding, so Manika had driven the Jeep to pick her up and the army had tried to stop her. The hole was in the front windshield, on the driver's side. They were shooting to kill. But they missed. And she shrugged it off.

She took me to see where the mine tailings have made the land sullen and lifeless, fetid and leached of green. Just gray dust and a dead river. Whitened, skeletal bones of trees scratch the sky, dead spikes of trunks. The river slinks, lank and toxic, away. Nothing will grow here.

The American Freeport-McMoRan is the largest and richest copper mine in the world and the third largest gold mine. It has been operating since the 1960s, and now the British company RTZ has a holding in the mine. The amount of rock shifted here is the equivalent of moving the Great Pyramid of Cheops every week. Every day, 120,000 tons of waste, including acid and heavy metals, are tipped into the Aikwa River.

And the whites strut around their specially built, well-fortified compound (with a supermarket and a church) like tubby lairds, fat from the spoils of someone else's land.

Ovid, Seneca, Pliny and the Stoics detested the idea of mining because it was an abuse of the earth as mother. In his "Metamorphoses," Ovid wrote of men digging into the earth to prize out

all that precious metal,
The root of evil. They found the guilt of iron,
And gold, more guilty still.

Edmund Spenser associated mining with avarice and lust and they combine in a clear image of sexual assault, while Shakespeare's *Timon of Athens* demonstrates the destructiveness of greed as Timon describes the earth as mankind's common mother and says the best use for gold is to stay buried in earth, for "here it sleeps, and does no hired harm."

I doubt if the Freeport wives, whom I met waiting for a plane, would bother with Shakespeare or read Ovid. There were two of them, white middle-class Americans, wealthy spouses of Freeport executives. I spoke to one.

"Do you have much contact with the local people here?" I asked.

"No."

"Is that your choice?"

"Yes."

"There are a lot of human rights abuses connected to Freeport."

"That isn't something I know much about."

"Why not? There's a lot of it going on. You must have heard about it."

She wrinkled her nose as if the subject were some unpleasant sexual perversion. "I'm not *inclined* that way," she said.

Her friend interjected at this point, "Freeport ex-pat ladies used to do volunteer projects."

"Such as?"

"Teaching local people about hygiene." She beamed smugly, and I turned away too angry to speak. For your greed you have poisoned people's drinking water and poured toxins in their food. You have angled your arsehole over a child's face and defecated till the child chokes. And then you have lectured the child's mother on hygiene.

For the local Amungme people, this mountain is a spiritual realm. All matter is alive, they believe: rocks, trees, rivers are enspirited. On their mountain, old and sacred groves may never be destroyed, and the mountains belong to their ancestors. "When our ancestors died, their souls traveled to the mountains and the rivers in the high places." Death translates them into land, so the ancestors merge, through metaphor and in spirit, with mountain. An

ancestory is immanent here, where ancestors and legend and meaning are re-
told in the land.

The mountain is the embodiment of "the mother." "We see our mother
as ourselves," they say, "and if they destroy our mother, they destroy us." I
met two Amungme men who told me how they see the mountain. One man
drew a picture of a woman on one side of a blackboard, and on the other, a
landscape. The head of the woman is the top of the mountain, they say. The
head is holy. The lower mountains are her breasts (she gives us milk, she feeds
her children) and there are the hills of her thighs and—"some places are
secret"—the taboo lands of her vagina. It is a prohibited area, not to be
shown to others. (Just as a woman will wear a grass skirt to hide that part of
herself from the sight of strangers, they say.) From the thighs to the feet is the
lowland areas, running down to the coast. It is an image of sacred geography,
sacred body and sacred land some fifty miles from mountaintop to sea.

The reclining figure is gigantic and inclusive, varying as a woman's body.
Little toes, each a mile long, rip-curl into the oceans, smelling of salt water and
seaweed. There are marshlands, silky wet for miles at her instep. Her ankles are
the rocky outcrops, her smooth wet calves the swamplands, and then, higher
up, the valleying lift of her thighs, the rivers running and running, the steep
slopes, buttocks to hips. Her ferns are dark, glossy and moss damp, an enchanted,
taboo crevasse, all mushroom of the jungle, musk and peat and a stringy metallic smell, a rock pool in the forest. Her belly is womb-dark and swelling with
life, and her breasts are hills, innocent as truth. Her exhalations, a body breathing from every pore, the susurration of chlorophyll and dew, from shore to
mountain a thousand smells, of cuscus and banana leaf and gourds. Her body
courses with underground streams, every trickle of every vein, dark, laughing at
its own secrecy. Her wrists like saplings singing of the future, the trunks of her
arms grown strong in sun and rain. The col of her neck, steep and slender, fragile with the weight of sudden snow. Her head, golden-minded and copper-
thoughted, scarved in cloud. Here is where the spirits are, where they can talk
freely with the ancestors, where people come with their hopes and dreams.

Freeport is mining the head of the mother. The face of the mountain is in
shock, her features blank and deadened. The jutting earth movers come, sinking a mine shaft, drilling into her head, against her will, a head fuck. And the
rivers that once ran with the mother's milk now are dank with deadly toxic-

ity. A nauseated landscape; slicks cling to the estuary like sick in the throat; no amount of washing will wash this away.

This mountain, this woman is the quintessential "interior" that the missionaries want "opened up." Open her legs for the mining company, entering the prohibited area, where they will shove their drill bits and tailings. The taboo lands of her thighs, which traditionally people are not allowed even to see, have been seized by Freeport as the place to dump their toxic sludge. The place of sweet sexuality is now a shrieking, filthy, scarred place, a stagnant sewer of poison in the rock pool. Her thighs are the site of refuse. A landscape made to loathe itself—a terrible contamination, a place of fecundity made the place of defecation. Where the mountain wore trees "like clothes," says a Papuan, the land has been forcibly stripped naked, bare with scars of tree stumps, torn clothes. And the land is mute, mute in the aftermath; no birds, no leaves, no children, no fish, no story, no dream, no songline, no words, no words, no words.

The mountain is minded, but the mine denies mind, savages the psyche. The mountains of the mind seared. The Amungme people have experienced psychological problems they did not know before. "They, especially the tribal leaders, they cry, just like children," says an OPM representative here.

Everywhere I went in West Papua, but here more than anywhere, I could hear the wavelengths of trauma. It was like being in an ultra-acoustic world where the air was weird and overcharged with the distorted, screaming transmissions of pain.

I met a Papuan man near the Freeport mine who was on the edge of insanity. His expression was furious and fearful at the same time. He jabbered about Indonesians poisoning his food, and was desperate to talk to me. He swaggered in a kind of boasting fear of "spies" everywhere, in expressions that looked almost comical in their exaggeration. He was obsequious in a way I never saw in any other Papuan, a fawning, neck-baring attitude that made me loathe him, but which seemed to me a reaction to deep trauma. I took him for supper in a quiet café and said, Tell me your story.

"I am witness by my eyes," he began. And his story would have made you weep. When he was in elementary school, he saw a hundred or more people tortured, the Indonesian soldiers putting iron rods in their ears. He saw needles stuck in people's eyes and people killed, axed in the head. He saw the soldiers putting iron rods in fires till they were red-hot, and putting them up people's anuses. People were killed that way, he said, as you would kill rabbits.

These kinds of tortures are attested to by other sources around the Freeport mine, and human rights workers also report how Amungme women from that area have been raped when they have protested against the mine, and how women have been held for weeks in a toilet flooded with human shit and repeatedly tortured. Other reports include people being slashed with razors till they bled to death. In 1995, people praying in church were attacked by the soldiers; children and the priest were murdered. On Christmas Day in 1994, people raised the Papuan flag in a village and were massacred. A man was recently killed here, his fingers cut off and his heart sliced open. A protest rally resulted in yet more mass murder, code-named "Operation Annihilation" by the Indonesian army. Thousands have been made homeless by Freeport. Hundreds, possibly thousands, have been murdered. Technically, these abuses are carried out not by Freeport but by the Indonesian military acting to "protect" the mine.

So murder is contracted out. Rape is outsourced. Good business practice.

When he spoke of these things, you could almost see the child's mind, tender and green, seared with the same red-hot iron rod so that much of his mind was scar tissue, burned dull, angry, bruised, his memory a bulge of putrefying flesh and all the nerve cells of his mind branded so that every thought and mind-message was accented with it. Every pathway between every neuron made crooked with it. He is tormented still: there are still needles in his eyes and no doctor could remove them. I am witness by my eyes, he says, as if there is a just jury somewhere, and he tries to shout, hoping to unleash a roar that would knock the world back into restitution. No roar comes, though if it did his tormentor would smash a mallet in his mouth for his temerity. And even if he did manage to call out, he would find that the rest of the world did not care, and his grief would collapse to permanent madness, for it is only the pity and outrage of others that bring justice back.

O the mind, mind has mountains; cliffs of fall
Frightful, sheer, no-man-fathomed
—GERARD MANLEY HOPKINS

It is midnight with the ancestors. Mist surrounds them and memory. There is language still in the wild air. The past lives here, the rocks sing with it, the unfrightened birds flock here. There is spirit here: do not come harshly, for the unhunted cuscus comes here to mate at midnight. It is always midnight here, now: be low, do not intrude, the air itself tolls still like a bell, then holds still like breath inheld. It is midnight with the ancestors at noon and dawn. Be silent near the tree fern and the rock beneath the snowy peaks. Mind matters here and finally. Mind is holy and wild. It is midnight with the ancestors now.

Wild Mind

THE WASTELAND OF TRAGEDY

did go to Outer Mongolia. Not in the way I would have wanted. Flung there rather than journeying there. Not discovering a place foreign to me, but thrown into a landscape that reflected my own state of mind. The trip happened when I was just—after seven years—at the point of finishing this book. I went because several months previously I had been invited to a Kazakh wedding. But in the enfolded truth of things, I went there because I was already there.

I had a lover, friend and partner who meant the world to me for all the years I'd known him. A few days before my flight, we broke up. And this parting pitched me into the wasteland of the psyche.

I went to stay for a time in an old Buddhist monastery, one of the very few that had not been destroyed by the Communists, possibly because it was so remote, even by Mongolian standards. The road was just an iced track through the mountains. There was no town anywhere near, and the nearest phone was fifty kilometers away (no mobile worked there either). The monastery was built in a flat circle of land, surrounded by a bowl of snowy mountains.

It was freezing—it was the end of a particularly fierce winter. In the mornings, I spent hours in the temple with the monks as they chanted and prayed, rang bells, blew conch shells and drummed up the sun. (In the temples, the young monks, chilly, would swish their golden capes with sky-blue cuffs and the smell of mutton would waft out from them, circling in the air.)

In the afternoons, I walked up the mountains, past prayer flags, cairns, vodka bottles and the brilliant blue scarves that stream out in the wind at every Mongolian shrine. This blue represents the sky, which is holy. "Why is the sky holy?" I asked a monk, who smiled back. "Because it is the sky," he replied, pure Zen. The sky itself was a waste of blue to me, and everything holy was dead.

I know that time is cyclic. But at that point it was worse than linear, it had stopped altogether. "Now," that precious thing, which I used to know as a transcendent idea, had become narrow as anguish, a cruel tightrope held up with a couple of broken drawing pins, a past too painful to remember and a future too bleak to consider. I saw a young monk on a bicycle, peddling on the ice for fun, falling off, laughing, getting back to his feet again, falling off again. Time is cyclic, but I couldn't see how I would cycle on.

In that state of mind and because of it, I saw wasteland everywhere. I saw bleakness, pale, wan and bleached, because devastation had sucked the marrow out of me. I was bleached, bleakness was all. One day when I was out walking, I saw a herder climbing a tree and chopping down branches for firewood. The branches cracked hollowly in the empty, cold air and I was the echo of that hollowness. Yet I was also huge with love, bloated with it, thick with love; the love I had was swollen in me like a bruise: I was a camel carcass in the desert swelling in the waste of sun.

I was all the stones of the Gobi Desert, that endless land of stones. And I felt an odd and entirely uncharacteristic longing for measurement, to know there is an end to stones. And is there an end to stones? There is. In this landscape, rocks are cracked by the heat of summer and the ice of winter, cracked by weather as we are harrowed by passion, seared till they crack and dust remains. There is an end to stones but not an end to devastation. Dust and gravel, gravel and dust. Dust and ashes was all that there was, all that I was.

And is there an end to dust and ashes? There is. After dust and ashes, silence. And the silenced mind is the worst wasteland there is. I was the silent wasteland. The mind's final, silent shriek. I was bleak and languageless as the pelican in the desert. In this wasteland, words don't carry across the devastated psyche. No intimate intricacy where conversation knots and bows and catscradles: here, there is no particularity, no peony, no pip, no piano, no parsley, no play—only the sound of the wind whistling through your mind, aeolian harp with all strings slunk across it, not singing the pitch of the wind but sagging uselessly, tunelessly dumb. That is the pitch of your mind. The wind has more existence, more body, more language, matters more.

I heard the silence underneath the keyboard. The ultimate resonant frequency of everything is—silence. I could hear it everywhere. Under the monk's gong and past the voice, after the blackbird. Below every sound, the silence. I heard the silence of outer space ringing in my ears far louder than the cheerful, muddy noise of people playing Frisbee on the Earth. From far enough away, the Earth wheels silent through the silent cosmos and I could hear silence where there has never been sound.

In this strange cracked-open state, in my silent unexistence, everything was pared down to essentials, love and death. Everything else was just dirty tinsel. Everything was gigantic and turned inside out. I saw the import of things before their surface. Meaning was more apparent than reality. I couldn't look at a mountain and see only mountain—rather I saw what a mountain might mean. Significance wouldn't stay in its place, below the surface; rather it erupted everywhere, breaking up through the stones. I felt a kind of radical empathy with everything. (Even months later, seeing a bird that had been shot out of the sky made me leap back in pain because I felt the stab of the bullet in me.)

There was a strange abeyance in the empty desert of days. I couldn't read or write because it took all my concentration to wash up and clean my socks. Empty weeks where I was a ghost in my own body. Exiled in emptiness. There were gaps between all the words. Chasms between all of us. Everywhere, lack. Loss unlinked me not only from him, but also from myself and everything else. I was empty in an empty world and emptiness was all, repeated in all empty directions. Only my soul, desolate, isolate, sole exile. As alone as the moon, my grief as perfect and as white. I was utterly lost for months. I was adrift and the compass was sick. It listed, lame and pointlessly limping, anywhere around the dial, where anywhere means nowhere and the lodestar was shrouded.

When grief felled me and I couldn't walk, I leaned on my friends physically. And they were strong enough. When grief felled me and I couldn't stop crying, I leaned on my friends for their hearts. And they were generous enough. And when grief felled me and I couldn't think, I leaned on my friends for their minds. I felt both demanding and diffident: I'm sorry but I seem to have lost my mind somewhere, do you mind if I borrow yours for a bit? As if mind were as casually lent as an old map book. And they were wise enough.

The shock of it left me in fear of everything. I am not a timorous person, but I became frightened of being alone, frightened of strangers, frightened of buying daffodils for a friend, frightened of streets, frightened of the future. Scared, in this alien world, this wasteland within, without him. Awake and frightened of sleep. Asleep and stalked by hooded nightmares.

For the first time, I understood the value of veils for those in mourning. I wanted widow's weeds to hide behind. I've never felt agoraphobic in my life, but for a time I became almost housebound. It shocked me. I wasn't scared of wide-open spaces but agora-phobic, scared of the agora, the marketplace, scared of going down to the shops, where strangers might stare at me. And I wanted to hide my eyes from strangers, because my eyes gave far too much away.

In the first night at the monastery, cold and dark in the *ger* (the Mongolian yurt), long after the stove fire had gone out and the toothpaste had frozen in the tube, the cold woke me. The moisture in my nose was frozen and I was cold to my core, but I knew one will, a will to survive so strong that Native Americans said it was the first command of Wakan Tanka, the Great Spirit: the need to endure.

A couple of days before we broke up, I'd been at an exhibition of Joseph Beuys. It became emblematic to me, for in the acuteness of grief, I felt as if I'd been in a terrible accident—in shock, in trauma, every bone smashed, every organ ruptured, every nerve screaming. (I couldn't get warm for days, no matter the temperature. Even in the hottest bath, I was frozen with shock.)

The plane fell out of the sky and crashed over one of the remotest parts of Mongolia. When I woke in the *ger* that night, I found myself alive. Breathing. Only but. And the local people wrapped me in felt and lit fires for me, insisted I eat animal fat and drink pints of hot tea. And in the temple, piled on the altar, were jars and pots of solid animal fat: sacrifice and survival, essential and life-saving. It was Beuys's experience. By a *ger* a mile away from the monastery, an old gray VW van was parked. I stared at it, in amazed recognition, as if Beuys's pack of sledges would come pouring out of it like dogs, each sledge strapped up with felt and fat and torches. (A few days later, on the mountainside, I did find a sledge. One runner broken, it was upended, useless in the snow. The young monks, many only eight or ten years old, the oldest twenty-five, had been using it to toboggan down the slopes.)

What I needed was what shamans know: How to keep walking. How to survive. How to understand this underneath world and how to resurge.

I was taken to see a Kazakh shaman who healed with herbs, and by reciting verses of the Qur'an, and with massage because, he said, he had electricity in his hands. His eyes were pale green and burning and he was very young, entirely unsmiling but compelling.

At first, he wanted to explain the theory, how he could help and heal people who were sick or who had been in an accident. And people who are sad? I asked. Yes, he nodded, and began to talk about the theory of how he could help. My arms lay across the table, my hands reaching toward him. I saw them as if they belonged to someone else, and they were beseeching. "Can you help me now?" I asked and the beg in my voice seemed to tear my throat.

He breathed over me and blew, rather than recited, verses of the Qur'an, and his hands shimmered around my head, as if my head were a thickly black winter night and his hands the Northern Lights. Afterward, I felt very faint and all the colors were very bright. I couldn't say I felt happier, but the weather in my head changed for a while.

I went to see a Mongolian shaman, who, when I arrived at his *ger*, was sitting in a battered silver Mercedes, parked in the snow. He was dressed in a highly embroidered sky-blue *del* (the traditional Mongolian coat), a pudgy man with false teeth and a cherry-nose from the vodka (empty bottles littered the *ger*). Inside, there were bearskins, flags and candles and a figure of Genghis Khan with a bottle of Gordon's gin by his side. Buddhist *tangkas* hung around the walls and everywhere hung stuffed birds with their wings outstretched, peacock feathers, gongs and horns. There were stuffed wolves, drums and a stuffed owl and a pile of white sugar cubes, a foot and a half high, with a plastic "Indian brave" on horseback at the top. ("I am like a god in Indiana," he had said.) On the opposite side of the *ger*, a fortuneteller in a pink kimono took cloakroom tickets to check people were coming in order.

The shaman said he was a messenger from heaven. And he sat on a bright throne.

"When you were a girl, the angels played with you," he said. "Why are you so sad?"

"I am lonely," I said.

"I also feel lonely, because there is no one perfect and clever like me," he said modestly.

He said he was a wise man, I thought he was a twit, but even he has his place on the stage, and his showmanship was wonderful.

He told me my aura was wounded and burnt a sprig of sage. "Look at me, and do not blink. Let your eyes fill with tears, and as they fall, your pain will fall away." He tried his best to give me faith in the future through faith in him, but his words meant less than nothing to me. I could find no reason to stop crying. I was engulfed, overwhelmed, in the sorrow of all water. An ocean of tears. My spirit was occluded and no light could reach those depths. And I would have swapped my cottage for a hug.

I staggered and fell. I felt as if I were falling off something, into an abyss that terrified me. I thought about suicide (don't we all?). It's easy. A piece of cake. Turn the oven on, Sylvia. The cake carelessly scorched in the oven one day when the sun was turned up too high. (You have to outstare it—look it right in the eyes and tell it to fuck off, little shit, suicide.)

I was mad with grief, Lear on the heath, as stricken as Cordelia without my favorite Fool.

And then, right at the very center, the sharpest heart of the storm, the pain so intense that it dazzled, a pain of midnight blue, it became electric: anguish like a lightning strike, vivid, elemental, night-defying. Lightning, scribbling its electric graffiti in the night, wildness tagging the wasteland because it wills to write.

Where the hemlock, there the stars, and this pain had the ferocious ambiguity of a rainbow in a violent sky.

Just at the point when you can no longer speak, sing. Just at the point when you can no longer get out of bed, fly. Pain can give you wings. (But don't stay indoors.)

At the center of the mountains was the monastery, in the center of Asia, as far from the sea as it's possible to be. And yet, there, right there, every morning, was the sound of the seashore as a monk blew a conch shell to the sun. At the center of the cold and silent circle of mountains, the monks were singing. And just so, right in the very heart of the psyche's wasteland, is the wildness, the vivid, life-loving wild.

In the depths of the ocean, when death and darkening seem all that there is, even there, life rolls up again, resurges up through lightening waters. Tragedy is not the heart of life. The saltwater tears, the ocean depths within, are not the end of the story. For from the fathoms of the ocean depths, in the dark and heavy waters of grief, sheer unfathomable levity perks up, the turning, quickening force.

While tragedy, in the midst of her nightmares, is weeping into the midnight pillows, right then, right there—*boink!*—comedy gets a hard-on and even tragedy can't resist a Puck.

My initial reason for planning to go to Mongolia was a friend's wedding feast. It seemed a discordant idea, that in my mourning I should go to a marriage, but it was actually wholly apt because the feast was where I needed most to be. The wisdom of the feast—a word linked to festival, fiesta and Feste the jester—is the wisdom of comedy. I was asked to festoon the wedding with flowers (festoon, too, is a linked word). And for two and a half weeks of Kazakh feasting (sheep fat and vodka, sweets and biscuits and wine) I had to eat though I had no appetite. Not to eat would have offended my hosts, and in a deeper way, not to eat what your life offers offends the spirit of life. For life survives through feast, not famine, and in this obviousness something oblique emerges: that in feast and festival, festooned with flowers, Comedy is a truer portrait of life than Tragedy.

THE WILDNESS OF COMEDY

I could no longer bear to live in my home. I had weeks of panicking despair and I was unable to finish this book. I needed a place apart, but with people, a place of safety. And so I came to Dial House, a place where artists, musicians and writers stay. Outside, a garden streaming with prayer flags and pennants, wood sculptures and a heron made of willow. A vegetable garden full of herbs and flowers: a real wort-yard, that lovely Anglo-Saxon word for garden. Indoors, a snug library full of books by the yard, books as well thumbed as the garden was well dug: a wort yard outside and a word yard inside.

Here, when I arrived, the runner beans were just beginning to grow ferociously on their bamboo assault course up to the sun—the wildness of life will force its way up to the light. And here the wildness of comedy couldn't help but defeat the wasteland of tragedy: a dyslexic stonemason was working in a studio in the garden, grinding inevitable accidental jokes on the gravestone. Here, out running one evening when the moon was full, I found a stone cracked open and in the heart of the dark stone, a round white center like the full moon shining. At the heart of the darkness of the wasteland, the mad and lovely moon, glowing, even within the flint.

And the Fool of this place said, in the kindest possible way: You have to stop fucking crying, and start fucking writing. And I had to.

Tragedy is set in the built environment, in the city, at court. Comedy is set in the garden. Comedy is feral and more vigorous—Arcadia trounces the Corinthian columns of Tragedy's citadel. The wildest plants are the toughest, the weeds that can crack open the paving stones. My tragedy didn't disappear but wild comedy busted through it, giant hogweed plunging up through the marble floor. Life wilts, wasted and wan, in the waste-courts of tragedy: it would rather be outside in the wildness, wanton with comedy. (Tragedy has its ghastly "nuptial bed," the grave of sex: Comedy has a self-delighting fuck in the woods.)

A wasteland is defined as a place without vegetation and so is tragedy. No greenery there, no bushes, no flowers in the halls and grim indoors, except those dead flowers cut for a grave. Wilderness and comedy alike are leguminous, a vegetable exuberance, tuber and root. An anthology of flowers and plants. (An anthology is literally a collection of flowers.)

Wildness and comedy alike, play. Wild things play in comedy, the gleeman cometh, playing havoc with the ice. The jester has the last word. "Jest," says the *Oxford English Dictionary*, is from the Latin *gesta*—"doings, exploits, performings." All action is (just) jest, suggests language: we are all players and life is ludic.

At the core of life is levity, and the force of levity is stronger than the force of gravity. Rising is ultimately easier than falling, because all that is alive has an upward swing, and the strength is there in us, in the tendril of the pea shoot, thrusting for the sun, in the oceans, in life itself. This levity is not a shallow thing: rather, levity matters more and is more profound than gravity. A joke is more important than a funeral wake, a comedy more serious and truer than tragedy. Mean academes of modernity purse their lips at this, insisting that if something is Important it must be Deadly Dull. If something is Funny, it can't be Deep. I disagree. Levity is far more than a laughing matter—in *levitas*, not *gravitas*, we think most wisely. The light lift of life is stronger than the grave gravitas of death. This is what lighthearted comedy knows, that the skull beneath the skin is not the end of the story. Tragedy can't withstand comedy, and in Ophelia's eyesockets, the damselfly will lay her eggs. On the one hand, death and the maiden waste; on the other, damsel life and the fecund wild.

What falls does rise and rise it must: the monk, cycling on ice, falls off laughing and gets to his feet again. The clown falls over and the children know they can laugh because he can bounce back up. We're all cycling on ice: and we must get up again because life and time are pedaling on, cyclic, and therefore so are we. The shaman goes deep down to the undermind and comes back up again. The philosophy of compost is the same, in its eternal risorgimento against the very idea of "waste." The force of this is feral, wild and tougher than any tragedy. The seed will explode the husk; spring will wrestle with winter and will win every time. ("For the red blood reigns in the winter's pale.") At the core of the dead and rotting apple is what? The pip. Tiny piece of pure braggadocio. *I will survive. I make trees 'n' time. Ha!*

The comedy of life is more stubborn and more agile than the tragedy of death. Wildness trumpets out the wasteland. The horn concerto matters more than the pauper's funeral, and underneath my widow's weeds, I have my clown costume on. Right at the heart of the starving austerity of grief is the feast, the abundance, the superfluity—the food laid out till the table buckles, the wine by the bucketful. In tragedy, all appetite is lost, but in comedy there is food galore and the appetite for it, the fundamental gusto of fundamental appetites. The wild god Dionysus, god of booze and revelry, was accompanied by the *komos*, the party of pissheads on the carouse. And the song of the *komos* was called the *komoidia*, from where the word *comedy* comes.

Wildness and comedy share a love of rudeness, tickling the pink with the horn of plenty. (This hairy arcadia will one day have a building historian's blue plaque solemnly recording that here was written "In Praise of Wanking.") And historians dutifully record that the Dionysiac revels included a phallus too large for one person to hold. Comedy comes nude—Bottom showing his bum at the birthday party—while tragedy, always clothed, stays indoors, wasting the midsummer sun. Comedy winks at the audience, robust as a turd in ground elder. Comedy is gregarious, seeking company; tragedy ends with an empty stage, the theater laid waste. Comedies end—for the moment—with the crowded stage. Comedy and wildness are promiscuous, spilling seeds and words (*now are frolic!*), fecund, rolling together a feck and a cunty ripeness. Tragedy wastes itself, celibate in the single bed.

Comedy is rude, very vulgar, that sensible word, of the common people. Comedy is of the underclass, the stage-for-all, the common or garden types, inclusive as common land, or a wilderness. Tragedy is exclusive—it has enclosed the common stage and privatized it for the aristocracy. Tragedy is classist in nature and depends on hierarchy, while comedy is an-archic. You have the Dignitaries of tragedy, and the undignified Bottom of comedy, the buffoon, and scaramouche, "born with the gift of laughter and a sense that the world was mad." Comedy amuses itself by knocking all pretensions of rank, in the natural world as in the human: bindweed and thistle here flourish as well as the violet. Comedy is as ecocratic as life itself, all wild weeds welcome. In comedy, antihierarchical, revelers are levelers all: stocky characters, tough as nettles, those through whom life survives. In its essential ecocratic character, wildness is political and it is tuned to comedy, which gives voice to pond life and weeds and peasants, the ruddy nub of life, demanding to be heard.

A wilderness is self-willed—the quality found in comedy too, a cheerful willfulness on the part of all the players. Wills are everywhere, flourishing up from the ground like grasses. Wildness is violently full of will, but will distinct from the malice of the tragic wasteland, where the land's will has been broken. Land made object. Object, abjectly so, distressed, demeaned, de-willed, dewilded. In tragedy, similarly, the will of the characters is overridden by the will of the fates or the will of god, imposed from above, the monovolio of the stony sky: My will be done.

Comedy suggests *What You Will* (as Will Shakespeare's *Twelfth Night* is alternatively titled), and that play is full of will: wild, self-willed mind. True to the spirit of comedy, the will of all has a voice. Feste is the good-will jester while the ill-willing Malvolio, that Puritan, wants to forbid Sir Toby Belch his cakes and ale.

Tragedy and the wasteland are places of obedience or forced submission to another's will. Comedy and the wilderness are the site of disobedience, insurrection, the insurgent resurgence of self-will, kicking against the pricks.

As the mountain wildernesses have always been the home of outlaws, so comedy is the natural home of the rebel (as the anticapitalist protesters who formed CIRCA, the Clandestine Insurgent Rebel Clown Army, so gloriously demonstrate). Humor is always rebellious, subverts expectation, quips at the rational, twists the linear, trips the predictable, surprises logic with lemon cake.

Comedy is carnival's cousin, and carnival is always upsetting the applecart, annoying the pants off the bourgeoisie, overthrowing the status quo. Carnival and comedy alike are the eruptions of necessary noise—vital wildness in the social wasteland—with the Lords of Misrule, the great inversions, Play putting a spanner in Work, the spirited, unbounded hullabaloo let loose till the rulers are nervous. Topsy-turvy as a twelfth-night revel.

To revel is to be rebellious. The two words are connected. To revel, "to be riotously festive," is from the Old French *reveler*, "to rebel, rejoice noisily," and the Old French word *revel* means "rebellion, tumult, disturbance, noisy mirth."

What is wild is rebellious, breaks the rules, subversive and quintessentially revelrous. Comedy rebels against tragedy, reverses it, subverts it. Life rebels against death. Anyone with any spittle rebels against the gray-willed suits of corporate modernity. Life blows a raspberry at the riot police and the clown has the final say, the rascal, the scamp, the rude man juggling his balls.

There are no spectators at the carnival: everyone is a player, comedy roundly demands audience participation. Tragedy, by contrast, insists on the sharp line dividing audience from actors. The stage a private enclosure, just as land is made waste by enclosure. In a wilderness, that comedy of land, there is no audience, no spectators: everything and everyone is a player in the harlequinade.

Finally, I laughed. After months, how sweet is fun. Funny word, that, from *funambuli*, the Roman tightrope walkers. My anguished tightrope walk was over because my tragedy, finally, could not fight the sheer vitality of comedy and, finally, had no wish to. The fool blows smoke rings through my tragic words and farts to amuse the cat. Tragedy slips on a fair-trade banana skin, artfully placed by the articulate rebel clown.

The fool is the personification of comedy. Playing the fool is a serious affair. Acting the ludic role means you may take the ludicrous line, where comedy is born of love and anger. His paraphernalia is unmistakable, the pipe and drum, the cap and bells, the coxcomb. The fool, the jester, is the joker in the pack of cards. Play the joker and you play the "wild" card (*ooooh, he is a card*), for the wild card expresses will, the will of the player. In the pack of cards, the joker comes up slap-bang against authority, outflouts the king and queen, overturns the will of the highest courts; the anarchic fool subverts the hierarchy, reverses all. The Shakespearean fool lives at court without fee, is paid spontaneously—or not. Being penniless, he is priceless. Never selling out, never fettered by a wage, the fool is wildly free, he can't be bought or directed by money. The fool is paid in laughter and in love, through gift, charity, that lovely word linked to *caritas* ("love") and to *grace*.

The fool and the shaman are one; fools, like Feste the jester, enter carrying their pipe and drum. Shamans too, all over the world, use drums and pipes. They are the original Pied Pipers, their music a wildly charismatic influence on all who hear it. (*Charisma*, too, is a word associated with grace.)

As the fool is the embodiment of wild comedy, the shaman is the embodiment of wild life. Shamans have an affinity with wild creatures, conversing with them, shape-shifting. (The witch's cat is virtually all we remember of this in modern culture.) The shaman-fool is a magnet to wildness; the free spirit, walking on the wild side. Shamanism is the universal religion of the wild earth, and even in societies like ours, which think they have forgotten their shamanic traditions, there are glimpses in probably every single household in the land—in a Complete Shakespeare or a pack of cards.

The shaman-fool understands the wastelands of the psyche, the underworld where souls are lost, and can find them well in the dark, as my soul was lost and found at the beginning of this book and at its end. The shaman-fool also understands the upper world of the mind like a kite. Shakespeare's Puck and Ariel are mind in flight, the messengers, winged as mercury, having an affinity with birds. The coxcomb, the fool's cap, represents the feathers of the cock's comb. Feathers are part of the clown's costume too, tickling you with a feather duster. Shamans too wear feathers, use them in ritual, to illustrate their ability to fly.

The insignia of comedy is the insignia of the wild.

The shaman-fool has a mind that is winged and can fly too high. Shamans and fools alike share a susceptibility to being called insane, or to occasional flights of mad-mindedness. The shaman-fool has license, the wild freedom to say anything, speaking in a wild grammar through wild, untaught intuition. Wildness speaks most incontrovertibly through the shaman-fool. This fool's license is absolute and untrammeled, but a freedom of speech is never bought so dearly—he pays with his whole life. Heckling the gods, the fool is the one through whom the wild word is spoken, so even at court there is one free to speak from the wild side. But because he is "mad" he is often ignored. Because his truths are ludic, they are often not taken seriously. Yet the mask of madness protects his license, for he is a beyonder of the psyche, and precisely because his words can be dismissed, he is free to say them.

The funny thing is, there is absolutely nothing unusual about this character. In shamanic societies, shamans are everywhere. Any diddly hamlet on any squiddly riverbank in the Amazon will have one or two. And even in societies like ours, which have temporarily misplaced their shamanism, shamans are not rare. Two extra for every fifty-two people, at a rough guess—the number of jokers tossed into a pack of cards. About 4 percent of us all. The percentage of the wisely mad, the instinctive healers and the original artists.

Shamans are liminal, creatures of the edge. They live on the border between the wild world and the ordinary one. In the Amazon, the shaman never lives in the middle of the village but hard by the great forests. The edge is also the place where wildness growls most furiously, the beast at the fence, the brambles on the edge of the golf course. In carnival tradition, the fool doesn't play in the band but takes his place at the edge of the crowd—neither-nor, he is not part of the band, nor part of the people. The Edge is also the psychological place of shamans; as mad people and artists, their minds are on the edge, on a tilt, on the brink of the utter wildness of insanity. They are on the edge of time, understanding both the past and future, they are on the edge of light, too, twilight-minded, living in two worlds, the bright day world of apparency and the dark night world of symbols.

The shaman-fool wears the motley coat, the variegated cape; Harlequin has his checkered costume, Pierrot the pied suit, the clown has diamond patches on his trews. In this, too, they are representatives of wildness. The multicolored and pied beauties belong to wild lands, which are places of diversity, the panthology of variegated life. The motley coat suits the shaman-fool, it fits his psyche, for he is motley minded. His mind is the creature of change, the mood-swinger, mercury-born, the changer, the transformer, the trickster, with the wisdom of reversal. "Now the melancholy god protect thee, and the tailor make thy doublet of changeable taffeta, for thy mind is a very opal," says Feste in *Twelfth Night*, where Olivia speaks of "sad and merry madness." Sad and merry madness? The motley? The *Pied* Piper? The melancholy god? The changeable taffeta? Those who can fly with the birds and sink to the underworld? It's the deepest meaning of manic-depression, that clowning curse that follows so many artists.

The Bible has nothing to say about humor. Not a joke in it. (I have one up my sleeve: Our Father, Who Art in Heaven, stay there.)

Christianity, Malvolio on the world stage, deadened the world with gray. Heaven was all white above and hell all black below, but this lovely multicolored rainbow world would be made dreary as the gray of gray friars. The Puritans personified the dead hand of tragedy, closing the theaters of comedy, their gray unvision enacting the gray and jealous will of their god, who detests this colorful, wild and self-willed Earth. Christianity, preaching life only after death, stores paradise stale in the attic, while heaven is here, right under our bare feet, and now, right at this bare moment. Christianity is on the side of death, and it doles out the book of Revelation, written—criminally—to encourage people to want the end of the world, for the heaven of Christianity means a holocaust for the Earth, and Revelation ends with a prayer to hasten the end of life here. Amen, so come Lord Jesus. Not.

For hundreds of years, the agents of the Christian Church, Christian states and Christian empires have attacked the wild wisdom of comedy in all its guises, banning carnival and corroboree, stealing and enclosing the common wild land where they took place, then enclosing the wild and bubbling human spirit. They banned the potlatch of Native Americans, banned the spirit of the gift, silenced the songlines of the wild Earth, killed shamans all over the . world, those who best understood wild mind, and they continue to do so now, the modern-day puritans, the capitalists, promulgators of Industry, the corporate suits, the board members. They ban the drugs that nature so jesterishly provides to trip us into the comedy, ban festivals, ban any extraordinary eruption of fun. Prohibition, prohibition everywhere, prohibiting liveliness, with their repulsive dogma of gray. Comedy is reduced to the leisure-industry and stand-up laugh merchants, selling their gags (and true comedy, stripped of its profundity, gags in the toilets).

But there is, thank fuck, rude rebellion and revelry running underground in the sheer force of exuberance: for life, that violent comedy, will not knuckle down to the sensible job in suburbia, nor kneel in the wasteland like a sinner being shriven. Comedy erupts on the wild side, gloriously demented, and moons at the church, gurning at the pope, sucking off a monk, tickling his fancy with a green rubber back-scratcher, and puts the Bible to good use—on the compost heap.

All of wild nature expresses time as a cycle and urges it to go on forever. Judeo-Christianity insisted that it was linear and prays for its end, so god could run it to ground like the last wild animal, and kill it at the end of the line.

Time in a wilderness is wild, motley and diverse, now slow as a slug, now quick as a kingfisher. It is unpredictable, chancy and cheeky. Time sprouts where it likes (and runs to seed some nights). Risky and opportunistic, wild time is pure spontaneity, that lovely word, that word on tiptoes, with *sponte* at its heart—of its own sweet will. Wild time is the eternal anarchist.

But time in a wasteland is trapped in schedule, tethered by routine, enclosed with deadlines. In the wasteland of tragedy, time follows the rules, straight as a ruler, ruling the lives of human rulers. Loki, god of mischief, lives in tricksy time and revels in comedy. But Loki doesn't get a look-in and Lady Luck is out of luck in tragedy. In tragedy, there are no second chances, for in the idea of the fatal flaw, wild time is prescribed, predicted and therefore caged. Tragedy, deterministic, shackles wild time so the future, which should be free, is a captive of the past, the story to come just the unfolding of the inevitable downfall.

In the wildness of comedy, there are second and third chances, chances galore, chances to infinity, to a number long as pi, in this pied time. Comedy throws a custard pie in the face of fate, belts out the refrain "It Ain't Necessarily So," and drums out an old scene to drum in a new one. Here, metamorphosis is not just possible but splendidly likely. Growth an absolute demand, the new shoots thrusting up, yearning for the free and open sky. In comedy, time is so cyclic it's positively curly, curly as kale, curling all our lives.

Tragedy and the wasteland brood with Malvolio, winding up his watch, hastening the end. Long before Benjamin Franklin's nasty little lie that "Time is Money," Malvolio made the same equation: "You waste the treasure of your time." But it is Feste who has the last word, knowing that "the whirligig of time brings in his revenges"—the curly-whirligig time of comedy, finally, will avenge itself on tragedy, and the spirits of wildness will defeat the agents of the wasteland.

Wastelands are manufactured by measurement—the anthropologists measuring human heads and penises (yes, they did), the Australian deserts measured in fences, the Amazon measured in weight of timber. Measurement destroys wildness both actually and conceptually. Measurement is a feature of tragedy, the precise meters of the verse, the measured payback for every action. Tragedy is bitterly mercantile, the contractual morality of fate.

In a Lithuanian folktale, the fairies give riches to humans, but if the riches are measured or counted, they turn to paper. The Amazon *riqueza* turned to pulp and paper money. The dollar a dolor, the pound pounding out a waste of worlds.

Wildness, though, persists in whatever is yet unmeasured, uncounted, the in-ordinate. Measurement is mean, while wildness is immoderately generous. Speech overflows all meters in comedy—there is abundance here and the spirit of gift. Here are the grace notes, unrepentantly unnecessary, which are not needed for any particular phrase but yet are absolutely essential to melody-at-large. Birds sing for reasons—sex, territory and alarm—and they also sing for fun, the grace notes of motive. They sing for sheer, shining gladness and as, all across the world, they are seen as messengers, their message is the essential comedy of the wild. Comedy has a generous, regenerative grace, fill it till it spills and lick it up again, a superfluity, an excess of it, which the thin-lipped agents of waste detest: *Too many notes, Herr Mozart.*

Tragedy is unforgiving—you get what you deserve—and it is therefore graceless. The grace of comedy means you get far more than you deserve. The idea of original sin—that disgusting waste of spirit—can only be countered by an aboriginal grace of wildness. Grace is at the heart of wildness and of comedy too.

Wild things have inherent grace, which is why all wild creatures are so bewitching—they are not just in, but they *are* a state of grace. They have that exquisite shimmer of sexual charisma that I knew with the jaguar in the Amazon. Life itself is a state of grace: at the heart of it all, there is this primeval wild comedy, and the Earth is hot with, bursting with, fermenting with, dizzy with, hooting with, gasping with—*life.*

In the wastes of the cosmos, the black holes and implosions, the voids devoid of life, the blanks of darkness and the blanks of unliving light, the famishing emptiness, the dead stars shining light-years away, light that has long ceased to be light, in the heart of the wasteland, there is this. The glad world gleaming in the dark, like the full moon in the flint.

Life. What are the chances? *Wildly improbable.* That in the wastes of space, there is this one wild and living planet, the complex, stonking grace of the thing: there is life here, now, and how it spins. Earth the feast in the famine of space, the festival in the desert. And even if Earth were home to just one iridescent dragonfly for just one morning, reeling one waltz over just one stream, it would still be enough, the flicker of grace. But life gives it more: another dragonfly, another stream, another pitcher plant, another Mozart. Life gives it extra, just for fun. Generous, promiscuous, *have another one.*

Earth, self-created, born of self-will and stardust, made her self-willed way her own, the aboriginal I Am. Willful and subversive planet that she is, grinning into the dark, roaring out her rebel yell, Earth is the rebel against the whole damn (solar) system; Earth, protesting against vacuum, in riot and revolt, throws her knickers at the space police. Wildness is subversive and Comedy's a rebel angel: Earth itself the ultimate wild comedian.

It is Earth that makes the eternal precession of the stars a harlequinade, primordial carnival in the puritan black. Earth the maenad, drunk on her own juices in the sober cosmos. Earth the vagrant, the flagrant minstrel, singing out her songlines to the universe. Earth the revelry, Earth the circus, doing a turn every day, with the stars for footlights and the sun the spot. Earth, clowning around the heavens, the joker in the pack of planets, the wild card. Earth in levity and gravity, rises and falls (and so holds her sway), jester to the stars. Earth with her (ice) cap and (hare)bells, the drum of the sun, penniless holder of the horn of plenty: Earth the shaman, Earth the fool, Earth, the most entire and sublime joker in the ultimate subversion, subverted deadness, made life out of laughing gas and quickened creatures from slow rain, made puns of the galaxies on the spiral of a snail. She was the original anarchist wit who cracked the first joke, which split the sides of the moon and, roaring with a dirty laugh fit to soil herself with good brown muck, said the first word—FUCK!—again and again. Earth the nomad, Earth the maenad, Earth the shaman, Earth the clown in boots too big, walks the wild way, the curly way, curling the stars, on, on, in fecund riot and feral grace.

Dedication

To David Holloway

Because this book began its ideahood with you.

Because it was nurtured by the fertility and comedy of your mind.

Because it was written with you in my heart in all my travels.

Because your bright love lit all my ways.

In Thanks

Before and during all my journeys I had advice, help, suggestions, hospitality, introductions, conversations, kindness and jokes from many people, and here my heartfelt thanks go to them all.

In the Amazon
Jeremy Narby, Juan Flores, Victor Mesa, Chinita Garcia, Perrico Garcia, Lily La Torre, Claus Kjaerby, Antonio Fernandini, Dick Smith, Carlos Peres, RACIMOS DE UNGURAHUI, FENAMAD, Tarzan and Matteo Jicca.

In the Arctic
John MacDonald, Larry Audlaluk, Mary Audlaluk, Hugh Lloyd, Alexina Kublu, Mick Mallon, Paul Amagoalik, Jaypeetee Akeagok, Looty Pijamini, John Arnatsiak, Susannah Singorie, Brock May, Henry Morgentaler and Yann Morgentaler.

In Oceans
Hal Whitehead and Richard Page.

In Australia
Robert Maclaurin and Jean Rankin, Rod Moss, Lareena Groves and Anjou Moss, Ernie Williams, Sandra Drover, Agnes Abbott, Jane Abbott, John Wolseley, Herb Wharton, Jenny Green, Myfanwy Turpin, Marlee Na-

purrula, Margaret-Kemarre Turner, Magdalene Johnson, Michael Nelson Jagamarra, Alison Ross and Jackie Margoungoun.

In West Papua
Eben Kirksey, Benny Giay, Thom Beanal, Neles Tebay and Adrian Arbib. Deepest thanks to people who cannot be named for their own safety, who guided me, translated for me, talked with me and sang into the night.

In pages of wildness
Authors whose work on wildness is passionate with wisdom and kindness, these I salute: Thor Heyerdahl, Rachel Carson, William Beebe, Henry Thoreau, Penny Rimbaud, Barry Lopez, Gary Snyder, Heathcote Williams, Hugh Brody, Gerardo Reichel-Dolmatoff, Vandana Shiva, Susan Griffin, Richard Nelson, Bill Neidjie, Robert Macfarlane and David Rothenberg.

In professional respect
Editors Simon Prosser and Sara Carder and Agent Godwin.

In stumping up the dosh
Relieved appreciation for stipends and awards from the following organizations: Nouvelle Planete, Barnes and Noble, and the Society of Authors. Thanks to Kenn Borek Air for help with flights in the Arctic.

In friendship
Hannah Scrase, Anna Jenkins, Ann Clare, Thea Stein, Clare Patey, Jan Parker, Russell Crockett, Margaret Moodie, Alex Moodie, Giuliana Becciu, Jim Thomas, Edd Thomas, Marina Chakyerkhan, Jason Torrance, Hugh Warwick, Zoe Broughton, Andy Warren, Susy Pegrum, Simon Key, Fiona Key, Rob Maclaurin, Jean Rankin, Naomi Saville, Narayan Acharaya, Ed Posey, Adrian Arbib, Ricarda Steinbrecher, Rowan Tilley, John Griffiths, Helen Griffiths, Malcolm Draper and Vic Worsley. Deep thanks to Penny Rimbaud for the love which made a wild home for me and for this book's completion.

Bibliography

Abbey, Edward. *Desert Solitaire*. Simon and Schuster, 1968.

———. *The Monkey Wrench Gang*. Lippincott Williams and Wilkins, 1975.

Abram, David. *The Spell of the Sensuous: Perception and Language in a More-Than-Human-World*. Random House, 1996.

Amarualik, Hubert. *Interview for the Igloolik Oral History Project*. Igloolik Research Centre, 1993.

Århem, Kaj. "The Cosmic Food Web: Human-nature Relatedness in the Northwest Amazon." In *Nature and Society: Anthropological Perspectives*, edited by Philippe Descola and Gísli Pálsson. Routledge, 1996.

Asher, Michael. *The Last of the Bedu: In Search of the Myth*. Viking, 1996.

Austin, Mary. *The Land of Little Rain*. Houghton Mifflin, 1903.

Bacon, Francis. *New Atlantis*. Edited by J. Weinberger. Harlan Davidson, 1980.

Bardon, Geoffrey. *Papunya Tula: Art of the Western Desert*. JB Books, 1991.

Barnes, Simon. *Rogue Lion Safaris*. HarperCollins, 1998.

Basso, Keith. "Stalking with Stories: Names, Places, and Moral Narratives Among the Western Apache." *Proceedings of the American Ethnological Society*, edited by Stuart Plattner, 1983.

Beebe, William. *The Arcturus Adventure*. G. P. Putnam's Sons, 1926.

———. *Half Mile Down*. Harcourt, Brace and Company, 1934.

Bell, Diane. *Daughters of the Dreaming*. George Allen and Unwin, 1983.

Bender, Barbara. *Landscape: Politics and Perspectives*. Berg, 1993.

Benterrak, Krim, Stephen Muecke, and Paddy Roe. *Reading the Country: Introduction to Nomadology*. Fremantle Arts Centre Press, 1984.

Bettex, Albert. *The Discovery of the World*. Thames and Hudson, 1960.

Bhathal, Ragbir, and Graeme White. *Under the Southern Cross: A Brief History of Astronomy in Australia*. Kangaroo Press, 1991.

Biehl, Janet, and Peter Staudenmaier. *Ecofascism: Lessons From the German Experience*. AK Press, 1995.

Bird-David, Nurit. "Tribal Metaphorization of Human-Nature Relatedness." In *Environmentalism: The View From Anthropology*, edited by K. Milton. Routledge, 1993.

Birket-Smith, Kaj. *The Eskimos*. Methuen, 1936. Published in Denmark, 1927.

Birtles, Dora. *North-West by North*. Cape, 1935.

Blixen, Karen (Isak Dinesen). *Out of Africa*. Penguin, 1954. First published 1937.

Boardman, Peter. *Sacred Summits*. Hodder and Stoughton, 1982.

Boas, Franz. *Kwakiutl Ethnography*. University of Chicago Press, 1966. Research notes, 1885.

Bonner, Raymond. *At the Hand of Man: Peril and Hope for Africa's Wildlife*. Simon and Schuster, 1993.

Bookchin, Murray. *The Ecology of Freedom*. Cheshire Books, 1982.

Bosworth-Toller. *Anglo-Saxon Dictionary*. Clarendon Press, 1898.

Boyd, David R., ed. *Northern Wild*. David Suzuki Foundation and Greystone Books, 2001.

Breckenridge, Keith, et al., ed. *Transformation: Critical Perspectives on Southern Africa*. University of Natal, 2000.

Bright, Michael, producer, *Wild Battlefields* (2003), television documentary.

Brody, Hugh. *Maps and Dreams*. Douglas and McIntyre, 1981.

———. *The Other Side of Eden: Hunter-Gatherers, Farmers and the Shaping of the World*. Faber, 2001.

———. *The People's Land: Eskimos and Whites in the Eastern Arctic*. Penguin, 1975.

Broome, Richard. *Aboriginal Australians Black Response to White Dominance, 1788–1980*. George Allen and Unwin, 1982.

Brown, Dee. *Bury My Heart at Wounded Knee: An Indian History of the American West*. Holt, Rinehart and Winston, 1970.

Bryson, Bill. *Mother Tongue: The English Language*. Penguin, 1990.

Bunney, Sarah. "Tracing our ancestral songlines." *New Scientist*, March 19, 1994.

Burger, Julian. *Aborigines Today: Land and Justice*. Anti-Slavery Society, 1988.

———. *Report From the Frontier: The State of the World's Indigenous Peoples*. Zed Books, 1987.

Butler, Tom, ed. *Wild Earth: Wild Ideas for a World Out of Balance*. Milkweed, 2002.

Byatt, Andrew, Alastair Fothergill, and Martha Holmes. *The Blue Planet: A Natural History of the Oceans*. BBC Worldwide, 2001.

Capra, Fritjof. *The Hidden Connections: A Science for Sustainable Living*. HarperCollins, 2002.

Carey, John, ed. *The Faber Book of Utopias*. Faber, 1999.

Carpenter, Edmund. *Eskimo Realities*. Holt, Rinehart and Winston, 1973.

Carroll, Lewis. *The Complete Illustrated Works*. Chancellor Press, 1982. First published 1865.

Carson, Rachel. *The Sea*. Readers Union, 1965.

Carter, Paul. *The Road to Botany Bay: An Essay in Spatial History*. Faber, 1987.

Caruana, Wally. *Aboriginal Art*. Thames and Hudson, 1993.

Caufield, Catherine. *In the Rainforest*. Picador, 1985.

Chapin, Mac. "Losing the Way of the Great Father" on the Kuna people of Panama. *New Scientist*, August 10, 1991.

Charlesworth, Max, Howard Morphy, Diane Bell, and Kenneth Maddock, eds. *Religion in Aboriginal Australia: An Anthology*. University of Queensland Press, 1984.

Cheesman, Evelyn. *Six-Legged Snakes in New Guinea*. Harrap, 1949.

Chomsky, Noam. *Powers and Prospects*. Pluto Press, 1996.

Clutton-Brock, Juliet. "How the Wild Beasts Were Tamed." *New Scientist*, February 15, 1992.

Cole, Thomas. *Essay on American Scenery*. 1835.

Conrad Joseph. *The Heart of Darkness*. Penguin, 1973. First published 1898–99.

———. *Typhoon; Falk; and The Shadow Line*. Wordsworth Classics, 1998. First published 1903 and 1917.

Cooper, Anthony Ashley. "The Moralists." 1711.

Cousteau, Jacques-Yves. *The Living Sea*. Hamish Hamilton, 1963.

———. *The Silent World*. Hamish Hamilton, 1953.

Crocker, Jon Christopher. *Vital Souls: Bororo Cosmology, Natural Symbolism and Shamanism*. University of Arizona Press, 1985.

Cullinan, Cormac. *Wild Law*. SiberInk, 2002.

Dahl, Jens, Jack Hicks, and Peter Jull. *Nunavut: Inuit Regain Control of Their Lands and Their Lives*. International Work Group for Indigenous Affairs (IWGIA), 2000.

Darby, Tom. *The Feast: Meditations on Politics and Time*. University of Toronto Press, 1982.

David, Bruno. *Landscapes, Rock-Art and the Dreaming: An Archaeology of Preunderstanding*. Leicester University Press, 2002.

Davis, Jack. *In Our Town*. Currency Press, 1992.

Davis, Jack, Mudrooroo Narogin, Stephen Muecke, and Adam Shoemaker, eds. *Paperbark: A Collection of Black Australian Writings*. University of Queensland Press, 1990.

Day, Stephen. "The Secret Language of Honeybees." *New Scientist*, March 21, 1992.

Dayton, Leigh. "Rock art evokes beastly echoes of the past." *New Scientist*, November 28, 1992.

———. "Killer whales communicate in distinct dialects." *New Scientist*, March 10, 1990.

Descola, Philippe. "*Les Cosmologies des Indiens D'Amazonie*." *La Recherche* 292, November 1996.

———. "Societies of Nature and the Nature of Society." In *Conceptualizing Society*, edited by Adam Kuper. Routledge, 1992.

De Quincey, Thomas. *Confessions of an English Opium Eater*. Oxford World's Classics, 1985.

Devall, Bill, and George Sessions. *Deep Ecology: Living as if Nature Mattered*. Gibbs Smith, 1985.

Diamond, Jared. *Guns, Germs and Steel: The Fates of Human Societies*. Jonathan Cape, 1997.

Dick, Lyle. *Muskox Land: Ellesmere Island in the Age of Contact*. University of Calgary Press, 2001.

Dillard, Annie. *Teaching a Stone to Talk: Expeditions and Encounters*. Pan Books, 1984. First published 1982.

Di Prima, Diane. *Pieces of a Song: Selected Poems*. City Lights Books, 1990.

Dobkin de Rios, Marlene. *Visionary Vine: Psychedelic Healing in the Peruvian Amazon*. Chandler Publications, 1972.

Doughty, C. M. *Passages from Arabia Deserta*. Selected by Edward Garnett, 1931. First published 1888.

Douglas, Mary. "In the Wilderness: The Doctrine of Defilement in the Book of Numbers." *Journal for the Study of the Old Testament, Supplement Series* 158, 1993.

————. *Purity and Danger: An Analysis of Concepts of Pollution and Taboo*. Routledge and Kegan Paul, 1966.

Draper, Malcolm. "In Quest of African Wilderness." *Seventh World Wilderness Congress Symposium*, comps. Alan Watson and Janet Sproull. 2001.

————. "Zen and the Art of Garden Province Maintenance: The Soft Intimacy of Hard Men in the Wilderness of KwaZulu-Natal, South Africa 1952–1997." *Journal of Southern African Studies*, 24, no. 4 (1998).

Draper, Malcolm, and Gerhard Maré. "Going In: The Garden of England's Gaming Zookeeper and Zululand." *Journal of Southern African Studies*, 29, no. 2 (2003).

Drayton, Michael. *Poly-Olbion*. 1612–1622.

Duerr, Hans Peter. *Dreamtime: Concerning the Boundary Between Wilderness and Civilization*. Blackwell, 1985. First published 1978.

Dunbar, Robin. Review of "Natural Theories of Mind, Evolution, Development and Simulation of Everyday Mindreading," ed. Andrew Whiten. *New Scientist*, June 29, 1991.

Dunsmore, Roger, ed. *The Poetics of Wilderness*. Proceedings of the 22nd Annual Wilderness Issues Lecture Series. University of Montana Wilderness Institute, 2001.

Durning, Alan Thein. "Guardians of the Land: Indigenous Peoples and the Health of the Earth." *Worldwatch Paper* 112, December 1992.

Eberhardt, Isabelle. *The Nomad*. Edited by Elizabeth Kershaw. Summersdale, 2002.

————. *The Oblivion Seekers and Other Writings*. Translated by Paul Bowles. Peter Owen, 1972.

————. *The Passionate Nomad: The Diary of Isabelle Eberhardt*. Virago, 1987.

Eidelson, Meyer. *The Melbourne Dreaming: A Guide to the Aboriginal Places of Melbourne*. Aboriginal Studies Press, 1997.

Eisenberg, Evan. *The Ecology of Eden*. Alfred A. Knopf, 1998.

El-Baz, Farouk. "Do People Make Deserts?" *New Scientist*, October 13, 1990.

Elick, John W. *An Ethnography of the Pichis Valley Campa of Eastern Peru*. Ph.D. diss., UCLA, 1969.

Elkin, A. P. *The Australian Aborigines*. Angus and Robertson, 1938.

Ellis, Jean A. *This Is the Dreaming: Australian Aboriginal Legends*. Collins Dove, 1994.

Emerson, Ralph Waldo. *Nature*. First published 1836.

Ereira, Alan. *From the Heart of the World*, television documentary on the Kogi people, 1990.

Feld, Steven. *Sound and Sentiment: Birds, Weeping, Poetics, and Song in Kaluli Expression*. University of Pennsylvania, 1982.

Ferry, Georgina. "Macaques strive to keep the peace." *New Scientist*, January 21, 1995.

Fichtelius, Karl-Erik, and Sverre Sjölander. *Man's Place: Intelligence in Whales, Dolphins and Humans*. Gollancz, 1973.

Firestone, Shulamith. *The Dialectic of Sex: The Case for Feminist Revolution*. The Women's Press, 1979.

Flanders, Michael, and Donald Swann. *At the Drop of Another Hat*. EMI, 2001. First recorded 1959.

Flannery, Tim, ed. *The Explorers: Epic First-Hand Accounts of Exploration in Australia*. Phoenix, 1999.

Flannery, Tim. *Throwim Way Leg*. Phoenix, 1998.

Fonseca, Isabel. *Bury Me Standing: The Gypsies and Their Journey.* Vintage, 1996.

Foreign Office briefing for the UK delegation to the UN General Assembly, September 10, 1969. FCO 24/449.

Foreman, Dave. *Confessions of an Eco-Warrior.* Crown, 1991.

Foucault, Michel. *Discipline and Punish.* Allen Lane, 1977.

Freedman, Françoise Barbira. "The Jaguar Who Would Not Say Her Prayers: Changing Polarities in Upper Amazonian Shamanism." In *Ayahuasca Reader: Encounters with the Amazon's Sacred Vine,* edited by Luis Eduardo Luna and Steven F. White. Synergetic Press, 2000.

Freeman, Minnie Aodla. *Life Among the Qallunaat.* Hurtig, 1978.

Friel, Brian. *Translations.* Faber, 1981.

Fugard, Athol. *Boesman and Lena.* Buren, 1969.

Furlong, Monica. *Flight of the Kingfisher: A Journey Among the Kukatja Aborigines.* Harper-Collins, 1996.

Gaffield, Chad, and Pam Gaffield. *Consuming Canada: Readings in Environmental History.* Copp Clark, 1995.

Gaski, Harald, ed. *Sami Prose and Poetry.* Davvi Girji, 1996.

Gebhart-Sayer, Angelika. "Una Terapia Estetica. Los Diseños Visionarios del Ayahuasca entre Los Shipibo-Conibo." *Handbook of Latin American Studies,* vol. 51, 1986.

Genet, Jean. *The Thief's Journal.* Penguin, 1967. First published 1949.

Giay, Benny. *Zakheus Pakage and His Communities: Indigenous Religious Discourse, Socio-Political Resistance, and Ethnohistory of the Me of Irian Jaya.* Vrije Universiteit, 1995.

Gilbert, Kevin. *Because a White Man'll Never Do It.* Angus and Robertson, 1973.

Gilbert, Kevin, ed. *Inside Black Australia: An Anthology of Aboriginal Poetry.* Penguin, 1988.

Golder, F. A. *Bering's Voyages.* American Geographical Society, 1922.

Goldman, Irving. *The Cubeo: Indians of the Northwest Amazon.* University of Illinois Press, 1963.

Gow, Peter. "River People: Shamanism and History in Western Amazonia." In *Shamanism, History, and the State,* edited by Nicholas Thomas and Caroline Humphrey. University of Michigan Press, 1994.

Graham, Stephen. *The Gentle Art of Tramping.* Robert Holden and Co., 1927.

Graves, Robert. *I, Claudius.* Barker, 1934.

———. *Lawrence and the Arabs.* Jonathan Cape, 1927.

Gray, Andrew. *The Arakmbut: Mythology, Spirituality and History in an Amazonian Community.* Berghahn Books, 1996.

———. *The Last Shaman: Change in an Amazonian Community.* Berghahn Books, 1997.

Green, Jenny. *A Learner's Guide to Eastern and Central Arrernte.* IAD Press, 1994.

Green, Rayna, ed. *That's What She Said: Contemporary Poetry and Fiction by Native American Women.* Indiana University Press, 1984.

Griffin, Sasha. *John Wolseley: Land Marks.* Craftsman House, 1998.

Griffin, Susan. *Woman and Nature: The Roaring Inside Her.* Harper & Row, 1978.

Grzimek, Bernhard. *Serengeti Shall Not Die.* Hamish Hamilton, 1960.

Guha, Ramachandra. "The Authoritarian Biologist and the Arrogance of Anti-Humanism: Wildlife Conservation in the Third World." *The Ecologist,* January 1997.

Hamilton-Paterson, James. *The Great Deep: The Sea and Its Thresholds*. Random Century, 1992.

Hardy, Jane, J.V.S. Megaw, and M. Ruth Megaw, eds. *The Heritage of Namatjira*. Heinemann, 1992.

Harper, Kenn. *Give Me My Father's Body: The Life of Minik, the New York Eskimo*. Steerforth Press, 2000. First published 1986.

Harrer, Heinrich. *I Come From the Stone Age*. Translated by Edward Fitzgerald. Dutton, 1965.

Hart, L. "Pacifying the Last Frontiers." *North American Congress on Latin America*, no. 10, 1973.

Harvey, Miles. *The Island of Lost Maps: A True Story of Cartographic Crime*. Weidenfeld and Nicolson, 2001.

Haslund-Christensen, Henning. *Men and Gods in Mongolia*. Kegan Paul, 1935.

Haulli, Sarah and Joe Haulli. *Interview for the Igloolik Oral History Project*. Igloolik Research Centre, 1987.

Haynes, Raymond, Roslynn Haynes, David Malin, and Richard McGee. *Explorers of the Southern Sky: A History of Australian Astronomy*. Cambridge University Press, 1996.

Haynes, Roslynn. *Seeking the Centre: The Australian Desert in Literature, Art and Film*. Cambridge University Press, 1998.

Heaney, Seamus. *North*. Faber, 1975.

Hemming, Steve, and Philip Jones. *Ngurunderi: An Aboriginal Dreaming*. South Australian Museum, 2000.

Herbert, Marie. *The Snow People: Life among the Polar Eskimos*. Pan, 1976.

Heyerdahl, Thor. *Fatu-Hiva: Back to Nature*. George Allen and Unwin, 1974.

———. *The Kon-tiki Expedition: By Raft Across the South Seas*. George Allen and Unwin, 1950.

Hildebrand, Martin von. In conversation, 2001.

Hillary, Edmund. *View From the Summit*. Book Club Associates, 1999.

Hitchcock, Robert K. *Bushmen and the Politics of the Environment in Southern Africa*. International Work Group for Indigenous Affairs, doc. No. 79, 1996.

Hoban, Russell. *Riddley Walker*. Jonathan Cape, 1980.

Hobsbawm, Eric. *Bandits*. Weidenfeld and Nicolson, 2000.

Holmes, Bob. "Dreams as big as an ocean." *New Scientist*, August 30, 1997.

Home, Stewart, ed. *What Is Situationism? A Reader*. AK Press, 1996.

Homer. *The Odyssey*. Translated by E. V. Rieu. Penguin, 1946.

Hooper, Meredith. *Inside Australia's Simpson Desert*. Cambridge University Press, 1997.

Huggins, Rita and Jackie Huggins. *Auntie Rita*. Aboriginal Studies Press, 1994.

Hume, Lynne. *Ancestral Power: The Dreaming, Consciousness and Aboriginal Australians*. Melbourne University Press, 2002.

Hunt, Matthew. Author of Internet information on the linguistic and social history of the cunt.

Huxley, Aldous. *Brave New World*. Chatto and Windus, 1932.

Hvalkof, Søren, and Peter Aaby, eds. *Is God an American? An Anthropological Perspective on the Missionary Work of the Summer Institute of Linguistics*. IWGIA and Survival International, 1981.

Ibsen, Henrik. *An Enemy of the People.* Translated by Michael Meyer. Methuen, 1974. First published 1882.

Ikummaq, Theo. *Interview for the Igloolik Oral History Project.* Igloolik Research Centre, 2000.

Illich, Ivan. H_2O *and the Waters of Forgetfulness.* Marion Boyars, 1986.

Illius, Bruno. "The Concept of Nihue among the Shipibo-Conibo of Eastern Peru." In *Portals of Power: Shamanism in South America*, edited by E. Jean Langdon and Gerhard Baer. University of New Mexico Press, 1992.

International Labor Organization convention no. 169. "Indigenous and Tribal Peoples Convention." U.N., 1989.

Indyk, Ivor, ed. *Burnt Ground.* Heat 4. Giramondo, 2002.

Irwin, Robert. *Night and Horses and the Desert: The Penguin Anthology of Classical Arabic Literature.* Penguin, 1999.

Iyer, Pico. *Falling off the Map.* Jonathan Cape, 1993.

Jabès, Edmond. *From the Desert to the Book: Dialogues with Marcel Cohen.* Station Hill Press, 1990.

———. *If There Were Anywhere but Desert: The Selected Poems of Edmond Jabès.* Translated by Keith Waldrup. Station Hill Press, 1988.

Jackson, Michael. *At Home in the World.* Duke University Press, 1995.

James, Barry. "Coral Reefs." *International Herald Tribune*, September 11, 2001.

Kamma, Freerk C. *Religious Texts of the Oral Tradition from Western New Guinea.* E. J. Brill, 1975.

Kane, Elisha Kent. *The Far North: Explorations in the Arctic Regions.* W. P. Nimmo, 1859.

Kappianaq, George. *Interview for the Igloolik Oral History Project.* Igloolik Research Centre, 2000.

Kappianaq, George Agiaq, and Cornelius Nutaraq. *Inuit Perspectives on the Twentieth Century: Travelling and Surviving on our Land.* Nunavut Arctic College, 1999.

Keneally, Thomas. *The Chant of Jimmie Blacksmith.* Angus and Robertson, 1972.

Kimber, R. G. *Man From Arltunga: Walter Smith, Australian Bushman.* The Arltunga Hotel and Hesperian Press, 1986.

Kolodny, Annette. *The Lay of the Land: Metaphor as Experience and History in American Life and Letters.* University of North Carolina Press, 1975.

Krakauer, Jon. *Into the Wild.* Doubleday, 1996.

Krupnik, Igor, and Dyanna Jolly. *The Earth Is Faster Now: Indigenous Observations of Arctic Environmental Change.* Smithsonian, 2002.

Kunnuk, Pauli. *Interview for the Igloolik Oral History Project.* Igloolik Research Centre, 1990.

Lacey, Roy, ed. *Wanderlust: A Travel Anthology.* Winchester Publications, 1948.

Laird, Gordon. "Losing the Cool." *Mother Jones*, March/April 2002.

Langdon, E. Jean, and Gerhard Baer, eds. *Portals of Power: Shamanism in South America.* University of New Mexico Press, 1992.

Langewiesche, William. *Sahara Unveiled.* Pantheon, 1996.

Langton, Marcia, and Nicolas Peterson, eds. *Aborigines, Land and Land Rights.* Australian Institute of Aboriginal Studies, 1983.

Latz, Peter. *Pocket Bushtucker: A Guide to the Plants of Central Australia and Their Traditional Uses.* Jukurrpa Books, 1999.

Lee, Dorothy. *Freedom and Culture.* Waveland Press, 1987.

Le Guin, Ursula. *Dancing at the Edge of the World: Thoughts on Words, Women, Places.* Gollancz, 1989.

Leopold, Aldo. *A Sand County Almanac: and Sketches Here and There.* Oxford University Press, 1949.

Lester, Yami. *Yami: The Autobiography of Yami Lester.* IAD Press, 1993.

Lévi-Strauss, Claude. *The Savage Mind.* Weidenfeld and Nicolson, 1962.

———. *Tristes Tropiques.* Translated by Jonathan Cape, 1973. Librairie Plon, 1955.

Lewis, D., and D. Rose. *The Shape of the Dreaming: The Cultural Significance of Victoria River Rock Art.* Aboriginal Studies Press, 1988.

Lindqvist, Sven. *Desert Divers.* Granta, 2000.

———. *A History of Bombing.* Granta, 2001.

Locke, John. *Second Treatise on Government.* First published 1690.

London, Jack. *The Call of the Wild.* Macmillan, 1903.

———. *White Fang.* Macmillan, 1906.

Lönnrot, Elias. *Kalevala.* Translated by Keith Bosley. Oxford University Press, 1999.

Lopez, Barry. *Arctic Dreams: Imagination and Desire in a Northern Landscape.* Scribner's, 1986.

———. *Desert Notes.* Andrews and McMeel, 1976.

Lowe, Pat, with Jimmy Pike. *Jilji: Life in the Great Sandy Desert.* Magabala Books, 1990.

Lowenthal, Marvin, ed. *The Autobiography of Michel de Montaigne.* Nonpareil Books, 1999.

Lucian. *Dialogues of the Sea Gods.* Translated by M. D. Macleod. Harvard University Press, 1961.

Luna, Luis Eduardo. *Vegetalismo: Shamanism among the Mestizo Population of the Peruvian Amazon.* Stockholm Studies in Comparative Religion No. 27, 1986.

Maalouf, Amin. *Samarkand.* Translated by Russell Harris. Quartet, 1992.

MacCormack, Carol P., and Marilyn Strathern, eds. *Nature, Culture and Gender.* Cambridge University Press, 1980.

MacDonald, John. *The Arctic Sky: Inuit Astronomy, Star Lore, and Legend.* Royal Ontario Museum/ Nunavut Research Institute, 1998.

Macfarlane, Robert. *Mountains of the Mind: A History of a Fascination.* Granta, 2003.

McKenna, Terence. *Food of the Gods.* Routledge, 1992.

McKibben, Bill. *The End of Nature.* Penguin, 1990.

McNeley, James Kale. *Holy Wind in Navajo Philosophy.* University of Arizona Press, 1981.

Madigan, C. T. *Crossing the Dead Heart.* Georgian House, 1946.

Mann, Charles C. "1491." *Atlantic Monthly,* March 2002.

Marika, Wandjuk. *Wandjuk Marika: Life Story.* As told to Jennifer Isaacs. University of Queensland Press, 1995.

Marvell, Andrew. "The Mower Against Gardens." 1681. *Complete Poetry,* Dent. 1984.

Marx, Leo. *The Machine in the Garden: Technology and the Pastoral Ideal in America.* Oxford University Press, 1964.

Mason, Georgia. "Fish Fathers Are Set Good Parenting Test." *New Scientist,* November 28, 1992.

Matthiessen, Peter. *At Play in the Fields of the Lord.* Vintage, 1991. First published 1965.

———. *Under the Mountain Wall.* Viking Press, 1962.

Midgley, Mary. *Beast and Man: The Roots of Human Nature.* Harvester Press, 1979.

Miller, James. *Koori: A Will to Win: The Heroic Resistance, Survival and Triumph of Black Australia.* Angus and Robertson, 1985.

Mitton, Robert. *The Lost World of Irian Jaya.* Oxford University Press, 1983.

Molina, Felipe S. "*Wa Huya Ania Ama Vutti Yo'oriwa*—The Wilderness World Is Respected Greatly." In *On Biocultural Diversity: Linking Language, Knowledge and the Environment,* edited by Luisa Maffi. Smithsonian Institution Press, 2001.

Monbiot, George. *No Man's Land: An Investigative Journey Through Kenya and Tanzania.* Macmillan, 1994.

———. *Poisoned Arrows: An Investigation in the Last Place in the Tropics.* Michael Joseph, 1989.

———. "Sleepwalking to Extinction." Article on climate change. *The Guardian,* August 12, 2003.

Moorhouse, Geoffrey. *The Fearful Void.* Hodder and Stoughton, 1974.

Moquin, Wayne, with Charles Van Doren. *Great Documents in American Indian History.* Da Capo Press, 1995.

Morgan, Fidelis. *A Misogynist's Sourcebook.* Jonathan Cape, 1989.

Morgan, Sally. *My Place.* Fremantle Arts Centre Press, 1987.

Morison, Samuel Eliot. *Spring Tides.* Houghton Mifflin, 1965.

Mowat, Farley. *People of the Deer.* McClelland and Stewart, 1952.

Mudrooroo. *Wildcat Screaming.* Angus and Robertson, 1992.

Muir, John. *A Thousand-Mile Walk to the Gulf.* Houghton Mifflin, 1916.

Müller, Fritz. *The Living Arctic.* Methuen, 1981.

Munn, Nancy D. *Walbiri Iconography.* Cornell University Press, 1973.

Myers, Fred R. *Pintupi Country, Pintupi Self: Sentiment, Place, and Politics among Western Desert Aborigines.* Smithsonian Institution Press, 1986.

Naess, Arne. *Ecology, Community and Lifestyle.* Cambridge University Press, 1989.

Nansen, Fridtjof. *The First Crossing of Greenland.* Longmans, 1890.

Narby, Jeremy. *The Cosmic Serpent.* Gollancz, 1998.

———. *Visions of Land.* Ph.D. diss., Stanford University, 1989.

Nash, Roderick Frazier. *Wilderness and the American Mind.* Yale University Press, 1967.

Neidjie, Bill. *Story About Feeling.* Magabala Books, 1989.

Ngabidj, Grant. *My Country of the Pelican Dreaming: The Life of an Australian Aborigine of the Gadjerong, 1904–1977.* As told to Bruce Shaw. Australian Institute of Aboriginal Studies, 1981.

Nicolson, Marjorie Hope. *Mountain Gloom and Mountain Glory: The Development of the Aesthetics of the Infinite.* Cornell University Press, 1959.

Niederland, William G., and Howard F. Stein, eds. *Maps From the Mind: Readings in Psychogeography.* University of Oklahoma Press, 1989.

Nietzsche, Friedrich. *Beyond Good and Evil.* Translated by Marion Faber. Oxford University Press, 1998. First published 1886.

Noonuccal, Oodgeroo (Kath Walker). *My People*. The Jacaranda Press, 1970.

———. *Stradbroke Dreamtime*. Angus and Robertson, 1992.

Novak, Barbara. *Nature and Culture: American Landscape and Painting 1825–1875*. Thames and Hudson, 1980.

Nunavut Arctic College. *Perspectives on Traditional Law: Interviewing Inuit Elders*. Iqaluit, 1999.

Oelschlaeger, Max. *The Idea of Wilderness*. Yale University Press, 1991.

Oosterzee, Penny van. *A Field Guide to Central Australia*. JB Books, 1999.

Orwell, George. *1984*. Secker and Warburg, 1949.

Paine, Barry. *The Green Centre*. BBC and André Deutsch, 1976.

Peake, Mervyn. *Letters From a Lost Uncle*. Eyre and Spottiswoode, 1948.

Peter, Sonja, and Pamela Lofts, eds. *Yarrtji: Six Women's Stories from the Great Sandy Desert*. Aboriginal Studies Press, 1997.

Pilger, John. *The New Rulers of the World*. Verso, 2002.

———. *A Secret Country*. Jonathan Cape, 1989.

Piugaattuk, Michel Kupaaq. *Interview for the Igloolik Oral History Project*. Igloolik Research Centre, 1990.

Pollan, Michael. *Second Nature: A Gardener's Education*. The Atlantic Monthly Press, 1991.

Ponting, Herbert. *The Great White South*. Duckworth, 1921.

Porteus, Alexander. *The Lore of the Forest*. George Allen and Unwin, 1928.

Posey, Darrell. "Native and Indigenous Guidelines for New Amazonian Development Strategies." In *Change in the Amazon Basin, Vol. 1*, edited by John Hemming. Manchester University Press, 1985.

Pospisil, Leopold. *The Kapauku Papuans of West New Guinea*. Holt, Rinehart and Winston, 1963.

Price, Tom. "Exiles of the Kalahari." *Mother Jones*, January/February, 2005.

Raban, Jonathan. *The Oxford Book of the Sea*. Oxford University Press, 1992.

Ransmayr, Christoph. *The Terrors of Ice and Darkness*. Paladin, 1992.

Rasing, W. C. E. *Too Many People: Order and Noncomformity in Iglulingmiut Social Process*. Nijmegen Katholieke Universiteit, 1994.

Rasmussen, Knud. *Intellectual Culture of the Copper Eskimos: Report of the Fifth Thule Expedition, Vol. IX*. Gyldendalske Boghandel, 1932.

———. *The Netsilik Eskimos: Report of the Fifth Thule Expedition, Vol. VIII*. Gyldendalske Boghandel, 1931.

Reader, John. *Man on Earth: A Celebration of Mankind*. University of Texas Press, 1988.

Reed, A. W. *Aboriginal Myths: Tales of the Dreamtime*. Reed New Holland, 2002.

Reed, Peter, and David Rothenberg. *Wisdom in the Open Air: The Norwegian Roots of Deep Ecology*. University of Minnesota, 1993.

Reichel-Dolmatoff, Gerardo. *The Forest Within: The World-View of the Tukano Amazonian Indians*. Themis Books, 1996.

———. "The Loom of Life: A Kogi Principle of Integration." *Journal of Latin American Lore* 4:1, 1978.

———. *Rainforest Shamans: Essays on the Tukano Indians of the Northwest Amazon*. Themis Books, 1997.

———. *The Shaman and the Jaguar: A Study of Narcotic Drugs Among the Indians of Colombia.* Temple University Press, 1975.

———. *Yurupari: Studies of an Amazonian Foundation Myth.* Harvard University Press, 1996.

Reid, Anna. *The Shaman's Coat: A Native History of Siberia.* Weidenfeld and Nicolson, 2002.

Rennie, Neil. *Far-Fetched Facts: The Literature of Travel and the Idea of the South Seas.* Clarendon, 1995.

Reynolds, Henry. *An Indelible Stain? The Question of Genocide in Australia's History.* Penguin, 2001.

Rich, Adrienne. *Selected Poems 1950–1995.* Salmon Publishing, 1996.

Rimbaud, Penny. "And Now It Rains." Poetry performed at the Vortex, London, 2006.

Rimbaud, Penny (Crass Agenda). "HOW?" Babel/Exitstencil, 2004.

Rival, Laura. "The Growth of Family Trees: Understanding Huaorani Perceptions of the Forest." In *MAN*, the *Journal of the Royal Anthropological Institute*, December, 1993.

Rival, Laura, ed. *The Social Life of Trees.* Berg, 1998.

Rogan, Mary. "Please Take Our Children Away." Article on Innu children in *The New York Times Magazine*, March 4, 2001.

Rolston, Holmes. "Values Gone Wild." *Inquiry* 26 (2), 1983.

Rosaldo, Michelle Zimbalist, and Louise Lamphere, eds. *Woman, Culture and Society.* Stanford University Press, 1974.

Rosaldo, Renato. *Culture and Truth: The Remaking of Social Analysis.* Beacon Press, 1989.

———. *Ilongot Headhunting: A Study in Society and History.* Stanford University Press, 1980.

Rose, Deborah Bird. *Country of the Heart: An Indigenous Australian Homeland.* Aboriginal Studies Press, 2002.

———. *Dingo Makes Us Human.* Cambridge University Press, 1992.

Rose, Gillian. *Feminism and Geography: The Limits of Geographical Knowledge.* Polity Press, 1993.

Rosenblum, Mort, and Doug Williamson. *Squandering Eden: Africa at the Edge.* Bodley Head, 1987.

Rothenberg, David. *Why Birds Sing.* Basic Books, 2005.

Rothenberg, David, ed. *Wild Ideas.* University of Minnesota Press, 1995.

Rothenberg, David, and Marta Ulvaeus, eds. *The World and the Wild.* University of Arizona Press, 2001.

Rothenberg, Jerome, ed. *Technicians of the Sacred.* University of California Press, 1968.

Rowell, Andrew. *Green Backlash: Global Subversion of the Environmental Movement.* Routledge, 1996.

Rubuntja, Wenten, with Jenny Green. *The Town Grew Up Dancing.* Jukurrpa Books, 2002.

Rytkheu, Yuri. *Reborn to a Full Life.* Novosti Press Agency Publishing House, Moscow, 1977.

Saayman, Graham, ed. *Modern South Africa in Search of a Soul.* Sigo Press, 1986.

Sabbioni, Jennifer, Kay Schaffer, and Sidonie Smith. *Indigenous Australian Voices: A Reader.* Rutgers University Press, 1998.

Satanta (Kiowa chief) quoted in *Autobiography* by Henry M. Stanley. Narrative Press, 2001. First published 1909.

Schopenhauer, Arthur. *The World as Will and Idea.* Everyman, 1995. First published 1819.

Schultes, Richard Evans. *Plants of the Gods: Origins of Hallucinogenic Use.* Hutchinson, 1980.

The Seafarer. Translated from Anglo-Saxon by John Wain. The Greville Press, 1980.

Sears, Cathy. "The Chimpanzee's Medicine Chest." *New Scientist,* August 4, 1990.

Sebald, W. G. *Austerlitz.* Hamish Hamilton, 2001.

Sennett, Richard. *The Uses of Disorder: Personal Identity and City Life.* Norton, 1970.

Shackleton, Ernest. *South: The Endurance Expedition.* Heinemann, 1919.

Shakespeare, William. *The Taming of the Shrew.*

———. *The Tempest.*

———. *Timon of Athens.*

———. *Twelfth Night.*

Shelley, Percy Bysshe. "Mont Blanc."

Shepard, Paul. *Coming Home to the Pleistocene.* Island Press, 1998.

———. *The Only World We've Got: A Paul Shepard Reader.* Sierra Club Books, 1996.

———. *The Others: How Animals Made Us Human.* Island Press, 1996.

Shephard, Mark. *The Simpson Desert: Natural History and Human Endeavour.* Corkwood Press, 1999.

Shipton, Eric. *Land of Tempest: Travels in Patagonia 1958–62.* Hodder and Stoughton, 1963.

———. *That Untravelled World.* Hodder and Stoughton, 1969.

———. *Upon That Mountain.* Hodder and Stoughton, 1943.

Shostak, Marjorie. *Nisa: The Life and Words of a !Kung Woman.* Allen Lane, 1982.

Shuker, Karl P. N. *Extraordinary Animals Worldwide.* Robert Hale, 1991.

Simpson, Joe. *Dark Shadows Falling.* Vintage, 1998.

———. *Touching the Void.* Jonathan Cape, 1988.

Simpson and Day. *Field Guide to the Birds of Australia.* Penguin, 1984.

Singh, Salina, et al. *Aboriginal Australia and the Torres Strait Islands.* Lonely Planet, 2001.

Smith, Adam. *The Wealth of Nations.* First published 1776.

Snyder, Gary. *Earth House Hold: Technical Notes and Queries to Fellow Dharma Revolutionaries.* New Directions, 1969.

———. *The Practice of the Wild.* North Point Press, 1990.

———. *Turtle Island.* New Directions, 1969.

Solnit, Rebecca. *Wanderlust: A History of Walking.* Penguin, 2000.

Solomon, Maui, and Leo Watson. "The Waitangi Tribunal and the Maori Claim to Their Cultural and Intellectual Heritage Rights Property." *Cultural Survival Quarterly.* Winter, 2001.

Soulé, Michael, and Gary Lease. *Reinventing Nature? Responses to Postmodern Deconstruction.* Island Press, 1995.

Souter, Gavin. *New Guinea: The Last Unknown.* Angus and Robertson, 1963.

Spufford, Francis. *I May Be Some Time: Ice and the English Imagination.* Faber, 1996.

Standing Bear, Chief. *Land of the Spotted Eagle.* Houghton Mifflin, 1933.

Stanner, W. E. H., *White Man Got No Dreaming: Essays, 1938–73.* Books Australia, 1979.

Stefansson, Vilhjalmur. *My Life with the Eskimos.* Harrap and Co., 1924.

Steinberg, Theodore. *Slide Mountain: or, The Folly of Owning Nature.* University of California Press, 1995.

Steiner, George. *George Steiner: A Reader.* Penguin, 1984.

———. *The Deeps of the Sea and Other Fiction.* Faber, 1996.

Stephen, David. *The San of the Kalahari.* Minority Rights Group Report No. 56, 1982.

Stevens, Stan, ed. *Conservation Through Cultural Survival: Indigenous Peoples and Protected Areas.* Island Press, 1997.

Stewart, Ian. "Mathematicians learn how to read the ant trails." *New Scientist,* June 26, 1993.

Storr, Anthony. *Solitude.* HarperCollins, 1989.

Stott, Rebecca. "The Dark Continent." *Feminist Review,* No. 32, 1989.

Strang, Veronica. *Uncommon Ground: Cultural Landscapes and Environmental Values.* Berg, 1997.

Strocchi, Marina. *Ikuntji: Paintings from Haasts Bluff, 1992–1994.* IAD Press, 1995.

Sullivan, Lawrence E. *Icauchu's Drum: An Orientation to Meaning in South American Religions.* Macmillan, 1988.

Sussman, Elizabeth, ed. *On the Passage of a Few People Through a Rather Brief Moment in Time: The Situationist International 1957–1972.* MIT Press, 1989.

Suzuki, David. *The Sacred Balance: Rediscovering Our Place in Nature.* Bantam Books, 1997.

Swaney, Deanna, ed. *The Arctic.* Lonely Planet, 1999.

Sweetman, David. *The Love of Many Things: A Life of Vincent van Gogh.* Hodder and Stoughton, 1990.

Swift, Jonathan. *Gulliver's Travels.* First published 1726.

Taylor, Rogan. *The Death and Resurrection Show: From Shaman to Superstar.* Blond and Briggs, 1985.

Temple, Philip. *Nawok! The New Zealand Expedition to New Guinea's Highest Mountains.* Dent, 1962.

Ten Bears (Comanche chief) in *The Worst Hard Time* by Timothy Egan. Houghton Mifflin, 2005.

Terborgh, John. *Requiem for Nature.* Island Press, 1999.

Theroux, Paul. *Dark Star Safari.* Hamish Hamilton, 2002.

Thesiger, Wilfred. *Desert, Marsh and Mountain: The World of a Nomad.* Collins, 1979.

Thomas, Elizabeth Marshall. *The Harmless People.* Secker and Warburg, 1959.

Thompson, E. P. *Customs in Common.* The New Press, 1991.

Thomson, James. *The Seasons.* 1726–1730.

Thoreau, Henry David. *Walden.* First published 1854.

Tilman, H. W. *China to Chitral.* Cambridge University Press, 1951.

Tonkinson, Robert. *The Mardu Aborigines: Living the Dream in Australia's Desert.* Holt, Rinehart and Winston, 1978.

Tookoome, Simon, with Sheldon Oberman. *The Shaman's Nephew: A Life in the Far North.* Stoddart, 1999.

Toulmin, Stephen. *Cosmopolis: The Hidden Agenda of Modernity.* University of Chicago Press, 1990.

Trakarnsuphakorn, Prasert. "The Wisdom of the Karen in Natural Resource Conservation." *National Geographic,* March 2000.

Tree, Isabella. *Islands in the Clouds: Travels in the Highlands of New Guinea.* Lonely Planet Publications, 1996.

Truth, Sojourner. *Narrative of Sojourner Truth; A Bondswoman of Olden Time.* Oxford University Press, 1991.

Tuan, Yi-Fu. *Topophilia: A Study of Environmental Perception, Attitudes, and Values.* Columbia University Press, 1974.

Tunbridge, Dorothy. *Flinders Ranges Dreaming.* Aboriginal Studies Press, 1988.

Turnbull, Colin. *The Forest People.* Jonathan Cape, 1961.

———. *The Mountain People.* Jonathan Cape, 1973.

Turner, Frederick. *Beyond Geography: The Western Spirit Against the Wilderness.* Rutgers University Press, 1983.

Turner, Jack. *The Abstract Wild.* University of Arizona Press, 1996.

Ulaajuruluk, Abraham. *Interview for the Igloolik Oral History Project.* Igloolik Research Centre, 1987.

Valadez, Susana Eger. "Wolf Power and Interspecies Communication in Huichol Shamanism." In *People of the Peyote: Huichol Indian History, Religion and Survival,* edited by Stacy B. Schaefer and Peter T. Furst. University of New Mexico, 1996.

Valkeapää, Nils-Aslak. *Greetings From Lappland: The Sami—Europe's Forgotten People.* Translated by Beverley Wahl. Zed Books, 1983. First published 1971.

———. *The Sun My Father.* Translated by Ralph Salisbury, Lars Nordström, and Harald Gaski. University of Washington Press, 1997. First published 1988.

Verrengia, Joseph. Article on the inhabitants of Shishmaref, Alaska. *The Independent,* September 20, 2002.

Waal, Frans de. *The Ape and the Sushi Master: Cultural Reflections by a Primatologist.* Allen Lane, 2001.

Waddell, Helen, translator. *Vitae Patrum: The Desert Fathers.* Constable, 1936.

Wessel, Ingrid, and Georgia Wimhöfer, eds. *Violence in Indonesia.* Abera, 2001.

West, Ida. *Pride Against Prejudice: Reminiscences of a Tasmanian Aborigine.* Australian Institute of Aboriginal Studies, 1984.

Whale and Dolphin Conservation Society, www.wdcs.org.

Wheeler, Sara. *Terra Incognita.* Jonathan Cape, 1996.

Whiten, Andrew, and Christophe Boesch. "The Cultures of Chimpanzees." *Scientific American,* January 2001.

Wilbert, Johannes. *Tobacco and Shamanism in South America.* Yale University Press, 1987.

Williams, Heathcote. *Whale Nation.* Jonathan Cape, 1988.

Williams, Raymond. *The Country and the City.* Chatto and Windus, 1973.

Wilson, Edward O. *Sociobiology.* Harvard University Press, 1976.

Wilson, Forbes. *The Conquest of Copper Mountain.* Atheneum, 1981.

Woodard, Colin. *Ocean's End: Travels Through Endangered Seas.* Basic Books, 2000.

Worsley, Peter. *Knowledges: What Different Peoples Make of the World.* Profile Books, 1997.

Yam, Eileen. "The Arctic and Global Warming." *National Geographic,* March 2000.

Younghusband, Francis. *The Heart of a Continent.* John Murray, 1937.

Zamyatin, Yevgeny. *We.* Dutton, 1924.

Zeldin, Theodore. *An Intimate History of Humanity.* Sinclair-Stevenson, 1994.

Index